# WHAT THEY SAY ABOUT THE JOB BANK SERIES...

".. A superior series of job hunt directories."

-Cornell University
Career Center
WHERE TO START

"A timely book for Chicago job hunters follows books from the same publisher that were well received in New York and Boston...A fine tool for job hunters..."

-Clarence Petersen
THE CHICAGO TRIBUNE

"Job hunting is never fun, but this book can ease the ordeal...The Southern California Job Bank will help allay fears, build confidence and avoid wheel-spinning."

-Robert W. Ross
THE LOS ANGELES TIMES

"This well-researched, well-edited job hunter's aid includes most major businesses and institutional entities in the New York metropolitan area...Highly recommended."

-Cheryl Gregory-Pindell
LIBRARY JOURNAL

"Here's the book for your job hunt...Trying to get a job in New York? I would recommend a good look through the Metropolitan New York Job Bank..."

-Maxwell Norton
NEW YORK POST

"Help on the job hunt...Anyone who is job-hunting in the New York area can find a lot of useful ideas in a new paperback called The Metropolitan New York Job Bank..."

-Angela Taylor
THE NEW YORK TIMES

"If you are looking for a job...before you go to the newspapers and the help-wanted ads, listen to Bob Adams, editor of The Metropolitan New York Job Bank."

-Tom Brokaw
NBC TELEVISION

"No longer can job seekers feel secure about finding employment just through want ads. With the tough competition in the job market, particularly in the Boston area, they need much more help. For this reason, The Boston Job Bank will have a wide and appreciative audience of new graduates, job changers, and people relocating to Boston. It provides a good place to start a search for entry-level professional positions."

-from a review in
THE JOURNAL OF
COLLEGE PLACEMENT

# What makes the JOB BANK SERIES the nation's premier line of employment guides:

 With vital employment information on thousands of the nation's largest companies, the **JOB BANK SERIES** is the most comprehensive and authoritative set of career directories available today.

 Each of the entries provides contact information, telephone numbers, addresses and a thumbnail sketch of the firm's business. Many entries also include a listing of the firm's typical professional job categories, the principal educational backgrounds sought, and the fringe benefits offered.

 All of the reference information in the **JOB BANK SERIES** is as up-to-date and accurate as possible. Every year, the entire database is thoroughly researched and verified, first by mail and then by telephone. More local **JOB BANK** books come out more often than any other comparable publications.

 In addition, the **JOB BANK SERIES** features important information about the local job scene--forecasts on which industries are the hottest, overviews of local economic trends, and even lists of regional professional associations, so you can get your job hunt started off right!

Looking for a particular kind of employer? Each **JOB BANK** Book features a comprehensive cross-index, which lists entries both by industry and, in multi-state job markets, by state. This means a person seeking a job in, say, finance, can identify major employers quickly and accurately.

 Hundreds of discussions with job-hunters show they prefer information organized geographically, because most people look for jobs in specific areas. The **JOB BANK SERIES** offers sixteen regional titles, from Minneapolis to Houston, and from Washington, D.C., to San Francisco. The future employee moving to a particular area can review the local employment data and get a feel not only for the type of industry most common to that region, but also for major employers.

 A condensed, but thorough, review of the entire job search process is presented in the chapter, 'The Basics of Job Winning', a feature that has received many compliments from career counselors. In addition, each **JOB BANK** directory is completed by a section on resumes and cover letters **The New York Times** has acclaimed as "excellent".

 The **JOB BANK SERIES** gives job-hunters the most comprehensive, most timely, and most accurate career information, organized and indexed to facilitate the job search. An entire career reference library, **JOB BANK** books are the consummate employment guides.

*Cover photograph courtesy of the Chicago Convention and Visitors Bureau.*

Published by Bob Adams, Inc.
260 Center Street, Holbrook MA 02343

Copyright © 1982, 1985, 1986, 1987, 1989, 1990, 1991, 1992
By Bob Adams, Inc.
All rights reserved.
No part of the material printed may be reproduced or utilized in any form or by any means, electronic or mechanical, including photo-copying, recording, or by any information storage retrieval system without written permission from the publisher.

The Greater Chicago JobBank and its cover design are trademarks of Bob Adams, Inc.

Brand name products mentioned in the employer listings are proprietary property of the applicable firm, subject to trademark protection, and registered with government offices.

While the publisher has made every reasonable attempt to obtain accurate information and verify same, occasional errors are inevitable due to the magnitude of data base. Should you discover an error, please write the publisher so that corrections may be made in future editions.

The appearance of a listing anywhere in this book does not constitute an endorsement from the publisher.

Cover design by Peter Weiss.

Manufactured in the United States of America.

ISBN: 1-55850-071-5

# The Greater Chicago JobBank 1992

**Managing Editor**
Carter Smith

**Associate Editor**
Peter Weiss

**Editorial Assistants**
Michelle Bevilacqua
Sharon C. Cook
Elizabeth Gale
Lynne Griffin

**BOB ADAMS, INC.**
PUBLISHERS
Holbrook, Massachusetts

**Top career publications from Bob Adams, Inc.:**

**THE JobBank SERIES:**

The Atlanta JobBank ($12.95)
The Boston JobBank ($12.95)
The Chicago JobBank ($12.95)
The Dallas-Ft. Worth JobBank ($12.95)
The Denver JobBank ($12.95)
The Detroit JobBank ($12.95)
The Florida JobBank ($12.95)
The Houston JobBank ($12.95)
The Los Angeles JobBank ($12.95)
The Minneapolis-St. Paul JobBank ($12.95)
The New York JobBank ($12.95)
The Ohio JobBank ($12.95)
The Philadelphia JobBank ($12.95)
The Phoenix JobBank ($12.95)
The San Francisco JobBank ($12.95)
The Seattle JobBank ($12.95)
The St. Louis JobBank ($12.95)
The Washington DC JobBank ($12.95)

The JobBank Guide to Employment Services (covers 50 states: $129.95)
The National JobBank ($199.95)

**CAREERS**

Campus-Free College Degrees ($9.95)
Careers and the College Grad ($12.95)
Careers and the Engineer ($12.95)
Careers and the MBA ($14.95)

The Complete Guide to Washington Internships ($12.95)
Cover Letters that Knock 'em Dead ($7.95)
The Elements of Job Hunting ($4.95)
Harvard Guide to Careers in Mass Media ($7.95)
How to Get a Job in Education ($6.95)
International Careers ($12.95)
Job Search Handbook ($6.95)
Knock 'em Dead with Great Answers to Tough Interview Questions ($6.95)
The Minority Career Book ($9.95)
Over 40 and Looking for Work ($7.95)
Resume Handbook ($5.95)
Resumes that Knock 'em Dead ($7.95)
Which Niche? (Answers to the Most Common Questions About Careers and Job Hunting) ($4.95)

To obtain a copy of any of these books, please check your local bookstore. If unavailable, please call 1-800-USA-JOBS toll free. (In Massachusetts call 617-767-8100).

# HOW TO USE THIS BOOK

A copy of *The Greater Chicago JobBank* is one of the most effective tools you can find for your professional job hunt. Use this guide for the most up-to-date information on most major businesses in Chicagoland. It will supply you with specific addresses, phone numbers, and personnel contact information.

Separate yourself from the flock of candidates who answer the help-wanted advertisements "looking for a job." The method this book offers, direct employer contact, boasts twice the success rate of any other. Exploit it.

Read and use *The Greater Chicago JobBank* to reveal new opportunities. Here's how:

Read the introductory economic overview section in order to gain insight on what the overall trends are for Greater Chicago's economy.

Map out your job-seeking strategy by reading the "Basics of Job Winning" section. It's a condensed review of the most effective job search methods.

Write a winning resume and learn how to sell yourself most effectively on paper, by using the "Resumes and Cover Letters" section.

Focus your career goals by reading the "Jobs in Each Industry" section. This chapter features descriptions of many of the most common professional occupations, as well as background requirements, and forecasts for future growth.

Formulate a target list of potential employers in your field. Consult the company listings in the "Primary Greater Chicago Employers" section. Use that information to supplement your own research, so that you'll be knowledgeable about the firm - before the interview.

Increase your knowledge of your field, as well as your connections within it, by using our listings of some of the region's major professional and trade associations.

Whether you are just out of college starting your first job search, looking for a new position in your current field, or entering an entirely new sector of the job market, *The Greater Chicago JobBank* will give you an idea of the incredible diversity of employment possibilities in one of the the country's most dynamic employment centers. Your ultimate success will largely depend upon how rigorously you use the information provided herein. This one-of-a-kind employment guide can lead you to a company, and a job, that would otherwise have remained undiscovered. With a willingness to apply yourself, a positive attitude, and the research within these covers, you can attain your career objective.

# TABLE OF CONTENTS

# INTRODUCTION/11

*A complete and informative economic overview designed to help you understand all of the forces shaping the Greater Chicago job market.*

# PART ONE: THE JOB SEARCH

**The Basics of Job Winning/17**

*A condensed review of the basic elements of a successful job search campaign. Includes advice on developing an effective strategy, time planning, preparing for interviews, interview techniques, etc.*

**Resumes and Cover Letters/33**

*Advice on creating a strong resume. Includes sample resumes and cover letters.*

# PART TWO: OCCUPATION PROFILES

**Jobs In Each Industry/51**

*Descriptions of many of the most common professional positions, with forecasts of their growth potential for the 1990's.*

# PART THREE: WHERE THE JOBS ARE

**Primary Greater Chicago Employers/109**

*Greater Chicago organized according to industry. Includes the address, phone number, description of the company's basic product lines and services, and for most firms, the name of the contact person for professional positions.*

*Accounting/Auditing/111*
*Advertising, Marketing and Public Relations/112*
*Amusement/Arts/Recreation/116*
*Apparel and Textile Manufacturing/117*
*Banking, Savings & Loan/119*
*Book and Magazine Publishing/126*

*Broadcasting/130*
*Charitable, Non-Profit and Humanitarian/132*
*Chemical & Related: Production, Processing & Disposal/134*
*Colleges and Universities/Education/139*
*Communications: Equipment & Services/143*
*Computers: Hardware, Software, and Services/145*
*Construction: Services, Materials & Related/148*
*Electrical & Electronic: Manufacturing & Distribution/154*
*Engineering and Architecture/163*
*Fabricated Metal Products/166*
*Financial Services/Management Consulting/174*
*Food & Beverage Related: Production/Trade/179*
*General Merchandise/Retail & Wholesale/188*
*Health Care & Pharmaceuticals/Products and Services/193*
*Highly Diversified/200*
*Hotels and Restaurants/201*
*Insurance/205*
*Legal Services/210*
*Manufacturing: Miscellaneous Consumer/212*
*Manufacturing: Miscellaneous Industrial/221*
*Miscellaneous Services/238*
*Newspaper Publishing/240*
*Paper, Packaging & Forest Products/Containers & Glass Products/241*
*Petroleum & Energy Related/Mining & Drilling/250*
*Printing/Graphic Arts/253*
*Real Estate: Services, Management, & Development/254*
*Research & Development/256*
*Rubber & Plastics/257*
*Transportation: Equipment & Services/260*
*Utilities/267*

**Professional Employment Services/271**

Includes the address, phone number, description of each company's services, contact name, and a list of positions commonly filled.

**Professional & Trade Associations/315**

Includes both local and national addresses and phone numbers for professional and trade associations in each field.

**Index/353**

# INTRODUCTION

# CHICAGO: AN ECONOMIC OVERVIEW

When Chicago -- long-known as America's "Second City", with a population historically second only to New York City's -- fell to number three behind Los Angeles, some saw it as an inevitable symptom of the decline of the midwestern "rust belt" economy. Traditionally, Chicago has served as the heart of the Midwest's economy, producing more fabricated metal and food products than any other metropolis in America.

Unfortunately, the shifting U.S. economy has turned these strengths into one of Chicago's greatest potential weaknesses. Since 1970, Chicago has lost more manufacturing jobs than any other city in the nation. Today, manufacturing accounts for only 22% of the jobs in the area, down from over 30%. The steel industry alone lost over 13,000 workers during the 1980's.

Perhaps Chicago's biggest dilemma has been attracting Big Business to settle in the city and then convincing them to stay. Some analysts have argued that Chicago is hampered by an unfavorable labor relations climate. Some corporations have shied away from Chicago because the city has no "right to work" laws, and because the city's laborers are so heavily unionized. Over 40 percent of the city's manufacturing employment is unionized; the national figure is about half that.

For all the despair in the manufacturing sector, Chicago's employment picture is really not all that gloomy. For instance, one recent study indicates that metropolitan Chicago actually created more jobs between 1983 and 1987 than any other area except Los Angeles. The key behind this encouraging news is that Chicago is beginning slowly but surely to adjust to the economic realities of the service-intensive 1990's. To those who view reliance on the larger players as more of a link to the past than to the future, there are encouraging developments on the small-business front. According to Dun and Bradstreet, new business incorporations climbed 40 percent in Chicago between 1980 and 1985. In 1986, the Chicago Capital Fund was started with the aim of granting smaller investments for firms passed over by the traditional investment community. While "seed" money is still perhaps a bit too difficult to come by for many entrepreneurs, the Capital Fund represents a new step welcomed by many business observers.

In addition, Chicago has been and will remain the financial powerhouse of the nation's midsection. In addition to a number of major banking institutions, the city is also home to the Midwest Stock Exchange (second largest securities exchange in the U.S. after NYSE), the 7th Federal Reserve Bank, and the Chicago Board of Trade (CBT). The CBT, founded in 1848, is the oldest exchange in the United States. The Chicago Mercantile Exchange is the busiest market for perishable goods. Between the CBT and the Mercantile Exchange, over 70% of all futures are traded through Chicago.

Cook Count, located to the city's northwest, has benefitted greatly from corporate relocations out of Chicago. Lured by low property taxes and extensive land, a number of large companies have relocated to Chicago's suburbs. In fact, suburbs now account for 60 percent of the metro area's population, and 60 percent of its jobs. Shopping centers, restaurants and recreational facilities have enabled the surrounding area to become more or less independent of downtown Chicago's facilities.

Lake and DuPage counties are taking advantage of local booms in the high tech area. In recent years, a number of small to mid-size companies specializing in software, pharmaceuticals and telecommunications are building a solid technological foundation. According to one are specialist, however, "The biggest impediment is that there's no technology-based institution of higher learning that serves the area the way MIT, Stanford, or even the University of Minnesota does."

Just as the Boston and Silicon Valley areas look to area schools as breeding grounds for innovation in high tech, Chicago must do the same. The city houses twelve major colleges and universities, among them the University of Chicago, Northwestern, and DePaul.

The health care sector is another in which area economists see hope for the future. At present, Chicago is third in numbers of health care facilities, maintaining 226 doctors for every 100,000 residents.

For those seeking to work in the city of Chicago, the next five to ten years should prove to be an interesting period. As reliance on the traditional companies and industries has been reassessed, the foundation for some innovative economic development has been laid. Particularly at the community level, Chicago has introduced a number of programs that have revealed promising results thus far. The increase in service sector and high technology employment have initiated a definitive transition in Chicago's economy. Although many of the area's most promising new companies operate away from the central metropolitan area, there remain avenues of very high potential for the resourceful job seeker.

## Chicagoland's Top 25 Employers

| Company | Location | No. of Employees |
|---|---|---|
| 1. Sears Roebuck & Co. | Chicago | 485,400 |
| 2. McDonald's Corporation | Oak Brook | 137,000 |
| 3. Motorola, Inc. | Schaumberg | 97,700 |
| 4. Sara Lee Corp. | Chicago | 92,400 |
| 5. Ameritech | Chicago | 71,871 |
| 6. Allegis Corporation | Chicago | 62,900 |
| 7. Baxter Travenol | Deerfield | 60,000 |
| 8. Caterpiller, Inc. | Peoria | 54,463 |
| 9. Firestone Inc. | Chicago | 53,500 |
| 10. Kraft, Inc. | Glenview | 50,000 |
| 11. Santa Fe Southern Pacific | Chicago | 48,769 |
| 12. Amoco Corporation | Chicago | 47,000 |
| 13. Walgreen Co. | Deerfield | 45,000 |
| 14. Deere & Co. | Moline | 37,931 |
| 15. Abbott Labs | North Chicago | 37,487 |
| 16. IC Industries | Chicago | 33,000 |
| 17. Quaker Oats Co. | Chicago | 30,000 |
| 18. Bally Manufacturing | Chicago | 29,365 |
| 19. Brunswick Corp. | Skokie | 28,400 |
| 20. FMC Corporation | Chicago | 25,000 |
| 21. Farley Industries | Chicago | 24,800 |
| 22. Premark Intl. | Deerfield | 22,800 |
| 23. Carson Pirie Scott | Chicago | 22,250 |
| 24. USG Corporation | Chicago | 22,200 |
| 25. Household Intl. | Sanders Heights | 22,029 |

# PART ONE: THE JOB SEARCH

The Basics of Job Winning

# THE BASICS OF JOB WINNING: A CONDENSED REVIEW

The best way to obtain a better professional job is to contact the employer directly. Broad-based statistical studies by the Department of Labor show that job seekers have found employment more successfully by contacting employers directly, than by using any other method.

However, given the current diversity, and increased specialization of both industry and job tasks it is possible that in some situations other job seeking methods may prove at least equally successful. Three of the other most commonly used methods are: relying on personal contacts, using employment services, and following up help wanted advertisements. Many professionals have been successful in finding better jobs using one of these methods. However, the Direct Contact method has an overall success rate twice that of any other method and it has been successfully used by many more professionals. So unless you have specific reasons to believe that another method would work best for you, the Direct Contact method should form the foundation of your job search effort.

**The Objective**

With any business task, you must develop a strategy for meeting a goal. This is especially true when it comes to obtaining a better job. First you need to clearly define your objectives.

Setting your job objectives is better known as career planning (or life planning for those who wish to emphasize the importance of combining the two). Career planning has become a field of study in and of itself. Since most of our readers are probably well-entrenched in their career path, we will touch on career planning just briefly.

If you are thinking of choosing or switching careers, we particularly emphasize two things. First, choose a career where you will enjoy most of the day-to-day tasks. Sure, this sounds obvious, but most of us have at one point or another been attracted by a glamour industry or a prestigious sounding job without thinking of the most important consideration: Would we enjoy performing the everyday tasks the position entailed?

The second key consideration is that you are not merely choosing a career, but also a lifestyle. Career counselors indicate that one of the most common problems people encounter in job seeking is a lack of consideration for how well-suited they are for a particular position or career. For example, some people, attracted to management consulting by good salaries, early responsibility and high level corporate exposure, do not adapt well to the long hours, heavy travel demands, and the constant pressure to produce. So be sure to determine both for your career as a whole and for each position that you apply for, if you will easily adapt to both the day-to-day duties that the position entails and the working environment.

## The Strategy

Assuming that you have now established your career objectives, the next step of the job search is to develop a strategy. If you don't take the time to develop a strategy and lay out a plan you will probably find yourself going in circles after several weeks making a random search for opportunities that always seem just beyond your reach.

Your strategy can be thought as having three simple elements:

1. Choosing a method of contacting employers.

2. Allocating your scarce resources (in most job searches the key scarce resource will be time, but financial considerations will become important in some searches too.)

3. Evaluating how the selected contact method is working and then considering adopting other methods.

We suggest you give serious consideration to using the Direct Contact method exclusively. However, we realize it is human nature to avoid putting all your eggs in one basket. So, if you prefer to use other methods as well, try to expend at least half your effort on the Direct Contact method, spending the rest on all of the other methods combined. Millions of other job seekers have already proven that Direct Contact has been twice as effective in obtaining employment, so why not benefit from their effort?

With your strategy in mind, the next step is to develop the details of the plan, or scheduling. Of course, job searches are not something that most people do regularly so it is difficult to estimate how long each step will take. Nonetheless, it is important to have a plan so that your effort can be allocated the way you have chosen, so that you can see yourself progressing, and to facilitate reconsideration of your chosen strategy.

It is important to have a realistic time frame in mind. If you will be job searching full-time, your search will probably take at least two months and very likely, substantially longer. If you can only devote part-time effort, it will probably take four months.

You probably know a few people who seem to spend their whole lives searching for a better job in their part time. Don't be one of them. Once you begin your job search on a part-time basis, give it your whole-hearted effort. If you don't really feel like devoting a lot of energy to job seeking right now, then wait. Focus on enjoying your present position, performing your best on the job, and storing up energy for when you are really ready to begin your job search.

Those of you currently unemployed should remember that job hunting is tough work physically and emotionally. It is also intellectually demanding -- requiring your best. So don't tire yourself out by working on your job campaign around the clock. It would be counter-productive. At the same time, be sure to discipline yourself. The most logical approach to time management is to keep your regular working hours.

For those of you who are still employed, job searching will be particularly tiring because it must be done in addition to your regular duties. So don't work yourself to the point where you show up to interviews appearing exhausted and slip behind at your current job. But don't be tempted to quit! The long hours are worth it - it is much easier to sell your skills from a position of strength (as someone currently employed).

If you are searching full-time and have decided to choose a mixture of contact methods, we recommend that you divide up each week allowing some time for each method. For instance, you might devote Mondays to following up newspaper ads because most of them appear in Sunday papers. Then you might devote Tuesdays, and Wednesday mornings to working and developing the personal contacts you have, in addition to trying a few employment services. Then you could devote the rest of the week to the Direct Contact method. This is just one plan that may succeed for you.

By trying several methods at once, job-searching will be more interesting for you, and you will be able to evaluate how promising each of the methods seems, altering your time allocation accordingly. Be very careful in your evaluation, however, and don't judge the success of a particular method just by the sheer number of interviews you obtain. Positions advertised in the newspaper, for instance, are likely to generate many more interviews per opening than positions that are filled without being advertised.

If you are searching part-time and decide to try several different contact methods, we recommend that you try them sequentially. You simply won't have enough time to put a meaningful amount of effort into more than one method at once. So decide how long your job search might take. (Only a guess, of course.) And then allocate so many weeks or months for each contact method you choose to use. (We suggest that you try Direct Contact first.)

If you are expected to be in your office during the business day, then you have an additional time problem to deal with. How can you work interviews into the business day? And if you work in an open office, how can you even call to set up interviews? As much as possible you should keep up the effort and the appearances on your present job. So maximize your use of the lunch hour, early in the morning and late in the afternoon for calling. If you really keep trying you will be surprised how often you will be able to reach the executive you are trying to contact during your out-of-office hours. The lunch hour for different executives will vary between 12 and 3. Also you can catch people as early as 8 AM and as late as 6 PM on frequent occasions. Jot out a plan each night on how you will be using each minute of your precious lunch break.

Your inability to interview at any time other than lunch just might work to your advantage. If you can, try to set up as many interviews as possible for your lunch hour. This will go a long way to creating a relaxed rapport. (Who isn't happy when eating?) But be sure the interviews don't stray too far from the agenda on hand.

Lunchtime interviews will be much easier for the person with substantial career experience to obtain. People with less experience will often find that they have no alternative other than taking time off for interviewing. If you have to take time off, you have to take time off. But try to do this as little as possible. Usually you should take the whole day off so that it is not blatantly obvious that you are job searching. Try to schedule in at least two, or at the most three, interviews for the same day. (It is very difficult to maintain an optimum level of energy at more than three interviews in one day.) Explain to the interviewer why you might have to juggle your interview schedule -- he/she should honor the respect you are showing your current employer by minimizing your days off and will probably appreciate the fact that another prospective employer is showing an interest in you.

Once again we need to emphasize if you are searching for a job, especially part-time, get out there and do the necessary tasks to the best of your ability and get it over with. Don't let your job search drag on endlessly.

Remember that all schedules are meant to be broken. The purpose of a schedule in your job search is not to rush you to your goal, its purpose is to map out the road ahead of you and evaluate the progress of your chosen strategy to date.

**The Direct Contact Method**

Once you have scheduled a time, you are ready to begin using the job search method that you have chosen. In the text we will restrict discussion to use of the Direct Contact method. Sideboards will comment briefly on developing your personal contacts and using newspaper advertisements.

The first step in preparing for Direct Contact is to develop a check list for categorizing the types of firms for which you would prefer working. You might categorize firms by their product line, their size, their customer-type (such as industrial or consumer), their growth prospects, or, of course by their geographical locations. Your list of important considerations might be very short. If it is, good! The shorter it is, the easier it will be to find appropriate firms.

Then try to decide at which firms you are most likely to be able to obtain employment. You might wish to consider to what degree your particular skills might be in demand, the degree of competition for employment, and the employment outlook at the firm.

Now you are ready to assemble your list of prospective employers. Build up your list to at least 100 prospects. Then separate your prospect list into three groups. The first tier of maybe 25 firms will be your primary target market, the second group of another 25 firms will be your secondary market, and remaining names you will keep in reserve.

## DEVELOPING YOUR CONTACTS

Some career counselors feel that the best route to a better job is through somebody you already know or through somebody to whom you can be introduced. The counselors recommend you build your contact base beyond your current acquaintances by asking each one to introduce you, or refer you, to additional people in your field of interest.

The theory goes like this: You might start with 15 personal contacts, each of whom introduces you to 3 additional people, for a total 45 additional contacts. Then each of these people introduces you to three additional people which adds 135 additional contacts. Theoretically, you will soon know every person in the industry.

Of course, developing your personal contacts does not usually work quite as smoothly as the theory suggests because some people will not be able to introduce you to several relevant contacts. The further you stray from your initial contact base, the weaker your references may be. So, if you do try developing your own contacts, try to begin with as large an initial group of people you personally know as possible. Dig into your personal phone book and your holiday greeting card list and locate old classmates from school. Be particularly sure to approach people who perform your personal business such as your lawyer, accountant, banker, doctor, stockbroker, and insurance agent. These people develop a very broad contact base due to the nature of their professions.

This book will help you greatly in developing your prospect list. Refer to the primary employers section of this book. You will notice that employer listings are arranged according to industry, beginning with Accounting, followed by Advertising, and so on through to Utilities. If you know of a firm, but you're unsure of what industry it would be classified under, then refer to the alphabetically ordered employer index at the rear of the book to find the page number that the firm's listing appears on.

At this stage, once you have gotten your prospect list together and have an idea of the firms for which you might wish to work, it is best to get to work on your resume. Refer to formats of the sample resumes included in the Resumes and Cover Letters section that follows this chapter.

Once your resume is at the printer, begin research for the first batch of 25 prospective employers. You will want to determine whether you would be happy working at the firms you are researching and also get a better idea of what their employment needs might be. You also need to obtain enough information to sound highly informed about the company during phone conversations and in mail correspondence. But don't go all out on your research yet! At some of these firms you probably will not be able to arrange interviews, so save your big research effort until you start to arrange interviews. Nevertheless, you should plan to spend about 3 or 4 hours, on average, researching each firm. Do your research in batches to save time and energy. Go into one resource at a time and find out what you can about each of the 25 firms in the batch. Start with the easiest resources to use (such as this book.) Keep organized. Maintain a folder on each firm.

If you discover something that really disturbs you about the firm (i.e. perhaps they are about to close their only local office) or if you discover that your chances of getting a job there are practically nil (i.e. perhaps they just instituted a hiring freeze) then cross them off your prospect list.

If possible, supplement your research efforts with contacts to individuals who know the firm well. Ideally you should make an informal contact with someone at the particular firm, but often a contact at a direct competitor, or a major supplier or customer will be able to supply you with just as much information. At the very least try to obtain whatever printed information that the company has available, not just annual reports, but product brochures and anything else. The company might very well have printed information about career opportunities.

**Getting The Interview**

Now it is time to arrange an interview, time to make the Direct Contact. If you have read many books on job searching you have probably noticed that virtually all tell you to avoid the personnel office like the plague. It is said that the personnel office never hires people, they just screen out candidates. In some cases you may be able to identify and contact the appropriate manager with the authority to hire you. However, this will take a lot of time and effort in each case. Often you'll be bounced back to personnel. So we suggest that you begin your Direct Contact campaign through personnel offices. If it seems that in the firms on your prospect list that little hiring is done through personnel, you might consider an alternative course of action.

The three obvious means of initiating Direct Contact are:

-Showing up unannounced
-Phone calls
-Mail

Cross out the first one right away. You should never show up to seek a professional position without an appointment. Even if you are somehow lucky enough to obtain an interview, you will appear so unprofessional that you will not even be seriously considered.

Mail contact seems to be a good choice if you have not been in the job market for a while. You can take your time to prepare a careful letter, say exactly what you want, tuck your resume in, and then the addressee can read the material at leisure. But employers receive many resumes every day. Don't be surprised if you do not get a response to your inquiry. So don't spend weeks waiting for responses that never come. If you do send a cover letter, follow it up (or precede it) with a phone call. This will increase your impact, and underscore both your interest in the firm and the fact that you are familiar with it (because of the initial research you did.)

Another alternative is to make a "Cover Call." Your Cover Call should be just like your cover letter: concise. Your first sentence should interest the employer in you. Then try to subtly mention your familiarity with the firm. Don't be overbearing; keep your introduction to three sentences or less. Be pleasant, self confident and relaxed. This will greatly increase the chances of the person at the other end of the line developing the conversation. But don't press. When you are asked to follow up "with something in the mail" don't try to prolong the conversation once it has ended. Don't ask what they want to receive in the mail. Always send your resume and a highly personalized follow-up letter, reminding the addressee of the phone conversation. Always include a cover letter even if you are requested to send a resume. (It is assumed that you will send a cover letter too.)

Unless you are in telephone sales, making smooth and relaxed cover calls will probably not come easily. Practice them on your own and then with your friends or relatives (friends are likely to be more objective and hence, better participants.)

If you obtain an interview over the telephone, be sure to send a thank you note reiterating the points you made during the conversation. You will appear more professional and increase your impact. However, don't mail your resume once an interview has been arranged unless it is specifically requested. Take it with you to the interview instead.

## DON'T BOTHER WITH MASS MAILING OR BARRAGES OF PHONE CALLS

Direct Contact does not mean burying every firm within a hundred miles with mail and phone calls. Mass mailings rarely work in the job hunt. This also applies to those letters that are personalized -- but dehumanized -- on an automatic typewriter. Don't waste your time or money on such a project; you will fool no one but yourself.

The worst part of sending out mass mailings or making unplanned phone calls is that you are likely to be remembered as someone with little genuine interest in the firm, as someone who lacks sincerity, and as somebody that nobody wants to hire.

## HELP WANTED ADVERTISEMENTS

Only a small fraction of professional job openings are advertised. Yet a majority of job seekers -- and a lot of people not in the job market -- spend a lot of time studying the help wanted ads. As a result, the competition for advertised openings is often much more severe.

A moderate-sized Manhattan employer told us about an experience advertising in the help wanted section of a major Sunday newspaper:

*It was a disaster. We had over 500 responses from this relatively small ad in just one week. We have only two phone lines in this office and one was totally knocked out. We'll never advertise for professional help again.*

If you insist on following up on help wanted ads, then research a firm before you reply to an ad so that you can ascertain if you would be a suitable candidate and that you would enjoy working at a particular firm. Also such preliminary research might help to separate you from all of the other professionals responding to that ad, many of whom will only have a passing interest in the opportunity. That said, your chances of obtaining a job through the want-ads are still much smaller than they are if you use the Direct Contact method.

## Preparing For The Interview

Once the interview has been arranged, begin your in-depth research. You have got to arrive at the interview knowing the company upside down and inside out. You need to know their products, their types of customers, their subsidiaries, their parent, their principal locations, their rank in the industry, their sales and profit trends, their type of ownership, their size, their current plans and much more. By this time you have probably narrowed your job search to one industry, but if you haven't then you need to be familiar with the trends in this firm's industry, the firm's principal competitors and their relative performance, and the direction that the industry leaders are headed. Dig into every resource you can! Read the company literature, the trade press, the business press, and if the company is public, call your stockbroker and ask for still additional information. If possible, speak to someone at the firm before the interview, or if not, speak to someone at a competing firm. Clearly the more time you spend, the better. Even if you feel extremely pressed for time, you should set aside at least 12 hours for pre-interview research.

If you have been out of the job market for some time, don't be surprised if you find yourself tense during your first few interviews. It will probably happen every time you re-enter the market, not just when you seek your first job after getting out of school.

Tension is natural during an interview, but if you can be relaxed you will have an advantage over the competition. Knowing you have done a thorough research job should help you relax for an interview. Also make a list of questions that you think might be asked in an interview. Think out your answers carefully. Then practice reviewing them with a friend. Tape record your responses to the questions he/she raises in the role as interviewer. If you feel particularly unsure of your interviewing skills, arrange your first interviews at firms in which you are not very interested. (But remember it is common courtesy to seem excited about the possiblity of working for any firm at which you interview.) Then practice again on your own after these first few interviews. Go over each of the questions that you were asked.

How important is the proper dress for a job interview? Buying a complete wardrobe of Brooks Brothers pinstripes, donning new wing tip shoes and having your hair trimmed every morning is not enough to guarantee your obtaining a career position as an investment banker. But on the other hand, if you can't find a clean, conservative suit and a narrow tie, or won't take the time to polish your shoes and trim and wash your hair -- then you are just wasting your time by interviewing at all.

Very rarely will the final selection of candidates for a job opening be determined by dress. So don't spend a fortune on a new wardrobe. But be sure that your clothes are adequate. Men applying for any professional position should wear a suit; women should either wear a dress or a suit (not a pant suit.) Your clothes should be at least as formal or slightly more formal and more conservative than the position would suggest.

Top personal grooming is more important than finding the perfect clothes for a job interview. Careful grooming indicates both a sense of thoroughness and self-confidence.

Be sure that your clothes fit well and that they are immaculate. Hair must be neat and clean. Shoes should be newly polished. Women need to avoid excessive jewelry and excessive makeup. Men should be freshly shaven, even if the interview is late in the day.

Be complete. Everyone needs a watch and a pen and pad of paper (for taking notes.) Finally a briefcase or folder (containing extra copies of your resume) will help complete the look of professionalism.

Sometimes the interviewer will be running behind schedule. Don't be upset, be sympathetic. He/she might be under pressure to interview a lot of candidates and to quickly fill a demanding position. So be sure to come to your interview with good reading material to keep yourself occupied. This will help increase your patience and ease your tenseness.

**The Interview**

The very beginning of the interview is the most important part because it determines the rapport for the rest of it. Those first few moments are especially crucial. Do you smile when you meet? Do you establish enough eye contact, but not too much? Do you walk into the office with a self-assured and confident stride? Do you shake hands firmly? Do you make small talk easily without being garrulous? It is human nature to judge people by that first impression, so make sure it is a good one. But most of all, try to be yourself.

Often the interviewer will begin, after the small talk, by proceeding to tell you about the company, the division, the department, or perhaps, the position. Because of your detailed research, the information about the company will be repetitive for you and the interviewer would probably like nothing better than to avoid this regurgitation of the company biography. So if you can do so tactfully, indicate to the interviewer that you are very familiar with the firm. If he/she seems intent on providing you with background information, despite your hints, then acquiesce. But be sure to remain attentive. If you can manage to generate a brief discussion of the company or the industry at this point, without being forceful, great. It will help to further build rapport, underscore your interests and increase your impact.

Soon (if it didn't begin that way) the interviewer will begin the questions. This period of the interview falls into one of two categories (or somewhere in between): either a structured interview, where the interviewer has a prescribed set of questions to ask; or an unstructured interview, where the interviewer will ask only leading questions to get you to talk about yourself, your experiences and your goals. Try to sense as quickly as possible which direction the interviewer wishes to proceed and follow along in the direction he/she seems to be leading. This will make the interviewer feel more relaxed and in control of the situation.

## SOME FAVORITE INTERVIEW QUESTIONS

Tell me about yourself...

Why did you leave your last job?

What excites you in your current job?

What are your career goals?

Where would you like to be in 5 years?

What are your greatest strengths?

What are your greatest weaknesses?

Why do you wish to work for this firm?

Where else are you seeking employment?

Why should we hire you?

Many of the questions will be similar to the ones that you were expecting and you will have prepared answers. Remember to keep attuned to the interviewer and make the length of your answers appropriate to the situation. If you are really unsure as to how detailed a response the interviewer is seeking, then ask. Query if he/she would prefer more details of a particular aspect.

As the interview progresses, the interviewer will probably mention what he/she considers to be the most important responsibilities of the position. If applicable, draw parallels between your experience and the demands of the position as seen by the interviewer. Describe your past experience in the same manner that you did on your resume: emphasizing results and achievements and not merely describing activities. If you listen carefully (listening is a very important part of the interviewing process) the interviewer might very well mention or imply the skills in terms of what he/she is seeking. But don't exaggerate. Be on the level.

Try not to cover too much ground during the first interview. This interview is often the toughest, with many candidates being screened out. If you are interviewing for a very competitive position, you will have to make an impression that will last. Focus on a few of your greatest strengths that are relevant to the position. Develop these points carefully, state them again in other words, and then try to summarize them briefly at the end of the interview.

Often the interviewer will pause towards the end and ask if you have any questions. Particularly in a structured interview, this might be the one chance to really show your knowledge of and interest in the firm. Have prepared a list of specific questions that are of real interest to you. Let your questions subtly show your research and your knowledge of the firm's activities. It is wise to have an extensive list of questions, as several of them may have already been answered during the interview.

Do not allow your opportunity to ask questions to become an interrogation. Avoid bringing your list of questions to the interview. And ask questions that you are fairly certain the interviewer can answer (remember how you feel when you cannot answer a question during an interview.)

Even if you are unable to determine the salary range beforehand, do not ask about it during the first interview. You can always ask about it later. Above all, don't ask about fringe benefits until you have been offered a position. (Then be sure to get all the details.) You should be able to determine the company's policy on fringe benefits relatively easily before the interview.

Try not to be negative about anything during the interview. (Particularly any past employer or any previous job.) Be cheerful. Everyone likes to work with someone who seems to be happy.

Don't let a tough question throw you off base. If you don't know the answer to a question, say so simply -- do not apologize. Just smile. Nobody can answer every question -- particularly some of the questions that are asked in job interviews.

Before your first interview, you may have been able to determine how many interviews the employer usually has for positions at your level. (Of

## YOU'RE FIRED!!

You are not the first and will not be the last to go through this traumatic experience. Thousands of professionals are fired every week. Remember, being fired is not a reflection on you as a person. It is usually a reflection of your company's staffing needs and its perception of your recent job performance. Share the fact with your relatives and friends. Being fired is not something of which to be ashamed.

Don't start your job search with a flurry of unplanned activity. Start by choosing a strategy and working out a plan. Now is not the time for major changes in your life. If possible, remain in the same career and in the same geographical location, at least until you have been working again for a while. On the other hand, if the only industry for which you are trained is leaving, or is severely depressed in your area, then you should give prompt consideration to moving or switching careers.

Register for unemployment compensation immediately. A thorough job search could take months. After all, your employers have been contributing to unemployment insurance specifically for you ever since your first job. Don't be surprised to find other professionals collecting unemployment compensation as well. Unemployment compensation is for everybody who is between jobs.

Be prepared for the question, "Why were you fired?", during job interviews. Avoid mentioning you were fired while arranging interviews. Try especially hard not to speak negatively of your past employer and not to sound particularly worried about your status of being temporarily unemployed. But don't spend much time reflecting on why you were fired or how you might have avoided it. Look ahead. Think positively. And be sure to follow a careful plan during your job search.

course it may differ quite a bit within one firm.) Usually you can count on at least three or four interviews, although some firms, such as some of the professional partnerships, are well-known to give a minimum of six interviews for all professional postions.

Depending on what information you are able to obtain you might want to vary your strategy quite a bit from interview to interview. For instance if the first interview is a screening interview then try to have a few of your strengths really stand out. On the other hand, if later interviews are primarily with people who are in a position to veto your hiring, but not to push it forward (and few people are weeded out at these stages), then you should primarily focus on building rapport as opposed to reiterating and developing your key strengths.

If it looks as though your skills and background do not match the position your interviewer was hoping to fill, ask him or her if there is another division or subsidiary that perhaps could profit from your talents.

**After The Interview**

Write a follow-up letter immediately after the interview, while it is still fresh in the interviewer's mind. Then, if you have not heard from the interviewer within seven days, call him/her to stress your continued interest in the firm and the position and to request a second interview.

A parting word of advice. Again and again during your job search you will be rejected. You will be rejected when you apply for interviews. You will be rejected after interviews. For every job you finally receive you will probably have received a multitude of rejections. Don't let these rejections slow you down. Keep reminding yourself that the sooner you go out and get started on your job search and get those rejections flowing in, the closer you will be to obtaining the better job.

# Resumes and Cover Letters

## RESUMES AND COVER LETTERS

## THIS SECTION CONTAINS:

1. Resume Preparation

2. Resume Format

3. Resume Content

4. Should You Hire A Resume Writer?

5. Cover Letters

6. Sample Resumes

7. General Model For A Cover Letter

8. Sample Cover Letters

9. General Model For A Follow-up Letter

## RESUMES/OVERVIEW

When filling a position, a recruiter will often have 100 plus applicants, but time to interview only the 5 or 10 most promising ones. So he or she will have to reject most applicants after a brief skimming of their resume.

Unless you have phoned and talked to the recruiter -- which you should do whenever you can -- you will be chosen or rejected for an interview entirely on the basis of your resume and cover letter. So your resume must be outstanding. (But remember -- a resume is no substitute for a job search campaign. YOU must seek a job. Your resume is only one tool.)

## RESUME PREPARATION

**One page, usually.**

Unless you have an unusually strong background with many years of experience and a large diversity of outstanding achievements, prepare a one page resume. Recruiters dislike long resumes.

**8 1/2 x 11 Size**

Recruiters often get resumes in batches of hundreds. If your resume is on small sized paper it is likely to get lost in the pile. If oversized, it is likely to get crumpled at the edges, and won't fit in their files.

**Typesetting**

Modern photocomposition typesetting gives you the clearest, sharpest image, a wide variety of type styles and effects such as italics, bold facing, and book-like justified margins. Typesetting is the best resume preparation process, but is also the most expensive.

**Word Processing**

The most flexible way to get your resume typed is on a good quality word processor. With word processing, you can make changes almost instantly because your resume will be stored on a magnetic disk and the computer will do all the re-typing automatically. A word processing service will usually offer you a variety of type styles in both regular and proportional spacing. You can have bold facing for emphasis, justified margins, and clear, sharp copies.

**Typing**

Household typewriters and office typewriters with nylon or other cloth ribbons are NOT good for typing the resume you will have printed. If you can't get word processing or typesetting, hire a professional with a high quality office typewriter with a plastic ribbon (usually called a "carbon ribbon.")

**Printing**

Find the best quality offset printing process available. DO NOT make your copies on an office photocopier. Only the personnel office may see the resume you mail. Everyone else may see only a copy of it. Copies of copies quickly become unreadable. Some professionally maintained, extra-high-quality photocopiers are of adequate quality, if you are in a rush. But top quality offset printing is best.

**Proofread your resume**

Whether you typed it yourself or had it written, typed, or typeset, mistakes on resumes can be embarrassing, particularly when something obvious such as your name is misspelled. No matter how much you paid someone else to type or write or typeset your resume, YOU lose if there is a mistake. So proofread it as carefully as possible. Get a friend to help you. Read your draft aloud as your friend checks the proof copy. Then have your friend read aloud while you check. Next, read it letter by letter to check spelling and punctuation.

If you are having it typed or typeset by a resume service or a printer, and you can't bring a friend or take the time during the day to proof it, pay for it and take it home. Proof it there and bring it back later to get it corrected and printed.

## RESUME FORMAT

(See samples)

**Basic data**

Your name, phone number, and a complete address should be at the top of your resume. (If you are a university student, you should also show your home address and phone number.)

**Separate your education and work experience**

In general, list your experience first. If you have recently graduated, list your education first, unless your experience is more important than your education. (For example, if you have just graduated from a teaching school, have some business experience and are applying for a job in business you would list your business experience first.) If you have two or more years of college, you don't need to list high schools.

**Reverse chronological order**

To a recruiter your last job and your latest schooling are the most important. So put the last first and list the rest going back in time.

**Show dates and locations**

Put the dates of your employment and education on the left of the page. Put the names of the companies you worked for and the schools you attended a few spaces to the right of the dates. Put the city and state or city and country where you studied or worked to the right of the page.

### Avoid sentences and large blocks of type

Your resume will be scanned, not read. Short, concise phrases are much more effective than long-winded sentences. Keep everything easy to find. Avoid paragraphs longer than six lines. Never go ten or more lines in a paragraph. If you have more than six lines of information about one job or school, put it in two or more paragraphs.

## RESUME CONTENT

### Be factual

In many companies, inaccurate information on a resume or other application material will get you fired as soon as the inaccuracy is discovered. Protect yourself.

### Be positive

You are selling your skills and accomplishments in your resume. If you achieved something, say so. Put it in the best possible light. Don't hold back or be modest, no one else will. But don't exaggerate to the point of misrepresentation.

### Be brief

Write down the important (and pertinent) things you have done, but do it in as few words as possible. The shorter your resume is, the more carefully it will be examined.

### Work experience

Emphasize continued experience in a particular type of function or continued interest in a particular industry. De-emphasize irrelevant positions. Delete positions that you held for less than four months. (Unless you are a very recent college grad or still in school.)

### Stress your results

Elaborate on how you contributed to your past employers. Did you increase sales, reduce costs, improve a product, implement a new program? Were you promoted?

**Mention relevant skills and responsibilities**

Be specific. Slant your past accomplishments toward the type of position that you hope to obtain. Example: Do you hope to supervise people? Then state how many people, performing what function, you have supervised.

**Education**

Keep it brief if you have more than two years of career experience. Elaborate more if you have less experience. Mention degrees received and any honors or special awards. Note individual courses or research projects that might be relevant for employers. For instance, if you are a liberal arts major, be sure to mention courses in such areas as: accounting, statistics, computer programming, or mathematics.

**Job objective?**

Leave it out. Even if you are certain of exactly the type of job that you desire, the inclusion of a job objective might eliminate you from consideration for other positions that a recruiter feels are a better match for your qualifications.

**Personal data**

Keep it very brief. Two lines maximum. A one-word mention of commonly practiced activities such as golf, skiing, sailing, chess, bridge, tennis, etc. can prove to be good way to open up a conversation during an interview. Do not include your age, weight, height, etc.

## SHOULD YOU HIRE A RESUME WRITER?

If you write reasonably well, there are some advantages to writing your resume yourself. To write it well, you will have to review your experience and figure out how to explain your accomplishments in clear, brief phrases. This will help you when you explain your work to interviewers.

If your write your resume, everything in it will be in your own words -- it will sound like you. It will say what you want it to say. And you will be much more familiar with the contents. If you are a good writer, know yourself well and have a good idea of what parts of your background employers are looking for, you may be able to write your own resume better than anyone else can. If you write your resume yourself, you should have someone who can be objective (preferably not a close relative) review it with you.

### When should you have your resume professionally written?

If you have difficulty writing in Resume Style (which is quite unlike normal written language), if you are unsure of which parts of your background you should emphasize, or if you think your resume would make your case better if it did not follow the standard form outlined here or in a book on resumes, then you should have it professionally written.

There are two reasons even some professional resume writers we know have had their resumes written with the help of fellow professionals. First, when they need the help of someone who can be objective about their background, and second, when they want an experienced sounding board to help focus their thoughts.

### If you decide to hire a resume writer

The best way to choose a writer is by reputation -- the recommendation of a friend, a personnel director, your school placement officer or someone else knowledgeable in the field.

You should ask, "If I'm not satisfied with what you write, will you go over it with me and change it?"

You should ask, "How long has the person who will write my resume been writing resumes?"

There is no sure relation between price and quality, except that you are unlikely to get a good writer for less than $50 for an uncomplicated resume and you shouldn't have to pay more than $300 unless your experience is very extensive or complicated. There will be additional charges for printing.

Few resume services will give you a firm price over the phone, simply because some people's resumes are too complicated and take too long to do at any predetermined price. Some services will quote you a price that applies to almost all of their customers. Be sure to do some comparative shopping. Obtain a firm price before you engage their services and find out how expensive minor changes will be.

## COVER LETTERS

Always mail a cover letter with your resume. In a cover letter you can show an interest in the company that you can't show in a resume. You can point out one or two skills or accomplishments the company can put to good use.

### Make it personal

The more personal you can get, the better. If someone known to the person you are writing has recommended that you contact the company, get permission to include his/her name in the letter. If you have the name of a person to send the letter to, make sure you have the name spelled correctly and address it directly to that person. Be sure to put the person's name and title on both the letter and envelope. This will ensure that your letter will get through to the proper person, even if a new person now occupies this position. But even if you are addressing it to the "Personnel Director" or the "Hiring Partner," send a letter.

Type cover letters in full. Don't try the cheap and easy ways like photocopying the body of your letter and typing in the inside address and salutation. You will give the impression that you are mailing to a multitude of companies and have no particular interest in any one. Have your letters fully typed and signed with a pen.

**Phone**

Precede or follow your mailing with a phone call.

**Bring extra copies of your resume to the interview**

If the person interviewing you doesn't have your resume, be prepared. Carry copies of your own. Even if you have already forwarded your resume, be sure to take extra copies to the interview, as someone other than the interviewer(s) might now have the first copy you sent.

## Chronological Resume
(Prepared on a Word Processor and Laser Printer.)

**WALLACE R. RECTORIAN**
412 Maple Court
Seattle, WA 98404
206/555-6584

**EXPERIENCE**

1984-present    THE CENTER COMPANY, Seattle, WA
*Systems Analyst*, design systems for the manufacturing unit. Specifically, physical inventory, program specifications, studies of lease buy decisions, selection of hardware the outside contractors and inside users. Wrote On-Site Computer Terminal Operators Manual. Adapted product mix problems to the LASPSP (Logistical Alternative Product Synthesis Program).

As *Industrial Engineer* from February 1984 to February 1986, computerized system design. Evaluated manufacturing operations operator efficiency productivity index and budget allocations. Analyzed material waste and recommended solutions.

**ADDITIONAL EXPERIENCE**

1980-1984    *Graduate Research Assistant* at New York State Institute of Technology.

1978-1980    *Graduate Teaching Assistant* at Salem State University.

**EDUCATION**

1982-1984    NEW YORK STATE INSTITUTE OF TECHNOLOGY, Albany, NY
M.S. in Operations Research. GPA: 3.6. Graduate courses included Advanced Location and Queueing Theories, Forecasting, Inventory and Material Flow Systems, Linear and Nonlinear Determination Models, Engineering Economics and Integer Programming.

1980-1982    M.S. in Information and Computer Sciences. GPA: 3.8
Curriculum included Digital Computer Organization & Programming. Information Structure & Process. Mathematical Logic, Computer Systems, Logic Design and Switching Theory.

1976-1980    SALEM STATE UNIVERSITY, Salem, OR
B.A. in Mathematics. GPA: 3.6.

**AFFILIATIONS**

Member of the American Institute of Computer Programmers, Association for Computing Machinery and the Operations Research Society of America.

**PERSONAL**

Married, three dependents, able to relocate.

## Chronological Resume
(Prepared on a Word Processor and Laser Printer.)

Angela Weatherstone
1009 Kilminster Drive
Los Angeles, CA 90013
213/555-0987

**Business experience**

1988-present  PACIFIC COMPUTER LEASING, Los Angeles, CA
**Manager of Debt Placement**
* Responsible for developing and maintaining bank and institutional debt sources.
* Structured leases for maximum tax advantages.
* Have documented and closed $120,000,000 of secured loans.
* Work closely with investment bankers and bank and institutional funding sources.

1981-1988  PRIME COMPUTER, INC., Natick, MA
**Customer Finance Marketing Manager, North America**
* Responsible for the profitable management of finance lease and tax exempt installment programs in the United States and Mexico used by government and business.
* Made certain pricing and documentation were suitable for sale of portfolio to funding institutions. Typical transaction exceeded $750,000.

1978-1981  COPPERBOTTOM INFORMATION SYSTEMS, Philadelphia, PA
**Manager of Marketing Proposal Analysis, Atlanta, GA**
* Advised field sales force in the initial stages of proposals with emphasis on the financial aspects of operating and finance leases, installment sales, and multi-party transactions.
**Sectional Revenue Manager, Winston-Salem, NC**
* Achieved planned lease purchase revenue mix, by appropriate pricing policies and financial agreements with customers.
**Sales Finance, Baltimore, MD**
* Implemented and administered Copperbottom's finance lease program. Educated field sales personnel in financial plans. Handled administration of equipment add-ons, replacements, handled contract amendments.

1975-1978  BAYBANK, N.A., Portland, OR
**Branch Manager**
* Responsible for the day-to-day operation of a branch bank.

**Education**
1970-1974  BABSON COLLEGE, Wellesley, MA
Bachelor of Science in Business Administration with a major in financial management, minor in mathematics.

**References**  References will be supplied upon request.

# Chronological Resume
(Prepared on a Word Processor and Laser Printer.)

**DAMIEN W. PINCKNEY**

U.S. Address:
15606 Center Street
Bottineau, ND 58777
701/555-9320

Jamaican Address:
Oskarrataan Building, Room 1234
Hedonism II
Negril, Jamaica
809/555-6634

**Experience**

1984-present   **HEDONISM II**, Negril, Jamaica
Resident Engineer for this publicly owned resort with main offices in Kingston. Responsibilities include:

Maintaining electrical generating and distribution equipment.

Supervising an eight-member staff in maintenance of refrigeration equipment, power and light generators, water purification plant, and general construction machinery.

1982-1984   **NEGRIL BEACH HOTEL**, Negril Beach, Jamaica
Resident Engineer for a privately held resort, assigned total responsibility for facility generating equipment.

Directed maintenance, operation and repair of diesel generating equipment.

1980-1982   Directed overhaul of turbo generating equipment in two Mid-Western localities and assisted in overhaul of a turbo generating unit in Mexico.

1975-1980   **CAPITAL CITY ELECTRIC**, Washington, DC
Service Engineer for the power generation service division of this regional power company, supervised the overhaul, maintenance and repair of large generators and associated auxiliary equipment.

**Education**

1972-1975   **FRANKLIN INSTITUTE**, Baltimore, MD
Awarded a degree of Associate of Engineering. Concentration in Mechanical Power Engineering Technology.

**Personal**   Willing to travel and relocate.
Interested in sailing, scuba diving, deep sea fishing.

**References available upon request.**

## Functional Resume
(Prepared on a Word Processor and Letter-Quality Printer.)

---

Michelle Hughes
430 Miller's Crossing
Essex Junction, VT 05452
802/555-9354

Solid background in plate making, separations, color matching, background definition, printing, mechanicals, color corrections, and supervision of personnel. A highly motivated manager and effective communicator. Proven ability to:

* **Create Commercial Graphics**
* **Produce Embossing Drawings**
* **Color Separate**
* **Analyze Consumer Acceptance**
* **Meet Graphic Deadlines**
* **Control Quality**
* **Resolve Printing Problems**
* **Expedite Printing Operations**

### Qualifications

**Printing:** Black and white and color. Can judge acceptability of color reproduction by comparing it with original. Can make four or five color corrections on all media. Have long developed ability to restyle already reproduced four-color artwork. Can create perfect tone for black and white match fill-ins for resume cover letters.

**Customer Relations:** Work with customers to assure specifications are met and customers are satisfied. Can guide work through entire production process and strike a balance between technical printing capabilities and need for customer approval.

**Management:** Schedule work to meet deadlines. Direct staff in production procedures. Maintain quality control from inception of project through final approval for printing.

**Specialties:** Make silk screen overlays for a multitude of processes. Velo bind, GBC bind, perfect bind. Have knowledge to prepare posters, flyers, and personalized stationery.

**Personnel Supervision:** Foster an atmosphere that encourages highly talented artists to balance high level creativity with a maximum of production. Meet or beat production deadlines. Am continually instructing new employees, apprentices and students in both artistry and technical operations.

### Experience

Professor of Graphic Arts, University of Vermont, Burlington, VT (1977-present).
Assistant Production Manager, Artsign Digraphics, Burlington, VT (1981-present) Part time.

### Education

Massachusetts Conservatory of Art, PhD 1977
University of Massachusetts, B.A. 1974

## Chronological Resume
(Prepared on a Word Processor and Laser Printer.)

Melvin Winter
43 Aspen Wall Lane
Wheaton, IL 60512
312/555-6923 (home)
312/555-3000 (work)

**RELATED EXPERIENCE**
1982-Present GREAT LAKES PUBLISHING COMPANY, Chicago, IL
Operations Supervisor (1986-present)
in the Engineering Division of this major trade publishing house, responsible for maintaining on line computerized customer files, title files, accounts receivable, inventory and sales files.

Organize department activities, establish priorities and train personnel. Provide corporate accounting with monthly reports of sales, earned income from journals, samples, inventory levels/value and sales and tax data. Divisional sales average $3 million annually.

Senior Customer Service Representative (1984-1986)
in the Construction Division. Answered customer service inquiries regarding orders and accounts receivable, issued return and shortage credits and expedited special sales orders for direct mail and sales to trade schools.

Customer Service Representative (1982-1983)
in the International Division. Same duties as for construction division except that sales were to retail stores and universities in Europe.

1980-1982 B. DALTON, BOOKSELLER, Salt Lake City, UT
Assistant Manager of this retail branch of a major domestic book seller, maintained all paperback inventories at necessary levels, deposited receipts daily and created window displays.

**EDUCATION**
1976-1980 UNIVERSITY OF MAINE, Orono, ME
Awarded a degree of Bachelor of Arts in French Literature.

**LANGUAGES**
Fluent in French. Able to write in French, German and Spanish.

**PERSONAL**
Willing to travel and relocate, particularly in Europe.

References available upon request.

## General Model for a Cover Letter

```
                                           Your Address
                                           Date

Contact Person Name
Title
Company
Address


Dear Mr./Ms._____:


Immediately explain why your background makes you the best can-
didate for the position that you are applying for. Keep the
first paragraph short and hard-hitting.

Detail what you could contribute to this company. Show how
your qualifications will benefit this firm. Remember to keep
this letter short; few recruiters will read a cover letter
longer than half a page.

Describe your interest in the corporation. Subtly emphasize
your knowledge about this firm (the result of your research ef-
fort) and your familiarity with the industry. It is common
courtesy to act extremely eager to work for any company that
you interview.

In the closing paragraph you should specifically request an in-
terview. Include your phone number and the hours when you can
be reached. Alternatively, you might prefer to mention that
you will follow up with a phone call (to arrange an interview
at a mutually convenient time within the next several days).



                                           Sincerely,

                                           (signature)

                                           Your full name (typed)
```

# Cover Letter

411 Looksee Avenue
Apt. 449
Medford, MA 02139
March 15, 1993

Mr. Benjamin Deiver
Sales Manager
Yankee Ski Products
456 Pillbox Lane
Denver, CO 80201


Dear Mr. Deiver:

I seek a position as a sales representative with Yankee Ski Products and I offer, in return, thorough industry experience and more than eleven years of solid practical background in sales.

As a sample of sales achievement, I increased my personal monthly gross sales volume to a point where it tripled the combined sales of three other full-time representatives for one ski manufacturer. Also, I have won numerous international and domestic sales awards.

As an experienced sales representative, I have succeeded in improving area or regional sales by employing a combination of aggressiveness, enthusiasm, and persistence, and I have been able to bring out these traits in those whom I have hired and trained in my capacity as National Sales Instructor for two companies.

I feel that your new line of competition skis offers an unbeatable price/performance combination for the serious racer. I am firmly convinced that I can improve your market penetration in the lucrative Upstate New York area at least to a top five position.

I am an avid skier. As such, I am familiar with not only the technical terms involved, but with the types of equipment available and the extent to which it is marketed.

I look forward to hearing from you.

Sincerely,

Christina Harges

## Cover Letter

1286 136th Avenue
Newark, NJ 07101
December 10, 1992

Mr. Edward Buchanan
Personnel Manager
Caufield & Compson Engineering Services, Inc.
Central Park Square Building
New York, NY 10019

Dear Mr. Buchanan:

My diversity as well as my depth of engineering experience in the wastewater treatment field could prove to be a particularly strong asset for Caufield & Compson given the firm's current and continued commitment to being a pioneering innovator in the engineering and construction of wastewater treatment facilities.

I offer an extensive background in investigating, reporting and designing multimillion dollar wastewater treatment facilities, pumping facilities and sewer lines in New Jersey and in Puerto Rico. In addition, I have experience in coordinating engineering services during construction of sewers and pumping facilities in Hawaii.

One of my basic strengths is my ability to act as liaison for diverse engineering and non-engineering individuals and groups to keep a project on schedule and in line with funding constraints.

I have come to a point in my career where I desire to expand into areas where I might apply over 8 years of solid engineering experience. These areas include hazardous waste treatment, industrial wastewater and water treatment, and water supply.

I will be glad to furnish any additional information you desire. You may reach me during the day at 201/555-1100. I look forward to hearing from you.

Sincerely,

Raymond A. Gatz

Enc. Resume

## General Model for a Follow-Up Letter

Your Address
Date

Contact Person Name
Title
Company
Address

Dear Mr./Ms._____:

Remind the interviewer of the position for which you were interviewed, as well as the date. Thank him/her for the interview.

Confirm your interest in the opening and the organization. Use specifics to emphasize both that you have researched the firm in detail and considered how you would fit into the company and the position.

Like in your cover letter, emphasize one or two of you strongest qualifications and slant them toward the various points that the interviewer considered the most important for the position. Keep the letter brief, a half-page is plenty.

If appropriate, close with a suggestion for further action, such as a desire to have additional interviews. Mention your phone number and the hours that you can best be reached. Alternatively, you may prefer to mention that you will follow up with a phone call in several days.

Sincerely yours,

(signature)

Your full name (typed)

# PART TWO: OCCUPATION PROFILES

## Jobs In Each Industry

## JOBS IN EACH INDUSTRY

*The following chapter includes descriptions of many of the most common occupations, with an emphasis on those that have especially strong growth outlooks for the 1990's. For each position, you will find a brief description of what the position entails, the background or qualification you would need for entering and advancing in that occupation, the salary expectations for various levels within the occupational category, and a forecast of the job's growth potential for the 1990's.*

**The occupations listed are as follows:**

Accountant/Auditor
Actuary
Administrator
Advertising Worker
Architect
Attorney
Bank Officer/Manager
Biochemist
Blue-Collar Worker Supervisor
Buyer/Merchandise Manager
Chemist
Claims Representative
Commercial Artist
Data Processing Specialist
Dietician/Nutritionist
Draftsperson
Economist
Engineer
Financial Analyst
Food Technologist
Forester
Geographer
Geologist/Geophysicist
Hotel Manager/Assistant Manager
Industrial Designer
Insurance Agent/Broker
Manager
Manaufacturer's Sales Worker
Personnel and Labor Relations Specialist
Physicist
Public Relations Worker

Purchasing Agent
Quality Control Supervisor
Reporter/Editor
Securities and Financial Services
Sales Representative
Statistician
Systems Analyst
Technical Writer/Editor
Underwriter

# ACCOUNTANT/AUDITOR

**DESCRIPTION:**

Accountants prepare and analyze financial reports that furnish important financial information. Four major fields are public, management, and government accounting, and internal auditing. Public accountants have their own businesses or work for accounting firms. Management accountants, also called industrial or private accountants, handle the financial records of their company. Government accountants examine the records of government agencies and audit private businesses and individuals whose dealings are subject to government regulation. Accountants often concentrate on one phase of accounting. For example, many public accountants may specialize in auditing, tax, or estate planning. Others specialize in management consulting and give advice on a variety of matters. Management accountants provide the financial information executives need to make sound business decisions. They may work in areas such as taxation, budgeting, costs, or investments. Internal auditing, a specialization within management accounting, is rapidly growing in importance. Internal auditors examine and ensure efficient and economical operation. Government accountants are often Internal Revenue Service agents or are involved in financial management and budget administration.

About 60 percent of all accountants do management accounting. An additional 25 percent are engaged in public accounting through independent firms. Other accountants work for government, and some teach in colleges and universities. Accountants and auditors are found in all business, industrial, and governmental organizations.

**BACKGROUND AND QUALIFICATIONS:**

Although many graduates of business schools are successful, most public accounting and business firms require applicants for accountant and internal auditor positions to have at least a BA in Accounting or a closely related field. Many employers prefer those with a Master's degree in Accounting. Most large employers prefer applicants who are familiar with computers and their applications in accounting and internal auditing.

Previous experience in accounting can help an applicant get a job. Many colleges offer students an opportunity to gain experience through summer or part-time internship programs conducted by public accounting firms. Such training is invaluable in gaining permanent employment in the field.

Professional recognition through certification or licensing also is extremely valuable. Anyone working as a certified public accountant (CPA) must hold a certificate issued by a state board of accountancy. All states use the four-part Uniform CPA Exam, prepared by the American Institute of Certified Public Accountants, to establish certification. The CPA exam is very rigorous, and candidates are not required to pass all four parts at once. Most states require applicants to have some public accounting experience for a CPA certificate, and those with BA's often need two years of experience. New trends require the candidate to have a BA plus 30 additional semester hours.

The Institute of Internal Auditors confers the Certified Internal Auditor (CIA) certificate upon graduates from accredited colleges and universities who have completed three years internal auditing and who have passed a four-part exam. The National Association of Accountants (NAA) confers the Certificate in Management Accounting (CMA) upon candidates who pass a series of uniform exams and meet specific educational and professional standards. A growing number of states require both CPA's and licensed public accountants to complete a certain number of hours of continuing education before licenses can be renewed. Increasingly, accountants are studying computer programming so they can adapt accounting procedures to data processing.

Junior public accountants usually start by assisting with auditing work for several clients. They may advance to intermediate positions with greater responsibility in one or two years, and to senior positions within another few years. Those who deal successfully with top industry executives often become supervisors, managers, or partners, or transfer to executive positions in private firms. Beginning management accountants often start as ledger accountants, junior internal auditors, or as trainees for technical accounting positions. They may advance to chief plant accountant, chief cost accountant, budget director, or manager of internal auditing. Some become controllers, treasurers, financial vice-presidents, or corporation presidents.

## OUTLOOK:

Employment of accountants and auditors is expected to grow much faster than the average for all occupations through the year 2000 due to the key role these workers play in the management of all types of businesses. Although increased demand will generate many new jobs, most openings win result from the need to replace workers who leave the occupation or retire. While accountants and auditors tend to leave the profession at a lower rate than members of most other occupations, replacement needs will be substantial because the occupation is large. Accountants rarely lose their jobs when other workers are laid off during hard economic times. Financial information must be developed and tax reports prepared regardless of the state of the economy.

# ACTUARY

## DESCRIPTION:

Actuaries design insurance and pension plans that can be maintained on a sound financial basis. They assemble and analyze statistics to calculate probabilities of death, sickness, injury, disability, unemployment, retirement, and property loss from accident, theft, fire, and other hazards. Actuaries use this information to determine the expected insured loss. The actuary calculates premium rates and determines policy contract provision for each type of insurance offered. Most actuaries specialize in either life and health insurance, or property and liability (casualty) insurance; a growing number specialize in pension plans. About two-thirds of all actuaries work for private insurance companies, the majority in life insurance. Consulting firms and rating bureaus employ about one-fifth of all actuaries. Other actuaries work for private organizations administering independent pension and welfare plans.

## BACKGROUND AND EXPERIENCE:

A good educational background for a beginning job in a large life or casualty insurance company is a Bachelor's degree in Mathematics or Statistics; a degree in Actuarial Science is preferred. Courses in accounting, computer science, economics, and insurance also are useful. Of equal importance, however, is the need to pass one or more of the exams offered by professional actuarial societies. Three societies sponsor programs leading to full professional status in the specialty. The Society of Actuaries gives nine actuarial exams for the life and health insurance, and pension fields; The Casualty Actuarial Society gives 10 exams for the property and liability fields; and the American Society of Pension Actuaries gives nine exams covering the pension field. Actuaries are encouraged to complete the entire series of exams as soon as possible; completion generally takes from five to ten years. Actuaries who complete five exams in either the life insurance segment of the pension series, or seven exams in the casualty series are awarded "associate" membership in their society. Those who have passed an entire series receive full membership and the title "Fellow".

Beginning actuaries often rotate among different jobs to learn various actuarial operations and to become familiar with different phases of insurance work. At first, their work may be routine, such as preparing tabulations for actuarial tables or reports. As they gain experience, they may supervise clerks, prepare correspondence and reports, and do research. Advancement to more responsible positions such as assistant, associate, or chief actuary depends largely on job performance and the number of actuarial exams passed. Many actuaries, because of their broad knowledge of insurance and related fields, are selected for administrative positions in other company activities, particularly in underwriting, accounting, or data processing. Many advance to top executive positions.

## OUTLOOK:

Employment of actuaries is expected to grow much faster than the average for all occupations through the year 2000. Most job openings, however, are expected to arise each year to replace actuaries who transfer to other occupations, or retire. Job opportunities should be favorable for college graduates who have passed at least two actuarial exams while still in school and have a strong mathematical and statistical background.

# ADMINISTRATOR

## DESCRIPTION:

Administrators perform a wide variety of office paperwork tasks. These tasks might range from preparing a summary of sales activity to filing and retrieving information. A lower-level administrator might serve primarily as a typist, office machine operator, or secretary, being closely supervised by an office superior. An upper-level administrator might supervise the work of many office workers and be responsible for a broad range of office duties that support an organization's activities.

## BACKGROUND AND QUALIFICATIONS:

Because of the broad range of duties and responsibilities of administrators at different levels or within different organizations, the actual job and its requisite background and experience may vary greatly from one firm to the next, and from one position to the next. However, all but the highest managerial levels of administrative work require strong office skills, such as fast and accurate typing and the ability to prepare business correspondence. In larger organizations with more complex office tasks, a college background is becoming an increasingly valuable asset. Also, experience or familiarity with computers, word processors, or data processing equipment greatly improves an applicant's employability and chances for promotion.

## OUTLOOK:

Despite the nearly universal use of computer and word processing automation in the office, administrative positions are still expected to offer above average growth. Also, with many new entrants to the job market trying to obtain junior managerial jobs and similar posts, administrative positions are likely to be less competitive than many other types of jobs. Administrators are found in all industries, but especially in banking, insurance, utilities, and other companies with a high volume of paperwork.

# ADVERTISING WORKER

**DESCRIPTION:**

There are several different occupations commonly associated with the field of advertising. Advertising managers direct the advertising program of the business for which they work. They determine the size of the advertising budget, the type of ad and the medium to use, and what advertising agency, if any, to employ. Managers who decide to employ an agency work closely with the advertising agencies to develop advertising programs for client firms and individuals. Copywriters develop the text and headlines to be used in the ads. Media directors negotiate contracts for advertising for advertising space or air time. Production managers and their assistants arrange to have the ad printed for publication, filmed for television, or recorded for radio.

**BACKGROUND AND QUALIFICATIONS:**

Most employers prefer college graduates. Some employers seek persons with degrees in advertising with heavy emphasis on marketing, business, and journalism; others prefer graduates with a liberal arts background; some employers place little emphasis on the type of degree. Opportunities for advancement in this field generally are excellent for creative, talented, and hard-working people. For example, copywriters and account executives may advance to more responsible work in their specialties, or to managerial jobs if they demonstrate ability in dealing with clients. Some especially capable employees may become partners in an existing agency, or they may establish their own agency.

**OUTLOOK:**

Employment of advertising managers is expected to increase faster than the average for all occupations through the year 2000 as increasingly intense domestic and foreign competition in products and services offered to consumers requires greater marketing and promotional efforts. In addition to rapid growth, many job openings will occur each year to replace managers who move into the top positions or retire. However, the ample supply of experienced professional and technical personnel and recent college graduates seeking these management positions may result in substantial job competition.

# ARCHITECT

**DESCRIPTION:**

Architects provide a wide variety of professional services to individuals, organizations, corporations, or government agencies planning a building project. Architects are involved in all phases of development of a building or project, from the initial discussion of general ideas through completion of construction. Their duties require a variety of skills, including design, engineering, managerial, and supervisory.

The architect and client first discuss the purposes, requirements, and cost of a project. The architect then prepares schematic drawings that show the scale and the mechanical and structural relationships of the building. If the schematic drawings are accepted, the architect develops a final design showing the floor plans and the structural details of the project.

Architects also specify the building materials and, in some cases, the interior furnishings. In all cases, the architect must ensure that the structure's design and specifications conform to local and state building codes, zoning laws, fire regulations, and other ordinances. After all drawings are completed, the architect assists the client in selecting a contractor and negotiating the construction contract. As construction proceeds, the architect visits the building site from time to time to ensure that the contractor is following the design using the specified materials.

Besides designing structures, architects may also help in selecting building sites, preparing cost and land-use studies, and long-range planning for site development. When working on large projects or for large architectural firms, architects often specialize in one phase of work, such as designing or administering construction contracts. This often requires working with engineers, urban planners, landscape architects, and others.

Most architects work for architectural firms or for builders, real estate firms, or other businesses that have large construction programs. Some work for governmental agencies. Although found in many areas, a large proportion of architects are employed in seven cities: Boston, Chicago, Los Angeles, New York, Philadelphia, San Francisco, and Washington, DC.

## BACKGROUND AND QUALIFICATIONS:

Every state requires individuals to be licensed before they may call themselves architects, or contract for providing architectural services. To qualify for the licensing exam, a person must have either a Bachelor of Architecture degree followed by three years of acceptable practical experience in an architect's office, or a Master of Architecture degree followed by two years of experience. As a substitute for formal training, most states accept additional experience (usually 12 years) and successful completion of a qualifying test for admission to the licensing examination. Many architectural school graduates work in the field although they are not licensed. However, a registered architect is required to take legal responsibility for all work. New graduates usually begin as drafters for architectural firms, where they prepare architectural drawings and make models of structures under the direction of a registered architect. After several years of experience, they may advance to Chief or Senior Drafter responsible for all major details of a set of working drawings, and for supervising other drafters. Others may work as designers, construction contract administrators, or specification writers who prepare documents that specify the building materials, their method of installation, the quality of finishes, required tests, and many other related details.

## OUTLOOK:

Employment of architects is expected to rise faster than the average for all occupations through the year 2000, although growth in employment will be slower than in recent years; however, demand for architects is highly dependent upon the level of construction, particularly of non-residential structures such as office buildings and shopping centers. Although rapid growth in this area is expected, construction is sensitive to cyclical changes in the economy. During recessions or slow periods for construction, architects will face competition for job openings or clients, and layoffs may occur.

# ATTORNEY

## DESCRIPTION:

Certain activities are common to nearly every attorney's work. Probably the most fundamental is interpretation of the law. Every attorney, whether representing the defendant in a murder trial, or the plaintiff in a lawsuit, combines an understanding of the relevant laws with knowledge of the facts in the case, to determine how the first affects the second. Based on this determination, the attorney decides what action would best serve the interests of the client.

A significant number specialize in one branch of law, such as corporate, criminal, labor, patent, real estate, tax, admiralty, probate, or international law. Communications lawyers, for example, may represent radio and television stations in their dealings with the Federal Communications Commission in such matters as preparing and filing license renewal applications, employment reports, and other documents required by the FCC on a regular basis. Lawyers representing public utilities before state and federal regulatory agencies handle matters involving utility rates. They develop strategy, arguments, and testimony, prepare cases for presentation, and argue the case. These attorneys also inform clients about changes in regulations and give advice about the legality of certain actions.

A single client may employ a lawyer full time. Known as House Counsel, this lawyer usually advises a company about legal questions that arise from business activities. Such questions might involve patents, governments regulations, a business contract with another company, or a collective bargaining agreement with a union. Some attorneys use their legal background in administrative or managerial positions in various departments of large corporations. A transfer from a corporation's legal department to another department is often viewed as a way to gain administrative experience and rise in the ranks of management. People may also use their legal background as journalists, management consultants, financial analysts, insurance claim adjusters, real estate appraisers, lobbyists, tax collectors, probation officers, and credit investigators.

**BACKGROUND AND QUALIFICATIONS:**

To practice law in the courts of any state, a person must be admitted to its bar. Applicants for admission to the bar must pass a written examination; however, a few states drop this requirement for graduates from its own law schools. Lawyers who have been admitted to the bar in one state may be admitted in another without taking an examination if they meet the state's standard of good moral character and have a specified period of legal experience. Federal courts and agencies set their own qualifications for those practicing before them. To qualify for the bar examination in most states, an applicant must complete at least three years of college, and graduate from a law school approved by the American Bar Association

## OUTLOOK:

Rapid growth in the nation's requirements for lawyers is expected to bring job openings into rough balance with the relatively stable number of law school graduates each year and result in an easing of competition for jobs through the year 2000. During the 1970's, the annual number of law school graduates more than doubled, even outpacing the rapid growth of jobs. Although graduates with superior academic records from well-regarded law schools continued to enjoy excellent opportunities, most graduates encountered increasingly keen competition for jobs. Growth in the yearly number of law school graduates has tapered off during the 1980's, but, nevertheless, the number remains at a level high enough to tax the economy's capacity to absorb them. The number of law school graduates is expected to continue to remain near its present level through the year 2000, allowing employment growth to bring the job market for lawyers back into balance.

Employment of lawyers has grown very rapidly since the early 1970's, and is expected to continue to grow much faster than the average for all occupations through the year 2000. Increased population and growing business activity help sustain the strong demand for attorneys. This demand also will be spurred by growth of legal action in such areas as employee benefits, consumer protection, the environment, and safety, and an anticipated increase in the use of legal services by middle-income groups through legal clinics and prepaid legal service programs.

Turnover of jobs in this occupation is low because its members are well paid and enjoy considerable social status, and a substantial educational investment is required for entry. Nevertheless, most job openings will stem from the need to replace lawyers who transfer to other occupations or retire.

## BANK OFFICER/MANAGER

### DESCRIPTION:

Because banks offer a broad range of services, a wide choice of careers is available. Loan officers may handle installment, commercial, real estate, or agricultural loans. To evaluate loan applications properly, officers need to be familiar with economics, production, distribution, merchandising, and commercial law, as well as have a knowledge of business operations and financial analysis. Bank officers in trust management must have knowledge of financial planning and investment research for estate and trust administration. Operations officers plan, coordinate, and control the work flow, update systems, and strive for administrative efficiency. Careers in bank operations include electronic data processing manager and other positions involving internal and customer services. A correspondent bank officer is responsible for relations with other banks; a branch manager, for all functions of a branch office; and an international officer, for advising customers with financial dealings abroad. A working knowledge of a foreign country's financial system, trade relations, and economic conditions is beneficial to those interested in international banking. Other career fields for bank officers are auditing, economics, personnel administration, public relations, and operations research.

**BACKGROUND AND QUALIFICATIONS:**

Bank officers and management positions generally are filled by management trainees, and occasionally by promoting outstanding bank clerks and tellers. A Business Administration degree with concentrations in finance or a liberal arts curriculum, including accounting, economics, commercial law, political science, or statistics, serves as excellent preparation for officer trainee positions. In large banks that have special training programs, promotions may occur more quickly. For a senior officer position, however, an employee usually needs many years of experience. Although experience, ability, and leadership are emphasized for promotion, advancement may be accelerated by special study. The American Bankers Association (ABA) offers courses, publications, and other training aids to officers in every phase of banking. The American Institute of Banking, an arm of the ABA, has long filled the same educational need among bank support personnel.

**OUTLOOK:**

Employment of financial managers is expected to increase about as fast as the average for all occupations through the year 2000. Expanding automation - such as use of computers for electronic funds transmission and for data and information processing - may make financial managers more productive. However, the growing need for skilled financial management in the face of increasing domestic and foreign competition, changing laws regarding taxes and other financial matters, and greater emphasis on accurate reporting of financial data should spur demand for financial managers. New jobs will also be created by the increasing variety and complexity of services - including financial planning - offered by financial institutions. However, most job openings will result from the need to replace those who transfer to other fields or retire.

# BIOCHEMIST

### DESCRIPTION:

Biochemists study the chemical composition and behavior of living things. They often study the effects of food, hormones, or drugs on various organisms. The methods and techniques of biochemists are applied in areas such as medicine and agriculture. More than three out of four biochemists work in basic and applied research activities. Some biochemists combine research with teaching in colleges and universities. A few work in industrial production and testing activities. About one-half of all biochemists work for colleges or universities, and about one-fourth for private industry, primarily in companies manufacturing drugs, insecticides, and cosmetics. Some biochemists work for non-profit research institutes and foundations; others for federal, state, and local government agencies. A few self-employed biochemists are consultants to industry and government.

### BACKGROUND AND QUALIFICATIONS:

The minimum educational requirement for many beginning jobs as a biochemist, especially in research and teaching, is an advanced degree. A PhD is a virtual necessity for persons who hope to contribute significantly to biochemical research and advance to many management or administrative jobs. A BS in Biochemistry, Biology, or Chemistry may qualify some persons for entry jobs as research assistants or technicians. Graduates with advanced degrees may begin their careers as teachers or researchers in colleges or universities. In private industry, most begin in research jobs, and with experience may advance to positions in which they plan and supervise research.

## OUTLOOK:

Employment of biochemists is expected to increase about as fast as the average for all occupations through the year 2000. Most growth will be in private industry, primarily in genetic and biotechnical research and in production - using newly developed biological methods. Efforts to preserve the environment should also result in growth.

Biochemists are less likely to lose their jobs during recessions than those in many other occupations since most are employed on long-term research projects or in agriculture, activities which are not much affected by economic fluctuations.

## BLUE-COLLAR WORKER SUPERVISOR

### DESCRIPTION:

Supervisors direct the activities of other employees and frequently ensure that millions of dollars worth of equipment and materials are used properly and efficiently. While blue-collar worker supervisors are most commonly known as foremen or forewomen, they also have many other titles. In the textile industry, they are referred to as second hands; on ships, they are known as boatswains, and in the construction industry, they are often called overseers, strawbosses, or gang leaders. Supervisors make work schedules and keep production and employee records. They must use judgement in planning and must allow for unforeseen problems such as absent workers, or machine breakdowns. Teaching employees safe work habits and enforcing safety rules and regulations are among other supervisory responsibilities. Supervisors also may demonstrate timesaving or laborsaving techniques to workers, and train new employees. Worker supervisors tell their subordinates about company plans and policies; recommend good workers for wage increases, awards, or promotions; and deal with poor workers by issuing warnings or recommending that they be fired. In companies where employees belong to labor unions, supervisors meet with union representatives to discuss work problems and grievances. They must know the provisions of labor management contracts and run their operations according to these agreements.

## BACKGROUND AND QUALIFICATIONS:

When choosing supervisors, employers generally look for experience, skill and leadership qualities. Most supervisors rise through the ranks; however, a growing number of employers are hiring trainees with a college background. This practice is most prevalent in industries with highly technical production processes, such as the chemical, oil, and electronics industries. Employers generally prefer backgrounds in business administration, industrial relations, mathematics, engineering, or science. The trainees undergo on-the-job training until they are able to accept supervisory responsibilities. Outstanding supervisors may move up to higher management positions. In manufacturing, for example, they may advance to jobs such as department head or plant manager. Some supervisors, particularly in the construction industry, use the experience and skills they gain to go into business for themselves.

## OUTLOOK:

Employment of blue-collar worker supervisors is expected to increase more slowly than the average for all occupation through the year 2000. Although rising incomes will stimulate demand for goods such as air-conditioners, home entertainment equipment, personal computers, and automobiles, employment in manufacturing industries will decline, due in part to increasing foreign competition. The production-related occupations in manufacturing, including blue-collar worker supervisors, will be the ones most adversely affected. Offsetting the decline in the number of supervisors in manufacturing, however, will be an increase in jobs in non-manufacturing industries, especially in the trade and service sectors. In addition to the jobs resulting in increased demand for supervisors, many openings will arise from the need to replace workers who leave the occupation. Supervisors have a relatively strong attachment to the occupation, but because the occupation is so large, turnover results in a large number of openings. Because blue-collar worker supervisors are so important to the successful operation of a firm, they are often protected from layoffs during a recession. Supervisors in the construction industry, however, may experience periodic layoffs when construction activity declines.

# BUYER/MERCHANDISE MANAGER

## DESCRIPTION:

All merchandise sold in a retail store appears in that store on the decision of a buyer. Although all buyers seek to satisfy their stores' customers and sell at a profit, the type and variety of goods they purchase depends on the store where they work. A buyer for a small clothing store, for example, may purchase its complete stock of merchandise. Buyers who work for larger retail businesses often handle a few related lines of goods, such as men's wear, ladies' sportswear, or children's toys, among many others. Some, known as foreign buyers, purchase merchandise outside the United States. Buyers must be familiar with the manufacturers and distributors who handle the merchandise they need. They also must keep informed about changes in existing products and the development of new ones. Merchandise Managers plan and coordinate buying and selling activities for large and medium-sized stores. They divide the budget among buyers, decide how much merchandise to stock, and assign each buyer to purchase certain goods. Merchandise Managers may review buying decisions to ensure that needed categories of goods are in stock, and help buyers to set general pricing guidelines.

Some buyers represent large stores or chains in cities where many manufacturers are located. The duties of these "market representatives" vary by employer; some purchase goods, while others supply information and arrange for store buyers to meet with manufacturer's representatives when they are in the area. New technology has altered the buyers' role in retail chain stores. Cash registers connected to a computer, known as point-of-sale terminals, allow retail chains to maintain centralized, up-to-the-minute inventory records. With these records, a single garden furniture buyer, for example, can purchase lawn chairs and picnic tables for the entire chain.

## BACKGROUND AND QUALIFICATIONS:

Because familiarity with the merchandise and with the retailing business itself is such a central element in the buyer's job, prior retailing experience sometimes provides sufficient preparation. More and more, however, employers prefer applicants who have a college degree. Most employers accept college grads in any field of study and train them on the job. In many stores, beginners who are candidates for buying jobs start out in executive training programs. These programs last from six to eight months, and combine classroom instruction in merchandising and purchasing with short rotations in various store jobs. This training introduces the new worker to store operations and policies, and provides the fundamentals of merchandising and management. The trainee's first job is likely to be that of assistant buyer. The duties include supervising sales workers, checking invoices on material received, and keeping account of stock on hand. Assistant buyers gradually assume purchasing responsibilities, depending upon their individual abilities and the size of the department where they work. Training as an assistant buyer usually lasts at least one year. After years of working as a buyer, those who show exceptional ability may advance to merchandise manager. A few find promotion to top executive jobs such as general merchandise manager for a retail store or chain.

### OUTLOOK:

Employment of buyers is expected to grow more slowly than the average for all occupations though the year 2000 as more wholesale and retail trade establishments automate and centralize their purchasing departments. Productivity gains resulting from the increased use of computers to control inventory, maintain records, and reorder merchandise will be the principal factor restraining employment growth. Most job openings, therefore, will result from replacement needs, which occur as experienced buyers transfer to other occupations in sales or management, change careers, or stop working altogether. The number of qualified jobseekers will continue to exceed the number of openings because merchandising attracts many college graduates. Prospects are likely to be best for qualified applicants who enjoy the competitive, fast-paced nature of merchandising.

# CHEMIST

### DESCRIPTION:

Chemists search for and put into practical use new knowledge about substances. Their research has resulted in the development of a tremendous variety of synthetic materials, such as nylon and polyester fabrics. Nearly one-half of all chemists work in research and development. In basic research, chemists investigate the properties and composition of matter and the laws that govern the combination of elements. Basic research often has practical uses. In research and development, new products are created or improved. Nearly one-eighth of all chemists work in production and inspection. In production, chemists prepare instructions (batch sheets) for plant workers that specify the kind and amount of ingredients to use and the exact mixing time for each stage in the process. At each step, samples are tested for quality control to meet industry and government standards. Other chemists work as marketing or sales representative because of their technical knowledge of the products sold. A number of chemists teach in colleges and universities. Some chemists are consultants to private industry and government agencies. Chemists often specialize in one of several subfields of chemistry: analytical chemists determine the structure, composition, and nature of substances, and develop new techniques; organic chemists at one time studied only the chemistry of living things, but their area has been broadened to include all carbon compounds; inorganic chemists study noncarbon compounds; and physical chemists study energy transformations to find new and better energy sources.

### BACKGROUND AND QUALIFICATIONS:

A BS with a major in Chemistry or a related discipline is sufficient for many entry-level jobs as a chemist. However, graduate training is required for many research jobs, and most college teaching jobs require a PhD. Beginning chemists with a Master's Degree can usually go into applied research. The PhD is generally required for basic research for teaching in colleges and universities, and for advancement to many administrative positions.

### OUTLOOK:

Employment of chemists is expected to grow more slowly than the average for all occupations through the year 2000.

## CLAIM REPRESENTATIVE

### DESCRIPTION:

The people who investigate insurance claims, negotiate settlements with policy holders, and authorize payments are known as claim representative - a group that includes claim adjusters and claim examiners. When a casualty insurance company receives a claim, the claim adjuster determines whether the policy covers it and the amount of the loss. Adjusters use reports, physical evidence, and testimony of witnesses in investigating a claim. When their company is liable, they negotiate with the claimant and settle the case. Some adjusters work with all lines of insurance. Others specialize in claims from fire, marine loss, automobile damage, workers' compensation loss, or product liability. A growing number of casualty companies employ special adjusters to settle small claims. These workers, generally called inside adjusters or telephone adjusters, contact claimants by telephone or mail and have the policy holder send repair costs, medical bills, and other statements to the company. In life insurance companies, the counterpart of the claim adjuster is the claim examiner, who investigates questionable claims or those exceeding a specified amount. They may check claim applications for completeness and accuracy, interview medical specialists, consult policy files to verify information on a claim, or calculate benefit payments. Generally, examiners are authorized to investigate and approve payment on all claims up to a certain limit; larger claims are referred to a senior examiner.

## BACKGROUND AND QUALIFICATIONS:

No specific field of college study is recommended. Although courses in insurance, economics, or other business subjects are helpful, a major in most college fields is adequate preparation. Most large insurance companies provide beginning claim adjusters and examiners with on-the-job training and home study courses. Claim representatives are encouraged to take courses designed to enhance their professional skills. For example, the Insurance Institute of America offers a six semester study program leading to an Associate's Degree in Claims Adjusting, upon successful completion of six exams. A professional Certificate in Insurance Adjusting also is available from the College of Insurance in New York City. The Life Office Management Association (LOMA), in cooperation with the International Claim Association, offers a claims education, program for life and health examiners. The program is part of the LOMA Institute Insurance Education Program leading to the professional designation FLMI (Fellow Life Management Institute) upon successful completion of eight written exams. Beginning adjusters and examiners work on small claims under the supervision of an experienced employee. As they learn more about claim investigation and settlement, they are assigned claims that are either higher in loss value or more complex. Trainees are promoted as they demonstrate competence in handling assignments and as they progress in their course work. Employees who show unusual competence in claims work or outstanding administrative skills may be promoted to department supervisor in a field office, or to a managerial position in the home office. Qualified adjusters and examiners sometimes transfer to other departments, such as underwriting or sales.

## OUTLOOK:

Employment of claim representatives is expected to grow faster than the average for all occupations as the increasing volume of insurance sales results in more insurance claims. Shifts in the age distribution of the population will result in a large increase in the number of people who assume career and family responsibilities. People in this group have the greatest need for life and health insurance, and protection for homes, automobiles, and other possessions. A growing demand for insurance coverage for working women is also expected. New or expanding businesses will need protection for new plants and equipment and for insurance covering their employees' health and safety. Opportunities should be particularly good for claim representatives who specialize in complex business insurance such as marine cargo, workers' compensation, and product and pollution liability insurance.

# COMMERCIAL ARTIST

## DESCRIPTION:

A team of commercial artists with varying skills and specializations often creates the artwork in newspapers and magazines, and on billboards, brochures, and catalogs. This team is supervised by an art director, whose main function is to develop a theme or idea for an ad or advertising campaign. After the art director has determined the main elements of an ad or design, he or she will turn the project over to two specialists for further refinement. The sketch artist, also called a renderer, does a rough drawing of any pictures required. The layout artist, who is concerned with graphics rather than art work, constructs or arranges the illustrations or photographs, plans the typography, and picks colors for the ad. Other commercial artists, usually with less experience, are needed to turn out the finished products. Letterers put together headlines and other words on the ad. Mechanical artists paste up an engraver's guide of the ad. Paste-up artists and other less experienced employees do more routine work, such as cutting mats, assembling booklets, or running errands. Advertising artists create the concepts and artwork for a wide variety of items. These include direct mail advertising, catalogs, counter displays, slides, and filmstrips. They also design or lay out newspapers, magazines, and advertising circulars. Some commercial artists specialize in producing fashion illustrations, greeting cards, or book illustrations, or in making technical drawings for industry.

**BACKGROUND AND QUALFICATIONS:**

Persons can prepare for a career in commercial art by attending either a 2- or 4-year trade school, community college, college, or university offering a program in commercial art.

**OUTLOOK:**

The graphic arts fields have a glamorous and exciting image. Because formal entry qualifications are few, many people with a love for drawing and creative ability qualify for entry. As a result, competition for both salaried jobs and freelance work is keen. Freelance work may be hard to come by, especially at first, and many free-lancers earn very little until they acquire experience and establish a good reputation.

# DATA PROCESSING SPECIALIST

**DESCRIPTION:**

The main function of a data processing specialist is to type data from documents such as checks, bills, and invoices quickly and accurately, and enter this information into a computer system. This is done with a variety of typewriter-like equipment. Many specialists use a machine that converts the information they type to magnetic impulses on tapes or disks. The information is then read into the computer from the tape or disk. Some specialists operate on-line terminals of the main computer system that transmit and receive data. Although brands and models of computer terminals and data entry equipment differ somewhat, their operation and keyboards are similar.

Some specialists working from terminals use data from the computer to produce business, scientific, and technical reports. In some offices, specialists also operate computer peripheral equipment such as printers and tape readers, and act as tape librarians.

**BACKGROUND AND QUALIFICATIONS:**

Employers usually require a high school education and the ability to key data in at a certain speed. Applicants are often tested for speed and accuracy. Some employers prefer applicants with experience or training in the operation of data entry equipment, and console operators are often required to have a college education. In some firms, other clerical workers such as tabulating and bookkeeping machine operators may be transferred to jobs as data processing specialists. Training in the use of data entry and similar keyboard equipment is available in high schools or private business schools.

**OUTLOOK:**

The employment rate of data processing specialists is expected to decline through the year 2000. Despite this decline, many openings, including part-time ones, will occur each year, due to the need to replace workers who transfer to other occupations or leave the labor force. Related occupations include secretaries, typists, receptionists, and typesetters and compositors.

## DIETITIAN/NUTRITIONIST

**DESCRIPTION:**

Dietitians, sometimes called nutritionists, are professionals trained in applying the principles of nutrition to food selection and meal preparation. They counsel individuals and groups; set up and supervise food service systems for institutions such as hospitals, prisons, and schools; and promote sound eating habits through education and administration. Dietitians also work on education and research. Clinical dietitians, sometimes called therapeutic dietitians, provide nutritional services for patients in hospitals, nursing homes, clinics, or doctors' offices. They assess patients' nutritional needs, develop and implement nutrition programs, and evaluate and report the results. Clinical dietitians confer with doctors and nurses about each patient in order to coordinate nutritional intake with other treatments-medications in particular.

Community dietitians counsel individuals and groups on sound nutrition practices to prevent disease and to promote good health. Employed in such places as home health agencies, health maintenance organizations, and human service agencies that provide group and home-delivered meals, their job is to establish nutritional care plans, and communicate the principles of good nutrition in a way individuals and their families can understand. Research dietitians are usually employed in academic medical centers or educational institutions, although some work in common programs. Using established research methods and analytical techniques, they conduct studies in areas that range from basic science to practical applications. Research dietitians may examine changes in the way the body uses food over the course of a lifetime, for example, or study the interaction of drugs and diet. They may investigate the nutritional needs of persons with particular diseases, behavior modification, as it relates to diet and nutrition, or applied topics such as food service systems and equipment.

**BACKGROUND/QUALIFICATIONS:**

The basic educational requirement for this field is a bachelor's degree with a major in foods and nutrition or institution management. To qualify for professional credentials as a registered dietitian, the American Dietetic Association (ADA) recommends one of the following educational paths: Completion of a grow-year coordinated undergraduate program which includes 900 to 1,000 hours of clinical experience; completion of a bachelor's degree from an approved program plus an accredited dietetic internship; completion of a bachelor's or master's degree from an approved program and six month's approved work experience.

# DRAFTSPERSON

**DESCRIPTION:**

Drafters prepare detailed drawings based on rough sketches, specifications, and calculations made by scientists, engineers, architects, and designers. Final drawings contain a detailed view of the object from all sides as well as specifications for materials to be used, procedures to be followed, and other information needed to carry out the job. There are two methods by which these drawings are prepared. In the traditional method, drafters sit at drawing boards and use compasses, dividers, protractors, triangles, and other drafting devices to prepare the drawing manually. In the new method, drafters use computer-aided drafting (CAD) systems. They sit at computer work stations and may make the drawing on a videoscreen. In some cases, the design may never be placed on paper. It may be stored electronically and, in some factories, may be used to guide automatic machinery. These systems free drafters from much routine drafting work and permit many variations of a design to be prepared easily. CAD systems allow a design to be viewed from various angles and perspectives not usually available with more traditional drafting methods so that design work can be better, faster, and more thorough. In addition to drafting equipment and CAD systems, drafters use technical handbooks, tables, and calculators in preparing drawings and related specifications.

**BACKGROUND/REQUIREMENTS:**

It is preferred that applicants have two years of post-high school training in technical institutes, junior and community colleges, or extension divisions of universities. Some persons receive training in the Armed Forces. Training for a career in drafting should include courses in mathematics, physical science, mechanical drawing, and drafting. Courses in shop practices and shop skills are also helpful, since most higher level drafting jobs require knowledge of manufacturing or construction methods. Many technical schools offer courses in structural design, architectural drawing, and engineering or industrial technology. Beginners usually start as junior drafters doing routine work under close supervision. After gaining experience, they do more difficult work with less supervision and may advance to senior drafter or supervisor with appropriate college education, they may become engineers, designers, or architects.

**OUTLOOK:**

Little change in employment of drafters is expected to occur through the year 2000. Related occupations include architects, engineering technicians, engineers, landscape architects, photogrammetrists, and surveyors.

# ECONOMIST

## DESCRIPTION:

Economists study the way a society uses scarce resources such as land, labor, raw materials, and machinery to produce goods and services. They analyze the costs and benefits of distributing and using resources in a particular way. Their research might focus on such topics as energy costs, inflation, business cycles, unemployment, tax policy, farm prices, and many other areas. Being able to present economic and statistical concepts in a meaningful way is particularly important for economists whose research is policy directed. Economists who work for business firms may be asked to provide management with information on which decisions such as the marketing or pricing of company products are made; to look at the advisability of adding new lines of merchandise, opening new branches, or diversifying the company's operations; to analyze the effects of changes in the tax laws; or to prepare economic or business forecasts. Business economists working for firms that carry on operations abroad may be asked to prepare forecasts of foreign economic conditions. About three of every economists work in private industry, including manufacturing firms, banks, insurance companies, securities and investment companies, economic research firms and management consulting firms. Some run their own consulting businesses. A number of economists combine a full-time job in government, business or an academic institution with part-time or consulting work in another setting.

## BACKGROUND AND QUALIFICATIONS:

A Bachelors degree in Economics is sufficient for many beginning research, administrative, management trainee, and business sales jobs. However, graduate training is increasingly necessary for advancement to more responsible positions as economists. In government research organizations and consulting firms, economists who have Master's degrees can usually qualify for more responsible research and administrative positions. A PhD may be necessary for top positions in some organizations. Experienced business economists may advance to managerial or executive positions in banks, industrial concerns, trade associations, and other orginzations where they formulate practical business and administrative policy.

## OUTLOOK:

Employment of economists is expected to grow faster than the average for all occupations through the year 2000. Most job openings, however, will result from the need to replace experienced economists who transfer to other occupations, retire, or leave the labor force for other reasons.

# ENGINEER

## DESCRIPTION:

Engineers apply the theories and principles of science and mathematics to tactical technical problems. Often, their work is the link between a scientific discovery and its useful application. Engineers design machinery, products, systems, and processes for efficient and economical performance. Engineering is a highly specialized field and the work an engineer does depends greatly upon the industry in which he/she is employed. The following descriptions outline the basic specialties and their respective employment outlooks.

### Aerospace Engineer:

Aerospace engineers design, develop, test, and help produce commercial and military aircraft, missiles, spacecraft, and related systems. They play an important role in advancing the state of technology in commercial aviation, defense and space exploration. Aerospace engineers often specialize in an area of work like structural design, navigational guidance and control, instrumentation and communication, or production methods. They also may specialize in one type of aerospace product, such as passenger planes, helicopters, satellites, or rockets.

### Outlook:

Employment of aerospace engineers is expected to grow more slowly than average for all occupations through the year 2000. During the 1980's, their employment grew very rapidly. However, because of recent Defense Department expenditure cuts for military aircraft, missiles and other aerospace systems, major growth is not expected.

### Chemical Engineer:

Chemical engineers are involved in many phases of the production of chemicals and chemical products. They design equipment and chemical plants as well as determine methods of manufacturing these products. Often, they design and develop chemical processes such as those used to remove chemical contaminants from waste materials. Because the duties of the chemical engineer cut across many fields, these professionals must have knowledge of chemistry, physics, and mechanical and electrical engineering. This branch of engineering is so diversified and complex that chemical engineers frequently specialize in a particular operation such as oxidation or polymerization. Others specialize in a particular area such as pollution control or the production of a specific product like plastics or rubber.

### Outlook:

Employment of chemical engineers is expected to grow about as fast as the average for all occupations through the year 2000.

### Civil Engineer:

Civil engineers, who work in the oldest branch of the engineering profession, design and supervise the construction of roads, harbors, airports, tunnels, bridges, water supply and sewage systems, and buildings. Major specialties within civil engineering are structural, hydraulic, environmental/ sanitary, transportation, urban planning, and soil mechanics. Many civil engineers are in supervisory or administrative positions ranging from supervisor of a construction site, to city engineer, to top level executive. Others teach in colleges and universities, or work as consultants.

### Outlook:

Employment of civil engineers is expected to increase faster than the average for all occupations through the year 2000.

### Electrical Engineer:

Electrical engineers design, develop, test and supervise the manufacture of electrical and electronic equipment. Electrical equipment includes power-generating and transmission equipment used by electrical utilities, electric motors, machinery controls, and lighting and wiring in buildings, automobiles, and aircraft. Electronic equipment includes radar, computers, communications equipment, and consumer goods such as television sets and stereos. Electrical engineers also design and operate facilities for generating and distributing electrical power.

Electrical engineers generally specialize in a major area, such as integrated circuits, computers, electrical equipment manufacturing, communications, or power distributing equipment, or in a subdivision of these areas, such as microwave communication or aviation electronic systems. Electrical engineers design new products, specify their uses, and write performance requirements and maintenance schedules.

### Outlook:

The outlook for electrical engineers is estimated to be good through the year 2000.

### Industrial Engineer:

Industrial engineers determine the most effective ways for an organization to use the basic factors of production--people, machines and materials. They are more concerned with people and methods of business organization than are engineers in other specialties, who generally are concerned more with particular products or processes, such as metals, power or mechanics. To solve organizational, production, and related problems most efficiently, industrial engineers design data processing systems and apply mathematical concepts. They also develop management control systems to aid in financial planning and cost analysis, design production planning and control systems to coordinate activities and control product quality, and design or improve systems for the physical distribution of goods and services. Industrial engineers also conduct plant location surveys, where they look for the best combination of sources of raw materials, transportation, and taxes, and develop wage and salary administration positions and job evaluation programs. Many industrial engineers move into managerial positions because the work is closely related.

**Outlook:**

Employment opportunities for industrial engineers are expected to be good; their employment is expected to grow faster than the average for all occupations through the year 2000. Most job openings, however, will result from the need to replace industrial engineers who transfer to other occupations or leave the labor force.

**Metallurgical Engineer:**

Metallurgical engineers develop new types of metals with characteristics that are tailored for specific requirements, such as heat resistance, lightweight strength, or high malleability. They also develop methods to process and convert metals into useful products. Most of these engineers generally work in one of three major branches of metallurgy: extractive or chemical, physical, or mechanical. Extractive metallurgists are concerned with extracting metals from ores, and refining and alloying them to obtain useful materials. Physical metallurgists deal with the nature, structure, and physical properties of metals and their alloys, and with the methods of converting refined metals into final products. Mechanical metallurgists develop methods to work and shape materials, such as casting, forging, rolling, and drawing.

**Outlook:**

Employment of metallurgical, ceramic, and materials engineers is expected to grow more rapidly than the average for all occupations through the year 2000.

**Mining Engineer:**

Mining engineers find, extract, and prepare minerals for manufacturing industries to use. They design open pit and underground mines, supervise the construction of mine shafts and tunnels in underground operations, and devise methods for transporting minerals to processing plants. Mining engineers are responsible for the economical and efficient operation of mines and mine safety, including ventilation, water supply, power, communications, and equipment maintenance. Some mining engineers work with geologists and metallurgical engineers to locate and appraise new ore deposits. Others develop new mining equipment or direct mineral processing operations, which involve separating minerals from the dirt, rock, and other materials they are mixed with. Mining engineers frequently specialize in the mining of one specific mineral such as coal or copper. With increased emphasis on protecting the environment, many mining engineers have been working to solve problems related to mined land reclamation, and water and air pollution.

**Outlook:**

The employment outlook for mining engineers is expected to remain constant through the year 2000, due to expected low growth in demand for coal, metals, and other minerals.

**Petroleum Engineer:**

Petroleum engineers are mainly involved in exploring and drilling for oil and gas. They work to achieve the maximum profitable recovery of oil and gas from a petroleum reservoir by determining and developing the best and most efficient methods. Since only a small proportion of the oil and gas in a reservoir will flow out under natural forces, petroleum engineers develop and use various artificial recovery methods, such as flooding the oil field with water to force the oil to the surface. Even when using the best recovery methods, about half the oil is still left in the ground. Petroleum engineers' research and development efforts to increase the proportion of oil recovered in each reservoir can make a significant contribution to increasing available energy resources.

**Outlook:**

Employment of petroleum engineers is expected to grow more slowly than the average for all occupations through the year 2000. With the drop in oil prices, domestic petroleum companies have curtailed exploration, resulting in poor employment opportunities.

**BACKGROUND AND QUALIFICATIONS:**

A bachelor's degree in engineering from an accredited engineering program is generally acceptable for beginning engineering jobs. College graduates trained in one of the natural sciences or mathematics also may qualify for some beginning jobs. Most engineering degrees may be obtained in branches such as electrical, mechanical, or civil engineering. College graduates with a degree in science or mathematics and experienced engineering technicians may also qualify for some engineering jobs, especially in engineering specialties in high demand. Graduate training is essential for engineering faculty positions but is not required for the majority of entry level engineering jobs. All 50 states require licensing for engineers whose work may affect life, health or property, or who offer their services to the public.

Beginning engineering graduates usually work under the supervision of experienced engineers, and in larger companies, may receive seminar or classroom training. As engineers advance in knowledge, they may become technical specialists, supervisors, or managers or administrators within the field of engineering. Some engineers obtain advanced degrees in business administration to improve their growth opportunities, while others obtain law degrees and become patent attorneys.

## FINANCIAL ANALYST

**DESCRIPTION:**

A financial analyst prepares the financial reports required by the firm to conduct its operations and satisfy tax and regulatory requirements. Financial analysts also oversee the flow of cash and financial instruments and develop information to assess the present and future financial status of the firm.

**BACKGROUND AND QUALIFICATIONS:**

A bachelor's degree in accounting or finance is suitable academic preparation for a financial manager. An MBA degree in addition to a bachelor's degree in any field is acceptable to many employers.

**OUTLOOK:**

Employment of financial managers is expected to increase about as fast as the average for occupations through the year 2000.

# FOOD TECHNOLOGIST

**DESCRIPTION:**

A food technologist studies the chemical, physical and biological nature of food to learn how to safely process, preserve, package, distribute, and store it. Some develop new products, while others insure quality standards. They are, like animal scientists, dairy scientists, horticulturists, soil scientists, animal and plant breeders, entomologists, and agriculturalists, classified generally as agricultural scientists by the U.S. Department of Labor.

**BACKGROUND AND QUALIFICATIONS:**

Educational requirements for the agricultural scientist depend a great deal upon the area and type of work performed. A PhD degree in agricultural science is usually required for college teaching, independent research, and for advancement to many administrative and management jobs. A bachelor's degree is sufficient for some sales, production management, inspection, and other nonresearch jobs, but, in some cases, promotions may be limited. Degrees in some related sciences such as biology, chemistry, or physics or in related engineering specialties also may be acceptable for some agricultural science jobs.

**OUTLOOK:**

Employment of agricultural scientists is expected to grow about as fast as the average for an occupations through the year 2000.

# FORESTER

**DESCRIPTION:**

Foresters plan and supervise the growing, protection and harvesting of trees. They plot forest areas, approximate the amount of standing timber and future growth, and manage timber sales. Some foresters also protect the trees from fire, harmful insects, and disease. Some foresters also protect wildlife and manage watersheds; develop and supervise campgrounds, parks, and grazing lands; and do research. Foresters in extension work provide information to forest owners and to the general public.

**BACKGROUND AND QUALIFICATIONS:**

A bachelor's degree in forestry is the minimum educational requirement for professional careers in forestry. In 1986, 55 colleges and universities offered bachelor's or higher degrees in forestry, 47 of these were accredited by the Society of American Foresters.

**OUTLOOK:**

Employment of foresters and conservation scientists is expected to grow more slowly than the average for all occupations through the year 2000.

# GEOGRAPHER

**DESCRIPTION:**

Geographers study the interrelationship of humans and the environment. Economic geographers deal with the geographic distribution of an area's economic activities. Political geographers are concerned with the relationship of geography to political phenomena. Physical geographers study physical processes in the earth and its atmosphere. Urban geographers study cities and metropolitan areas, while regional geographers specialize in the physical, climatic, economic, political and cultural characteristics of a particular region or area. Medical geographers study the effect of the environment on health.

**BACKGROUND AND QUALIFICATIONS:**

The minimum educational requirement for entry-level positions is a BA or BS degree in Geography. However, a Masters degree is increasingly required for many entry level positions. Applicants for entry level jobs would find it helpful to have training in a specialty such as cartography, photogrammerty, remote sensing data interpretation, statistical analysis including computer science, or environmental analysis. To advance to a senior research position in private industry and perhaps gain a spot in management, a geographer would probably be required to have an advanced degree.

**OUTLOOK:**

Average growth is predicted throughout the 1990's.

## GEOLOGISTS AND GEOPHYSISICTS

**DESCRIPTION:**

Geologists study the structure, composition and history of the earth's crust. By examining surface rocks and drilling to recover rock cores, they determine the types and distribution of rocks beneath the earth's surface. They also identify rocks and minerals, conduct geological surveys, draw maps, take measurements, and record data. Geological research helps to determine the structure and history of the earth, and may result in significant advances, such as in the ability to predict earthquakes. An important application of geologists' work is locating oil and other natural and mineral resources. Geologists usually specialize in one or a combination of general areas: earth materials, earth processes, and earth history.

Geophysicists study the composition and physical aspects of the earth and its electric, magnetic and gravitational fields. Geophysicists usually specialize in one of three general phases of the science -- solid earth, fluid earth, and upper atmosphere. Some may also study other planets.

**BACKGROUND AND QUALIFICATIONS:**

A Bachelor's degree in geology or geophysics is adequate for entry to some lower level geology jobs, but better jobs with good advancement potential usually require at least a master's degree in geology or geophysics. Persons with strong backgrounds in physics, mathematics, or computer science also may qualify for some geophysics jobs. A PhD is essential for most research positions.

**OUTLOOK:**

Employment of geologists and geophysicists is expected to grow more slowly than the average for all occupations through the year 2000, mainly due to the reduction in energy exploration by oil companies.

# HOTEL MANAGER/ASSISTANT MANAGER

**DESCRIPTION:**

Hotel managers are responsible for operating their establishments profitably and satisfying guests. They determine room rates and credit policy, direct the operation of the food science operation, and manage the housekeeping, accounting, security, and maintenance departments of the hotel. Handling problems and coping with the unexpected are important parts of the job. A small hotel or motel requires only a limited staff, and the manager may have to fill various front office duties, such as taking reservations or assigning rooms. When management is combined with ownership, these activities may expand to include all aspects of the business. General managers of large hotels usually have several assistants or department heads who manage various part of the operation. Because hotel restaurant and cocktail lounges are important to the success of the entire establishment, they are almost always operated by managers with experience in the restaurant field. Other areas that are usually handled separately include advertising, rental of banquet and meeting facilities, marketing and sales, personnel and accounting. Large hotel and motel chains often centralize some activities, such as purchasing and advertising, so that individual hotels in the chain may not need managers for these departments. Managers who work for chains may be assigned to organize a newly-built or purchased hotel, or to reorganize an existing hotel or motel that is not operating successfully.

**BACKGROUND AND QUALIFICATIONS:**

Experience is the most important consideration in selecting hotel managers. However, employers are increasingly emphasizing college education. A BA in Hotel/Restaurant Administration provides particularly strong preparation for a career in hotel management. Most hotels promote employees who have proven their ability, usually front office clerks, to assistant manager, and eventually to general manager. Hotel and motel chains may offer better employment opportunities because employees can transfer to another hotel or motel in the chain, or to the central office if an opening occurs

**OUTLOOK:**

Employment of salaried hotel managers is expected to grow much faster than the average for all occupations through the year 2000 as more large hotels and motels are built.

# INDUSTRIAL DESIGNER

**DESCRIPTION:**

Industrial designers combine artistic talent with a knowledge of marketing, materials, and methods of production to improve the appearance and functional design of products so that they compete favorably with similar goods on the market. Although most industrial designers are engaged in product design, others are involved in different facets of design. To create favorable public images for companies and for government service, some designers develop trademarks or symbols that appear on the firm's products, advertising, brochures, and stationery. Some design containers and packages that both protect and promote their contents. Others prepare small display exhibits or the entire layout for industrial fairs. Some design the interior layout of special purpose commercial buildings such as restaurants and supermarkets.

Corporate designers usually work only on products made by their employer. This may involve filling the day-to-day design needs of the company, or long-range planning of new products. Independent consultants who serve more than one industrial firm often plan and design a great variety of products. Most designers work for large manufacturing companies designing either consumer or industrial products, or for design consulting firms. Others do freelance work, or are on the staffs of architectural and interior design firms.

### BACKGROUND AND QUALIFICATIONS:

The normal requirement for entering this field of work involves completing a course of study in industrial design at an art school, university, or technical college. Most large manufacturing firms hire only industrial designers who have a Bachelor's degree in the field. Beginning industrial designers frequently do simple assignments. As they gain experience, they may work on their own, and many become supervisors with major responsibility for the design of a product or group of products. Those who have an established reputation and the necessary funds may start their own consulting firms.

### OUTLOOK:

Employment in design occupations is expected to grow faster than the average for all occupations through the year 2000. Continued emphasis on product quality and safety, on design of new products for businesses and offices, and on high-technology products in medicine and transportation should expand the demand for industrial designers.

## INSURANCE AGENT/BROKER

### DESCRIPTION:

Agents and brokers usually sell one or more of the three basic types of insurance: life, casualty, and health. Underwriters offer various policies that, besides providing health benefits, may also provide retirement income, funds for education, or other benefits. Casualty insurance agents sell policies that protect individual policyholders from financial losses resulting from automobile accidents, fire, or theft. They also sell industrial or commercial lines, such as workers' compensation, products liability, or medical malpractice insurance. Health insurance policies offer protection against the high costs of hospital and medical care, or loss of income due to illness or injury. Many agents also offer securities, such as mutual fund shares or variable annuities.

An insurance agent may be either an insurance company employee or an independent who is authorized to represent one or more insurance companies. Brokers are not under exclusive contract with any single company, instead, they place policies directly with the company that best meets a company's needs.

Insurance agents spend most of their time discussing insurance needs with prospective and existing clients. Some time must be spent in office work to prepare reports, maintain records, plan insurance programs that are tailored to prospects' needs, and draw up lists of prospective customers. Specialists in group policies may help an employer's accountant set up a system of payroll deductions for employees covered by the policy.

### BACKGROUND AND QUALIFICATIONS:

All insurance agents and most insurance brokers must obtain a license in the state where they plan to sell insurance. In most states, licenses are issued only to applicants who pass written examinations covering insurance fundamentals and the state insurance laws. Agents who plan to sell mutual fund shares and other securities also must be licensed by the state. New agents usually receive training at the agencies where they will work, and frequently at the insurance company's home office. Beginners sometimes attend company-sponsored classes to prepare for the examination. Others study on their own and accompany experienced sales workers when they call on prospective clients.

### OUTLOOK:

Employment of insurance agents and brokers is expected to grow about as fast as the average for all occupations through the year 2000. Turnover is high because many beginners are able to establish a sufficiently large clientele in this highly competitive business. Most individuals and businesses consider insurance a necessity, regardless of economic conditions. Therefore, agents are not likely to face unemployment because of a recession.

# MANAGER

**DESCRIPTION:**

Managers supervise employees and are accountable for the overall success of the operation which they direct. The scope and nature of a manager's responsibilities depend greatly upon the position and the size of his or her organization.

A department manager at a retail store, for example, may actually spend most of his or her time waiting on customers, and his or her managerial duties may be limited to scheduling employees' work shifts to properly staff the department, or to training new employees in such simple tasks as operating the check-out terminal, processing credit card purchases, and displaying merchandise.

A branch manager, even in a small store or service operation, might have considerably broader duties and responsibilities. He or she might, in addition to supervising and training employees, be responsible for hiring and firing decisions. He or she might have a limited ability to purchase items, and might have some control over a local advertising budget. He or she might also deal with local suppliers of goods and services. Some organizations, however, prefer to delegate rather limited responsibility to branch managers, and instead rely upon a strong network of regional managers who travel from branch to branch, making key operating decisions.

Factories or service firms with extensive processing requirements employ operations and production managers. While these managers typically supervise many people, their primary responsibility is the overall success of the operation, which may be dependent upon equipment, raw material, purchased goods, or outside vendors. The operations manager at a bank, for example, remains heavily dependent upon data processing equipment, and usually will have an extensive background in this area. The production manager at a petroleum refinery, for another example, remains heavily dependent upon a large variety of specialized equipment, and will usually have a background in engineering or chemistry.

The general manager is responsible for the overall day-to-day operations of the firm or operating unit. He or she must be acquainted with each part of the operation. In a small store, the general manager may spend most of his or her time performing nonmanagerial tasks such as making purchases, or even waiting on customers. In a large corporation, on the other hand, the general manager (who is often the executive vice president) will spend much of his or her time meeting with key executives in each department to ensure that company operations are being conducted successfully.

**BACKGROUND AND QUALIFICATIONS:**

The educational background of managers and top executives varies as widely as the nature of their diverse responsibilities. Most general managers and top executives have a bachelor's degree in liberal arts or business administration. Graduate and professional degrees are common. Many managers in administrative, marketing, financial, and manufacturing activities have a master's degree in business administration. Larger firms usually have some form of management training program, usually open to recent college graduates. While such programs are usually competitive, they generally offer an excellent opportunity to quickly familiarize oneself with many different aspects of a firm's business. Also, such programs are often open to a broad range of candidates, including both candidates with a BS in business administration, and liberal arts graduates as well.

**OUTLOOK:**

Employment of general managers and top executives is expected to grow about as fast as the average for all occupations through the year 2000.

## MANUFACTURERS' SALES WORKERS

**DESCRIPTION:**

Most manufacturers employ sales workers to market their products to other businesses, mainly to other producers, wholesalers, and retailers. Manufacturers also sell directly to institutions such as schools, hospitals, and libraries. The sales workers who represent a manufacturer to prospective buyers are usually called manufacturers' representatives, although the job title may vary by product line.

Manufacturers' sales workers visit prospective buyers to inform them about the products they sell, analyze the buyer's needs, suggest how their products can meet these needs, and take orders. Sales workers visit firms in their territory, using an approach adapted to their line of merchandise. Sometimes sales workers promote their company's products at trade shows and conferences.

Manufacturers' sales workers spend most of their time visiting prospective customers. They also prepare reports on sales prospects or customers' credit ratings, plan their work schedules, draw up lists of prospects, contact the firm to schedule appointments, handle correspondence, and study literature about their products.

## BACKGROUND AND QUALIFICATIONS:

Although a college degree is increasingly desirable for a job as a manufacturer's sales worker, many employers hire individuals without a degree who have previous sales experience. Most entrants to this occupation, even those with college degrees, transfer from other occupations, but some are recent graduates. Entrants are older, on the average, than entrants to other occupations. Sales representatives who have good sales records and leadership ability may advance to sales supervisor, branch manager, or district manager. Those with managerial ability eventually may advance to sales manager or other executive positions; many top executives in industry started as sales representatives. Some people eventually go into business for themselves as independent representatives, while others find opportunities in advertising and marketing research.

## OUTLOOK:

Little or no change in employment is expected in the occupation through the year 2000. Increased reliance on electronic ordering systems and a trend toward increased utilization of wholesale distribution channels will limit future employment growth.

# PERSONNEL AND LABOR RELATIONS SPECIALIST

## DESCRIPTION:

Personnel and labor relations specialists provide the necessary link between management and employees which helps management make effective use of employees' skills, and helps employees find satisfaction in their jobs and working conditions. Personnel specialists interview, select, and recommend applicants to fill job openings. They handle wage and salary administration, training and career development, and employee benefits. Labor relations specialists usually deal in union-management relations, and people who specialize in this field work primarily in unionized businesses and government agencies. They help management officials prepare for collective bargaining sessions, participate in contract negotiations with the union, and handle day-to-day matters of labor relations agreements.

In a small company, personnel work consists mostly of interviewing and hiring, and one person usually handles all phases. By contrast, a large organization needs an entire staff, which might include recruiters, interviewers, counselors, job analysts, wage and salary analysts, education and training specialists, as well as technical and clerical workers. Personnel work often begins with the personnel recruiter or employment interviewer who travels around the country, often to college campuses, in the search for promising job applicants. These specialists talk to applicants, and then select and recommend those who appear qualified to fill vacancies. They often administer tests to applicants and interpret the results. Job analysts and salary and wage administrators examine detailed information on jobs, including job qualifications and worker characteristics, in order to prepare manuals and other materials for these courses, and look into new methods of training. They also counsel employees participating in training opportunities, which may include on-the-job, apprentice, supervisory, or management training.

Employee benefits supervisors and other personnel specialists handle the employer's benefits programs, which often include health insurance, life insurance, disability insurance, and pension plans. These specialists also coordinate a wide range of employee services, including cafeterias and snack bars, health rooms, recreational facilities, newsletters and communications, and counseling for worker-related personal problems. Counseling employees who are reaching retirement age is a particularly important part of the job. Labor relations specialists give advice on labor management relations. Nearly three out of four work in private industry, for manufacturers, banks, insurance companies, airlines, department stores, and virtually every other business concern.

**BACKGROUND AND QUALIFICATIONS:**

The educational backgrounds of personnel training, and labor relations specialists and managers vary considerably due to the diversity of duties and level of responsibility. While some employers look for graduates with degrees in Personnel Administration or Industrial and Labor Relations, others prefer graduates with a general business background. Still others feel that a well-rounded liberal arts education is the best preparation. A college degree in Personnel Administration, Political Science, or Public Administration can be an asset in looking for personnel work with a government agency. Graduate study in industrial or labor relations is often required for work in labor relations. Although a law degree is often required for entry-level jobs, most of the people who are responsible for contract negotiations are lawyers, and a combination of industrial relations courses and a law degree is becoming highly desirable. New personnel specialists usually enter formal or on-the-job training programs to learn how to classify jobs, interview applicants, or administer employee benefits. Next, new workers are assigned to specific areas in the employee relations department to gain experience. Later, they may advance within their own company, transfer to another employer, or move from personnel to labor relations work. Workers in the middle ranks of a large organization often transfer to a top job in a smaller company. Employees with exceptional ability may be promoted to executive positions, such as director of personnel or director of labor relations.

## OUTLOOK:

The number of jobs in this field is projected to increase through the year 2000, although most job openings will be due to replacement needs. The job market is likely to remain competitive in view of the abundant supply of college graduates and experienced workers with suitable qualifications.

# PHYSICIST

## DESCRIPTION:

Through systematic observation and experimentation, physicists describe the structure of the universe and the interaction of matter and energy in fundamental terms. Physicists develop theories that describe the fundamental forces and laws of nature. The majority of physicists work in research and development. Some do basic research to increase scientific knowledge. Some engineering-oriented physicists do applied research and help develop new products. Many physicists teach and do research in colleges and universities. A small number work in inspection, quality control and other production-related jobs in industry, while others do consulting work.

Most physicists specialize in one or more branches of the science. A growing number of physicists are specializing in fields that combine physics and a related science. Furthermore, the practical applications of a physicist's work have become increasingly merged with engineering. Private industry employs more than one half of all physicists, primarily in companies manufacturing chemicals, electrical equipment, and aircraft and missiles. Many others work in hospitals, commercial laboratories, and independent research organizations.

### BACKGROUND AND QUALIFICATIONS:

Graduate training in physics or a closely related field is almost essential for most entry-level jobs in physics, and for advancement into all types of work. A PhD is normally required for faculty status at colleges and universities, and for industrial or government jobs administering research and development programs. Those with a Master's Degree qualify for many research jobs in private industry and in the Federal Government. In colleges and universities, some teach and assist in research while studying for their PhD degrees. Those with a BA may qualify for some applied research and development positions in private industry and in government, and some holding Bachelor's degrees are employed as research assistants in colleges and universities while studying for advanced degrees. Many also work in engineering and other scientific fields. Physicists often begin their careers performing routine laboratory tasks. After gaining some experience, they are assigned more complex tasks and may advance to work as project leaders or research directors. Some work in top management jobs. Physicists who develop new products sometimes form their own companies or join new firms to exploit their own ideas.

### OUTLOOK:

Physicists with a PhD should experience good employment opportunities by the late 1990s. The employment of physicists is expected to improve as retirements increase. Related industries: chemistry, geology, and geophysics.

## PUBLIC RELATIONS WORKER

### DESCRIPTION:

Public relations workers aid businesses, government, universities, and other organizations build and maintain a positive public image. They apply their talents and skills in a variety of different areas, including press, community, or consumer relations, political campaigning, interest-group representation, fund-raising, or employee recruitment. Public relations is more than telling the employer's story, however. Understanding the attitudes and concerns of customers, employees, and various other public groups, and effectively communicating this information to management to help formulate policy is an important part of the job.

Public relations staffs in very large firms may number 200 or more, but in most firms the staff is much smaller. The director of public relations, who is often a vice-president of the company, may develop overall plans and policies with a top management executive. In addition, large public relations departments employ writers, research workers, and other specialists who prepare material for the different media, stockholders, and other groups the company wishes to reach.

Manufacturing firms, public utilities, transportation companies, insurance companies, and trade and professional associations employ many public relations workers. A sizeable number work for government agencies, schools, colleges, museums, and other educational, religious, human service and other organizations. The rapidly expanding health field also offers opportunities for public relations work. A number of workers are employed by public relations consulting firms which furnish services to clients for a fee. Others work for advertising agencies.

## BACKGROUND AND QUALIFICATIONS:

A college education combined with public relations experience is excellent preparation for public relations work. Although most beginners in the field have a college degree in communications, public relations, or journalism, some employers prefer a background in a field related to the firm's business. Other firms want college graduates who have worked for the news media. In fact, many editors, reporters, and workers in closely related fields enter public relations work. Some companies, particularly those with large public relations staffs, have formal training programs for new workers. In other firms, new employers work under the guidance of experienced staff members.

Promotion to supervisory jobs may come as workers demonstrate their ability to handle more demanding and creative assignments. Some experienced public relations workers start their own consulting firms. The Public Relations Society accredits public relations officers who have at least five years of experience in the field and have passed a comprehensive six-hour examination.

**OUTLOOK:**

Employment of public relations workers is expected to increase much faster than the average for all occupations through the year 2000.

## PURCHASING AGENT

**DESCRIPTION:**

Purchasing agents, also called industrial buyers, obtain goods and services of the quality required at the lowest possible cost, and see that adequate supplies are always available. Agents who work for manufacturing maintenance and repair supplies; those working for government agencies may purchase such items as office supplies, furniture, business machines, or vehicles, to name some.

Purchasing agents usually specialize in one or more specific groups of commodities. Agents are assigned to sections, headed by assistant purchasing managers, who are responsible for a group of related commodities. In smaller organizations, purchasing agents generally are assigned certain categories of goods. About half of all purchasing agents work for manufacturing firms.

**BACKGROUND AND QUALIFICATIONS:**

Most large organizations now require a college degree, and many prefer applicants who have an MBA degree. Familiarity with the computer and its uses is desirable in understanding the systems aspect of the purchasing profession. Following the initial training period, junior purchasing agents usually are given the responsibility of purchasing standard and catalog items. As they gain experience and develop expertise in their assigned areas, they may be promoted to purchasing agent and then senior purchasing agent. Continuing education is essential for purchasing agents who want to advance their careers. Purchasing agents are encouraged to participate in frequent seminars offered by Professional societies, and to take courses in the field at local colleges and universities.

The recognized mark of experience and professional competence is the designation certified purchasing manager (CPM). This designation is conferred by the National Association of Purchasing Management, Inc. upon candidates who have passed four examinations and who meet educational and professional experience requirements

## OUTLOOK:

Employment of purchasing agents and managers is expected to increase more slowly than the average for all occupations during the 1990's. Computerization of purchasing coupled with an increased reliance on a smaller number of suppliers should boost the productivity of purchasing personnel.

## QUALITY CONTROL SUPERVISOR

### DESCRIPTION:

A quality control supervisor may either be involved in the spot checking of items being manufactured or processed or in assuring that the proper processes are being followed. A quality control system involves selection and training of personnel, product design, the establishment of specifications, procedures and tests, the design and maintenance of facilities and equipment, the selection of materials, and recordkeeping. In an effective quality control system, all these aspects are evaluated on a regular basis, and modified and improved when appropriate.

### BACKGROUND AND QUALIFICATIONS:

While some quality control positions involved with the supervision of the production of simpler items might require little background besides on-the-job training, many require a specialized degree in engineering, chemistry, or biology. While all manufacturing firms require some degree of quality control, this is especially important in the chemistry, food and drug industries. Some drug manufacturers for example, may assign one out of six production workers to quality assurance functions alone

### OUTLOOK:

Varies greatly, depending upon the industry.

# REPORTER/EDITOR

**DESCRIPTION:**

Newspaper reporters gather information on current events and use it to write stories for daily or weekly newspapers. Large dailies frequently assign teams of reporters to investigate social, economic, or political conditions, and reporters are often assigned to beats, such as police stations, courthouses, or governmental agencies, to gather news originating inthese places. General assignment reporters write local news stories on a wide range of topics, from public meetings to human interest stories.

Reporters with a specialized background or interest in a particular area write, interpret, and analyze the news in fields such as medicine, politics, foreign affairs, sports, fashion, art, theater, consumer affairs, travel, finance, social events, science, education, business, labor, religion, and other areas. Critics review literary, artistic, and musical works and performances while editorial writers present viewpoints on topics of interest. Reporters on small newspapers cover all aspects of local news, and may also take photographs, write headlines, lay out pages, and write editorials. On some small weeklies, they may also solicit advertisements, sell subscriptions, and perform general office work. Reporters must be highly motivated, and are expected to work long hours.

**BACKGROUND AND QUALIFICATIONS:**

Most newspapers will only consider applicants with a degree in journalism, which includes training in the liberal arts in addition to professional training in journalism. Others prefer applicants who have a bachelor's degree in one of the liberal arts and a master's degree in journalism. Experience as a part-time "stringer" is very helpful in finding full time employment as a reporter. Most beginning reporters start on weekly or small daily newspapers, with a small number of outstanding journalism graduates finding work with large daily newspapers, although this is a rare exception. Large dailies generally look for at least three years of reporting experience, acquired on smaller newspapers.

Beginning reporters are assigned duties such as reporting on civic and community meetings, summarizing speeches, writing obituaries, interviewing important community leaders or visitors, and covering police, government, or courthouse proceedings. As they gain experience, they may report on more important events, cover an assigned beat, or specialize in a particular field. Newspaper reporters may advance to large daily newspapers or state and national newswire services. However, competition for such positions is fierce, and news executives are flooded with applications from highly qualified reporters every year. Some experienced reporters become columnists, correspondents, editorial writers, editors, or top executives; these people represent the top of the field, and competition for these positions is extremely keen. Other reporters transfer to related fields, such as public relations, writing for magazines, or preparing copy for radio or television news programs.

OUTLOOK:

Employment of reporters and correspondents is expected to grow through the year 2000, primarily due to the anticipated increase in the number of small-town and suburban daily and weekly newspapers.

## SECURITIES AND FINANCIAL SERVICES SALES REPRESENTATIVES

DESCRIPTION:

**Securities Sales Representatives:**

Most investors, whether they are individuals with a few hundred dollars or large institutions with millions to invest, use securities sales representatives when buying or selling stocks, bonds, shares in mutual funds, or other financial products. Securities sales representatives also provide many related services for their customers. Depending on a customer's knowledge of the market, the representative may explain the meaning of stock market terms and trading practices, offer financial counseling, devise an individual financial portfolio including securities, corporate and municipal bonds, life insurance, annuities, and other investments, and offer advice on the purchase or sale of particular securities.

**Financial Services Sales Representative:**

Financial services sales representatives call on various businesses to solicit applications for loans and new deposit accounts for banks or savings and loan associations. They also locate and contact prospective customers to present their bank's financial services and to ascertain the customer's banking needs. At most small and medium-sized banks, branch managers and commercial loan officers are responsible for marketing the bank's financial services. As banks offer more and increasingly complex financial services, for example, securities brokerage and financial planning - the job of financial services sales representatives - will assume greater importance.

BACKGROUND AND QUALIFICATIONS:

A college education is becoming increasingly important, as securities sales representatives must be well informed about economic conditions and trends. Although employers seldom require specialized academic training, courses in business administration, economics, and finance are helpful. Securities sales representatives must meet state licensing requirements, which generally include passing an examination and, in some cases, furnishing a personal bond. In addition, sales representatives must register as representatives of their firm according to the regulations of the securities exchanges where they do business or the National Association of Securities Dealers, Inc. (NASD). Before beginners can qualify as registered representatives, they must pass the General Securities Registered Representative Examination. Banks and other credit institutions prefer to hire college graduates for financial services sales jobs. A business administration degree with a specialization in finance or a liberal arts degree including courses in accounting, economics, and marketing serves as excellent preparation for this job. Financial services sales representatives learn through on-the-job training under the supervision of bank officers. Outstanding performance can lead to promotion to managerial positions.

OUTLOOK:

The demand for securities sales representatives fluctuates as the economy expands and contracts. Employment of securities sales representatives is expected to expand as economic growth, rising personal incomes, and greater inherited wealth increase the funds available for investment. Employment of financial services sales representatives is also expected to increase through the year 2000, as banks and credit institutions expand the financial services they offer, and issue more loans for personal and commercial use.

# STATISTICIAN

## DESCRIPTION:

Statisticians devise, carry out, and interpret the numerical results of surveys and experiments. In doing so, they apply their knowledge of statistical methods to a particular subject area, such as economics, human behavior, the natural sciences, or engineering. They may use statistical techniques to predict population growth or economic conditions, develop quality control tests for manufactured products, or help business managers and government officials make decisions and evaluate the results of new programs. Over half of all statisticians are in private industry, primarily in manufacturing, finance, and insurance firms.

## BACKGROUND AND QUALIFICATIONS:

A bachelor's degree in statistics or mathematics is the minimum educational requirement for many beginning jobs in statistics. For other entry-level jobs in the field, however, a BA with a major in an applied field of study such as economics or a natural science, and a minor in statistics is preferable. A graduate degree in mathematics or statistics is essential for college and university teaching. Most mathematics statisticians have at least a BA in mathematics and an advanced degree in statistics. Beginning statisticians who have a BA often spend their time performing routine work under the supervision of an experienced statistician. Through experience, they may advance to positions of greater technical and supervisory responsibility. However, opportunities for promotion are best for those with advanced degrees.

## OUTLOOK:

Employment opportunities for persons who combine training in statistics with knowledge of computer science or a field of application - such as biology, economics or engineering - are generally expected to be favorable through the year 2000.

# SYSTEMS ANALYST

**DESCRIPTION:**

Systems analysts plan efficient methods of processing data and handling the results. Analysts use various techniques, such as cost accounting, sampling, and mathematical model building to analyze a problem and devise a new system. The problems that systems analysts solve range from monitoring nuclear fission in a powerplant to forecasting sales for an appliance manufacturing firm. Because the work is so varied and complex, Analysts usually specialize in either business or scientific and engineering applications. Most systems analysts work in manufacturing firms, banks, insurance companies, and data processing service organizations. In addition, large numbers work for wholesale and retail businesses and government agencies.

**BACKGROUND AND QUALIFICATIONS:**

College graduates are almost always sought for the position of systems analyst. For some of the more complex positions, persons with graduate degrees are preferred. Employers usually seek analysts with a background in accounting, business management, or economics for work in a business environment, while a background in the physical sciences, mathematics, or engineering is preferred for work in scientifically oriented organizations. A growing number of employers seek applicants who have a degree in Computer Science, Information Systems, or Data Processing. Regardless of the college major, employers seek those who are familiar with programming languages.

In order to advance, systems analysts must continue their technical education. Technological advances come so rapidly in the computer field that continuous study is necessary to keep computer skills up to date. Training usually takes the form of one and two-week courses offered by employers and software vendors. Additional training may come from professional development seminars offered by professional computing societies. An indication of experience and professional competence is the Certificate in Data Processing (CDP). This designation is conferred by the Institute for Certification of Computer Professionals, and is Granted to candidates who have five years experience and have passed a five-part examination.

## OUTLOOK:

The demand for systems analysts is expected to rise through the year 2000, as advances in technology lead to new applications for computers. Factory and office automation, advances in telecommunications technology, and scientific research are just a few areas where use of computers will expand.

# TECHNICAL WRITER/EDITOR

## DESCRIPTION:

Technical writers and technical editors research, write, and edit technical materials, and also may produce publications and audiovisual materials. To ensure that their work is accurate, Technical Writers must be expert in the subject area in which they are writing. Editors are also responsible for the accuracy of material on which they work. Some organizations use job titles other than technical writer/editor, such as staff writer, publications engineer, communications specialist, publications engineer, communications specialist, industrial writer, industrial materials developer, and others.Technical writers set out either to instruct or inform, and in many instances they do both. They prepare manuals, catalogs, parts lists, and instructional materials needed by sales representatives who sell machinery or scientific equipment and by the technicians who install, maintain, and service it. Technical writers are often part of a team, working closely with scientists, engineers, accountants, and others. Technical editors take the material Technical writers produce and further polish it for final publication and use. Many writers and editors work for large firms in the electronics, aviation, aerospace, ordinance, chemical, pharmaceutical, and computer manufacturing industries. Firms in the energy, communications, and computer software fields also employ many technical writers, and research laboratories employ significant numbers.

## BACKGROUND AND QUALIFICATIONS:

Employers seek people whose educational background, work experience, and personal pursuits indicate they possess both writing skills and appropriate scientific knowledge. Knowledge of graphics and other aspects of publication production may be helpful in landing a job in the field. An understanding of current trends in communication technology is an asset, and familiarity with computer operations and terminology is increasingly important. Many employers prefer candidates with a degree in science or engineering, plus a minor in English, journalism, or technical communications. Other employers emphasize writing ability and look for candidates whose major field of study was journalism, English, or the liberal arts. Depending on their line of business, these employees almost always require course work or practical experience in a specific subject as well, computer science, for example.

People with a solid background in science or engineering are at an advantage in competing for such jobs. Those with BA's or MA's in Technical Writing are often preferred over candidates with little or no technical background. Beginning technical writers often assist experienced writers by

With large writing staffs may eventually move to the job of technical editor, or shift to an administrative position in the publication or technical information departments. The top job is usually that of publications manager (and other titles), who normally supervises an of the people directly involved in producing the company's technical documents. The manager supervises not only the technical writers and editors, but also staff members responsible for illustrations, photography, reproduction, and distribution.

### OUTLOOK:

Through the year 2000, the outlook for writing and editing jobs is expected to continue to be keenly competitive. With the increasing complexity of industrial and scientific equipment, more users will depend on the technical writer's ability to prepare precise but simple explanations and instructions.

## UNDERWRITER

### DESCRIPTION:

Underwriters appraise and select the risks their company will insure. Underwriters decide whether their insurance company will accept risks after analyzing information in insurance applications, reports from loss control consultants, medical reports, and actuarial studies. Most Underwriters specialize in one of the three major categories of insurance: life, casualty, and health. They further specialize in group or individual policies.

## BACKGROUND AND QUALIFICATIONS:

For beginning underwriters, most large insurance companies seek college graduates with degrees in liberal arts or business administration. Underwriter trainees begin by evaluating routine applicants under the close supervision of an experienced risk appraiser. Continuing education is a necessity if the underwriter expects to advance to senior level positions. Insurance companies generally place great emphasis on completion of one or more of the many recognized independent study programs. Many companies pay tuition and the cost of books for those who successfully complete underwriting courses; some offer salary increases as an additional incentive. Independent study programs are available through the American Institute of Property and Liability Underwriters, the Health Insurance Association of America, and the Life Office Management Association.

As underwriters gain experience, they can qualify as a "Fellow" of the Academy of Life Underwriters by passing a series of examinations and completing a research paper on a topic in the field. Exams are given by the Institute of Home Office Underwriters and the Home Office Life Underwriters Association. The designation of "Fellow" is recognized as a mark of achievement in the underwriting field. Experienced underwriters who complete a course of study may advance to chief underwriter or underwriting manager. Some underwriting managers are promoted to senior managerial positions after several years.

## OUTLOOK:

Employment of underwriters is expected to rise faster than the average for all occupations through the year 2000 as insurance sales continue to expand. Most job openings, however, are expected to result from the need to replace underwriters who transfer to other occupations or stop working altogether.

# PART THREE: WHERE THE JOBS ARE

**Primary Greater Chicago Employers**

# ACCOUNTING AND AUDITING

For more information on professional employment opportunities in the accounting and auditing industries, contact the following professional and trade organizations, as listed beginning on page 315:

AMERICAN INSTITUTE OF CERTIFIED PUBLIC ACCOUNTANTS
THE EDP AUDITORS ASSOCIATION
INDEPENDENT ACCOUNTANTS ASSOCIATION OF ILLINOIS
INSTITUTE OF INTERNAL AUDITORS/CHICAGO CHAPTER
NATIONAL SOCIETY OF PUBLIC ACCOUNTANTS

**CLIFTON GUNDERSON & COMPANY**
301 South West Adams
Peoria IL 61602
309/671-4560
Contact Director of Personnel. A full-service accounting firm.

**COMPREHENSIVE BUSINESS SERVICES OF CANADA**
2111 Comprehensive Drive
Aurora IL 60505
708/898-3145
Contact Leo Lauzen, President. A franchisor of accounting services.

**KPMG/PEAT MARWICK**
303 East Wacker Drive
Chicago IL 60601
312/938-1000
Contact Patricia Gamble, Director of Human Resources. One of the largest CPA firms in the world.

**PRICE WATERHOUSE**
200 East Randolph
Chicago IL 60601
312/565-1500
Contact Mark Ormond, Recruitment Director. One of the largest international public accounting firms, with 115 United States offices and more than 400 offices in 100 countries. Common positions include: Accountant; Auditor; Attorney (Tax); Computer Programmer; Management Consultant; Systems Analyst; Technical Writer/Editor; Tax Specialist. Principal educational backgrounds sought: Accounting; Computer Science; Economics; Engineering. Training programs offered; Internships offered. Company benefits include: medical insurance; dental insurance; pension plan; life insurance; tuition assistance; disability coverage; daycare assistance; profit sharing; savings plan; 25 days vacation. United States headquarters

location: New York, NY. World headquarters location: London, England. Operations at this facility include: regional headquarters; service.

## ADVERTISING, MARKETING & PUBLIC RELATIONS

For more information on professional employment opportunities in the advertising and public relations industries, contact the following professional and trade organizations, as listed beginning on page 315:

AMERICAN ADVERTISING FEDERATION
AMERICAN ASSOCIATION OF ADVERTISING AGENCIES
AMERICAN MARKETING ASSOCIATION
BUSINESS-PROFESSIONAL ADVERTISING ASSOCIATION
FINANCIAL RELATIONS BOARD INC.
TELEVISION BUREAU OF ADVERTISING/CHICAGO
PUBLIC RELATIONS SOCIETY OF AMERICA
TELEVISION BUREAU OF ADVERTISING


ADAMS ADVERTISING AGENCY
111 North Canal Street
Chicago IL 60606
312/930-9446
Contact Personnel. An advertising and sales promotion company.

ADVERTISING METAL DISPLAY
4620 West 19th Street
Cicero IL 60650
708/863-8900
Contact Valerie Kikinder, Personnel. Manufactures and sells point of purchase displays.

N.W. AYER INC
515 North State, Suite 2100
Chicago IL 60610
312/644-2937
Contact Department of interest. The Chicago office of the nationally recognized advertising agency.

BBDO CHICAGO INC.
410 North Michigan Avenue
Chicago IL 60611
312/337-7860
Contact Michelle Shotts, Vice President, Human Resources. Chicago office of the nationally known advertising agency. Common positions include: Advertising Worker; Buyer; Commercial Artist; Marketing Specialist;

Personnel & Labor Relations Specialist; Public Relations Specialist; Statistician; Systems Analyst. Principal educational backgrounds sought: Art/Design; Business Administration; Communications; Computer Science; Finance; Liberal Arts; Marketing; Mathematics. Training programs offered; Internships offered. Company benefits include: medical, dental, and life insurance; profit sharing. Corporate headquarters location: New York, NY. Parent company: Omnicom. Operations at this facility include: administration; service.

## BOZELL
625 North Michigan Avenue
Chicago IL 60611
312/988-2000
Contact Barbara King, Manager, Human Resources. Area offices of a major international advertising agency. Services include marketing and community relations.

## LEO BURNETT COMPANY, INC.
35 West Wacker Drive
Chicago IL 60601
312/220-5959
Contact Cathy Norris, Employee Relations Associate. One of the nation's largest and most prestigious full-service advertising agencies. Employs 4,795. Corporate headquarters location.

## CHICAGO DISPLAY COMPANY
1301 West Armitage Avenue
Melrose Park IL 60160
312/379-8500
Contact Joan Maddocks, Personnel Manager. Makes advertising displays for merchandisers & manufacturers.

## DDB NEEDHAM WORLDWIDE
303 East Wacker Drive
Chicago IL 60601
312/861-0200
Contact Patricia DuBoux, V.P., Director of Human Resources. An advertising agency. Corporate headquarters location: New York, NY. Parent company: Omnicom. Common positions include: Account Executive; Account Supervisor; Media Planner; Media Buyer; Research Supervisor; Copywriter; Art Director; Creative Director; Secretary; Accounting Clerk. Principal educational backgrounds sought: Art/Design; Business Administration; Communications; Liberal Arts; Marketing; Mathematics. Company benefits include: medical insurance; dental insurance; life insurance; tuition assistance; disability coverage; profit sharing; employee discounts; savings plan. Operations at this facility include: research/marketing; administration; service.

## FOOTE CONE AND BELDING COMMUNICATIONS
101 East Erie
Chicago IL 60611
312/751-7000
Contact Robert Vogel, Director of Personnel. Ranks as the 8th largest advertising agency in the U.S.

## HADDON ADVERTISING, INC.
919 North Michigan Avenue
Chicago IL 60611
312/943-6266
Contact Jackie Ames, Director of Personnel. An advertising agency.

## BERNARD HODES ADVERTISING
205 West Wacker Drive, Suite 1300
Chicago IL 60606
312/222-5800
Contact Mrs. Greta Sherman, Branch Manager. Chicago office of a national recruitment advertising agency.

## INFORMATION RESOURCES, INC.
150 North Clinton Street
Chicago IL 60661
312/726-1221
Contact Thomas Quinn, Senior Corporate Recruiter. A major metropolitan Chicago marketing research firm. Common positions include: Accountant; Computer Programmer; Electrical Engineer. Principal educational backgrounds sought: Accounting; Computer Science; Marketing. Company benefits include: medical, dental, and life insurance; tuition assistance; disability coverage; employee discounts; savings plan. Corporate headquarters location. Operations at this facility include: divisional headquarters; research/development; sales.

## KETCHUM COMMUNICATIONS, INC.
142 East Ontario
Chicago IL 60611
312/266-4550
Contact Paula Williams, Administrative Assistant. A Chicago area public relations agency. Common positions include: Public Relations Specialist; Technical Writer/Editor. Principal educational backgrounds sought: Business Administration; Communications; Marketing. Training programs offered; Internships offered. Corporate headquarters location: Pittsburgh, PA. Operations at this facility include: regional headquarters.

## SAATCHI SAATCHI DFS
225 North Michigan, Suite 900
Chicago IL 60601
312/856-1046

Contact Mary Palmer, Broadcast Director. Chicago office of the nationally known advertising agency.

**TATHAM-LAIRD & KUDNER**
980 North Michigan Avenue
Chicago IL 60611
312/337-4400
Contact Eileen Haggerty, Director of Personnel. A major advertising agency.

**J. WALTER THOMPSON USA INC.**
900 North Michigan Avenue
Chicago IL 60611
312/951-4000
Contact Melinda Weaver, Personnel Manager. Chicago office of the well-known company engaged in advertising, public relations, research, and related activites. Subsidiares include J. Walter Thompson Company, one of the world's largest advertising agencies, which plans and creates consumer, direct response, trade, and corporate advertising, recruitment and medical advertising, and other services, including the design and production of merchandising and sales promotion programs and a wide range of consumer, media, and market research; Hill and Knowlton, Inc., the world's largest public relations firm; Lord, Geller, Federico, Einstein, Inc., a New York-based full-service agency noted for its creative flair and effective execution; and Simmons Market Research Bureau, Inc., a syndicated market research firm, and one of the leading United States authorites on magazine readership and demographics. Company employs more than 8,600 people worldwide.

**YOUNG & RUBICAM/CHICAGO**
1 South Wacker Drive, Suite 1800
Chicago IL 60606
312/845-4000
Contact Larry Claypoll, Vice President, Business Manager. A major international advertising agency, with 126 agency offices throughout the world. Operates through three divisions: Young & Rubicam International, with offices throughout the world; Marsteller Inc., a worldwide leader in business-to-business and consumer advertising, with offices throughout the Unites States and worldwide, with subsidiary Burson-Marsteller providing public relations services throughout the world; and Young & Rubicam USA, with 14 consumer advertising agencies operating through four regional groups (except Young & Rubicam Detroit), and five specialized advertising/marketing agences. Corpoate headquarters location: New York, NY.

## AMUSEMENT/ARTS/RECREATION

For more information on professional employment opportunities in the arts, entertainment, or leisure industries, contact the following professional and trade organizations, as listed beginning on page 315:

AMERICAN ASSOCIATION OF ZOOLOGICAL PARKS & AQUARIUMS
AMERICAN FEDERATION OF MUSICIANS
AMERICAN FEDERATION OF MUSICIANS/CHICAGO
AMERICAN FEDERATION OF TELEVISION AND RADIO ARTISTS
NATIONAL ENDOWMENT FOR THE ARTS
NATIONAL ENDOWMENT FOR THE ARTS/CHICAGO
NATIONAL RECREATION AND PARKS ASSOCIATION/CHICAGO
THEATRE COMMUNICATIONS GROUP

**BALLY MANUFACTURING**
8700 West Bryn Mawr Avenue
Chicago IL 60631
312/399-1300
Contact Mrs. Lois Balodis, Personnel Director. Major manufacturers of pinball, video, slot and exercise machines. Also engaged in the ownership and operation of health clubs, hotels, and casinos.

**CHICAGO NATIONAL LEAGUE BALL CLUB, INC.**
Wrigley Field, 1060 West Addison Street
Chicago IL 60613
312/404-2827
Contact Wendy Lewis, Director of Human Resources. Operates the Chicago Cubs professional baseball club.

**CHICAGO STADIUM CORP.**
1800 West Madison Street
Chicago IL 60612
312/733-5300
Contact Jim DeMaria, Director of Public Relations. Operators of a 20,000 seat arena.

**FAIRMONT RACE TRACK/
OGDEN FAIRMONT INC.**
Route 40
Collinsville IL 62234
618/345-4300
Contact Brian Zander, General Manager. A major area race track specializing in horse racing. Employs over 400.

## FIELD MUSEUM OF NATURAL HISTORY
Roosevelt Road at Lake Shore Drive
Chicago IL 60605
312/922-9410
Contact Human Resources Administrator. A research and education museum.

## MOTIVATION MEDIA, INC.
1245 Milwaukee Avenue
Glenview IL 60025
708/297-4740
Contact Shirley Emil, Personnel Coordinator. Produces business-related slide presentations, motion pictures, and videotapes.

## MUSEUM OF SCIENCE & INDUSTRY
57th Street and Lake Shore Drive
Chicago IL 60637
312/684-1414
Contact Judy Kupfer, Personnel Coordinator. One of the largest museums of science and industry in the world. Corporate headquarters location.

## SIX FLAGS GREAT AMERICA
P.O. Box 1776
Gurnee IL 60031
708/249-1776
Contact Rosemary Monahan, Personnel Manager. A family entertainment company operating amusement parks. A subsidiary of S.F. Acquisition Inc.

---

## APPAREL & TEXTILES MANUFACTURING

For more information on professional employment opportunities in the apparel, textile or fashion industries, contact the following professional and trade organizations, as listed beginning on page 315:

AMERICAN APPAREL MANUFACTURERS ASSOCIATION
AMERICAN TEXTILE MANUFACTURERS INSTITUTE
NORTHERN TEXTILE ASSOCIATION
TEXTILE RESEARCH INSTITUTE

## ARATEX SERVICES, INC.
1834 Walden Office Square, #450
Schaumburg IL 60173
708/397-9500
Contact John Regan, Area Human Resource Manager. Aratex is the largest uniform service company in the world serving the varied needs of close to 400,000 clients across the nation. Common positions include: Industrial

Engineer; Department Manager; General Manager; Management Trainee; Operations/Production Manager; Sales Representative. Principal educational backgrounds sought: Business Administration; Communications; Liberal Arts; Marketing. Training programs offered. Company benefits include: medical insurance; dental insurance; pension plan; life insurance; tuition assistance; disability coverage; profit sharing; savings plan. Corporate headquarters location: Burbank, CA. Parent company: ARA Services, Inc. Operations at this facility include: regional headquarters.

**ARTEX INTERNATIONAL INC.**
1405 S. Walnut Street
Highland IL 62249. 618/654-2114
Contact Personnel Department. Major area apparel company, specializing in the manufacture of dyed and imprinted tablecloths and napkins. Employs over 100.

**BELLEVILLE SHOE MANUFACTURING COMPANY**
P.O. Box 508
Belleville IL 62222
618/233-5600
Contact Bill Tripp, Plant Manager. Manufacturers of men's and boy's shoes. Employs over 300.

**R.A. BRIGGS & COMPANY**
650 North Church Street
Lake Zurich IL 60047.
Contact Vincent P. Smyth, Personnel Director. Specializes in textiles with silk screening and embroidery.

**FLORSHEIM SHOE COMPANY**
130 South Canal Street
Chicago IL 60606
312/559-0009
Contact Personnel Manager. A retailer and manufacturer of footwear.

**HARTMARX CORPORATION**
101 North Wacker Drive
Chicago IL 60606
312/372-6300
Contact Human Resources Coordinator. A manufacturer and retailer of men's and women's apparel.

**O'BRYAN BROTHERS**
4220 West Belmont Avenue
Chicago IL 60641
312/283-3000

Contact Denis B. O'Keefe, Director of Personnel. An apparel manufacturer specializing in ladies' loungewear and lingerie. Corporate headquarters location.

## OXFORD CLOTHES
1220 West Van Buren Street
Chicago IL 60607
312/829-3600
Contact Robert Stepman, Personnel Manager. Manufacturer of men's and boys' suits and coats. A subsidiary of Koracorp Industries, Inc. Corporate headquarters location.

## OZITE CORPORATION
1755 Butterfield Road
Libertyville IL 60048
708/362-8210
Contact Kathy Foxx, Personnel/Payroll Manager. Manufactures commercial, automotive, industrial and specialty carpeting and wall covering. Corporate headquarters location. Common positions include: Accountant; Administrator; Bank Officer/Manager; Blue-Collar Worker Supervisor; Buyer; Chemist; Claim Representative; Computer Programmer; Credit Manager; Customer Service Representative; Industrial Engineer; Personnel & Labor Relations Specialist; Purchasing Agent; Quality Control Supervisor; Sales Representative; Statistician; Transportation & Traffic Specialist. Principal educational backgrounds sought: Accounting; Business Administration; Computer Science; Engineering; Finance; Liberal Arts; Marketing. Company benefits include: medical insurance; dental insurance; life insurance; tuition assistance; disability coverage; profit sharing; employee discounts; savings plan; 401K. Operations at this facility include: manufacturing; research/development; administration; sales.

## QST INDUSTRIES
231 South Jefferson Street
Chicago IL 60661
312/930-9400
Contact Personnel. A major manufacturer, importer, and exporter of textiles. Employs 350.

## BANKING/SAVINGS AND LOAN

For more information on professional employment opportunities in the banking industry, contact the following professional and trade organizations, as listed beginning on page 315:

AMERICAN BANKERS ASSOCIATION
BANK ADMINISTRATION INSTITUTE

COMMUNITY BANKERS ASSOCIATION OF ILLINOIS
ILLINOIS BANKERS ASSOCIATION
INDEPENDENT BANKERS ASSOCIATION OF AMERICA
INSTITUTE OF FINANCIAL EDUCATION
NATIONAL COUNCIL OF SAVINGS INSTITUTIONS

**AETNA BANK**
2401 North Halsted
Chicago IL 60614
312/935-6000
Contact Janet Toledo, Personnel. A banking association. A subsidiary of Aetna Bancorp.

**ALBANY BANK & TRUST COMPANY N.A.**
3400 West Lawrence Avenue
Chicago IL 60625
312/267-7300
Contact Mrs. Lee Weisman, Personnel Director. A bank operating as a subsidiary of Albank Corporation.

**AMERICAN NATIONAL BANK AND TRUST**
33 North La Salle Street
Chicago IL 60690
312/661-6907
Contact Ron Yenerich, Vice President of Human Resources. Provides banking services to corporate clients.

**AUSTIN BANK OF CHICAGO**
5645 West Lake Street
Chicago IL 60644
312/287-5412
Contact Pamela Robinson, Personnel Director. A banking institution.

**BEVERLY BANK**
1357 West 103rd Street
Chicago IL 60643
312/881-2200
Contact Personnel. A major banking institution.

**BOATMEN'S NATIONAL BANK OF BELLEVILLE**
23 Public Square
Belleville IL 62222
618/233-6600
Contact Personnel Officer. A full-service St. Louis area bank. Employs over 100. Corporate headquarters location: St. Louis MO. Parent company: Boatmen's Bancshares, Inc. Common positions include: Bank Office/Manager; Customer Service Representative; Branch Manager;

Department Manager. Principal educational backgrounds sought: Accounting; Business Administration; Finance. Company benfits include: medical, dental, and life insurance; pension plan; tuition assistance; disability coverage; employee discounts; savings plan.

**BOULEVARD BANK NATIONAL ASSOCIATION**
410 North Michigan Avenue
Chicago IL 60611
312/836-6505
Contact Barbara Kessner, Vice President of Human Resources. A full-service bank; the 13th largest in the state of IL.

**CITIBANK FSB**
One South Dearborn Street
Chicago IL 60603
312/977-5000
Contact Ian Ostergard, Vice President, Human Resources. A full service consumer banking institution.

**COLE TAYLOR BANK**
350 East Dundy, Suite 201
Chicago IL 60090
708/459-6666
Contact Personnel. A bank operating as a subsidiary of Cole Taylor Group.

**CONTINENTAL ILLINOIS NATIONAL BANK**
231 South LaSalle Street
Chicago IL 60697
312/828-2345
Contact Joseph Thompson, Personnel Director. One of the largest banks in the Chicago Area.

**FEDERAL RESERVE BANK OF CHICAGO**
230 South LaSalle Street
Chicago IL 60604
312/322-5496
Contact Human Resource Services. A member of the Federal Reserve, the nation's central bank

**FIRST CHICAGO CORPORATION**
1 First National Plaza, Suite 0016
Chicago IL 60670-0016
312/407-4908
Contact Cynthia Causey, Executive Recruiter. A holding company that is primarily concerned with the operation of The First National Bank of Chicago. The bank provides a broad range of commercial and investment banking, trust services, financial and other services on a worldwide basis to individuals, businesses and governmental units. Maintains 14 major

departments dealing with the different aspects of operation: Commercial Lending, Trading Products, Corporate Trust Services, Retail Banking (including Personal Trust), Financial Products, Service Products, Risk Insurance, Credit Policy, Community Affairs, Personnel, Systems & MIS, Corporate Planning, Credit Administration, Law, Control, Audit, Bond, Economics, Communications and Administration. Corporate headquarters location. International. New York Stock Exchange. Common positions include: Accountant; Attorney; Seasoned Commercial Lender; Computer Programmer; Customer Service Representative; Mining Engineer; Petroleum Engineer; Financial Analyst; Systems Analyst; Mergers & Acquisitions Specialist; Leveraged Buyout Specialist. Principal educational backgrounds sought: Accounting; Business Administration; Computer Science; Finance; Law. Company benefits include: medical insurance; pension plan; life insurance; tuition assistance; disability coverage; 401K.

**FIRST FINANCIAL BANK, FSB**
6550 North Illinois
Fairview Heights IL 62208
618/632-7421, ext. 203
Contact Bill Bright, Employee Relations Manager. First Financial is a federal savings bank. Common positions include: Accountant; Administrator; Advertising Worker; Computer Programmer; Customer Service Representative; Financial Analyst; Branch Manager; Management Trainee; Personnel and Labor Relations Specialist. Principal educational backgrounds sought: Accounting; Business Administration; Computer Science; Finance; Marketing. Training programs offered. Company benefits include: medical insurance; dental insurance; pension plan; life insurance; tuition assistance; disability coverage; profit sharing; savings plan. Corporate headquarters location: Stevens Point, WI. Operations at this facility include: regional headquarters; administration; service; sales.

**FIRST NATIONAL BANK OF BELLEVILLE**
19 Public Square
Belleville IL 62220
618/234-0020
Contact Les Mehrtens, Personnel Director. A leading St. Louis area national banking institution. Employs over 300.

**GERMANIA FEDERAL SAVINGS AND LOAN ASSOCIATION**
543 E. Broadway
Alton IL 62002
618/465-5543
Contact Alenna Wehnemeyer, Asst. Vice President, Personnel Officer. Federal savings and loan association. Employs over 100.

## HARRIS TRUST AND SAVINGS BANK
P.O. Box 775
Chicago IL 60690
312/461-2121
Contact Human Resources Department. A full service banking institution.

## LAKE SHORE NATIONAL BANK
605 North Michigan Avenue
Chicago IL 60611
312/787-1900
Contact Richard W. Nevell, Manager of Human Resources. A banking institution. Common positions include: Financial Analyst; Sales Representative. Principal educational backgrounds sought: Business Administration; Finance. Training programs offered; Internships offered. Company benefits include: medical insurance; pension plan; life insurance; tuition assistance; disability coverage; profit sharing; savings plan. Corporate headquarters location. Parent company: Lake Shore Bancorp., Inc. Operations at this facility include: regional headquarters; administration; sales. NASDAQ.

## LANDMARK BANK
1223 Broadway, P.O. Box 70
Highland IL 62249
618/654-4511
Contact Marsh Kennett, Personnel Director. Bank holding company; national member of Federal Reserve System. Employs over 100.

## LASALLE BANK LAKE VIEW
3201 North Ashland Avenue
Chicago IL 60657
312/525-2180
Contact Carolyn K. Cacal, Personnel Administrator. Lasalle Bank Lake View is part of one of the world's largest banking conglomerates: ABN AMRO. It is a full service bank that caters to the middle market. four Chicagoland locations. Common positions include: Accountant; Bank Officer/Manager; Credit Manager; Customer Service Representative; Financial Analyst; Branch Manager; Department Manager; Management Trainee; Personnel and Labor Relations Specialist. Principal educational backgrounds sought: Accounting; Business Administration; Communications; Economics; Finance; Liberal Arts. Training programs offered. Company benefits include: medical insurance; dental insurance; pension plan; life insurance; tuition assistance; disability coverage; profit sharing; savings plan. Corporate headquarters location.

**LASALLE NATIONAL**
135 South LaSalle Street
Chicago IL 60603
312/443-2000
Contact Joan Schellhorn, Employment Manager. A commercial middle market bank. Member of FDIC.

**MERCHANDISE NATIONAL BANK**
Merchandise Mart, Suite 2400
Chicago IL 60654
312/836-8120
Contact Mrs. Metcalfe, Director of Personnel. A commercial bank. Offices in Germania Club, as well as in Merchandise Mart. Corporate headquarters location. Common positions include: Accountant; Bank Officer/Manager; Credit Manager; Customer Service Representative; Teller. Principal educational backgrounds sought: Accounting; Business Administration; Finance. Company benefits include: medical insurance; dental insurance; pension plan; life insurance; tuition assistance; disability coverage; employee discounts; savings plan.

**MICHIGAN AVENUE NATIONAL BANK OF CHICAGO**
30 North Michigan Avenue
Chicago IL 60602
312/641-1000
Contact Personnel. A major banking institution.

**THE NORTHERN TRUST COMPANY**
50 South LaSalle
Chicago IL 60675
312/630-6000
Contact Personnel Department. A major full service bank engaged in commercial lending, trust and financial services, bond, financial management, operations and capital markets among other services.

**NORTHWEST NATIONAL BANK**
4747 W. Irving Park
Chicago IL 60641
312/777-7700
Contact Vice President of Personnel. A commercial bank. A subsidiary of Northwestco, Inc. Corporate headquarters location.

**OLD KENT BANK**
Sears Tower
Chicago IL 60606
312/876-4200
Contact Personnel Recruiter. Engaged in the commercial banking and trust business, including taking deposits, making secured and unsecured loans, financing commercial transactions, underwriting municipal obligations,

renting safe deposit boxes, providing travel services, and performing corporate, pension, and personal trust services.

## PIONEER BANK & TRUST COMPANY
4000 West North Avenue
Chicago IL 60639
312/772-8600
Contact Donna Evinger, Personnel Manager. A banking association.

## ST. PAUL FEDERAL BANK FOR SAVINGS
6700 West North Avenue
Chicago IL 60635
312/622-5000
Contact Dawn Jensen, Employment Manager. Federally chartered savings and loan association. There are multiple branch locations in Chicago and the suburbs. Corporate headquarters location. Common positions include: Accountant; Customer Service Representative; Sales Representative. Principal educational backgrounds sought: Accouting; Finance. Training programs offered. Company benefits include: medical, dental, and life insurance; pension plan; tuition assistance; disability coverage; profit sharing; employee discounts; savings plan. Operations at this facility include: administration; service; sales.

## TALMAN HOME FEDERAL SAVINGS AND LOAN ASSOCIATION OF ILLINOIS
5501 South Kedzie Avenue
Chicago IL 60629
312/434-3322
Contact Christen Nelson, Director of Human Resources. One of the nation's largest savings and loan associations. Branch offices throughout Chicago and its suburbs, and central Illinois. It owns two subsidiaries: Talman Insurance Services, Inc. and Talman Home Mortgage Corporation, which has offices nationwide. Common positions include: Accountant; Advertising Worker; Attorney; Bank Officer/Manager; Claim Representative; Consumer Loan Officer; Credit Manager; Customer Service Representative; Financial Analyst; Financial Counselor; Insurance Agent/Broker; Branch Manager; Department Manager; Consumer Loan Officer; Mortgage Loan Officer; Personnel & Labor Relations Specialist; Public Relations Worker; Purchasing Agent; Systems Analyst; Underwriter. Principal educational backgrounds sought: Accounting; Business Administration; Communications; Computer Science; Economics; Finance; Liberal Arts; Marketing. Company benefits include: medical, dental, and life insurance; pension plan; tuition assistance; disability coverage; savings plan. Corporate headquarters location: 30 West Monroe Street, Chicago, IL 60603. Operations at this facility include: regional headquarters; divisional headquarters; administration; service.

## BOOK AND MAGAZINE PUBLISHING

For more information on professional employment opportunities in the book and magazine publishing industries, contact the following professional and trade organizations, as listed beginning on page 315:

AMERICAN BOOKSELLERS ASSOCIATION
ASSOCIATION OF AMERICAN PUBLISHERS
MAGAZINE PUBLISHERS ASSOCIATION
WRITERS GUILD OF AMERICA EAST, INC.
WRITERS GUILD OF AMERICA WEST, INC.

**AMERICAN LIBRARY ASSOCIATION**
50 East Huron Street
Chicago IL 60611
312/944-6780
Contact Human Resources. A major national association for the library industry.

**BELL & HOWELL CO.**
5215 Old Orchard Road
Skokie IL 60077
708/470-7685
Contact Cheryl Haas, Corporate Human Resource Manager. Offices of the information services company. Common positions include: Accountant; Administrator; Computer Programmer; Credit Manager; Financial Analyst; Personnel and Labor Relations Specialist; Sales Representative; Systems Analyst. Prinipal educational backgrounds sought: Accounting; Business Administration; Computer Science; Finance. Internships offered. Company benefits include: medical insurance; dental insurance; life insurance; tuition assistance; disability coverage; profit sharing; employee discounts; savings plan; gain sharing plan. Corporate headquarters location.

**CHILDREN'S PRESS**
5440 North Cumberland Avenue
Chicago IL 60656
312/693-0800
Contact Carol Werkmeister, Personnel Assistant. Children's Press publishes a wide list of children's books. Common positions include: Accountant; Computer Programmer; Customer Service Representative; Sales Representative; Editor. Company benefits include: medical insurance; dental insurance; pension plan; life insurance; disability coverage; savings plan. Corporate headquarters location: Danbury, CT. Parent company is Grolier, Inc. Operations at this facility include: manufacturing; administration; sales.

**CHRISTIANITY TODAY, INC.**
465 Gundersen Drive
Carol Stream IL 60188
708/260-6200
Contact Kate V. Bryant, Personnel Coordinator. A major Chicago area publisher of religious magazines. Common positions include: Accountant; Commercial Artist; Credit Manager; Marketing Specialist; Personnel and Labor Relations Specialist; Reporter/Editor; Sales Representative; Fullfillment Manager; Market Research Analyst. Principal educational backgrounds sought: Accounting; Art/Design; Business Administration; Communications; Liberal Arts; Marketing; Journalism. Internships available. Company benefits include: dental insurance; pension plan; life insurance; tuition assistance; disability coverage; employee discounts. Corporate headquarters location.

**COMMERCE CLEARING HOUSE, INC.**
4700 Lake Cook Road
Riverwoods IL 60015
312/583-8500
Contact Darde Gaertner, Personnel Director. Publishes current information, primarily regarding taxes and law.

**DAVID C. COOK PUBLISHING COMPANY**
850 North Grove Avenue
Elgin IL 60120
312/741-2400
Contact Stephan Barney, Employment Coordinator. Creates, designs, produces, prints, markets, and distributes non-demoninational Christian education material. Common positions include: Accountant; Blue Collar Worker Supervisor; Buyer; Computer Programmer; Customer Service Representative; Department Manager; Operations/Production Manager; Marketing Specialist; Personnel & Labor Relations Specialist; Public Relations Specialist; Purchasing Agent; Sales Representative; Statistician; Systems Analyst. Principal educational backgrounds sought: Accounting; Art/Design; Business Administration; Communications; Computer Science; Finance; Marketing; Mathematics; Religion. Training programs available. Company benefits include: medical, dental, and life insurance; tuition assistance; disability coverage; employee discounts; 401K. Operations at this facility include: manufacturing; research/development; administration; service; sales.

**DON TECH**
205 North Michigan Avenue
Chicago IL 60601
312/861-2551
Contact Brian Grant, Personnel Selection Manager. Engaged in the publishing and selling of Yellow Pages.

## ENCYCLOPAEDIA BRITANNICA
Brittannica Centre
310 S. Michigan Avenue
Chicago IL 60604
312/347-7277
Contact Corporate Human Resources. An international publisher of reference books and educational materials. A privateley held corporation wholly owned by the William Benton Foundation, and Illinois Not for Profit Corporation. There are six principal income producing divisions of Encyclopaedia Britannica, Inc. They are: Encyclopaedia Britannica USA, Encyclopaedia Britannica International; Merriam-Webster, Encylopaedia Britannica Educational Corporation, American Learning Corporation, and Britannica Software. The company has approximately 1,800 employees and more than 2,000 independent contractor and sales representatives in the United States. Outside the U.S. there are approximately 4,500 employees, independent contractor and sales representatives. Area locations include: distribution centers located in Chicago and Skokie; a full-service telemarketing agency/bureau (Britcom), with offices in Joliet and Lombard, Illinois, as well as in Merrillville, Indiana; and a regional sales office in Oakbrook Terrace. Corporate headquarters. International. Common positions include: Accountant; Computer Programmer; Customer Services Representative; Buyer; Copy Editor; Indexer; Systems Analyst. Company benefits include: medical insurance; life insurance; disability coverage; pension plan; savings plan; educational assistance; employee discounts.

## FRANCISCAN HERALD PRESS
1434 West 51st Street
Chicago IL 60609
312/254-4462
Contact Personnel. A book publisher.

## JOHNSON PUBLISHING CO.
820 South Michigan Avenue
Chicago IL 60605
312/332-9200
Contact Personnel. One of the nation's leading magazine publishers. Publications include Ebony, Jet, and others. Company is also engaged in broadcasting, television production, cosmetics, and haircare products. Corporate headquarters location.

## CHARLES LEVY CIRCULATING COMPANY
1200 North North Branch Street
Chicago IL 60622
312/440-4400
Contact Frances Lefkow, Personnel Director. A major area magazine, book and newspaper distributor.

## McMILLAN INFORMATION SERVICES GROUP
3004 Glenview Road
Wilmette IL 60091
708/256-6067
Contact Jane McCarthy, Human Resource Manager. Subsidiary of Macmillan, Inc. Publishers of specialized directories for advertising agencies. Corporate headquarters location.

## PLAYBOY ENTERPRISES
680 North Lakeshore Drive
Chicago IL 60611
312/751-8000
Contact Ms. Carol Devine, Personnel Director. Publishes a major magazine. Also operates licensed cable television services.

## RAND McNALLY & COMPANY
8255 Central Park Avenue
Skokie IL 60076-2970
708/673-9100
Contact Employment Manager. A major book and map publisher. Well-known products include road atlases. Corporate headquarters location.

## SCOTT, FORESMAN AND COMPANY
1900 East Lake Avenue
Glenview IL 60025
708/729-3000
Contact Human Resources Department. A subsidiary of SFN Companies, Inc. Publisher of elementary, secondary and college textbooks and materials; also adult and continuing education, and educational software. Common positions include: Accountant; Advertising Worker; Computer Programmer; Credit Manager; Customer Service Representative; Department Manager; Editor; Marketing Specialist; Personnel Specialist; Sales Representative; Systems Analyst. Principal educational backgrounds sought: Accounting; Art/Design; Business Administration; Computer Assisted Instruction; Computer Science; Finance; Liberal Arts; Marketing; Mathematics. Company benefits include: medical insurance; dental insurance; pension plan; life insurance; tuition assistance; disability coverage; profit sharing; employee discounts; savings plan; benefit reimbursement account. Parent company is Time Warner, Inc. American Stock Exchange. Corporate, regional headquarters location. Operations at this facility include: service; sales.

## SCRIPTURE PRESS PUBLICATIONS
1825 College Avenue
Wheaton IL 60187
708/668-6000
Contact Douglas Walton, Employment Manager. Scripture Press and Victor Books are publishers of Christian Education materials, providing Sunday School curriculum, books, training, and resources for all ages. Common

positions include: Accountant; Advertising; Commercial Artist; Customer Service Representative; Marketing Specialist; Purchasing Agent; Sales Representative; Writer/Editor. Principal educational backgrounds sought: Accounting; Art/Design; Communications; Liberal Arts; Marketing. Company benefits include: medical insurance; dental insurance; pension plan; life insurance; disability coverage; profit sharing; employee discounts; employee credit union. Corporate headquarters location. Operations include: product development; production; marketing; administration; service; sales; distribution.

**STANDARD EDUCATIONAL CORPORATION**
200 West Monroe Street, Room 200
Chicago IL 60606
312/346-7440
Contact Personnel. Publishers of the New Standard Encyclopedia.

**TYNDALE HOUSE PUBLISHERS, INC.**
P.O. Box 80
Wheaton IL 60189
708/668-8300
Contact Pamela Orr, Employment and Training Coordinator. Publishes bibles and religious books. Common positions include: Buyer; Commercial Artist; Credit Manager; Customer Service Representative; Department Manager; Operations/Production Manager; Marketing Specialist; Purchasing Agent; Reporter/Editor; Sales Representative. Principal educational backgrounds sought include: Art/Design; Business Administration; Communications; Liberal Arts; Marketing. Training programs available. Company benefits include: medical insurance; dental insurance; pension plan; life insurance; tuition assistance; disability coverage; profit sharing; employee discounts. Corporate headquarters location.

**U.S. SAMPLE COMPANY, INC.**
1840 North Marcey Street
Chicago IL 60614
312/528-4200
Contact Personnel. A publisher of sample books.

**BROADCASTING**

For more information on professional employment opportunities in the broadcasting industry, contact the following professional and trade organizations, as listed beginning on page 315:

**BROADCAST EDUCATION ASSOCIATION**
**CABLE TELEVISION ASSOCIATION**
**FEDERAL COMMUNICATIONS COMMISSION**

ILLINOIS CABLE TELEVISION ASSOCIATION
INTERNATIONAL RADIO AND TV SOCIETY
NATIONAL ASSOCIATION OF BRAODCASTERS
NATIONAL ASSOCIATION OF BROADCASTERS/ILLINOIS
NATIONAL ASSOCIATION OF BUSINESS AND EDUCATIONAL RADIO
TELEVISION BUREAU OF ADVERTISING
TELEVISION BUREAU OF ADVERTISING/CHICAGO
WOMEN IN RADIO AND TV, INC.


**CHICAGO EDUCATIONAL TELEVISION ASSOCIATION**
5400 North St. Louis Avenue
Chicago IL 60625
312/583-5000
Contact Gene Caylor, Personnel Director. A major public television station.

**JONES INTERCABLE COMPANY**
8 East Galena Boulevard
Aurora IL 60506
708/897-2288
Contact Jim Vrkota, Personnel. A cable television operator.

**MIDWEST TELEVISION, INC.**
509 South Neil Street
P.O. Box 777
Champaign IL 61824-0777
217/356-8333
Contact department of interest. A major television and radio broadcasting company.

**NATIONAL BROADCASTING COMPANY, INC.**
NBC Tower
454 North Columbus Drive
Chicago IL 60611-5555
312/836-5750
Contact Personnel. Resumes can only be accepted for positions that are open. To learn of these opportunities, please call one of the hotlines. Job hotline: ext. 2574; Internship hotline: ext. 2573. Operating facilities for one television station and a regional office for the national television sales network. Parent company: GE. Common positions include: Accountant; Advertising Worker; Broadcast Engineer and Technician; Broadcast Professional; Electrical Engineer; Financial Analyst; Reporter/Editor; Sales Representative. Principal educational backgrounds sought: Accounting; Business Administration; Communications; Engineering; Finance; Journalism; Liberal Arts. Internships offered. Company benefits include: medical insurance; dental insurance; pension plan; life insurance; tuition assistance; disability coverage; employee discounts; savings plan; dependent

life insurance. Regional headquarters location. Corporate headquarters: New York, NY.

**A.C. NIELSEN**
Nielsen Plaza
Northbrook IL 60062
708/498-6300
Contact Personnel. Provides demographic and related information for the consumer goods industry, such as television audience-rating services and consumer polling. Corporate headquarters location.

**SALTER BROADCASTING COMPANY**
P.O. Box C 1730
Aurora IL 60507
708/898-6668
Contact Chuck Filippi, General Manager. A radio broadcasting firm.

**TRIBUNE COMPANY/BROADCASTING DIVISION**
435 North Michigan Avenue, Suite 1900
Chicago IL 60611
312/222-9100
Contact Personnel. Operates several radio and television stations.

## CHARITABLE, NON-PROFIT, HUMANITARIAN

For more information on professional employment opportunities with charitable, non-profit or humanitarian organizations, contact the following professional and trade associations, as listed beginning on page 315:

NATIONAL ASSOCIATION OF SOCIAL WORKERS
NATIONAL ORGANIZATION FOR HUMAN SERVICE EDUCATION

**AMERICAN RED CROSS**
43 East Ohio Street
Chicago IL 60611
312/440-2236.
Contact Janet Dixon, Employment Specialist. A social services organization committed to the health and safety needs of the community.

**INTERNATIONAL ASSOCIATION OF LIONS CLUBS**
300 22nd Street
Oak Brook IL 60521-8842
708/571-5466
Contact Peggy Malenchik, Personnel Manager. A major international service club organinzation.

## KNOX COUNTY COUNCIL FOR DEVELOPMENTAL DISABILITIES
2015 Windish Drive
Galesburg IL 61401
309/344-2600
Contact Mary Crittenden, Assistant Administrator. A not-for-profit agency serving developmentally disabled. Common positions include: Accountant; Administrator; Blue-Collar Worker Supervisor; Industrial Manager; Department Manager; Operations/Production Manager; Marketing Specialist. Principal educational backgrounds sought: Nursing; Occupational Therapy; Teaching; Social Work; Human Service Fields. Training programs offered. Company benefits include: medical insurance; pension plan; life insurance; tuition assistance; disability coverage; savings plan. Operations at this facility include: administration.

## NATIONAL SAFETY COUNCIL
444 North Michigan Avenue
Chicago IL 60611
312/527-4800
Contact Stacey Donovan, Human Resources Department. A non-governmental, not-for-profit public service organization. Common positions include: Accountant; Advertising Worker; Computer Programmer; Credit Manager; Customer Service Representative; Chemical Engineer; Industrial Hygienest; Mining Engineer; Financial Analyst; Marketing Specialist; Personnel & Labor Relations Specialist; Public Relations Specialist; Purchasing Agent; Reporter/Editor; Statistician; Systems Analyst; Technical Writer/Editor; Transportation & Traffic Specialist; Warehouse Worker; Data Entry Operator; Administrative Secretary; Warehouse Supervisor; Product Developer. Principal educational backgrounds sought: Accounting; Business Administration; Communications; Computer Science; Finance; Journalism; Marketing. Company benefits include: medical insurance; dental insurance; pension plan; life insurance; tuition assistance; disability coverage; savings plan. Corporate headquarters location. Operations at this facility include: regional headquarters; administration; sales.

## THE WOODLAWN ORGANIZATION
6040 South Harper Street
Chicago IL 60637
312/288-5840
Contact Personnel Director. Neighborhood community organization founded to serve the needs of Woodlawn residents. Provides social services, detox center, child abuse center, mental health facilities, two early childhood development programs, secretarial and word-processing training programs, a youth try-out employment project, and real estate management of property owned by HUD. Social services are available citywide, not limited to Woodlawn residents. Common positions include: Accountant; Administrator; Computer Programmer; Financial Analyst; Department Manager; Purchasing Agent; Social Worker; Alcoholism/Drug Counselor; Nurse; Early

Childhood Development Teacher. Principal educational backgrounds sought: Accounting; Business Administration; Computer Science; Finance; Liberal Arts. Company benefits include: medical, dental and life insurance; tuition assistance. Corporate headquarters location. Operations at this facility include: administration.

## CHEMICALS & RELATED:
## PRODUCTION, PROCESSING AND DISPOSAL

For more information on professional employment opportunities in the chemical industry, contact the following professioanl and trade organizations, as listed beginning on page 315:

AMERICAN CHEMICAL SOCIETY
AMERICAN INSTITUTE OF CHEMICAL ENGINEERING
AMERICAN INSTITUTE OF CHEMICAL ENGINEERING/CHICAGO
AMERICAN INSTITUTE OF CHEMISTS
AMERICAN INSTITUTE OF CHEMISTS/CHICAGO
ASSOCIATION OF STATE & INTERSTATE
WATER POLLUTION CONTROL ADMINISTRATORS
WATER POLLUTION CONTROL FEDERATION

**CF INDUSTRIES**
Salem Lake Drive
Long Grove IL 60047
708/438-9500
Contact Carolyn Taylor, Supervisor, Corporate Placement. Manufactures and distributes chemical fertilizer products. Common positions include: Accountant; Computer Programmer; Agricultural Engineer; Electrical Engineer; Mechancial Engineer; Financial Analyst; Operations/Production Manager; Marketing Specialist; Personnel and Labor Relations Specialist; Sales Representative; Statistician; Systems Analyst; Transportation and Traffic Specialist. Educational backgrounds sought include: Accounting; Computer Science; Engineering; Marketing. Company benefits include: medical insurance; dental insurance; pension plan; life insurance; tuition assistance; disability coverage; profit sharing; on-site fitness center. Operations at this facility include: regional headquarters location; research and development; administration; service; sales.

**CHEMICAL WASTE MANAGEMENT**
3001 Butterfield Road
Oak Brook IL 60521
708/218-1500
Contact Dave Coleman, Vice President of Human Resources. A garbage and refuse removal company.

**FMC CORPORATION**
200 East Randolph Drive
Chicago IL 60601
Contact Staffing Manager. Manufactures and sells a broad range of chemical products.

**GENERAL FIRE EXTINGUISHER CORPORATION**
1685 Shermer Road
Northbrook IL 60062
312/272-7500
Contact Personnel Supervisor. Manufactures a complete line of fire extinguishers.

**W.R. GRACE/DEARBORN**
300 Genessee Street
Lake Zurich IL 60047
312/438-8241
Contact Director of Human Resources. Markets industrial waste water treatment products.

**HARCROS PIGMENTS INC.**
2001 Lynch Avenue
East St. Louis IL 62205
618/271-4700
Contact Dave Goeddel, Personnel Director. Manufacture synthetic, natural & magnetic iron oxides, colors, extender pigments, and barytes.

**HYSAN CORPORATION**
1400 Touhy Avenue, Suite 260
Des Plaines IL 60018
708/390-8100
Contact David Taylor, Director of Human Resources. A major chemical manufacturer and distributor.

**INTERNATIONAL MINERALS AND CHEMICAL CORPORATION**
2315 Sanders Road
Northbrook IL 60062
312/564-8600
Contact Personnel. A producer of phosphate and potash plant nutrient. Products also include fertilizers, pharmaceuticals, medical products, and a wide variety of other products.

## MORTON INTERNATIONAL INC./ AUTO AND INDUSTRIAL FINISHES
2700 East 170th Street
Lansing IL 60438
708/868-7270
Contact David Bonko, Manager, Human Resources. A multi-national manufacturer of specialty chemical products. Common positions include: Accountant; Chemist; Computer Programmer; Customer Service Representative; Personnel and Labor Relations Specialist. Principal educational backgrounds sought: Business Administration; Chemistry; Engineering. Training programs offered. Company benefits include: medical insurance; dental insurance; pension plan; life insurance; tuition assistance; disability coverage; profit sharing. Corporate headquarters location. Parent company: Morton International. Operations at this facility include· manufacturing; research/development; administration; service; sales. New York Stock Exchange.

## MORTON THIOKOL, INC.
100 North Riverside Plaza
Chicago IL 60606
312/807-2000
Contact Personnel. A highly diversified manufacturer of such products as high technology propulsion systems, chemicals, and Morton salt. Employs 19,600.

## NALCO CHEMICAL COMPANY
1 Nalco Center
Naperville IL 60563-1198
708/305-1000
Contact Karen Nordquist, Employment Manager. Several area locations including: Naperville, Northbrook. Engaged primarily in the manufacture and sale of highly specialized service chemicals used in water treatment, pollution control, energy conservation, oil production and refining, steelmaking, papermaking, mining and other industrial processes. Corporate headquarters location. International. New York Stock Exchange.

## OLIN CORPORATION
P.O. Box 2219
Patterson Road
Joliet IL 60434
815/727-4901
Contact Vince Cimino, Personnel Manager. Several area locations, including Oak Brook. Manufacturer of organic and inorganic chemicals, specializing in those used in industry and agriculture. Also manufactures metal and paper products, sports and recreational equipment, and energy systems. Operations at this facility include: manufacturing. Corporate headquarters location: Stamford, CT. New York Stock Exchange. International. Common positions include: Accountant; Chemical Engineer; Industrial Engineer; Mechanical

Engineer; Operations/Production Manager; Personnel & Labor Relations Specialist. Principal educational backgrounds sought: Business Administration; Engineering. Company benefits include: medical insurance; dental insurance; pension plan; life insurance; tuition assistance; disability coverage; profit sharing; employee discounts; savings plan.

## OLIN CORPORATION/
## BRASS AND WINCHESTER GROUPS
427 North Shamrock Street
East Alton IL 62024
618/258-2909
Contact Mr. Schnieder, Personnel. A major St. Louis company engaged in the manufacture of commercial and military ammunition; ramset powder activated fastening systems; copper and alloy sheet and strip, stamped and drawn parts and clad metals.

## RHONE-POULENC BASIC CHEMICALS COMPANY
1245 East Diehl Road
Naperville IL 60563
708/505-1450
Contact Glen R. Hanson, Regional Employee Relations Manager. Several area locations, including: Chicago Heights and Hammond, IN. A chemical manufacturer specializing in agricultural, specialty and industrial chemicals; and food ingredients. Division headquarters location: Shelton, CT. International. New York Stock Exchange.

## RUST-OLEUM CORPORATION
11 Hawthorne Parkway
Vernon Hills IL 60061
708/367-7700
Contact Steve Gillmann, Manager of Human Resources. Several area locations including: Vernon Hills and Evanston. Leading manufacturer of rust-preventative paints and coatings. Corporate headquarters location.

## SHERWIN-WILLIAMS COMPANY
11541 South Champlain
Chicago IL 60628
312/821-3011
Contact Mr. Murphy, Personnel Director. Operates nationally in six segments: Retail Stores, Coatings, Chemicals, Packaging Products, Specialty Products, and International. Products include Sherwin-Williams, Dutch Boy, Martin Seymour, Baltimore and Kem paints, as well as such related packaging products as paint cans, sprays and labels. Corporate headquarters location: Cleveland, OH. International. New York Stock Exchange.

## STEPAN COMPANY
22 West Frontage Road
Northfield IL 60093
708/446-7500

Contact Mr. Richard Larsen, Corporate Personnel Manager. Several area locations. Develops, manufactures, and markets a wide range of chemical intermediates sold to producers of such consumer products as shampoos, toothpastes, household detergents, and other personal care items. Products also used as ingredients in industrial detergents and cleansers, agricultural fertilizers, herbicides, and pesticides, as well as petroleum-based detergents for recovering additional oil from known reservoirs. A major producer of phthalic anhydride, an essential ingredient in plastics and polyesters, and also manufactures urethane foam systems and other specialty products. Has eight production plants; five in United States, including near Joliet, IL. Corporate headquarters location. Operations include: research/development; administration; sales. Common positions include: Accountant; Chemist; Customer Service Representative; Chemical Engineer; Sales Representative; Systems Analyst. Principal educational backgrounds sought: Accounting; Biology; Chemistry; Engineering; Finance; Liberal Arts. Company benefits include: medical, dental, and life insurance; pension plan; tuition assistance; disability coverage; profit sharing; savings plan; employee stock ownership plan. American Stock Exchange.

## SUN CHEMICAL CORPORATION/ GENERAL PRINTING INK
135 West Lake Street
Northlake Il 60164
708/562-0550

Contact Nick Hiller, Personnel Director. One of the world's largest producers of printing inks and organic pigments. Also designs and manufactures graphic arts equipment, aircraft and military instrumentation and a number of diversified products including specialty chemicals, flexible laminates, and automobile cigarette lighters. Products sold primarily by own sales force. Printing ink facilities are located in Chicago, Kankakee, and Northlake. Corporate headquarters location: New York, NY. International. New York Stock Exchange.

## WASTE MANAGEMENT INC.
3003 Butterfield Road
Oak Brook IL 60521
708/572-8800

One of the nation's leading providers of waste collection and disposal services. Employs 24,416.

## WITCO CORPORATION/
## MIDWEST REGIONAL OFFICE
2701 West Lake Street
Melrose Park IL 60160
708/344-4300
Contact Ms. D. E. Thoren, Manager, Personnel Services. Produces a wide range of special purpose chemical and petroleum products for industrial and consumer use. Two business segments: Chemical Group, which manufactures chemicals sold to OEMs for use in the manufacture of rubber, plastics, cosmetics, pharmaceuticals, petroleum lubricants, fungicidal compounds, automobiles, building materials, paper, and textiles; and Petroleum Group, which manufactures white oils, petrolatums, natural and synthetic petroleum sulfonates, microcrystalline waxes, greases and other petroleum specialties from refined and semi-refined oils, as well as operating two refineries which primarily produce lubricating oils sold under the Kendall and Amalie trademarks. These products are used in the pharmaceutical, cosmetics, food processing, animal husbandry, paper converting, plastics, chemical processing, textile, and agricultural industries. Other Illinois facilities include four chemical group manufacturing plants in Chicago. Common positions include: Buyer; Credit Manager; Customer Service Representative; Purchasing Agent; Sales Representative. Principal educational backgrounds sought: Business Administration; Marketing. Company benefits include: medical insurance; dental insurance; pension plan; life insurance; tuition assistance; disability coverage; savings plan. Corporate headquarters location: New York, NY. Operations at this facility include: regional headquarters; divisional headquarters; administration; service; sales. International. New York Stock Exchange.

## COLLEGES AND UNIVERSITIES

For more information on professional employment opportunities with colleges and universities, contact the following professional and trade organizations, as listed beginning on page 315:

**AMERICAN ASSOCIATION OF SCHOOL ADMINISTRATORS**
**ASSOCIATION OF AMERICAN UNIVERSITIES**

## BELLEVILLE AREA COLLEGE
2500 Carlyle Road
Belleville IL 62221
618/235-2700 ext. 255
Contact Larry Friederich, Director of Personnel. A public, two year community college located in the metropolitan St. Louis area. Company benefits include: medical insurance; pension plan; life insurance; tuition

assistance; disability coverage; daycare assistance; employee discounts; savings plan. Corporate headquarters location.

**BRADLEY UNIVERSITY**
1501 West Bradley Avenue
Peoria IL 61625
309/677-3223
Contact Personnel Department. A major university

**CHICAGO STATE UNIVERSITY**
95th at King Drive
Chicago IL 60628
312/995-2000
Contact Personnel Department. A major state university

**COLUMBIA COLLEGE**
600 South Michigan
Chicago IL 60605
312/663-1600
Contact Personnel Department. A major college

**DePAUL UNIVERSITY**
243 South Wabash
Chicago IL 60604
312/362-8000
Contact Personnel Department. A major university.

**EASTERN ILLINOIS UNIVERSITY**
Charleston IL 61920
217/581-3463
Contact Personnel Department. A major university.

**GOVERNORS STATE UNIVERSITY**
University Park IL 60466
708/534-5000
Contact Personnel Department. A major state university.

**ILLINOIS INSTITUTE OF TECHNOLOGY**
3300 South Federal
Chicago IL 60616
312/567-3000
Contact Personnel Director. A major institute of technology.

**ILLINOIS STATE UNIVERSITY**
Normal IL 61761
309/438-8311
Contact Personnel Department. A major state university.

## LEWIS & CLARK COMMUNITY COLLEGE
5800 Godfrey Road
Godfrey IL 62035
618/466-3411
Contact Dr. Dale Chapman, V.P. of Administration and Finance. A major area 2-year Junior college.

## LOYOLA UNIVERSITY AND MEDICAL CENTER
820 North Michigan Avenue
Chicago IL 60611
Contact Mimi Winter, Director, Human Resources. A private Catholic Jesuit University and medical center with national standing. Loyola has four campuses in the Greater Chicago are, including Loyola Medical Center in Maywood, IL; Lake Shore and Water Tower campuses both in Chicago; Millinckrodt Campus in Wilmett, IL.

## McKENDREE COLLEGE
701 College Road
Lebanon IL 62254
618/537-4481
Contact Mary Ann Newcomb, Personnel Director. A major St. Louis area educational institution with 28 academic majors and an enrollment of over 1,000.

## NATIONAL LOUIS UNIVERSITY
2840 Sheridan Road
Evanston IL 60201
708/475-1100
Contact Personnel Department. A well known school of education.

## NORTHEASTERN ILLINOIS UNIVERSITY
5500 North St. Louis
Chicago IL 60625
312/583-4050, ext. 3275
Contact Personnel Department. A major university.

## NORTHERN ILLINOIS UNIVERSITY
DeKalb IL 60115
815/753-1000
Contact Personnel Department. A major university.

## NORTHWESTERN UNIVERSITY
720 University Place
Evanston IL 60208
708/491-7507
Contact Personnel Department. A major university.

**ROOSEVELT UNIVERSITY**
430 South Michigan
Chicago IL 60605
312/341-3560
Contact Personnel Director. A major four-year university.

**SOUTHERN ILLINOIS UNIVERSITY AT CARBONDALE**
Carbondale IL 62901
618/453-2121
Contact Personnel Services. A major university.

**SOUTHERN ILLINOIS UNIVERSITY AT EDWARDSVILLE**
Box 1222
Edwardsville IL 62026
618/692-2000
Contact Personnel Services. A state university offering several graduate programs as well as a 4-year bachelor's degree program.

**UNIVERSITY OF CHICAGO**
1100 East 57th Street
Chicago IL 60637
312/702-8757
Contact Personnel Department. A major university.

**UNIVERSITY OF ILLINOIS AT CHICAGO**
1140 South Paulina
Chicago IL 60680
312/996-0840
Contact Personnel Department. A major Illinois university.

**UNIVERSITY OF ILLINOIS AT URBANA-CHAMPAIGN**
52 East Gregory Drive
Champaign IL 61820
217/333-3950
Contact Personnel Services. A location of the major university.

**WESTERN ILLINOIS UNIVERSITY**
900 West Adams Street
Macomb IL 61455
309/298-1971
Contact Personnel Department. A major university.

## COMMUNICATIONS: EQUIPMENT & SERVICES

For more information on professional employment opportunities in the communications industry, contact the following professional and trade organizations, as listed beginning on page 315:

COMMUNICATIONS WORKERS OF AMERICA
COMMUNICATIONS WORKERS OF AMERICA/CHICAGO
UNITED STATES TELEPHONE ASSOCIATION


**ALLTEL ILLINOIS, INC.**
300 North Maplewood Street
Rantoul IL 61866
217/892-9661
Contact Julie Blodgett, Director of Personnel. Provides telephone communication. A subsidiary of Alltel Communication. A subsidiary of Alltel Corp.

**AMERITECH SERVICES**
1900 East Golf Road, Floor 3
Schaumberg IL 60173
708/605-2299
Contact Joe Poehlmann, Manager of Employment. Provides services to its five telecommunications companies.

**ANDREW CORPORATION**
10500 West 153rd Street
Orland Park IL 60462
708/349-3300
Contact Roger Blaylock, Personnel Manager. A diverse telecommunications hardware firm.

**ANIXTER BROTHERS, INC.**
4711 Golf Road
Skokie IL 60076
708/677-2600
Contact Ed O'Donnell, Personnel. Distributes wire and cable to the telecommunications industry.

**CENTEL CORPORATION**
8725 West Higgins Road
Chicago IL 60631
312/399-2500
Contact Liz Legenza, Staff Coordinator. A major telephone and electric service company.

**CONTINENTAL TELEPHONE COMPANY OF ILLINOIS**
112 West Elm Street
Sycamore IL 60178
815/895-5151
Contact Jim Ward, Human Resources Director. A telephone service company.

**COOK ELECTRIC DIVISION**
6201 Oakton Street
Morton Grove IL 60053
708/967-6600
Contact Kathy Brosmith, Director of Personnel. Manufactures telephone equipment including central office protectors.

**ILLINOIS BELL**
212 West Washington Street, Floor 2G
Chicago IL 60606
312/727-7861
Contact Management Employment Office. Provides communications systems and services.

**ILLINOIS CONSOLIDATED TELEPHONE COMPANY**
121 South 17th Street
Mattoon IL 61938
217/235-3311
Contact Carol O'Neill, Personnel Director. Provides telephone communications.

**RELIABLE ELECTRIC COMPANY**
11333 West Addison
Franklin Park IL 60131
708/455-8010
Contact Scott Hodal, Personnel Manager. Manufactures connectors for telecommunication devices used by the telephone industry and power utilities. Corporate headquarters location.

**ROCKWELL INTERNATIONAL**
8245 South Lemont Road
Downers Grove IL 60516
708/985-9000
Contact Kevin Weiss, Director of Human Resources. Designs and manufactures telecommunications products and systems including digital PBX (private branch exchange), switching systems, PCM transmission multiplexers, and miscellaneous telecommunications equipment. A subsidiary of Rockwell International (Pittsburgh, PA). Divisional headquarters location. International.

**TELEPHONE & DATA SYSTEMS INC.**
30 North Lasalle Street, Suite 1000
Chicago IL 60602
312/630-1900
Contact Office Manager. A conglomerate, owning out-of-state telephone companies.

## COMPUTER RELATED:
## HARDWARE, SOFTWARE AND SERVICES

For more information on professional employment opportunities in the computer industry, contact the following professional and trade organizations, as listed beginning on page 315:

ADAPSO/THE COMPUTER SOFTWARE AND SERVICES INDUSTRY ASSOCIATION
ASSOCIATION FOR COMPUTER SCIENCE
ASSOCIATION FOR COMPUTING MACHINERY
IEEE COMPUTER SOCIETY
SEMICONDUCTOR INDUSTRY ASSOCIATION

**ADVANCED SYSTEM APPLICATIONS INC./
DIVISION OF POLICY MANAGEMENT SYSTEMS CORPORATION**
One ASA Plaza, P.O. Box 385
Bloomingdale IL 60108
708/893-9055
Contact Robert Farrell, Recruiting Supervisor. A computer services company specializing in on-lines claim adjustment for the insurance industry. Common positions include: Computer Programmer. Principal educational backgrounds sought include: Computer Science. Training programs offered; Internships offered. Company benfits include: medical, dental, and life insurance; tuition assistance; savings plan; 401K, fitness center. Corporate headquarters location: Columbia, SC. Parent company: PMSC. Operations at this facility include: divisional headquarters.

**APPLIED LEARNING INTERNATIONAL**
1751 W. Diehl Road
Naperville IL 60563
708/369-3000
Contact Julie Ann Roberts, Manager of Human Resources. Applied Learning is a world leader in providing technology management strategies and information processing skills training for national and international clients. Courseware is concentrated in five key areas: Information Processing Professional Skills; Technology Management; Personal and Departmental Computing; Human Resources Development; Manufacturing and Industrial

Skills. Common positions include: Accountant; Administrator; Attorney; Computer Programmer; Customer Service Representative; Branch Manager; Department Manager; General Manager; Operations/Production Manager; Marketing Specialist; Personnel and Labor Relations Specialist; Quality Control Supervisor; Reporter/Editor; Sales Representative; Systems Analyst; Technical Writer/Editor. Principal educational backgrounds sought: Accounting; Art/Design; Business Administration; Communications; Computer Science; Economics; Engineering; Finance; Liberal Arts; Marketing. Training programs offered; Internships offered. Company benefits include: medical insurance; dental insurance; life insurance; tuition assistance; disability coverage; profit sharing; savings plan. Corporate headquarters location. Parent company: National Education Corporation. Operations at this facility include: regional headquarters; manufacturing; research/development; administration; service; sales. New York Stock Exchange.

**BARNES & REINECKE, INC.**
2201 Estes Avenue
Elk Grove Village IL 60007
708/640-7200
Contact Scott Wirig, Human Resources Manager. Provides computer and business services.

**COMDISCO**
6111 North River Road
Rosemont IL 60018
708/698-3000
Contact Lucie Buford, Vice President, Personnel. A company engaged in the leasing of computer equipment to businesses.

**COMPUTER POWER GROUP**
823 Commerce Drive
Oak Brook IL 60521
708/654-3030
Contact James Verri, Personnel Director. A computer company involved primarily in data processing and consulting services.

**HONEYWELL INC.**
1500 W. Dundee Road
Arlington Heights IL 60004
708/394-4000
Contact Mark Hoggay, Senior Human Resources Administrator. An international company dedicated to advanced technology and offering high quality products and services in the fields of information processing, automation, and controls. Chicago area facilities include computer marketing offices, and plants manufacturing temperature control and security devices, and commercial building controls. Corporate headquarters: Minneapolis, MN. Common positions include: Accountant; Administrator; Buyer;

Computer Programmer; Customer Service Representative; Draftsperson; Electrical Engineer; Industrial Engineer; Mechanical Engineer; Technical Writer/Editor. Principal educational backgrounds sought: Accounting; Business Administration; Computer Science; Engineering; Liberal Arts. Company benefits include: medical insurance; dental insurance; pension plan; life insurance; tuition assistance; disability coverage; employee discounts; savings plan. Operations include: manufacturing; research/development; administration. New York Stock Exchange.

**IBM**
One IBM Plaza
Chicago IL 60611
312/245-4040
Contact Senior Recruiter, Manager of Central Employment. A leading corporation in information technology.

**THE CHARLES LEVY COMPANY**
1200 North Branch Street
Chicago IL 60622
312/440-4400
Contact Personnel. A wholesaler of computer software.

**MAY & SPEH DATA PROCESSING**
1501 Opus Place
Downers Grove IL 60515
708/964-1501
Contact Claudia Colalillo, Director/Human Resources. Provides data processing services to business and industry. Common position: Computer Programmer. Corporate headquarters location.

**NCR CORPORATION**
405 South Washington Boulevard
Mundelein IL 60060
708/566-4350
Contact Christine Sitko, Personnel Manager. Multiple area locations include: Rolling Meadows, Mundelein, Niles, Chicago, and Springfield IL; Kansas City, St. Louis, and Springfield MO. Develops, manufactures, markets, installs, and services total business information processing systems for selected worldwide markets. These markets are primarily in retail, financial, commercial, industrial, health care, education, and government sectors. The NCR total systems concept encompasses one of the broadest hardware and software product lines in the industry. NCR computers range from small business systems to the most powerful general-purpose processors, and are suported by a complete spectrum of terminals, processors, data communications networks, and an extensive library of software products. Supplemental services and products include field engineering, data centers, systems services, educational centers, and a comprehensive line of media. Common positions include: Sales Representative. Principal educational

backgrounds sought: Business Administration; Computer Science; Marketing. Company benefits include: medical insurance, dental insurance, pension plan, life insurance, tuition assistance, disability coverage, profit sharing, employee discounts, savings plan. Corporate headquarters location: Dayton, OH. International. Regional headquarters location. Operations at this facility include: administration; sales. New York Stock Exchange.

**PANSOPHIC SYSTEM, INC.**
2400 Cabot Drive
Lisle IL 60532
708/505-6000
Contact Ron Gruenberg, Manager of Corporate Employment. Manufactures, sells, and services software products.

**SYSTEM SOFTWARE ASSOCIATES, INC.**
500 West Madison, Suite 3200
Chicago IL 60661
312/641-2900
Contact Mr. James Colello, Personnel. A major computer programming and software firm.

**WALLACE COMPUTER SERVICES INC.**
4600 West Roosevelt Road
Hillside IL 60162
312/626-2000
Contact Barry White, Personnel Director. A company engaged in the manufacture and sale of computer oriented business forms, commercial printing, computer labels, machine ribbons, computer software, and computer accessory supplies.

**CONSTRUCTION: SERVICES, MATERIALS, & RELATED**

For more information on professional employment opportunities in the construction industry, contact the following professional and trade organizations, as listed beginning on page 315:

**BUILDING OFFICIALS AND CODE ADMINISTRATORS INTERNATIONAL, INC.**
**CONSTRUCTION INDUSTRY MANUFACTURERS ASSOCIATION**
**HOME BUILDERS ASSOCIATION OF GREATER CHICAGO**
**INTERNATIONAL CONFERENCE OF BUILDING OFFICIALS**
**NATIONAL ASSOCIATION OF HOME BUILDERS**

## ANNING-JOHNSON CO.
1959 Anson Drive
Melrose Park IL 60160
708/681-1300
Contact John R. Andrzejewski, Sr. Vice President. A construction company dealing in specialty contracting.

## APPLETON ELECTRIC CO.
1701 W. Wellington
Chicago IL 60657
312/327-7200
Contact L.W. McElhinny, Vice President/Industrial Relations. Manaufactures electrical conponents.

## BARBER-GREENE CO.
3000 Barber-Greene Road
DeKalb IL 60115
815/756-5600
Contact Corporate Personnel Manager. Designs, manufactures and sells construction machinery.

## CECO CORPORATION
1 Tower Lane
Oak Brook Terrace IL 60181
708/242-2000
Contact Personnel. Manufacturers of products for the contruction industry. Employs 5,300.

## CONTRACTING & MATERIAL COMPANY
165 Hintz Road
Wheeling IL 60090
708/541-2550
Contact Fran Seabert, Office Manager. Involved in electrical and pipeline, heavy, and highway construction.

## ECONOMY MECHANICAL INDUSTRIES
77 Wheeling Road
Wheeling IL 60090
708/541-8700
Contact Personnel Director. A mechanical contracting firm; works in commercial plumbing.

## GLOBE INDUSTRIES
2638 East 126th Street
Chicago IL 60633
312/646-1300
Contact Vice President/Industrial Relations. Manufactures and sells roofing products.

## GOLD BOND BUILDING PRODUCTS
1400 East Touhy Avenue, Suite 106
Des Plaines IL 60018
708/296-9800
Contact Christel King, Office Manager. A diversified manufacturer of construction products. Common positions include: Customer Service Representative. Educational backgrounds sought include: Liberal Arts; Marketing. Training programs available. Company benefits include: medical insurance; dental insurance; life insurance; tuition assistance; employee discounts; savings plan. Parent company: National Gypsum (Charlotte, NC). Operations at this facility include: regional headquarters; administration; service; sales.

## EDWARD GRAY CORPORATION
12233 Avenue O
Chicago IL 60633
312/221-8400
Contact W. Jed Mundell, Treasurer. Engaged in all phases of industrial construction.

## H.H. HALL CONSTRUCTION COMPANY
211 South 15th Street
P.O. Box 2439
East St. Louis IL 62202
618/274-2500
Contact Personnel Department. A major area contracting firm engaged in industrial and commercial construction work. Also manufactures ready mix concrete.

## HOEFFKEN BROS. INC.
P.O. Box 405
Belleville IL 62222
618/233-0268
Contact Leon Linneman, Personnel Director. An area heavy construction firm specializing in roads and bridges.

## THE HOFFMAN GROUP, INC.
300 Park Boulevard
Itasca IL 60143
708/250-7878
Contact Personnel. A land developer and residential construction company.

## KENNY CONSTRUCTION COMPANY
250 Northgate Parkway
Wheeling IL 60090
708/541-8200

Contact Ronald P. Smith, Corporate Secretary. A heavy duty construction contractor.

## MILLER-DAVIS COMPANY
4300 North Avenue
Melrose Park IL 60165
312/626-0957
Contact Herman Weissmann, Vice-President. A major regional general contracting firm. Common positions include: Accounting; Engineering. Company benefits include: medical insurance; pension plan; disability coverage; profit sharing; ESOP. Divisional headquarters location. Corporate headquarters location: Kalamazoo, MI.

## F.E. MORAN
2265 Carlson Drive
Northbrook IL 60062
708/498-4800
Contact Richard Maloni, President. Mechanical contractors specializing in fire detection, heating, air conditioning, plumbing, and ventilation systems. Corporate headquarters location. International.

## W.E. O'NEIL CONSTRUCTION
2751 North Clybourn Avenue
Chicago IL 60614
312/327-1611
Contact Personnel Department. A construction company. Common positions include: Civil Engineer; Electrical Engineer; Civil Engineer; Mechanical Engineer; Construction Engineer. Principal education background sought: Engineering. Company benefits include: medical insurance; dental insurance; life insurance; disability coverage include: profit sharing; savings plan. Corporate headquarters location.

## PASCHEN CONTRACTORS INC.
2739 North Elston Avenue
Chicago IL 60647
312/278-4700
Contact William Paschen, Vice President. A construction company with 28 different payrolls, including construction sites at the deep tunnel, CTA, and others. Corporate headquarters location.

## PEPPER COMPANIES
643 North Orleans Street
Chicago IL 60610
312/266-4703
Contact Personnel. A leading Chicago building contractor and construction management company.

## PHILLIPS, GETSCHOW COMPANY
1913 South Briggs Street
Joliet IL 60433
312/644-6116
Contact Joyce Wilson, Personnel Director. Another area facility is in Joliet. A construction company working in the areas of mechanical and nuclear construction. Corporate headquarters location.

## R&D THIEL INC.
1700 Rand Road
Palatine IL 60074
708/359-7150
Contact Personnel Director. A general contractor. Corporate headquarters location.

## RICHARDS BRICK COMPANY
234 Springer Avenue, Box 407
Edwardsville IL 62025
618/656-0230
Contact John Motley, Plant Superintendant. A major manufacturer of building bricks.

## THE ROBERTSON-CECO CORPORATION
One Tower Lane
Oak Brook Terrace IL 60181
312/242-2000
Contact Manager, Human Resources. Manufactures, distributes, & sells products for construction industry.

## SHEFFIELD STEEL CORPORATION
Industry Avenue
P.O. Box 727
Joliet IL 60434-0727
815/723-9335
Contact Bill Winkler, Personnel Manager. Operates the largest subsidiary component of Penn Dixie Industries, a multi-product corporation primarily serving the construction industry, although companies operate independently. Manufactures steel, industrial and welding wire, nails, fence, welded wire fabric, and other products (Kokomo, IN); and hot-rolled steel merchant bars and lightweight structural steel shapes (Joliet, IL). Other facilities operate in several western and midwestern states. Corporate headquarters location: Kokomo, IN.

## GEORGE SOLLITT CONSTRUCTION COMPANY
790 North Central
Wooddale IL 60191
708/860-7333

Contact Office Manager. General contractors for schools and hospitals; also public works projects such as sewage treatment plants. Corporate headquarters location.

## SYMONS CORPORATION
200 East Touhy
Des Plaines IL 60018
708/298-3200
Contact Richard M. Wolter, Corporate Personnel Manager. Manufacturer of concrete forming equipment: standard, custom and fiberglass. Common positions include: Accountant; Advertising Worker; Buyer; Computer Programmer; Credit Manager; Customer Service Representative; Draftsperson; Civil Engineer; Industrial Engineer; Personnel & Labor Relations Specialist; Purchasing Agent; Quality Control Supervisor; Sales Representative. Principal educational backgrounds sought: Business Administration; Computer Science; Engineering; Marketing; Structural Engineering. Company benefits include: medical insurance; dental insurance; pension plan; life insurance; tuition assistance; disability coverage; employee discounts; savings plan. Corporate headquarters location. Operations at this facility include: manufacturing; administration; sales. International.

## USG CORPORATION
101 South Wacker Drive
Chicago IL 60606
312/606-4390
Contact Greg Puchalski, Manager of Employment and Development. A major manufacturer of building materials in the United States. Produces a wide range of products for use in new building construction, repair and remodeling, and in many industry processes. Operates more than 100 plants in the United States, Canada, Mexico, and Europe. Corporate headquarters location. International. New York Stock Exchange. Common positions include: Accountant; Attorney; Buyer; Computer Programmer; Chemical Engineer; Civil Engineer; Electrical Engineer; Industrial Engineer; Mechanical Engineer; Mining Engineer; Financial Analyst; Industrial Designer; Systems Analyst; Technical Writer/Editor. Principal educational backgrounds sought: Accounting; Art/Design; Business Administration; Engineering; Finance; Liberal Arts; Marketing. Company benefits include: medical insurance; dental insurance; pension plan; life insurance; tuition assistance; disability coverage; employee discounts; savings plan. Operations at this facility include: administration.

## WOODWORK CORPORATION OF AMERICA
1432 West 21st Street
Chicago IL 60608
312/226-4800
Contact Bruce Stulik, Controller. Manufacturers of architectural woodwork. Corporate headquarters location.

## ELECTRICAL AND ELECTRONICS: MANUFACTURING & DISTRIBUTION

For more information on professional employment opportunities in the electrical and electronics industries, contact the following professional and trade organizations, as listed beginning on page 315:

AMERICAN ELECTROPLATERS AND SURFACE FINISHERS SOCIETY
AMERICAN ELECTROPLATERS AND SURFACE FINISHERS SOCIETY/CHICAGO BRANCH
ELECTROCHEMICAL SOCIETY
ELECTRONIC INDUSTRIES ASSOCIATION
ELECTRONICS TECHNICIANS ASSOCIATION
INSTITUTE OF ELECTRICAL AND ELECTRONICS ENGINEERS
INSTITUTE OF ELECTRICAL AND ELECTRONICS ENGINEERS/CHICAGO
INTERNATIONAL BROTHERHOOD OF ELECTRICAL WORKERS
INTERNATIONAL SOCIETY OF CERTIFIED ELECTRONICS TECHNICIANS
NATIONAL ELECTRICAL MANUFACTURERS ASSOCIATION
NATIONAL ELECTRONICS SALES AND SERVICES ASSOCIATION

**ADVANCE TRANSFORMER CO.**
10275 West Higgins Road
Wooddale IL 60018
708/390-5000
Contact Personnel Director. Manufactures ballasts for lighting components.

**APPLETON ELECTRIC CO.**
1701 W. Wellington
Chicago IL 60657
312/327-7200
Contact L.W. McElhinny, Vice President/Industrial Relations. Manaufactures electrical components.

**BASLER ELECTRIC COMPANY**
Route 143
P.O. Box 269
Highland IL 62249
618/654-2341
Contact Marilyn Frey, Personnel Director. Manufacturers of transformers and electronic systems. Employs over 400.

## BLUE M ELECTRIC COMPANY
2218 W. 138th Street
Blue Island IL 60406-3248
708/385-9000
Contact Bruce Leonard, Manager of Human Resources. Designs equipment with special temperature controls.

## BODINE ELECTRIC COMPANY
2500 West Bradley Place
Chicago IL 60618
312/478-3515
Contact David C. McClenahan, Director, Human Resources. Manufacturer of specialized electrical equipment.

## BRUSH FUSES INC.
2070 Maple Street
Des Plaines IL 60018
708/299-2211
Contact Richard Cettone, Employee Relations Manager. Manufactures fuses. Common positions include: Accountant; Blue-Collar Worker Supervisor; Buyer; Computer Service Representative; Draftsperson; Industrial Engineer; Mechanical Engineer; Financial Analyst; General Manager; Operations/Production Manager; Personnel & Labor Relations Specialist; Purchasing Agent; Quality Control Supervisor. Educational backgrounds sought: Accounting; Business Administration; Computer Science; Engineering; Finance. Company benefits include: medical insurance; dental insurance; life insurance; tuition assistance; disability coverage; profit sharing. Corporate headquarters location. Parent company: Hawker Siddeley. Operations at this facility include: manufacturing; research/development; administration; sales. London Stock Exchange.

## THE CHERRY CORPORATION
3600 Sunset Avenue
Waukegan IL 60087
708/662-9200
Contact Gloria Jordan, Personnel Representative. Operates in electrical products, electronic products, & semiconductor products.

## COMMERCIAL LIGHT COMPANY
245 Fencl Lane
Hillside IL 60162
708/449-6900
Contact Mike Sorden, Personnel Director. An electrical contractor.

## COOPER POWER SYSTEMS
510 North Pearl Street
Macomb IL 61455
309/833-4171
Contact Larry Baker, Personnel Manager. A subsidiary of Cooper Industries in Houston, TX. Manufactures electrical porcelain insulators. Operations at this facility include: manufacturing. Corporate headquarters location: Rolling Meadows, IL. New York Stock Exchange. Common positions include: Accountant; Buyer; Draftsperson; Engineer; Ceramics Engineer; Industrial Engineer; Mechanical Engineer; Personnel & Labor Relations Specialist; Quality Control Supervisor. Principal educational backgrounds sought: Accounting; Business Administration; Engineering. Company benefits include: medical insurance; dental insurance; life insurance; pension plan; tuition assistance; disability coverage; profit sharing; savings plan.

## R. DRON ELECTRICAL COMPANY INC.
P.O. Box 753
Granite City IL 62040
618/452-1363
Contact Linda Gilley, Office Manager. An on-site electrical contracting company. Employs over 100.

## DUCHOSSOIS INDUSTRIES, INC.
845 Larch Avenue
Elmhurst IL 60126
708/279-3600
Contact Chris Wright, Corporate Recruiter. A diversified manufacturer of electronic products.

## DYNASCAN CORPORATION
6460 West Cortland Street
Chicago IL 60635
312/889-8870
Contact Celeste Boucher, Human Resources Director. Designs and markets consumer electronics products.

## EATON CONTROLS DIVISION
191 East North Avenue
Carol Stream IL 60188
708/260-3400
Contact Nick Blaukwiekel, Manager of Staffing & Recruitment. Designs, manufactures, and sell electronic and electromechanical devices to automotive, appliance, and air conditioning and refrigeration manufacturers.

## FURNAS ELECTRIC COMPANY
100 KcKee Street
Batavia IL 60510
708/879-6000

Contact Leslie H. Nord, Manager of Professional Employment. Furnas Electric Company, founded in 1932, develops, manufactures, and markets an expanding line of electronic control products and systems for a wide variety of industrial applications. It is a medium sized company with sales volume growing into the $100 million range in recent years. Approximately 1,500 are employed in five modern manufacturing plants in Illinois, Iowa, and Massachusetts, and in sales offices throughout the U.S. Common positions include: Accountant; Buyer; Computer Programmer; Customer Service Representative; Draftsperson; Electrical Engineer; Industrial Engineer; Mechanical Engineer; Industrial Manager; Department Manager; General Manager; Management Trainee; Operations/Production Manager; Marketing Specialist; Purchasing Agent; Quality Control Supervisor; Sales Representative. Principal educational backgrounds sought: Accounting; Business Administration; Engineering; Marketing. Training programs and internships available. Company benefits include: medical insurance; dental insurance; pension plan; life insurance; tuition assistance; disability coverage; savings plan. Corporate headquarters location. Operations at this facility include: manufacturing; research/development; administration; service; sales.

## G&W ELECTRIC COMPANY
3500 West 127th Street
Blue Island IL 60406
708/388-5010
Contact Personnel Director. Produces power cable terminals, switches, and splices.

## GUARDIAN ELECTRIC MANUFACTURING CO.
1425 Lake Avenue
Woodstock IL 60098
815/337-0050
Contact Sharon McFarlin, Director of Personnel. Manufactures electromechanical components and relays.

## HYRE ELECTRIC COMPANY
2320 West Ogden Avenue
Chicago IL 60608
312/738-7200
Contact Rick Freeman, Treasurer. An electrical contracting company.

## INTERMATIC, INC.
Intermatic Plaza
Spring Grove IL 60081
815/675-2321
Contact Director, Employee Relations. A manufacturer of electromechanical and electronic timers, photo controls, Malibu lights, outdoor lighting systems, and portable heaters.

**JAKEL INCORPORATED**
400 Broadway
Highland IL 62249
618/654-2371
Contact Human Resources. Manufacture sub-fractional horse power electric motors.

**JOHNSON CONTROLS**
270 South Glengarry
Geneva IL 60134
708/232-4270
Contact Donna Brucher, Personnel Director. Manufactures storage batteries for sale to private labels.

**KALMUS & ASSOCIATES, INC.**
2424 South 25th Avenue
Broadview IL 60153
708/343-7004
Contact Colleen Brown, Personnel Manager. Manufactures printed circuit boards.

**KNOWLES ELECTRONICS, INC.**
1151 Maplewood Road
Itaska IL 60143
708/250-5100
Contact Richard Lane, Personnel Director. Manufactures miniature electronic components.

**LLOYD'S ELECTRONICS/
A DIVISION OF DYNASCAN CORPORATION**
700 North Commerce Street
P.O. Box 2066
Edison IL 60507-2066
708/820-6699
Contact Carol Kurth, Human Resources. Designs, imports, and markets home and portable audio entertainment products for sale to dealers throughout the United States. The company also markets its products on a minor scale in Latin America and South Africa. Leading products include home stereo systems, portable radios and didital clock radios, cassette recorders and personal tape players. Company purchases its home entertainment products and components from several manufactureres in Taiwan, South Korea, China, Japan, the Philippines, and Hong Kong. International. Common positions include: Accountant; Administator; Blue Collar Worker Supervisor; Customer Service Representative; Financial Analyst; Department Manager; Operations/Production Manager; Sales Representative; Computer Operator. Principal educational backgrounds sought: Accounting; Business Administration; Finance; Marketing. Company

benefits include: medical, dental, and life insurance; disability coverage. Operations at this facility include: administration; sales; warehouse.

**METHODE ELECTRONICS INC.**
7444 West Wilson Avenue
Chicago IL 60656
708/867-9600
Contact Personnel Manager. Several area locations. Manufactures component devices that connect, convey, and control electrical and electronic energy and pulse. Products include printed circuit boards, connectors, and transportation control and connection components. Chief customers include the telecommunications, computer, transportation, military, aerospace, industrial, and entertainment electronics industries. Operates seven facilities in the Chicago area: Harwood Heights, housing headquarters and manufacturing facilities; Chicago (manufacturing facility); Skokie (currently being leased); Rolling Meadows (manufacturing); and three facilities in Chicago Ridge. Also has facilities in Carthage and Warsaw, IL. Corporate headquarters location.

**MOLEX INCORPORATED**
2222 Wellington Court
Lisle IL 60532
708/969-4550
Contact Director/Employee Relations. Several area locations including: Downers Grove, Schaumburg, Addison. Designs, manufactures, and distributes electrical and electronic devices such as terminals, connectors, switches, and related application tooling. Products are used by television, stereo, home computer, electronic game, audio, video, refrigeration, laundry, and many other consumer manufacturing firms, as well as by the automotive, truck, leisure vehicle, and farm equipment industries. Sold through independent sales representatives located throughout the United States. Corporate headquarters location. International.

**MOTOROLA INC.**
1303 East Algonquin Road
Schaumburg IL 60196
708/576-5260
Contact Jim Donnelly, V.P. & Corporate Director of Personnel. Several area locations including: Carol Stream, Franklin Park. One of the world's leading manufacturers of electronic equipment and components, engaged in the design, manufacture, and sale of a diversified line of products such as 2-way radios and other electronic communication systems; semiconductors, including integrated circuits, and other components, primarily for aerospace use; electronic engine controls; digital appliance controls; automobile radios, citizens band radios, and other automotive and industrial electronic equipment; and data communication products such as low, medium and high speed modems, multiplexers, and network processors. In addition to Schaumburg executive offices, other Illinois facilities include plants in Carol

Stream, Franklin Park, and a manufacturing plant in Schaumburg. Corporate headquarters location. International. New York Stock Exchange.

**NEWARK ELECTRONICS**
4801 North Ravenswood Avenue
Chicago IL 60640
312/784-5100
Contact James D. Runtz, Director of Recruitment. A broad-line electronics distributor with sales offices throughout North America and Europe. Divisional headquarters: Premium Industrial Corporation. Corporate headquarters location: Cleveland, OH. New York Stock Exchange. Common positions include: Accountant; Advertising Worker; Buyer; Computer Programmer; Credit Representative; Financial Analyst; Industrial Engineer; Branch Manager; Management Trainee; Purchasing Agent; Sales Representative; Systems Analyst. Principal educational backgrounds sought: Accounting; Business Administration; Communications; Computer Science; Engineering; Finance; Liberal Arts; Marketing. Company benefits include: medical insurance; pension plan; life insurance; tuition assistance; disability coverage; employee discounts; savings plan; stock options. Operations at this facility include: divisional headquarters.

**OAK SWITCH SYSTEMS INC./**
**SUBSIDIARY OF OAK INDUSTRIES INC.**
100 South Main Street
P.O. Box 517
Crystal Lake IL 60014
815/459-5000
Contact Martin Davis, Director/Employee Relations. Components division manufactures products such as electrical switches, controls and components for home appliances, high frequency crystals, oscillators, and potentiometers. Parent company: Oak Industries Inc. Illinois facilities in Crystal Lake, Hinsdale, Mt. Prospect, Princeton, and Sterling. Common positions include: Accountant; Blue-Collar Worker Supervisor; Buyer; Computer Programmer; Credit Manager; Draftsperson; Electrical Engineer; Industrial Engineer; Mechanical Engineer; Marketing Specialist; Purchasing Agent; Quality Control Supervisor; Sales Representative; Systems Analyst. Principal educational backgrounds sought: Accounting; Business Administration; Computer Science; Engineering; Marketing; Physics. Company benefits include: medical insurance; dental insurance; pension plan; life insurance; tuition assistance; disability coverage; savings plan; stock purchase plan. Operations at this facility include: manufacturing; research/development; administration; sales. Divisional headquarters location. Corporate headquarters location: Rancho Bernardo, CA. International facilities. New York Stock Exchange.

## RAULAND-BORG CORPORATION
3450 West Oakton
Skokie IL 60076
708/679-0900
Contact Carl Bank, Personnel Manager. Manufactures electronic communications and professional sound equipment. Corporate headquarters location.

## RICHARDSON ELECTRONICS, LTD.
40W267 Keslinger Road
La Fox IL 60147
Contact Patricia A. Salas, Employment & Benefits Manager. Distributes and manufactures industrial and electronic components. Common positions include: Accountant; Computer Programmer; Credit Manager; Customer Service Representative; Electrical Engineer; Financial Analyst; Marketing Specialist; Purchasing Agent; Quality Control Supervisor; Sales Representative; Systems Analyst. Principal educational backgrounds sought: Accounting; Business Administration; Computer Science; Engineering; Finance; Marketing. Company benefits include: medical, dental and life insurance; tuition assistance; disability coverage; profit sharing; savings plan. Corporate headquarters location. International. Operations at this facility include: manufacturing; research/development; administration; service; sales.

## S&C ELECTRIC
6601 North Ridge Boulevard
Chicago IL 60626
312/338-1000
Contact Personnel Department. Manufacturer of high voltage fuses and switches.

## SCHUMACHER ELECTRIC CORPORATION
7474 North Rogers Avenue
Chicago IL 60626
312/973-1600
Contact Ralph Cernohouz, Controller. Manufactures transformers.

## SHURE BROTHERS INC.
222 Hartrey Avenue
Evanston IL 60202-3696
708/866-2228
Contact Bob Lovell, Employment Manager. Several area locations. Manufactures electronics equipment. Corporate headquarters location. Principal educational backgrounds sought include: Engineering. Company benefits include: medical, dental, and life insurance; pension plan; tuition assistance; disability coverage; employee discounts; savings plan. Corporate headquarters location. Operations at this facility include: manufacturing; research/development; administration; service; sales.

## SOLA ELECTRIC
1717 Busse Road
Elk Grove Village IL 60007
708/439-2800
Contact Jack Allen, Employee Relations Manager. Manufactures transformers, power supplies, and voltage regulators. A unit of General Signal Corporation. Corporate headquarters location.

## SQUARE D COMPANY
1415 South Roselle
Palatine IL 60067-7399
708/397-2600
Contact Linda Berny, Personnel Manager. Several area locations. An electronics firm operating in two major business segments: Electrical Equipment and Electronics Products. Electrical Equipment segment designs, manufactures and sells a broad range of products generally used in the distribution and control of electricity. Products include circuitbreakers, safety switches, panel boards, switchboards, switchgear, busways, transformers, and wiring devices; motor-starters, relays, limit switches, pressure switches, vacuum switches, programmable controllers, and energy management systems. Electronics Products segment includes the manufacture and sale of electro-deposited copper foil through subsidiary Yates Electronics. Other products include semiconductor devices manufactured by subsidiary General Semiconductor Industries. Corporate headquarters location. International. New York Stock Exchange.

## SWITCHCRAFT, INC.
5555 North Elston Avenue
Chicago IL 60630
708/792-2700
Contact Elaine Lysandrou, Human Resource Manager. Manufacturer of such electronic components as switches. A subsidiary of Raytheon (Lexington, MA). Corporate headquarters location.

## WEBER MARKING SYSTEMS, INC.
711 West Algonquin Road
Arlington Heights IL 60005
708/364-8500
Contact Mrs. Shirley A. Hurley, V.P./Human Resources. Several area locations. International distributor of product identification addressing, labeling, industrial marking machines and devices. Corporate headquarters location. Common positions include: Accountant; Buyer; Chemist; Computer Programmer; Customer Service Representative; Electrical Engineer; Industrial Engineer; Electrical Engineer; Marketing Specialist; Purchasing Agent; Sales Representative. Principal educational backgrounds sought include: Accounting; Business Administration; Chemistry; Computer Science; Engineering; Finance; Marketing. Company benefits include: medical insurance; life insurance; disability coverage; profit sharing; savings plan.

**WELLS-GARDNER ELECTRONICS CORPORATION**
2701 North Kildare Avenue
Chicago IL 60639
312/252-8220
Contact Mary Ann Mikol, Director of Industrial Relations. Business activities in three industry segments: video monitors, including game and display monitors sold to arcade game and computer manufacturers; television receivers; and intrusion alarms. All manufacturing, sales, and administration at Chicago facility. Corporate headquarters location.

## ENGINEERING AND ARCHITECTURE

For more information on professional employment opportunities in the engineering and architecture industries, contact the following professional and trade organizations, as listed beginning on page 315:

AMERICAN INSTITUTE OF ARCHITECTS
AMERICAN SOCIETY OF CIVIL ENGINEERS
AMERICAN SOCIETY FOR ENGINEERING EDUCATION
AMERICAN SOCIETY OF HEATING, REFRIGERATING AND AIR
    CONDITIONING ENGINEERS
AMERICAN SOCIETY OF HEATING, REFRIGERATING AND AIR
    CONDITIONING ENGINEERS/CHICAGO
AMERICAN SOCIETY OF LANDSCAPE ARCHITECTS/CHICAGO
AMERICAN SOCIETY OF NAVAL ENGINEERS
AMERICAN SOCIETY OF PLUMBING ENGINEERS
AMERICAN SOCIETY OF SAFETY ENGINEERS
ILLUMINATING ENGINEERING SOCIETY OF NORTH AMERICA
INSTITUTE OF INDUSTRIAL ENGINEERS
INSTITUTE OF INDUSTRIAL ENGINEERS/CHICAGO
NATIONAL ACADEMY OF ENGINEERING
NATIONAL SOCIETY OF PROFESSIONAL ENGINEERS
SOCIETY OF FIRE PROTECTION ENGINEERS
SOCIETY OF FIRE PROTECTION ENGINEERS/CHICAGO
UNITED ENGINEERING TRUSTEES

**ABB RAYMOND COMBUSTION ENGINEERING INC.**
650 Warrenville Road
Lisle IL 60532
708/971-2500
Contact Rob Sentell, Vice President, Human Resources. Several local facilities, including Lisle and Naperville. Other locations in Cleveland, OH; Abilene, Kansas; Enterprise, Kansas; and Concordi, Kansas. Engineering, sales, and manufacturing firm serving the power, cement, gypsum, chemical,

mineral, and environmental and foundry industries. Common positions include: Accountant; Buyer; Computer Programmer; Draftsperson; Chemical Engineer; Electrical Engineer; Mechanical Engineer; Department Manager; Marketing Specialist; Personnel & Labor Relations Specialist; Purchasing Agent; Sales Representative; Systems Analyst. Principal educational backgrounds sought: Accounting; Business Administration; Computer Science; Engineering; Finance; Marketing. Company benefits include: medical, dental, and life insurance; pension plan; tuition assistance; disability coverage; profit sharing; savings plan. Corporate headquarters location: Stamford, CT. Parent company: Asea Brown Boveri. Operations at this facility include: divisional headquarters; research/development. New York Stock Exchange.

**AUSTIN COMPANY**
2001 Rand Road
Des Plaines IL 60016
708/391-4300
Contact Ranjit Roy, Manager of Engineering. A design/building company providing architectural services. Common positions include: Architect; Civil Engineer; Electrical Engineer; Mechanical Engineer. Principal educational backgrounds sought: Economics. Company benefits include: medical insurance; dental insurance; pension plan; life insurance; tuition assistance; savings plan. Corporate headquarters location: Cleveland, OH. Operations at this facility include: regional headquarters.

**CONSOER, TOWNSEND, & ASSOCIATES, INC.**
303 East Wacker Drive, Suite 600
Chicago IL 60601
312/938-0300
Contact Carla Hickey, Director of Human Resources. Consulting engineers.

**ELGIN NATIONAL INDUSTRIES**
120 South Riverside Plaza
Chicago IL 60606
312/454-1900
Contact Administration. Business company involved in engineering and coal manufacturing.

**FLOUR DANIEL**
200 W. Monroe Street
Chicago IL 60606
312/368-3681
Contact Director of Personnel. Provides a wide range of services to the power industry.

**GREELEY AND HANSEN**
222 South Riverside Plaza, Suite 900
Chicago IL 60606
312/648-1155
Contact Personnel Administrator. A consulting engineering firm specializing in wastewater.

**DAVY McKEE CORPORATION**
300 South Riverside, Suite 1800
Chicago IL 60606
312/669-7000
Contact John G. Gatto, Director/Human Resources. Provides industrial engineering and contracting services to industries such as food service and pharmaceuticals. Above address is Midwest region sales and administrative offices location. Parent company: Davy Ltd., London. Common positions include: Chemical Engineer; Civil Engineer; Electrical Engineer; Mechanical Engineer; Structural Engineer. Principal educational background sought: Engineering. Company benefits include: medical insurance; pension plan; life insurance; tuition assistance; disability coverage; savings plan. Divisional headquarters location. Corporate headquarters: Pittsburgh, PA. London Exchange.

**SALEM TECHNICAL SERVICES**
1333 Butterfield Road
Downers Grove IL 60515. 800/323-7200
Contact Recruiting. This office recruits for the company's 30 offices nationally from coast to coast. Salem is one of the nation's largest and most respected contract technical service firms with 30 offices nationally: contract or temporary assignments are available throughout the US in all engineering disciplines - from aircraft to nuclear. Common positions include: Architect; Computer Programmer; Draftsperson; Aerospace Engineer; Agricultural Engineer; Biomedical Engineer; Ceramics Engineer; Chemical Engineer; Civil Engineer; Electrical Engineer; Industrial Engineer; Mechanical Engineer; Metallurgical Engineer; Mining Engineer; Petroleum Engineer; Systems Analyst; Technical Writer/Editor; Aviation Mechanics. Principal educational backgrounds sought: Engineering. Company benefits include: medical insurance; life insurance. Corporate and national headquarters location. Parent company: The SEC Companies.

**SARGENT & LUNDY**
55 East Monroe Street
Chicago IL 60603
312/269-3578
Contact Carol Talaronek, Supervisor of Employment. A consulting engineering firm engaged in the design of nuclear and fossil fueled power plants for the electric utility industry. Employs 4,500 people. Corporate headquarters location. Common positions include: Computer Programmer; Draftsperson; Civil Engineer; Electrical Engineer; Mechanical Engineer;

Reporter/Editor; Systems Analyst; Technical Writer/Editor. Principal educational backgrounds sought: Engineering; Chemical Engineering; Instrumentation Engineering. Company benefits include: medical insurance; dental insurance; pension plan; life insurance; tuition assistance; disability coverage; employee discounts; savings plan.

**SCHMIDT, GARDEN & ERIKSON, INC.**
104 South Michigan Avenue
14th Floor
Chicago IL 60603
312/332-5070
Contact Mary Ann Underhill, Personnel Director. A full-service architectural/engineering firm. Specializes in the design of commercial and industrial space, hospitals and schools. Corporate headquarters location. Common positions include: Architect; Draftsperson; Engineer; Civil Engineer; Electrical Engineer; Mechanical Engineer; Quality Control Supervisor; Sales Representative. Principal educational backgrounds sought: Architectural; Engineering; Interior Design; Marketing. Company benefits include: medical insurance; dental insurance; life insurance; disability coverage.

**TAD TECHNICAL SERVICES CORPORATION**
1717 North Naper Boulevard, Suite 101
Naperville IL 60563
708/505-1913
Contact Personnel. A contract engineering services company serving the Midwest since 1944. Common positions include: Architect; Biochemist; Blue-Collar Worker Supervisor; Chemist; Commercial Artist; Computer Programmer; Draftsperson; Biomedical Engineer; Ceramics Engineer; Civil Engineer; Electrical Engineer; Industrial Engineer; Mechanical Engineer; Metallurgical Engineer; Petroleum Engineer; Quality Control Supervisor; Systems Analyst; Technical Writer/Editor; Computer Aided Designer; Machine and Product Designer. Principal educational backgrounds sought: Art/Design; Biology; Chemistry; Communications; Engineering; Mathematics; Physics. Training programs offered; Internships offered. Company benefits include: medical, dental, and life insurance. Corporate headquarters location: Cambridge, MA. Operations at this facility include: divisional headquarters; research/development; administration; service; sales.

## FABRICATED METAL PRODUCTS/PRIMARY METALS

**For more information on professional employment opportunities in the fabricated metal products industries, contact the following professional and trade organizations, as listed beginning on page 315:**

AMERICAN CASTE METALS ASSOCIATION
AMERICAN POWDER METALLURGY INSTITUTE
ASSOCIATION OF IRON AND STEEL ENGINEERS
NATIONAL ASSOCIATION OF METAL FINISHERS


**ALLSTEEL INC.**
Allsteel Drive
Aurora IL 60507-0871
708/844-7191
Contact Employee Relations Representative. Manufacturer of steel office furniture systems.

**AMERICAN SPRING AND WIRE SPECIALTY CO.**
816 North Spaulding Avenue
Chicago IL 60651
312/826-0800
Contact Patti A. Buffington, Vice President. Manufacturer of springs and wire formed products. Training programs offered; Internships offered. Company benefits include: medical insurance; pension plan; life insurance; tuition assistance; disability coverage; profit sharing; employee discounts; savings plan. Corporate headquarters location.

**AMERICAN STEEL FOUNDRIES**
1700 Walnut St.
Granite City IL 62040
618/452-2111
Contact Gwen Pitchford, Personnel Director. Manufacturers of railroad castings, and wholesalers of steel castings. Employs over 1,000.

**B-LINE SYSTEMS INC.**
509 W. Monroe
Highland IL 62249
618/654-2184
Contact Personnel Department. A leading greater St. Louis metal fabricating company, engaged primarily in the production of roll formers, and the welding of all sorts of steel and aluminum products for the electrical and mechanical industry. Employs over 400.

**BIG RIVER ZINC CORPORATION**
Route 3 and Monsanto Ave.
Sauget IL 62201
618/274-5000
Contact Valerie Fulbright, Personnel Supervisor. A major area foundry, producing primary zinc. Common positions include: Chemist; Computer Programmer; Metallurgical Engineer; Industrial Engineer; General Manager; Operations/Production Manager; Personnel and Labor Relations Specialist; Sales Representative; Sales Manager. Principal educational

backgrounds sought: Accounting; Business Administration; Chemistry; Engineering. Company benefits include: medical insurance; dental insurance; life insurance; tuition assistance; disability coverage; profit sharing; savings plan; 401K. Corporate headquarters location: Clayton, MO. Parent company: Big River Mineral. Operations at this facility include: divisional headquarters; manufacturing; research/development; sales.

**CBI INDUSTRIES INC.**
800 Jorie Boulevard
Oak Brook IL 60522
708/572-7722
Contact Personnel Director. Designs, fabricates, and constructs large metal plate structures and related systems

**A.M. CASTLE & COMPANY**
3400 North Wolf Road
Franklin Park IL 60131
708/455-7111
Contact Tom Prendergast, Director of Corporate Human Resources. A large metals service center company.

**CENTRAL STEEL AND WIRE COMPANY**
3000 West 51st Street
Chicago IL 60632
312/471-3800
Contact Mr. Kukowski, Personnel Director. Distributes processed and non-processed ferrous metals.

**DANVILLE METAL STAMPING COMPANY, INC.**
20 Oakwood Avenue
Danville IL 61832
217/446-0647
Contact Greg Allard, Personnel Director. Develops and produces fabricated metal components for the aerospace industry.

**FERALLOY CORPORATION**
8755 Higgins Road
Chicago IL 60631
312/380-1500
Contact Personnel. Processors and wholesalers of flat-rolled steel.

**A. FINKL & SONS**
2011 North Southport Avenue
Chicago IL 60614
312/975-2622
Contact Personnel Manager. A steel mill that manufactures custom forgings.

## GRANITE CITY STEEL DIVISION/ NATIONAL STEEL COMPANY
20th and State Streets
Granite City IL 62040
618/451-3456
Contact Troy Ward, Director/Human Resources. A major area manufacturer of steel. Employs over 3,000.

## HANDY BUTTON MACHINE
1750 North 25th Avenue
Melrose Park IL 60160
708/450-9000
Contact Corinne Amati, Personnel Director. Manufactures metal stampings and forms.

## HARRIS-HUB/DRESHER
7200 South Mason
P.O. Box 8
Bedford Park IL 60499
708/331-5030
Contact Personnel Director. Manufacturer of metal furniture for the consumer market.

## INLAND STEEL INDUSTRIES
30 West Monroe Street
Chicago IL 60603
312/346-0300
Contact Personnel Supervisor. A large integrated steel manufacturer.

## KROPP FORGE DIVISION
5301 West Roosevelt Road
Chicago IL 60650
312/242-1900
Contact Frank Greco, Personnel Director. A producer of steel forgings.

## LINDBERG CORPORATION
6133 North River Road, Suite 700
Wooddale IL 60018
708/823-2021
Contact Office Manager. Operating in the field of metallurgical processing.

## MODERN DROP FORGE COMPANY
13810 South Western Avenue
P.O. Box 429
Blue Island IL 60406
708/388-1806, 568-3030
Contact Mike Vogelsang, Personnel Manager. Operates a steel forging plant. Corporate headquarters location.

### NATIONAL CASTINGS DIVISION
1400 South Laramie Avenue
Cicero IL 60650
708/863-4800
Contact Personnel Manager. Operates a steel foundry, as part of the heavy industry division of Midland-Ross. Corporate headquarters location: Cleveland, OH.

### NATIONAL METALWARES INC.
900 North Russell Avenue
Aurora IL 60506
708/892-9000
Contact Katrina Smith, Management Recruiter. Wholly-owned subsidiary of Varlen Corporation. Manufacturer of fabricated steel tubing. Corporate headquarters location.

### NATIONAL STEEL CORPORATION
2850 West Golf Road, Suite 402
Rolling Meadows IL 60008
708/640-3300
Contact Bill Levendoski, Personnel Manager. A widely diversified company engaged in a wide range of metal products manufacturing. Engaged in the following business segments: Transportation (steel for automotive and rail markets); Containers; Service Centers (36 stores specializing in cut-to-order steel sheet); Metal Buildings and Components; Appliances; Tubing (for cars, chairs, and chemicals); Electrical Products and Components; Construction Products (steel used for doors, heating and cooling systems); Research and Development; National Mineral Resources; and Environment. Chicago area subsidiaries include Midwest Steel (which is involved in Appliances, Tubing, and Construction products divisions). Common positions include: Customer Service Representative; Management Trainee; Sales Representative. Principal educational backgrounds sought: Business Administration; Communications; Marketing. Training programs offered. Company benefits include: medical, dental, and life insurance; pension plan; tuition assistance; disability coverage; profit sharing; savings plan. Corporate headquarters location: Pittsburgh, PA. Parent company: NKK/NII. Operations at this facility include: sales. New York Stock Exchange.

### NESCO STEEL BARREL COMPANY
P.O. Box N
Granite City IL 62040
618/452-1190
Contact Albert Zamarione, President. A leading manufacturer of steel drums for food, chemicals and oil.

## NORTHWESTERN STEEL AND WIRE COMPANY
121 Wallace Street
Sterling IL 61081
815/625-2500, ext. 2700
Contact Don Simpson, Manager of Employment. A producer of basic steel and wire products. Operations at this facility include: manufacturing; sales. Corporate headquarters location. Common positions include: Accountant; Blue-Collar Worker Supervisor; Buyer; Chemist; Computer Programmer; Credit Manager; Draftsperson; Engineer; Electrical Engineer; Industrial Engineer; Mechanical Engineer; Metallurgical Engineer; Financial Analyst; Department Manager; Management Trainee; Marketing Specialist; Operations/Production Manager; Personnel & Labor Relations Specialist; Quality Control Supervisor; Sales Representative. Principal educational backgrounds sought: Accounting; Business Administration; Chemistry; Computer Science; Engineering; Finance; Marketing; Mathematics. Company benefits include: medical insurance; dental insurance; pension plan; life insurance; disability coverage; profit sharing; ESOP. Corporate headquarters location.

## PARKVIEW METAL PRODUCTS
4931 West Armitage
Chicago IL 60639
312/622-8414
Contact John Harrington, Personnel Director. A metal stampings manufacturer servicing metal trades industries nationwide. Builds and maintains progressive dies. Common positions include: Blue-Collar Worker Supervisor; Mechanical Engineer; Operations/Production Manager; Purchasing Agent; Quality Control Supervisor. Principal educational backgrounds sought: Business Administration; Engineering. Company benefits include: medical insurance; life insurance; disability coverage; profit sharing. Corporate headquarters location. Operations at this facility include: manufacturing; administration; sales.

## REYNOLDS METALS COMPANY
1st Avenue and 47th Street
McCook IL 60525
708/485-9000
Contact Cornell Ward, Manager, Industrial Relations. A producer of primary aluminum and fabricated aluminum products. Founded in 1928. Operates 50 plants in the United States. Mines and processes bauxite, refines it into alumina, reduces it to aluminum and then processes finished product. It produces Reynolds Wrap foil, beverage cans, plastic films, electric wire and cable, building products, and solar hot water heating systems. Operations include: manufacturing. Corporate headquarters location: Richmond, VA. International. New York Stock Exchange. Common positions include: Accountant; Chemist; Computer Programmer; Customer Service Representative; Draftsperson; Electrical Engineer; Industrial Engineer; Mechanical Engineer; Metallurgical Engineer; Operations/Production

Manager; Personnel & Labor Relations Specialist; Quality Control Supervisor; Systems Analyst; Technical Writer/Editor; Transportation & Traffic Specialist. Principal educational backgrounds sought: Accounting; Business Administration; Computer Science; Engineering; Liberal Arts; Marketing. Company benefits include: medical insurance; dental insurance; pension plan; life insurance; tuition assistance; disability coverage; savings plan.

**ROESCH INC.**
100 North 24th Street
P.O. Box 328
Belleville IL 62222
618/233-2760
Contact Bonnie Voges, Personnel Director. Major Southern Illinois manufacturers of steel stampings and porcelain enameling, refrigerated ice merchandisers.

**TARACORP INDUSTRIES**
1200 16th Street
Granite City IL 62040
618/451-4400
Contact Carla R. Jones, Personnel Administrator. Manufactures and sells lead products. Common positions include: Accountant; Administrator; Blue-Collar Worker Supervisor; Buyer; Chemist; Claim Representative; Customer Service Representative; Engineer; Industrial Engineer; Purchasing Agent; Quality Control Supervisor; Transportation & Traffic Specialist. Currently in a hiring freeze. Principal educational backgrounds sought: Accounting; Chemistry; Engineering. Company benefits include: medical insurance; pension plan; life insurance; disability coverage; profit sharing. Divisional headquarters location. Corporate headquarters location: Atlanta, GA. Operations at this facility include: manufacturing; sales.

**TEMPEL STEEL COMPANY**
1939 West Bryn Mawr
Chicago IL 60660
312/282-9400
Contact Arthur Canning, Manager Industrial Relations. Several area locations including: Arlington Heights, Elk Grove Village. Manufacturer of magnetic steel laminations for electric motors and transformers. Corporate headquarters location.

**THOMPSON STEEL COMPANY**
9470 King Street
Franklin Park IL 60131
708/678-0400
Contact Personnel Director. Cold-roll reducers of strip steel. Corporate headquarters location.

## USS/A DIVISION OF USX CORPORATION
3426 East 89th Street
Chicago IL 60617
312/933-3012
Contact Corporate Employment Manager. Several area locations, including: Joliet, Chicago Heights, and Moline. One of the world's largest vertically integrated steel manufacturers. Also involved in mining, transporting, processing and construction. Active in many other industries including chemicals, cement, plastics and wire products. Divisions include: USS Products, USS Supply, USS Chemicals and Plastics, USS Agri-Chemicals, USS Realty, American Bridge, Oilwell Supply, Universal Atlas Cement. Local operations include Illinois Manufacturing Division: Chicago Plant (South Works): produces steel ingots, billets. Steel Supply Division: produces strapping, strapping equipment, wire rope, fence, metal conveyor belts, nails, paint, and containers. Corporate headquarters location: Pittsburgh, PA. New York Stock Exchange.

## UDDEHOLM CORPORATION
4902 Tollview Drive
Rolling Meadows IL 60008
312/577-2220
Contact Personnel Office. A major area steel distributorship. Corporate headquarters location. Common positions include: Accountant; Administrator; Advertising Worker; Buyer; Computer Programmer; Credit Manager; Metallurgical Engineer; Financial Analyst; Department Manager; General Manager; Operations/Production Manager; General Manager; Marketing Specialist; Personnel and Labor Relations Specialist; Purchasing Agent; Quality Control Supervisor; Reporter/Editor; Systems Analyst. Principal educational backgrounds sought: Accounting; Business Administration; Computer Science; Economics; Finance; Liberal Arts; Marketing. Company benefits include: medical insurance; dental insurance; life insurance; pension plan; disability coverage; savings plan. Operations at this facility include: divisional headquarters location; administration.

## VERSON
## A DIVISION OF ALLIED PRODUCTS CORP
1355 East 93rd Street
Chicago IL 60619
312/933-8303
Contact Larry Farnesi, Manager, Employee Relations. Designs and manufactures metal forming equipment. Corporate headquarters location. Common positions include: Computer Programmer; Customer Service Representative; Electrical Engineer; Industrial Engineer; Mechanical Engineer; Sales Representative. Principal educational backgrounds sought: Computer Science; Engineering; Mathematics. Company benefits include: medical and life insurance; tuition assistance; disability coverage; savings plan; 401K. Corporate headquarters location: Chicago, IL. Parent company:

Allied Products Corp. Operations at this facility include: divisional heaquarters; manufacturing. New York Stock Exchange.

**WELDED TUBE COMPANY OF AMERICA**
1855 East 122nd Street
Chicago IL 60633
312/646-4500
Contact John Perish, Personnel Director. Engaged in the manufacture and sale of welded steel tubing, in square, rectangular, and special shapes and sizes. Manufacturing facilities are located in Chicago. Products are used in low-and-medium-rise construction; automotive, railroad and industrial equipment; farm implements and equipment; boat, car, and truck trailers; and industrial storage facilities. Future plans include supplying the oil and gas industries with a line of tubular products, to be added to the current Chicago manufacturing plants. Corporate headquarters location: Philadelphia, PA. American Stock Exchange.

**WELLS MANUFACTURING COMPANY**
7800 North Austin Avenue
Skokie IL 60077
708/966-5050
Contact Robert Engelhardt, Vice President & Personnel Director. Several area locations. National distributor of electric furnace gray and alloyed iron castings, and cast iron bar stock. Corporate headquarters location.

## FINANCIAL SERVICES/MANAGEMENT CONSULTING

For more information on professional employment opportunities in the financial services industry, contact the following professional and trade organizations, as listed beginning on page 315:

AMERICAN FINANCIAL SERVICES ASSOCIATION
AMERICAN SOCIETY OF APPRAISERS
AMERICAN SOCITY OF APPRAISERS/CHICAGO
ASSOCIATION OF MANAGEMENT CONSULTING FIRMS
CHICAGO ASSOCIATION OF BUSINESS ECONOMISTS
CHICAGO ASSOCIATION OF CREDIT MANAGEMENT
COUNCIL OF CONSULTANT ORGANIZATIONS
FEDERATION OF TAX ADMINISTRATORS
FINANCIAL ANALYSTS FEDERATION
FINANCIAL ANALYSTS FEDERATION/CHICAGO
FINANCIAL EXECUTIVES INSTITUTE
FINANCIAL EXECUTITVES INSTITUTE/CHICAGO
INSTITUTE OF FINANCIAL EDUCATION
INSTITUTE OF MANAGMENT CONSULTANTS/GREATER CHICAGO CHAPTER

NATIONAL ASSOCIATION OF CREDIT MANAGEMENT
NATIONAL ASSOCIATION OF REAL ESTATE INVESTMENT TRUSTS
NATIONAL CORPORATE CASH MANAGEMENT ASSOCIATION
NORTHWEST CASH MANAGEMENT ASSOCIATION
SECURITIES INDUSTRY ASSOCIATION

## ANDERSEN CONSULTING
33 West Monroe Street
Chicago IL 60603
312/580-0033
Contact Julie Arndorfer, Recruiting Manager. Andersen Consulting provides services to help organizations effectively apply technology for their business advantage. By combining general business knowledge with information systems skills, the company develops solutions that help clients in many industries manage technology. Common positions include: Computer Programmer; Systems Analyst; Staff Consultant. Principal educational backgrounds sought: Business Administration; Computer Science; Economics; Engineering; Finance; Mathematics. Company benefits include: medical insurance; dental insurance; pension plan; life insurance; tuition assistance; disability coverage; daycare assistance; profit sharing; employee discounts; savings plan. Corporate headquarters location. Parent company: Arthur Andersen & Co.

## AUTOMATIC DATA PROCESSING
7350 West Lawrence Avenue
Chicago IL 60656
708/867-6400
Contact Jean McGann, Senior Employment Specialist. Engaged in the data processing services business. Provides payroll processing, payroll tax filing and unemployment compensation management among other services. Common positions include: Accountant; Administrator; Computer Programmer; Customer Service Representative; Department Manager; Personnel and Labor Relations Specialist; Sales Representative; PC Trainer; Technical Support. Principal educational backgrounds sought: Accounting; Business Administration; Communications; Liberal Arts; Marketing. Training programs offered. Company benefits include: medical insurance; dental insurance; pension plan; life insurance; tuition assistance; disability coverage; employee discounts; savings plan; employee stock ownership plan. Corporate headquarters location: Roseland, NJ. Operations at this facility include: regional headquarters; administration; service; sales. New York Stock Exchange.

## CHICAGO BOARD OF OPTIONS EXCHANGE
400 South LaSalle
Chicago IL 60605
312/786-5600
Contact Human Resources Department. A financial institution engaged in the trading of options.

## THE CHICAGO BOARD OF TRADE
141 West Jackson Boulevard, A-30
Chicago IL 60604
312/435-3494
Contact Amy Smith, Employment Specialist. Commodity futures exchange. Common positions include: Computer Programmer; Economist; Financial Analyst; Auditors. Principal educational backgrounds sought include: Accounting; Computer Science; Economics; Finance. Training programs available. Company benefits include: medical insurance; dental insurance; pension plan; life insurance; tuition assistance; disability coverage; savings plan. Corporate headquarters location.

## CHICAGO MERCANTILE EXCHANGE
30 South Wacker Drive
Chicago IL 60606
312/930-8243
Contact Steven Timmons, Employment Manager. A large commodities exchange company.

## CHICAGO METROPOLITAN MUTUAL ASSURANCE COMPANY
4455 Martin Luther King Jr. Drive
Chicago IL 60653
312/285-3030
Contact Alzater Timmons, Personnel Director. Mortgage holders. Corporate headquarters location.

## CHICAGO MILWAUKEE CORPORATION
547 West Jackson Boulevard, Suite 1510
Chicago IL 60661
312/822-0400
Contact Dianne Barango, Personnel Director. A financial investment company with two subsidiaries involved in real estate sales.

## THE CONTINENTAL CORPORATION
200 South Wacker Drive
Chicago IL 60606
312/876-5000
Contact Joyce E. Heidemann, AVP Human Resources. A large diversified financial company.

## DRESSER KOMATSU DIVISION
3201 North Wolf Road
Franklin Park IL 60131
708/451-3500
Contact Debra Zeman, Personnel Department. Offers finance services.

## EQUIFAX INC.
P.O. Box 3115
Naperville IL 60566
708/505-1099
Contact Personnel Department. A diversified credit reporting agency.

## HELLER FINANCIAL
200 North LaSalle
Chicago IL 60601
312/621-7700
Contact Susan Gallen, V.P. of Organizational Staffing. Provides businesses with a variety of financial services.

## HOUSEHOLD INTERNATIONAL
2700 Sanders Road
Prospect Heights IL 60070
708/564-6119
Contact Laura Bennett, Manager, Human Resources. A multi-billion dollar fiancial services company. Common positions include: Accountant; Administrator; Attorney; Bank Officer/Manager; Credit Manager; Financial Analyst; Management Trainee; Marketing Specialist; Personnel and Labor Relations Specialist; Public Relations Specialist; Purchasing Agent; Systems Analyst. Principal educational backgrounds sought: Accounting; Business Administration; Communications; Computer Science; Economics; Finance; Liberal Arts; Marketing; Mathematics. Training programs offered; Internships offered. Company benefits include: medical insurance; dental insurance; pension plan; life insurance; disability coverage; daycare assistance; profit sharing; employee discounts; savings plan. Corporate headquarters location. Operations at this facility include: administration; service. New York Stock Exchange.

## A.T. KEARNEY, INC.
222 South Riverside Plaza
Chicago IL 60606
312/648-0111
Contact V.P./Executive Search Department. A general management consulting firm.

**LESTER B. KNIGHT & ASSOCIATES, INC.**
549 West Randolph Street
Chicago IL 60661
312/346-2100
Contact Jim Turner, Director of Human Resources. A management consulting firm.

**MERRILL LYNCH**
33 West Monroe Street, 25th Floor
Chicago IL 60604
312/269-5000
Contact Mia Merkel, Director of Personnel. Provides financial services in securities, extensive insurance, and real estate and related areas. Its major subsidiary, Merrill Lynch, Pierce, Fenner & Smith, Inc., is one of the largest securities brokerage firms in the United States. It also brokers commodity futures and options, is a dealer in corporate and municipal securities, and engages in investment banking activities. Other major subsidiaries include Merrill Lynch Government Securities, Inc., Family Life Insurance Company and AMIC Corporation. Corporate headquarters location: New York, NY. New York Stock Exchange.

**MIDWEST STOCK EXCHANGE INC.**
440 South LaSalle, Suite 425
Chicago IL 60605
312/663-2012
Contact Nancy Neilsson, Employee Relations Specialist. The second largest stock exchange in the United States. Securities trading and depository services. Common positions include: Accountant; Computer Programmer; Customer Service Representative; Financial Analyst; Department Manager; Operations/Production Manager; Technical Writer/Editor; Research Analyst. Company benefits include: medical insurance; dental insurance; pension plan; life insurance; tuition assistance; disability coverage; savings plan. Corporate headquarters location. New York Stock Exchange and American Stock Exchange.

**STEIN ROE & FARNHAM**
1 South Wacker Drive
Chicago IL 60606
312/368-7705
Contact Susan C. Esque, Manager, Human Resources. Investment counsel offering professional advice and service to individuals, institutions and other organizations. Also manages several no-load mutual funds. Approximately 60 officers and 400 employees. Regional offices in Arizona, New York, Cleveland, Minneapolis, Ft. Lauderdale, and Puerto Rico. Corporate headquarters location. Common positions include: Accountant; Administrator; Attorney; Computer Programmer; Customer Service Representative; Economist; Financial Analyst; Department Manager; Operations/Production Manager; Department Manager; Statistician;

Systems Analyst; Research Assistant. Principal educational backgrounds sought: Accounting; Business Administration; Finance; MBA for Analyst or Manager of Investment. Company benefits include: medical insurance; life insurance; tuition assistance; disability coverage; profit sharing.

**WASHINGTON NATIONAL CORPORATION**
1630 Chicago Avenue
Evanston IL 60201
708/570-3186
Contact Michael Richardson, Human Resources Department. A financial services holding company with subsidiaries engaged primarily in marketing and underwriting life insurance, annuities, and health insurance for groups and individuals. With life insurance in force of $30 billion and assets of $2.9 billion, Washington National Corporation had 1989 revenues of over $800 million. Washington National also involved in real estate development. Corporate headquarters location. New York Stock Exchange. Common positions include: Accountant; Actuary; Computer Programmer; Financial Analyst; Sales Representative; Systems Analyst; Underwriter. Principal educational backgrounds sought: Accounting; Business Administration; Computer Science; Finance; Marketing; Mathematics. Training programs offered; Internships offered. Company benefits include: medical, dental, and life insurance; pension plan; tuition assistance; disability coverage; employee discounts; savings plan; health club membership discounts.

**FOOD & BEVERAGE RELATED:**
**PRODUCTION AND DISTRIBUTION/WHOLESALE & RETAIL**

For more information on professional employment opportunities in the food industries, contact the following professional and trade organizations, as listed beginning on page 315:

AMERICAN ASSOCIATION OF CEREAL CHEMISTS
AMERICAN SOCIETY OF AGRICULTURAL ENGINEERS
AMERICAN SOCIETY OF BREWING CHEMISTS
DAIRY AND FOOD INDUSTRIES SUPPLY ASSOCIATION
NATIONAL AGRICULTURAL CHEMICALS ASSOCIATION
NATIONAL DAIRY COUNCIL
UNITED FOOD AND COMMERCIAL WORKERS INTERNATIONAL UNION

## ARCHER DANIEL MIDLAND CO.
P.O. Box 1470
Decatur IL 62525
217/424-5239
Contact Sheila Witts-Mannweiler, Personnel Manager. One of the nation's leading agricultural products firms.

## GEORGE J. BALL, INC.
622 Town Road
West Chicago IL 60185
708/231-3500
Contact Dennis Johnson, Personnel Director. Chicago-area horticultural business.

## BEATRICE CORPORATION
2 North LaSalle
Chicago IL 60602
312/558-4000
Contact Personnel. One of the nation's largest producers of consumer foods. Products include a wide variety of well-known brand names. Employs 22,000.

## BOISE CASCADE OFFICE PRODUCTS
800 West Bryn Mawr Avenue
Itasca IL 60143
708/773-5000
Contact Human Resource Administrator. One of the nation's leading distributors of office products. Distributes in both wholesale and consumer markets. Common positions include: Accountant; Blue-Collar Worker Supervisor; Computer Programmer Customer Service Representative; Marketing Specialist; Sales Representative. Principal educational backgrounds sought include: Accounting; Business Administration; Computer Science; Marketing. Internships available. Company benefits include: medical insurance; dental insurance; pension plan; life insurance; tuition assistance; disability coverage; profit sharing; employee discounts; savings plan. Corporate headquarters location: Boise, Idaho. Operations at this facility include: regional headquarters; division headquarters; service; sales. New York Stock Exchange.

## CPC INTERNATIONAL/BEST FOODS DIVISION
P.O. Box 448
6400 South Archer
Argo IL 60501
708/458-8686
Contact Robert Swanson, Human Resources Manager. A worldwide family of food and related businesses. Common positions include: Blue-Collar Worker Supervisor; Chemist. Principal educational backgrounds sought include: Chemistry; Management. Training programs available. Company benefits include: medical insurance; dental insurance; pension plan; life

insurance; tuition assistance; disability coverage; savings plan. Corporate headquarters location: Englewood Cliffs, NJ. Operations at this facility include: manufacturing. New York Stock Exchange.

**CENTRAL GROWERS COOPERATIVE, INC.**
3701 North Centrella Street
Franklin Park IL 60131
708/678-0660
Contact Personnel. A leading grocery wholesaler.

**CERTIFIED GROCERS MIDWEST, INC.**
Certified Drive
Hodgkins IL 60525
708/585-7000
Contact Personnel. A cooperative food wholesaler, employing 1,093.

**CLARK FOODSERVICE, INC.**
950 Arthur Avenue
Elk Grove Village IL 60007
312/956-1730
Contact Personnel. A food service distributor.

**CONTINENTAL GRAIN COMPANY**
10 South Riverside Plaza
Chicago IL 60606
312/930-1050
Contact Mr. Jochum, Personnel Director. An international food company, involved mostly in grain.

**CULINARY FOODS, INC.**
1240 West George Street
Chicago IL 60657
312/528-7300
Contact Howard Davis, President. Buys raw food products, processes and distributes them.

**DOMINICK'S FINER FOODS**
505 Railroad Avenue
Northlake IL 60164
708/562-1000
Contact Gary J. Bosco, Human Resources Manager. Retail grocery firm.

**EDWARD DON & COMPANY**
2500 South Harlem Avenue
North Riverside IL 60546
708/442-9400
Contact Jim Walsh, Human Resources Manager. Distributor of food service equipment and supplies.

**ENVIRODYNE INDUSTRIES, INC.**
701 Harger Road
Oak Brook IL 60521
708/571-8800
Contact Personnel Department. A holding company for sausage casing and disposable plastic cutlery and straws company.

**FLOUR MILLS DIVISION/
CON-AGRA**
145 West Broadway
Alton IL 62002
618/463-4411
Contact Cindy Holt, Office Manager. A major division of the national agricultural products corporation, specializing in the manufacture of grain terminal operators, and the production of millers-flour and animal feed.

**GOLDEN GRAIN**
7700 W. 71st Street
Bridgeview IL 60455
708/458-7020
Contact David Futts, General Manager. Producers of Rice-a-roni. Makers of all types of macaroni.

**GONNELLA BAKING COMPANY**
2002-14 West Erie Street
Chicago IL 60612
312/733-2020
Contact Lou Pasquesi, Jr., Personnel. Makers of bread and other bakery products.

**GROEN COMPANY
DOVER CORPORATION**
1900 Pratt Boulevard
Elk Grove Village IL 60007
708/439-2400
Contact Personnel Director. Manufactures food processing equipment.

**ILLINOIS FARM BUREAU**
1701 Towanda Avenue
Bloomington IL 61701
309/557-2209
Contact Jack Fowler, Director of Employment & Training. Company sells production supplies, provides insurance protection, markets farm products and provides business and personal services for members.

## INTERSTATE BRANDS CORPORATION
40 East Garfield Boulevard
Chicago IL 60615
312/536-7700
Contact William Schwab, Associate Personnel Manager. Manufacturer & wholesaler of bread products. Common positions include: Route Salesperson. Training programs offered. Corporate headquarters location: Kansas City, MO. Operations at this facility include: manufacturing.

## JAY'S FOODS, INC.
825 East 99th Street
Chicago IL 60628
312/731-8400
Contact Personnel Director. Produces and distributes popcorn & potato chips.

## KEEBLER COMPANY
One Hollow Tree Lane
Elmhurst IL 60126
708/833-2900
Contact Roger L. Gansauer, Manager, Management Staffing. A national manufacturer and marketer of cookies, crackers and salty snacks. Positions recruited for at the corporate office require specific functional and/or industry experience. Formal management development training or internship programs are not offered. Positions commonly available include: programmer, food scientist, product manager, accountant, project engineer, market research manager. Hiring for sales (marketing/account representative, store merchandiser, route sales driver), distribution (driver, warehouse worker) and manufacturing (production worker, maintenance mechanic, qa/qc technician, production supervisor). These positions are handled at individual locations throughout the U.S. Principal educational backgrounds sought: Acocounting; Business Administration; Computer Science; Engineering; Marketing; Food Science. Company benefits include: medical insurance; dental insurance; pension plan; life insurance; tuition assistance; disability coverage; employee discounts; savings plan. Corporate headquarters location. Parent company: United Biscuit (Holdings) PLC. Operations at this facility include: research/development; administration.

## KITCHENS OF SARA LEE
500 Waukegan Road
Deerfield IL 60015
Contact Human Resources/Staffing. Mailed inquiries only. An area producer of frozen baked goods. Parent company, Sara Lee Corporation, is a diversified consumer goods company (see separate listing). Common positions include: Accountant; Buyer; Chemist; Computer Programmer; Industrial Engineer; Mechanical Engineer; Packaging Engineer; Financial Analyst; Food Technologist; Experimental Baker. Principal educational backgrounds sought: Business Administration; Computer Science;

Engineering; Finance; Marketing; Packaging Design. Company benefits include: medical, dental, and life insurance; pension plan; tuition assistance; disability coverage; employee discounts. Corporate, regional and divisional headquarters location. Operations at this facility include: research/development; administration; service; sales.

**KRAFT HOLLEB**
800 Supreme Drive
Bensonville IL 60106
708/595-1200
Contact Personnel Director. Distributes prepared foods to institutional customers.

**KRAFT, INC.**
2211 Sanders Road
Northbrook IL 60062
312/498-8000
Contact Chris Niko, Manager of Employee Relations. An international leader in consumer food products.

**LEAF, INC.**
2355 Waukegan Road
Bannockburn IL 60015
708/940-7500
Contact Joel Dant, Vice President, Personnel. A confectionery and candy company (manufacturing & sales).

**NATIONAL BAKING COMPANY**
5001 West Polk
Chicago IL 60644
312/261-6000
Contact Harry Carson, Executive Vice President/General Manager. Specializes in preparation and baking of breads and rolls. Trucks deliver products east of the Rocky Mountains. Institutional route system locally. Corporate headquarters location.

**NESTLE FOODS CORPORATION**
2101 Adams Street
Granite City IL 62040
618/225-4242
Contact Steve Drummond, Manager, Human Resources. The St. Louis office of the nationally-known manufacturer of a wide range of food products. Also produces a wide range of ingredients for the food-processing and beverage industries. A wholly-owned subsidiary of Nestle SA (Vevey, Switzerland), a major international food products firm. Corporate headquarters: Purchase, NY. Common positions include: Accountant; Blue-Collar Worker Supervisor; Draftsperson; Chemical Engineer; Industrial Engineer; Mechanical Engineer; General Manager; Management Trainee;

Operations/Production Manager; Personnel & Labor Relations Specialist; Quality Control Supervisor. Principal educational backgrounds sought: Engineering. Company benefits include: medical, dental, and life insurance; pension plan; tuition assistance; disability coverage; savings plan. Operations at this facility include: manufacturing.

## ORVAL KENT FOOD COMPANY
120 West Palatine Road
Wheeling IL 60090
708/459-9000
Contact Personnel Department. Producers of refrigerated salads. Employs 1,350.

## OSCAR MAYER FOODS CORPORATION
320 West Scott Street
Chicago IL 60610
312/642-1200
Contact Don Culburson, Assistant Personnel Manager. Operates meat packing and processing facilities in the United States and abroad. Company produces more than 750 food service and consumer processed meat products, including wieners, sausage, bacon, sandwich spreads, turkey products, and ham products, as well as many others. Company's products are sold throughout the United States by approximately 450 salespersons operating out of 32 distribution centers in most major cities. A processing plant in Chicago. Company has a distribution center in Chicago, and subsidiary Claussen Pickle Company is located in Woodstock. Operates 20 processing plants nationwide. Operations at this facility include: manufacturing. Corporate headquarters location: Madison, WI. Parent company: Phillip Morris. New York Stock Exchange. International. Common positions include: Accountant; Blue-Collar Worker Supervisor; Buyer; Credit Manager; Engineer; Customer Service Representative; Draftsperson; Chemical Engineer; Electrical Engineer; Industrial Engineer; Mechanical Engineer; Food Technologist; Department Manager; Operations/Production Manager; Personnel & Labor Relations Specialist; Purchasing Agent; Quality Control Supervisor. Principal educational backgrounds sought: Accounting; Biology; Business Administration; Computer Science; Engineering; Finance; Food Science; Liberal Arts. Company benefits include: medical insurance; dental insurance; pension plan; life insurance; tuition assistance; disability coverage; employee discounts; profit sharing; savings plan

## PRAIRIE FARMS DAIRY INC.
1800 Adams Street
Granite City IL 62040
618/451-5600
Contact Personnel Department. Major St. Louis area producer and wholesaler of dairy products.

## THE QUAKER OATS COMPANY
P.O. Box 9001
Chicago IL 60604-9001
Contact Placement Office for information. Engaged in research, manufacturing, and marketing of foods, pet foods, toys and specialty retailing. Established in 1877. Employs 32,000 people worldwide. Corporate headquarters location. New York Stock Exchange.

## SARA LEE
3 First National Plaza
70 West Madison
Chicago IL 60602
312/726-2600
Contact Vice President of Human Resources. The corporate office of the international food and consumer products company.

## SHURFINE-CENTRAL CORPORATION
2100 North Mannheim Road
Northlake IL 60164
708/681-2000
Contact Personnel. A provider of private label brands to grocery distribution warehouses.

## SUNSHINE-SALEMO, INC.
7777 North Caldwell Avenue
Niles IL 60648
312/774-2000
Contact Sue Malarski, Manager of Human Resources. A producer and distributor of cookies and crackers.

## SUNSTAR FOODS INCORPORATED
707 Skokie Boulevard, Suite 220
Northbrook IL 60062
708/564-5270
Contact Human Resources. A company engaged primarily in the production of peanut butter, syrups, honey, and Jero cocktail mixes.

## SUPERIOR COFFEE COMPANY
990 Supreme Drive
Bensenville IL 60106
708/860-1400
Contact Mr. Lee Ashmann, V.P./Human Resources Department. Several area locations, including: Bensenville, Chicago, Elk Grove Village. Produces and sells coffee, tea, salad dressings, syrups, and vending products. Corporate headquarters location.

## SYSCO FOOD SERVICES
250 Wieboldt Drive
Des Plaines IL 60017
708/699-5400
Contact Personnel Department. Manufactures, sells, and distributes food products.

## TOPCO ASSOCIATES, INC.
7711 Gross Point Road
Skokie IL 60076
312/676-3030
Contact Garry J. Lunt, Employment Manager. Cooperative buying organization engaged in procurement of private label grocery products, meat products, produce and general merchandise items. Serves 35 member supermarket chains located nationwide. Common positions include: Accountant; Food Technologist; Transportation & Traffic Specialist; Food & Non-food Buyers; Marketing Research Analyst; Produce Buyer. Principal educational backgrounds sought: Accounting; Biology; Business Administration; Computer Science; Finance; Liberal Arts; Marketing. Company benefits include: medical, dental, and life insurance; pension plan; tuition assistance; disability coverage; savings plan. Corporate headquarters location. Operations at this facility include: administration; procurement; finance; MIS; Accounting; Marketing; Quality Assurance.

## VIENNA BEEF LTD.
2501 North Damen Avenue
Chicago IL 60647
312/278-7800
Contact Mr. Jamie Eisenberg, Vice President, Personnel. National distributor and processor of meat and sausage. Also a meat cutting facility. Corporate headquarters location. International. Common positions include: Accountant; Computer Programmer; Customer Service Representative; Food Technologist; Sales Representative. Principal educational backgrounds sought: Accounting; Business Administration; Computer Science. Company benefits include: medical, dental, and life insurance; pension plan; disability coverage; profit sharing; employee discounts. Operations at this facility include: regional headquarters; manufacturing; administration; service; sales.

## WHITE HEN PANTRY
660 Industrial Drive
Elmhurst IL 60126
312/883-3100
Contact Personnel. Offices of the convenience food and deli stores.

### WORLD'S FINEST CHOCOLATE
4801 South Lawnddale
Chicago IL 60632
312/847-4600
Contact Greg Serratore, Personnel Director. Manufactures chocolate and cocoa products. Corporate headquarters location. International.

### WM. WRIGLEY, JR. COMPANY
410 North Michigan Avenue
Chicago IL 60611
312/644-2121
Contact Edgar W. Swanson, Vice President/Personnel. Several area locations. Manufactures and markets chewing gums, under such well-known name brands as Wrigley's Spearmint, Doublemint, Juicy Fruit, Freedent, Big Red, Orbit, Spurt, Hubba Bubba, and others, in 14 factories worldwide. Gum factories are located in Chicago and Naperville, a raw materials processing plant is located in West Chicago, and the Wrigley Building is located in Chicago (houses corporate offices). A Fortune 500 company. New York Stock Exchange.

## GENERAL MERCHANDISE: RETAIL AND WHOLESALE

For more information on professional employment opportunities in the retail and wholesale industries, contact the following professional organization, as listed beginning on page 315:

### NATIONAL RETAIL MERCHANTS ASSOCIATION


### BRADFORD EXCHANGE
9333 North Milwaukee Avenue
Niles IL 60648
708/966-2770
Contact Personnel. Engaged in the direct mail marketing of collectibles. Employs 650.

### COTTER COMPANY
2740 North Clybourn Avenue
Chicago IL 60614-1088
312/975-2700
Contact A. Fred Lobo, Director of Human Resources. A member-owned wholesaler of hardware, variety and related products.

## EVANS, INC.
36 South State Street
Chicago IL 60603
312/855-2000
Contact Dean Obrecht, Personnel Director. A retailer of fur garments, cloth coats and suits.

## FIRESTONE TIRE
205 North Michigan Avenue
Chicago IL 60601
312/819-0001
Contact Personnel Director. Operates a chain of 280 retail outlets marketing tires and automotive services in Ohio, Michigan, Indiana, Illinois, Wisconsin, Minnesota, Iowa, Nebraska, North Dakota, and South Dakota. 1,400 retail outlets nationally.

## FOLLETT CORPORATION
1000 West Washington Boulevard
Chicago IL 60607
312/666-4300
Contact Carl Dickes, Director of Human Resources. Primarily concerned with the distribution of educational textbooks, library books, and software systems for library management. Largest operation of college bookstores in the United States.

## GATELY'S PEOPLE STORE
6901 West 159th Street
Tinley Park IL 60477
708/429-2400
Contact Mary Walsh, Director of Personnel. A retail department store. Corporate headquarters location.

## HOME NURSERY GREENHOUSES INC.
P.O. Box 307
Edwardsville IL 62025
618/656-1790
Contact Carol Balke, Personnel Director. A major area nursery engaged in the wholesale and retail sales of lawn and garden supplies.

## K'S MERCHANDISE
3103 North Charles Street
Decatur IL 62526
217/875-1440
Contact John Bell, Director of Personnel. An expanding retail catalog showroom chain.

**KROCH'S & BRENTANO'S, INC.**
29 South Wabash Avenue
Chicago IL 60603
312/332-7500
Contact Maureen Como, Vice President, Human Resources. Company operates service oriented retail bookstores, selling books and related merchandise. Common positions include: Bookseller; Sales Associate; Operational Support Worker. Principal educational backgrounds sought: Business Administration; Communications; Liberal Arts; Marketing. Training programs offered. Company benefits include: medical insurance; dental insurance; life insurance; disability coverage; employee discounts; employee stock option plan. Corporate headquarters location. Operations at this facility include: regional headquarters; administration; service; sales.

**LANE BRYANT, INC.**
75 Oakbrook Center
Oak Brook IL 60521
708/573-8602
Contact Richard Martin, Regional Manager. Purchases, distributes, & sells apparel, shoes, etc.

**LERNER STORES CORPORATION**
4190 East North Harlem Avenue
Chicago IL 60634
312/625-3991
Contact Regional Office. Sells moderately priced women's fashions, except shoes.

**MONTGOMERY WARD & COMPANY**
One Montgomery Ward Plaza
Chicago IL 60671
312/467-2000
Contact Human Resources. Nationwide mass merchandiser in the retail and catalog areas. Operates more than 300 stores. Corporate headquarters location. International.

**J.C. PENNEY COMPANY INC./
NORTHWEST REGION**
1750 East Golf Road
Schaumburg IL 60173-5049
708/517-4600
Contact Don Brewer, Regional Career Development Coordinator. Multiple area locations including: Schaumburg, Ford City, Lombard, North Riverside. A national, $14-billion retail merchandise sales and service corporation. Regional headquarters. Corporate headquarters location: Dallas, TX. International. New York Stock Exchange. Common positions include: Buyer; Department Manager; Management Trainee. Principal educational backgrounds sought: Accounting; Business Administration; Communications;

Computer Science; Liberal Arts; Economics; Marketing. Company benefits include: medical insurance; dental insurance; pension plan; life insurance; disability coverage; profit sharing; employee discounts; savings plan.

**POLK BROTHERS**
8311 West North Avenue
Melrose Park IL 60160
708/216-3030
Contact Mike Crane, Personnel Director. Multiple area locations. A furniture and appliances sales company selling a wide variety of products with name brands. Corporate headquarters location.

**SAKS FIFTH AVENUE**
700 North Michigan
Chicago IL 60611
312/944-6500
Contact Mrs. Christine Warman, Personnel Director. Fashion-forward, specialized department store chain. Branches of greatly varying sizes in 30 cities throughout the country. Soft goods products only, particularly apparel for men, women and children. Emphasis on high-quality fashion items. Subsidiary companies conduct a catalogue operation and a corporate gift service. A subsidiary of Gimbel Brothers, Inc., but is operated autonomously with respect to current operations, personnel, merchandising, purchasing, etc. Corporate headquarters location: New York, NY.

**SAXON PAINT & HOME CARE CENTERS**
3840 West Fullerton
Chicago IL 60647
312/252-8100
Contact Howard R. Kraus, Director of Personnel. Several area locations. A chain of retail stores in northern Illinois, Indiana, and Wisconsin. 44 stores are located in the Chicago metropolitan area. Saxon specializes in paint, wallpaper, window fashions and other home decorating products. Also manufacture own paint. Corporate headquarters location. Common positions include: Advertising Worker; Buyer; Management Trainee; Store Manager; Salesperson. Principal educational backgrounds sought: Accounting; Art/Design; Liberal Arts. Training programs offered. Company benefits include: medical, dental, and life insurance; disability coverage; profit sharing; employee discounts; savings plan.

**SEARS, ROEBUCK & COMPANY**
Sears Tower, D-707-2
Chicago IL 60684
312/875-2500
Contact Mary Misar, Professional Employment. One of the world's largest retailers with subsidiaries engaged in the insurance, securities brokerage, and real estate businesses. The company's principal business groups are: Merchandise, which distributes broad lines of merchandise and services in

the United States through more than 850 retail stores and 2,700 sales offices and other facilities; Allstate, which engages in the property/liability insurance, life insurance and financial services businesses, principally in the United States and Canada; Coldwell Banker, which invests in, develops, and operates real estate and performs financial services, which include savings and loan, mortgage banking and mortgage guaranty insurance activities; and Dean Witter Reynolds, which provides a complete range of securities brokerage services. The company employs approximately 390,000 people worldwide, including part-time employees. Corporate headquarters location. International. New York Stock Exchange.

**SHERWIN-WILLIAMS COMPANY**
11541 South Champlain
Chicago IL 60628
312/821-3011
Contact Mr. Murphy, Personnel Director. Operates nationally in six segments: Retail Stores, Coatings, Chemicals, Packaging Products, Specialty Products, and International. Products include Sherwin-Williams, Dutch Boy, Martin Seymour, Baltimore and Kem paints, as well as such related packaging products as paint cans, sprays and labels. Corporate headquarters location: Cleveland, OH. International. New York Stock Exchange.

**JOHN M. SMYTH'S HOMEMAKERS**
1013 Butterfield Road
Downers Grove IL 60515
708/960-4100
Contact Rex Slocum, Personnel Director. Multiple area locations. Large, high-quality retail furniture chain. One store in downtown Chicago and five suburban locations. Corporate headquarters location. Common positions include: Administrator; Buyer; Customer Service Representative; Department Manager; Management Trainee; Sales Representative. Principal educational backgrounds sought: Art/Design; Business Administration; Liberal Arts; Marketing. Company benefits include: medical insurance; life insurance; disability coverage; employee discounts

**UNITED STATIONERS SUPPLY COMPANY**
2200 East Golf Road
Des Plaines IL 60016
708/699-5000
Contact Mrs. Pat Zatto, Personnel Director. Wholesale distributors of office furniture, office machines, stationery, and a variety of writing instruments. Corporate headquarters location.

**VENTURE STORES**
17 West 734 22nd Street
Oakbrook Terrace IL 60181
708/627-9750

Contact Bob Hensley, Regional Personnel Manager. Department store chain. A subsidiary of May Department Stores Company. Corporate headquarters location.

**F.W. WOOLWORTH COMPANY**
915 Lee Street
Des Plaines IL 60016
708/827-7731
Contact Roger Boe, Regional Director of Personnel. An international retailing firm with more than 6,000 retail stores and leased departments in the United States, Puerto Rico, U.S. Virgin Islands, Canada, Germany, Mexico, Spain, Australia, Great Britain, Ireland, and the Caribbean Islands, operating under the names Woolworth, Woolco, Kinney, and Richman, as well as other names regionally. Annual sales in excess of $6 billion. Corporate headquarters location: New York, NY. International. New York Stock Exchange.

## HEALTH CARE & PHARMACEUTICALS: PRODUCTS & SERVICES

For more information on professional employment opportunities in the health care industries, contact the following professional and trade organizations, as listed beginning on page 315:

AMERICAN ACADEMY OF PHYSICIAN ASSISTANTS
AMERICAN COLLEGE OF HEALTHCARE EXECUTIVES
AMERICAN DENTAL ASSOCIATION
AMERICAN HEALTH CARE ASSOCIATION
AMERICAN MEDICAL ASSOCIATION
AMERICAN OCCUPATIONAL THERAPY ASSOCIATION
AMERICAN PHARMACEUTICAL ASSOCIATION
AMERICAN PHYSICAL THERAPY ASSOCIATION
AMERICAN SOCIETY FOR BIOCHEMISTRY AND MOLECULAR BIOLOGY
AMERICAN SOCIETY OF HOSPITAL PHARMACISTS
AMERICAN VETERINARY MEDICAL ASSOCIATION
CARDIOVASCULAR CREDENTIALING INTERNATIONAL
CHICAGO PHYSICAL THERAPY ASSOCIATION
ILLINOIS ACADEMY OF PHYSICIAN ASSISTANTS
ILLINOIS SOCIETY OF HOSPITAL PHARMACISTS
MEDICAL GROUP MANAGEMENT ASSOCIATION
MEDICAL GROUP MANAGEMENT ASSOCIATION/SPRINGFIELD BRANCH
NATIONAL HEALTH COUNCIL
NATIONAL MEDICAL ASSOCIATION

## ABBOTT LABORATORIES
Abbott Park
Corporate Placement (AP6D)
North Chicago IL 60064
Contact Michael Omelanuk, Manager of Corporate Placement. Manufactures a wide variety of health care products, including pharmaceuticals, hospital products, diagnostic products, chemicals, and nutritional products. Common positions at this facility include: Accountant; Attorney; Biochemist; Biologist; Chemist; Computer Programmer; Biomedical Engineer; Chemical Engineer; Civil Engineer; Electrical Engineer; Mechanical Engineer; Financial Analyst; Personnel & Labor Relations Specialist; Systems Analyst. Principal educational backgrounds sought: Accounting; Biology; Business Administration; Chemistry; Computer Science; Engineering; Personnel/Industrial Relations. Company benefits include: medical insurance; dental insurance; pension plan; life insurance; tuition assistance; disability coverage; profit sharing; employee discounts; savings plan. Corporate headquarters location. Operations at this facility include: divisional headquarters; manufacturing; research/development; administration; service; sales. New York Stock Exchange.

## ALBERTO-CULVER CO.
2525 Armitage Avenue
Melrose Park IL 60160
708/450-3000
Contact Cindy Lang, Manager of Staffing. Develops, manufactures and promotes personal use products.

## ALTON MEMORIAL HOSPITAL
1 Memorial Drive
Alton IL 62002
618/463-7320
Contact N. Dawn Wakeford, Manager of Human Resources. A major St. Louis area general acute care hospital. Common positions include: Health Care RN; OT; PT; MT. Principal educational backgrounds sought: Appropriate health care major. Internships offered. Company benefits include: medical insurance; dental insurance; pension plan; life insurance; tuition assistance; disability coverage; savings plan; TSA. Corporate headquarters location: St. Louis, MO. Parent company: Christian Health Services.

## ALTON MENTAL HEALTH CENTER
4500 College Avenue
Alton IL 62002
618/465-5593
Contact Joe Foehrkolv, Head of Personnel. A major metropolitan St. Louis medical facility, specializing in treatment of psychiatric developmental disabilities. Employs over 300.

## AMERICAN DENTAL ASSOCIATION
211 E. Chicago Ave.
Chicago IL 60611-9985
312/440-2500
Contact Thomas Dorsch, Director of Human Resources. A professional association serving the dental community.

## AMERICAN HOSPITAL ASSOCIATION
840 N. Lake Shore Drive
Chicago IL 60611
312/280-6092
Contact Cal Gilbert, Recruitment Manager. A $50 million organization serving the medical industry.

## BAXTER HEALTHCARE
One Baxter Parkway
Deerfield IL 60015
708/948-2000
Contact Robert DeBaun, Corporate Recruitment Director. A multinational manufacturer and distributor of a wide range of products and services used primarily in the health care field. Sells domestically and internationally to hospitals, clinical and medical research laboratories, medical and dental offices, rehabilitation centers, nursing homes, and related facilities and institutions. Company operates in three domestic market segments (Hospital, Laboratory, Medical Specialties), and one international market segment. A small sampling of the company's products include disposable medical and surgical instruments, hospital apparel and furniture, disposable plastic products, food service products and systems, blood-typing serums, laboratory controls, specialty glassware, diagnostic reagents and associated instrumentation, a wide range of medical and dental devices and instruments, diagnostic equipment, prosthetic devices, plastic lenses, intravenous fluids and fluid delivery systems, and ethical pharmaceuticals, Corporate headquarters location. International. New York Stock Exchange.

## BEVERLY FARM FOUNDATION INC.
6301 Humbert Road
Godfrey Il 62035
618/466-0367
Contact Rebecca Hutt, Personnel Director. A residential care facility for mentally handicapped children and adults from ages 5 to 85. Employs over 200.

## CENTREVILLE TOWNSHIP HOSPITAL
5900 Bond Avenue
Centerville IL 62207
618/332-3060
Contact Administrative Assistant. A major area medical facility. Employs over 300.

## HELENE CURTIS INDUSTRIES, INC.
325 North Wells
Chicago IL 60610
312/661-0222
Contact Vice President, Human Resources. Operates in beauty & hair products, & sealing products.

## DAMON LABS
3231 South Euclid
Berwyn IL 60402
312/282-9500
Contact Georgianna Casey, Personnel Manager. An around-the-clock clinical testing lab.

## FOUR FOUNTAINS CONVALESCENT
101 S. Belt West
Belleville IL 62220
618/277-7700
Contact Personnel Department. A major area skilled nursing care facility. Employs over 100.

## FOXMEYER
520 East North Avenue
Carol Stream IL 60188
708/681-5300
Contact Personnel. A wholesaler of drugs, sundries and assorted health care products.

## HUMISTON-KEELING, INC.
233 East Erie Street
Chicago, IL 60611
312/943-6066
Contact Personnel. A wholesale pharmaceutical distributor.

## IMCERA GROUP
2315 Sanders Road
Northbrook IL 60062
708/564-8600
Contact Sandra E. Doran, Manager, Administration. Fortune 300 company. Involved in medical products, animal health and specialty chemicals. Common positions include: Accountant; Attorney; Computer Programmer;

Financial Analyst. Principal educational backgrounds sought: Accounting; Business Administration; Computer Science; Finance. Company benefits include: medical insurance; dental insurance; pension plan; life insurance; tuition assistance. Corporate headquarters location.

## MEDLINE INDUSTRIES
1 Medline Place
Mundelein IL 60060
708/949-5500
Contact Personnel. A leading manufacturer and distributor of hospital supplies.

## MEMORIAL HOSPITAL
4501 North Park Drive
Belleville IL 62223
618/233-7750
Contact Barbara Nicely, Director of Personnel. A major St. Louis general hospital with 346 adult and pediatric beds and 32 cribs.

## PACKARD INSTRUMENT COMPANY
2200 Warrenville Road
Downers Grove IL 60515
708/969-6000
Contact Manager, Human Resources. A division of Canberra Industries, Inc. (Meriden, CT). Company manufactures biomedical instruments such as the scintillation gamma counter (tests blood for disease). Sells to hospitals and universities. Corporate headquarters location: Meriden, CT. International. Company benefits include: medical, dental, and life insurance; pension plan; tuition assistance; disability coverage; profit sharing; savings plan. Parent company: Canberra Industries. Operations at this facility include: manufacturing; research/development; service. Common positions include: Chemist; Electrical Engineer; Mechanical Engineer; Electronics Technician. Principal educational backgrounds sought: Business Administration; Engineering; Liberal Arts.

## PITMAN-MOORE, INC.
421 E. Hawley Street
Mundelein IL 60060
708/949-3300
Contact George Hyland, Manager, Human Resources. A leader in the animal health and nutrition businesses worldwide and the nation's largest supplier of feed-grade phosphates and potassium products. Common positions include: Accountant; Biochemist; Biologist; Computer Programmer; Customer Service Representative; Marketing Specialist; Systems Analyst. Principal educational backgrounds sought: Accounting; Biology; Computer Science; Marketing.

## RESPIRATORY CARE INC. (RCI)
900 West University Drive
Arlington Heights IL 60004
708/259-7400
Contact Althea Schuler, Human Resource Manager. Specialized manufacturer of sterile disposable products for respiratory therapy. Common positions include: Accountant; Blue-Collar Worker Supervisor; Buyer; Computer Programmer; Credit Manager; Customer Service Representative; Draftsperson; Biomedical Engineer; Chemical Engineer; Electrical Engineer; Industrial Engineer; Mechanical Engineer; Department Manager; General Manager; Operations/Production Manager; Purchasing Agent; Quality Control Supervisor; Transportation & Traffic Specialist. Principal educational backgrounds sought: Accounting; Business Administration; Chemistry; Computer Science; Engineering; Liberal Arts. Company benefits include: medical insurance; dental insurance; pension plan; life insurance; tuition assistance; disability coverage; employee discounts. Corporate headquarters location: Temecula, CA. Parent company: Hudson Respiratory Care Inc. Operations at this facility include: manufacturing; research/development; administration; service; sales.

## ST. ANTHONY'S HOSPITAL
P.O. Box 340
Alton IL 62002-0340
618/463-5151
Contact Personnel Director. A major Southern Illinois general hospital.

## ST. CLEMENT HOSPITAL
325 Spring Street
Red Bud IL 62278
618/282-3831
Contact Human Resource Director. A St. Louis/Illinois area general hospital. Common positions include: Accountant; Administrator; Credit Manager; Personnel and Labor Relations; Purchasing Agent; RNs; Radiology Technicians; Lab Technicians. Educational backgrounds sought: Business Administration; Finance; Nursing; Health Care. Company benefits include: medical insurance; pension plan; life insurance; tuition assistance; disability coverage; employee discounts; savings plan. Corporate headquarters location: O'Fallon, IL. Parent company ASC Health System. Operations at this facility include: administration; service.

## ST. ELIZABETH'S HOSPITAL
211 South 3rd Street
Belleville IL 62222
618/234-2120
Contact Norman Theisman, Personnel Director. A major Southern Illinois general hospital.

## ST. JOSEPH HOSPITAL
1515 Main Street
Highland IL 62249
618/654-7421
Contact Kim Kampwerth, Personnel Assistant. A major Southern Illinois general hospital. Company benefits include: medical, dental, and life insurance; pension plan; tuition assistance; disability coverage.

## ST. PAUL'S HOMES FOR THE AGED
1021 West E Street
Belleville IL 62220
618/233-2095
Contact Arthur H. Peters, Administrator. Residential and nursing care for the aged.

## G.D. SEARLE & COMPANY
5200 Old Orchard Road
Skokie IL 60677
708/982-7000
Contact Human Resources. Engaged in four groups: Research and Development, Pharmaceutical/Consumer Products, Medical Products, and the Optical Group. Products include ethical pharmaceuticals, healthcare products, high-purity compressed gases, eyewear, lenses and sunglasses. Corporate headquarters location. International. New York Stock Exchange.

## WESLEY-JESSEN CORP.
400 West Superior Street
Chicago IL 60610
312/751-6200
Contact Jeff Mustardo, Employment Manager. Develops, manufactures and markets contact lenses and lens care products. A wholly owned subsidiary of Schering-Plough Corporation (Madison, NJ). Common positions include: Accountant; Administrator; Blue-Collar Worker Supervisor; Buyer; Chemist; Computer Programmer; Credit Manager; Customer Service Representative; Draftsperson; Industrial Engineer; Mechanical Engineer; Financial Analyst; Industrial Manager; Marketing Specialist; Personnel & Labor Relations Specialist; Purchasing Agent; Quality Control Supervisor; Sales Representative; Statistician; Systems Analyst; Technical Writer/Editor. Principal educational backgrounds sought: Accounting; Chemistry; Communications; Computer Science; Plastics Engineering; Finance; Liberal Arts; Marketing. Internships offered. Company benefits include: medical insurance; dental insurance; pension plan; life insurance; tuition assistance; disability coverage; profit sharing; employee discounts; savings plan. Divisional headquarters location. Operations include: manufacturing; research/development; administration; sales. Corporate headquarters location: Madison, NJ. New York Stock Exchange.

**WOOD RIVER TOWNSHIP HOSPITAL**
Edwardsville Road
Wood River IL 62095
618/254-3821
Contact Personnel Department. A major general hospital.

## HIGHLY DIVERSIFIED

**FARLEY INDUSTRIES**
233 S. Wacker Drive
Chicago IL 60606
312/876-7000
Contact Human Resources Director. A diversified holding company.

**ITEL**
2 North Riverside Plaza
Chicago IL 60606
312/902-1515
Contact Gloria Waber, Manager of Corporate Relations. A company with 4 current sources of cash flow: railcar leasing, marine dredging & wiring systems products for voice data and video communications. Common positions include: Accountant; Financial Analyst. Principal educational backgrounds sought· Accounting; Business Administration; Finance. Company benefits include: medical insurance; pension plan; life insurance; tuition assistance; disability coverage; savings plan. Corporate headquarters location.

**NEWELL**
29 East Stephenson Street
Freeport IL 61032
815/235-4171
Contact Manager, Corporate Recruitment. Newell Company is a manufacturer of staple, volume comsumer and industrial products for the volume purchaser. Manufacturing is decentralized by product line. Common positions include: Accountant; Administrator; Credit Manager; Financial Analyst; General Manager; Personnel & Labor Relations Specialist; Systems Analyst; Technical Writer/Editor. Principal educational backgrounds sought: Accounting; Business Administration; Computer Science; Finance; Mathematics. Company benefits include: medical, dental, and life insurance; pension plan; tuition assistance; disability coverage; profit sharing; employee discounts; credit union. Operations at this facility include: administration. New York Stock Exchange.

## ST. LOUIS NATIONAL STOCK YARDS COMPANY
P.O. Box 97
National Stock Yards IL 62071
618/271-2405
Contact Personnel Department. A diversified livestock company engaged in a variety of activities, including livestock marketing; the operation of public stock yards and dry bulk warehousing; the operation of a switching railroad system; the operation of area restaraunts; and the sale of real estate.

## UNR INDUSTRIES, INC.
332 South Michigan Avenue
Chicago IL 60604
312/341-1234
Contact Personnel Department. Several area locations including: Evanston, IL, and Hammond, Paris and Peoria, IN. A diversified corporation with five operating groups: Industrial Products, Commercial Products, Consumer Products, Communications Products and Transportation Products. The first group manufactures and sells mechanical and structural electric resistance-welded steel tubing. The commercial products group manufactures and sells grocery shopping carts, self-service luggage carts, office and other carts and continuous shelving systems. The consumer products group includes the wholesale and retail sale of Unarco-West Corporation. Sales include name brand appliances, TV and sound equipment. Also, manufactures roller skate wheels, outdoor barbecue grills, a line of casual indoor/outdoor furniture, and stainless steel sinks. The communications group includes the manufacture and marketing of towers with related accessories used principally to support communications equipment for microwave transmissions, broadcasting, home television and amateur broadcasting. The transportation group includes the manufacture and sale of loading equipment and box car doors for railroads. Corporate headquarters location. New York Stock Exchange.

## HOTEL AND RESTAURANT RELATED

For more information on professional employment opportunities in the hotel and restaurant related industries, contact the following professional and trade organizations, as listed beginning on page 315:

THE AMERICAN HOTEL AND MOTEL ASSOCIATION
COUNCIL ON HOTEL, RESTAURANT AND INSTITUTIONAL
    EDUCATION
THE EDUCATION FOUNDATION OF THE NATIONAL RESTAURANT
    ASSOCIATION

**ARA SERVICES**
2000 Spring Road, Suite 300
Oak Brook IL 60521
708/572-2800
Contact Mary Jo McLaughlin, Human Resources Director. A leading provider of institutional dining services.

**CARSON PIRIE SCOTT**
1 South State Street
Chicago IL 60603
312/641-8000
Contact Mark Case, College Recruitment. Provides hotel management and direct mail marketing.

**CHURCH'S CHICKEN INC.**
10600 West Higgins Road, Suite 512
Wooddale IL 60018
708/699-9980
Contact Regional Personnel Management. A chain of fast food restaurants specializing in fried chicken.

**COLLINSVILLE HOLIDAY INN**
1000 Eastport Plaza Drive
Collinsville IL 62234
618/345-2800
Contact Eva Kisow, Personnel Department. Operates a full service hotel as part of the Holiday Inn chain, whose operations include the management of more than 1,750 company-owned and franchised hotels, gaming operations, restaurants, and a sea transportation subsidiary. Corporate headquarters location: Memphis, TN. Employs over 100.

**COLLINSVILLE MAC INC./**
**McDONALD'S RESTAURANT OFFICE**
3673 Highway 111
Granite City IL 62040
618/931-2100
Contact Dave Embry, Head of Operations. A regional home office which owns and operates 15 area fast food restaurants. Parent company is a worldwide developer, operator, franchisor, and servicer of a system of restaurants which process, package, and sell a limited menu of fast foods. Internationally, company is one of the largest restaurant chains, and the largest food service organization, operating more than 6,000 McDonald's restaurants in all 50 states and in more than 25 foreign countries. Corporate headquarters location: Oak Brook, IL. New York Stock Exchange. Employs over 100.

## DRAKE HOTEL
140 East Walton Place
Chicago IL 60611
312/787-2200
Contact Miss Bodell, Human Resources Director. A Hilton International hotel and restaurant.

## EXECUTIVE HOUSE HOTEL
71 East Wacker Drive
Chicago IL 60601
312/346-7100
Contact Margaret Lord, Personnel Director. A major Chicago hotel.

## FABER ENTERPRISES
55 E. Monroe Street
Chicago IL 60603
312/558-8989
Contact Personnel Manager. A chain of restuarants, retail drug and gift stores.

## FISCHER'S RESTAURANT
2100 W. Main Street
Belleville IL 62223
618/233-1131
Contact Vel Crabtree, Manager. A major area restaurant which also provides catering services. Employs over 100.

## HOLIDAY INNS, INC.
300 East Ohio Street
Chicago IL 60611
708/932-9600
Contact Regional Human Resources Director. One of the world's largest hotel chains.

## HYATT REGENCY CHICAGO
151 East Wacker Drive
Chicago IL 60601
312/565-1234
Contact Carla Thomas, Director of Human Resources. A regional office for the Hyatt chain of hotels.

## McDONALD'S CORPORATION
One McDonald's Plaza
Oak Brook IL 60521
708/385-6500
Corporate headquarters location of the internationally recognized fast food restaurant chain.

**PHEASANT RUN INC.**
4051 East Main Street
St. Charles IL 60174-5200
708/584-6300
Contact Debbie Edwards, Personnel Director. Operates a hotel. Corporate headquarters location. Common positions include: Department Manager. Company benefits include: medical insurance.

**RAMADA HOTEL O'HARE**
6600 North Mannheim Road
Wooddale IL 60018
708/827-5131
Contact Terry Lopez, Personnel Director. Operates a major hotel as part of the international hotel chain. Parent company: Ramada Inns Inc. Common positions include: Accountant; Credit Manager; Hotel Manager/Assistant Manager; Department Manager; Personnel & Labor Relations Specialist; Purchasing Agent; Sales Representative. Principal educational backgrounds sought: Accounting; Business Administration; Communications; Finance; Liberal Arts; Marketing. Company benefits include: medical insurance; dental insurance; pension plan; life insurance; tuition assistance; disability coverage; profit sharing; employee discounts; savings plan; stock options. Corporate headquarters location: Phoenix, AZ. New York Stock Exchange.

**RITZ CARLTON HOTEL**
160 East Pearson Street
Chicago IL 60611
312/266-1000
Contact Darren Oliver, Director of Human Resources. An exclusive Chicago hotel with convention and banquet facilities. A subsidiary of Four Seasons Hotels, Ltd. Common positions include: Accountant; Administrator; Credit Manager; Customer Service Representative; Hotel Manager/Assistant Manager; Department Manager; General Manager; Management Trainee; Marketing Specialist; Personnel & Labor Relations Specialist; Purchasing Agent; Sales Representative. Principal educational backgrounds sought: Business Administration; Hotel Administration; Marketing. Company benefits include: medical insurance; dental insurance; pension plan; life insurance; tuition assistance; disability coverage; profit sharing; employee discounts; savings plan. Operations at this facility include: service; sales. Corporate headquarters location: Toronto, Canada.

**THE WESTIN HOTEL, CHICAGO**
909 North Michigan Avenue
Chicago IL 60611
312/943-7200
Contact Human Resources. A 740-room hotel with 2 restaurants, 24 hour room service; health club; 18 fully equipped meeting rooms; two ballrooms; parking facilities. Located on Chicago's Magnificent Mile. Common positions include: Accountant; Hotel Manager/Assistant Manager; Sales

Representative; Restaurant Manager. Educational backgrounds sought: Accounting; Business Administration; Marketing. Company benefits include: medical insurance; dental insurance; pension plan; life insurance; disability coverage; savings plan. Corporate headquarters location: Seattle, WA. Parent company: Westin Hotels & Resorts. Operations include: administration; service; sales.

**TRI-R VENDING SERVICE**
1401 West North Avenue
Chicago IL 60622
312/235-9100
Contact Ms. Shelley Hundley, Personnel Director. Provides vending and food services throughout the Chicago area. Corporate headquarters location.

## INSURANCE

For more information on professional employment opportunities in the insurance industry, contact the following professional and trade organizations, as listed beginning on page 315:

ALLIANCE OF AMERICAN INSURERS
AMERICAN COUNCIL OF LIFE INSURANCE
AMERICAN INSURANCE ASSOCIATION
INSURANCE INFORMATION INSTITUTE
INSURANCE INFORMATION INSTITUTE OF CHICAGO
NATIONAL ASSOCIATION OF LIFE UNDERWRITERS
SOCIETY OF ACTUARIES

**AON CORPORATION**
123 North Wacker Drive, 14th Floor
Chicago IL 60606
312/701-3200
Contact Rebecca Hogue, Director of Corporate Staffing. A leading metropolitan Chicago insurance agency specializing in accident and health coverage but also provides life, property, and casualty insurance and brokerage and related services. Common positions include: Accountant; Actuary; Administrator; Claim Representative; Customer Service Representative; Branch Manager; Department Manager; Personnel & Labor Relations Specialist. Company benefits include: medical, dental, and life insurance; pension plan; tuition assistance; disability coverage; profit sharing; employee discounts; savings plan. Corporate headquarters location. New York Stock Exchange.

## ALLSTATE INSURANCE CO.
Allstate Plaza South, Building G1C
Northbrook IL 60062
708/402-7182
Contact Deborah Cross, Employment Manager. One of the nation's largest insurance companies.

## BANKERS LIFE AND CASUALTY
4400 W. Lawrence Avenue
Chicago IL 60630
312/777-7000
Contact Director of Human Resources. Specializes in life and health insurance policies.

## BENEFIT TRUST LIFE INSURANCE CO.
400 Field Drive
Lake Forest IL 60045
708/615-1500
Contact Diane Peterson, Manager of Human Resources. A legal reserve life insurance company with operations in every state and the District of Columbia. Issues a wide variety of individual and group life, disability, annuity, hospital and medical policies, as well as administrative service-only arrangements for larger groups. Common positions include: Accountant; Actuary; Claim Representative; Customer Service Representative; Marketing Specialist; Systems Analyst; Technical Writer/Editor; Underwriter; Programmer Analyst; Software Engineer. Principal educational backgrounds sought: Accounting; Business Administration; Computer Science; Liberal Arts; Mathematics. Company benefits include: medical insurance; dental insurance; pension plan; life insurance; disability coverage; savings plan. Corporate headquarters location. Operations at this location include: administration; service; sales.

## CNA INSURANCE COMPANIES
CNA Plaza, Floor 41S
Chicago IL 60685
312/822-4100
Contact Employment Manager. A multiline insurer underwriting a variety of policies.

## THE COUNTRY COMPANIES
1701 Towanda Avenue
Bloomington IL 61701
309/557-2786
Contact Ruth Woeful, Personnel. A multi-line insurance and financial services organization.

**FEDERAL KEMPER INSURANCE COMPANY**
2001 East Mound Road
Decatur IL 62526
217/877-9510
Contact Linda Koter, Personnel Manager. An insurance agency.

**FOURTH DEARBORN LIFE INSURANCE COMPANY**
233 North Michigan Avenue
Chicago IL 60601
Contact Karen Metzger, Personnel Director. Group life insurance company. Multiple area locations. Common positions include: Accountant; Actuary; Attorney; Claim Representative; Customer Service Representative; Insurance Agent/Broker; Branch Manager; General Manager; Marketing Specialist; Personnel and Labor Relations Specialist; Sales Representative; Underwriter. Principal educational backgrounds sought include: Accounting; Business Administration; Finance; Marketing. Company benefits include: medical insurance; dental insurance; pension plan; life insurance; tuition assistance; disability coverage; 401k plan. Corporate headquarters location. Operations at this facility include: administration; service; sales.

**ILLINOIS FARMERS INSURANCE COMPANY**
2245 Sequoia Drive
Aurora IL 60507
708/801-3200
Contact Mr. J.R. Radecki, Human Resources Manager. A subsidiary of Farmers Insurance Company, Los Angeles, CA. Farmers maintains a regional office and four branch claims offices in the area. Handles property, life, and casualty insurance. Corporate headquarters location. Common positions at this facility include: Accountant; Claim Representative; Management Trainee; Underwriter. Principal educational backgrounds sought: Accounting; Business Administration; Finance; Marketing; All majors qualify. Company benefits include: medical insurance; pension plan; life insurance; tuition assistance; disability coverage; profit sharing. Regional headquarters.

**LIBERTY MUTUAL INSURANCE GROUP**
555 West Pierce Road
Itasca IL 60143-2691
708/250-7100
Contact Roland Stanton, Director of Human Resources. Several area locations including: Lisle, Des Plaines, Matteson. A full-line insurance firm offering life, medical, and business insurance, as well as investment and retirement plans. Common positions include: Accountant; Administrator; Attorney; Claim Representative; Computer Programmer; Electrical Engineer; Industrial Engineer; Mechanical Engineer; Financial Analyst; Insurance Agent/Broker; Management Trainee; Sales Representative; Systems Analyst; Underwriter. Principal educational backgrounds sought: Accounting; Art/Design; Business Administration; Communications;

Computer Science; Economics; Engineering; Finance; Liberal Arts; Marketing; Mathematics. Company benefits include: medical, dental, and life insurance; pension plan; tuition assistance; disability coverage; employee discounts; savings plan. Corporate headquarters location: Boston, MA. Operations at this facility include: divisional headquarters (midwest only).

**NORTH AMERICAN COMPANY
FOR LIFE & HEALTH INSURANCE**
222 South Riverside Plaza
Chicago IL 60606
312/648-7600
Contact Mary Bresnahan, Staffing and Development Specialist. Writes a wide variety of individual life insurance policies. Common positions include: Accountant; Actuary; Attorney; Claim Representative; Computer Programmer; Customer Service Representative; Purchasing Agent; Systems Analyst; Underwriter; Insurance Clerk. Principal educational backgrounds sought: Accounting; Business Administration; Communications; Computer Science; Finance; Liberal Arts; Marketing; Mathematics. Company benefits include: medical insurance; dental insurance; pension plan; life insurance; tuition assistance; disability coverage; employee discounts. Corporate headquarters location. Operations at this facility include: administration; service; sales.

**SAFECO INSURANCE COMPANIES**
2900 West Higgins Road, Suite 1100
Hoffman Estates IL 60196
708/490-2900
Contact Christopher Higman, Personnel Manager. An insurance company offering personal lines insurance, homeowners and auto; commercial insurance, all lines in property and casualty; and life and health insurance products. Common positions include: Attorney; Claim Representative; Customer Service Representative; Financial Analyst; Management Trainee; Sales Representative; Underwriter. Principal educational backgrounds sought: Accounting; Art/Design; Biology; Business Administration; Chemistry; Communications; Computer Science; Economics; Engineering; Finance; Geology; Liberal Arts; Marketing; Mathematics; Physics; all educational backgrounds accepted. Training programs and internships available. Company benefits include: medical insurance; dental insurance; pension plan; life insurance; disability coverage; profit sharing; employee discounts; savings plan. Corporate headquarters location: Seattle, WA. Operations at this facility include: regional and divisional headquarters

**SENTRY INSURANCE COMPANY**
75 Executive Drive
Aurora IL 60504
312/844-8105,800-323-0863
Contact Thomas Skillman, Human Resources Manager. Concentrates on the business insurance market. Sentry is a multi-line insurer that primary

markets are: hardware stores, autoparts stores, printers, metal workers, and other small businesses. Common positions include: Insurance Agent/Broker; Sales Representative. Principal educational backgrounds sought: Business Administration; Communications; Finance; Liberal Arts. Company benefits include: medical, dental, and life insurance; pension plan; disability coverage; profit sharing; savings plan. Corporate headquarters location: Stevens Point, WI. Operations at this facility include: divisional headquarters.

**TICOR TITLE INSURANCE**
203 North LaSalle Street, Suite 1400
Chicago IL 60601
312/621-5128
Contact Gail A. Beicher, Personnel Representative. Several area locations, including Schaumberg, Joliet, and Oaklawn. Specializes in real estate title insurance and escrow services. Corporate headquarters location: Los Angeles, CA

**TRAVELERS INSURANCE COMPANY**
100 Park Street
Naperville IL 60566-1029
708/961-8700
Contact Ralph Schulz, Associate Personnel Administrator. One of the world's largest investor-owned financial service organizations. Offers many different financial services including every principal form of insurance for life, health and property. Corporate headquarters location: Hartford, CT. New York Stock Exchange. International.

**UNITED EQUITABLE INSURANCE GROUP**
7373 North Cicero
Lincolnwood IL 60646
708/677-4800
Contact Human Resources Office. Provides accident, health, and life insurance as well as extended service contracts for automobiles. Common positions include: Accountant; Actuary; Claim Representative; Computer Programmer; Customer Service Representative; Financial Analyst; Marketing Specialist; Systems Analyst; Underwriter. Principal educational backgrounds sought: Accounting; Business Administration; Computer Science; Marketing; Mathematics; Actuarial Science. Company benefits include: medical insurance; dental insurance; life insurance; tuition assistance; long-term disability coverage; profit sharing; credit union. Corporate headquarters location.

**WAUSAU INSURANCE COMPANIES**
901 Warrenville Road, Suite 500
Lisle IL 60532-4307
708/719-9700
Contact James Hofman, Personnel Specialist. Regional office for major insurance company; offers a full line of business insurance services in 17

regional offices and 200 service offices across the United States. Common positions include: Claim Representative; Sales Representative; Underwriter. Principal educational backgrounds sought: Business Administration; Communications; Economics; Finance; Marketing. Company benefits include: medical, dental, and life insurance; pension plan; tuition assistance; disability coverage; savings plan. Corporate headquarters location: Wausau, WI. Operations at this facility include: regional headquarters.

**ZURICH-AMERICAN INSURANCE COMPANIES**
1400 American Lane
Schaumburg IL 60196
708/605-6000
Contact Dan Borbas, Vice-President/Human Resources. A large international insurance company with worldwide operations. Corporate headquarters location.

## LEGAL SERVICES

For more information on professional employment opportunities in the legal services industries, contact the following professional and trade organizations, as listed beginning on page 315:

AMERICAN BAR ASSOCIATION
FEDERAL BAR ASSOCIATION
NATIONAL ASSOCIATION FOR LAW PLACEMENT
NATIONAL ASSOCIATION OF LEGAL ASSISTANTS
NATIONAL FEDERATION OF PARALEGAL ASSOCIATIONS
NATIONAL PARALEGAL ASSOCIATION

**AMERICAN BAR ASSOCIATION**
750 N. Lake Shore Drive
Chicago IL 60611
Contact Manager of Employment. The world's largest voluntary professional association.

**ARNSTEIN AND LEHR**
120 South Riverside Plaza, Suite 1200
Chicago IL 60606
312/876-7100
Contact Jackie Van Fossan, Personnel Director. A general practice legal services firm.

**BAKER & McKENZIE**
One Prudential Plaza
130 East Randolph Street
Chicago IL 60601
312/861-2905
Contact Ann Rohaly, Recruiter. A metropolitan Chicago law firm.

**CHAPMAN AND CUTLER**
111 West Monroe Street, 18th Floor
Chicago IL 60603
312/845-3000
Contact Linda O'Donnell, Personnel Director. A leading area general practice law firm.

**GARDNER, CARTON, & DOUGLAS**
Quaker Tower, Suite 3400
321 North Clark Street
Chicago IL 60610-4795
312/644-3000
Contact Lynn Sanchez, Assistant Personnel Director. A Chicago area law firm concentrating on corporate and real estate law.

**KECK, MAHIN, & CATE**
8300 Sears Tower
233 S. Wacker Drive
Chicago IL 60606-6589
312/876-3400
Contact Personnel Director. A metropolitan Chicago general practice law firm

**LORD, BISSELL, & BROOK**
115 South LaSalle Street, Suite 3400
Chicago IL 60603
312/443-0700
Contact Jean Bouslog, Personnel Director. A leading Chicago law firm specializing in corporate law.

**PETERSON, ROSS, SCHLOERB & SEIDEL**
200 East Randolph Street
Suite 7300
Amoco Building
Chicago IL 60601
312/861-1400
Contact Laura Geyer, Manager of Personnel. An area law firm offering a variety of legal services. Common positions include: Accountant. Company benefits include: medical, dental, and life insurance; pension plan; disability coverage; savings plan. Corporate headquarters location. Operations at this facility include: service.

**RUDNICK & WOLFE**
203 North LaSalle Street, Suite 1500
Chicago IL 60601
312/368-4000
Contact Personnel. A metropolitan Chicago law firm

**VEDDER, PRICE, KAUFMAN, & KAMMHOLZ**
222 North LaSalle Street, Suite 2600
Chicago IL 60601-1003
312/609-7500
Contact Leslie Thomas, Personnel. A firm engaged in a variety of legal services including labor, litigation, corporate, health, and pro bono law.

## MANUFACTURING: MISCELLANEOUS CONSUMER

**ACCO INTERNATIONAL**
770 South Acco Plaza
Wheeling IL 60090
708/541-9500. Contact Joan Petitt, Human Resources. Manufacturer of school, office and computer supplies.

**ACE HARDWARE CORPORATION**
2200 Kennsington Court
Oak Brook IL 60521
708/990-6600
Contact Don Wallner, Human Resources Representative. A wholesaler of hardware and related products.

**ARTRA GROUP**
500 Central Avenue
Northfield IL 60093
708/441-6650
Contact Personnel Director.

**BALLY MANUFACTURING/GAMING DIVISION**
90 O'Leary Drive
Bensenville IL 60106
708/860-7777
Contact Scott D. Robinson, Director of Human Resources/Administration. A manufacturer of electronic/mechanical slot machines, and gaming equipment. Divisional headquarters location. common positions include: Accountant; Blue Collar Worker Supervisor; Buyer; Computer Programmer; Credit Manager; Customer Service Representative; Draftsperson; Electrical Engineer; Industrial Engineer; Mechanical Engineer; Operations/Production Manager; Marketing Specialist; Personnel & Labor Relations Specialist;

Purchasing Agent; Quality Control Supervisor; Systems Analyst; Transportation & Traffic Specialist. Principal educational backgrounds sought: Accounting; Computer Science; Engineering; Finance. Company benefits include: medical, dental, and life insurance; pension plan; tuition assistance; disability coverage; profit sharing; employee discounts; savings plan. Corporate headquarters location: chicago, IL. Operations at this facility include: divisional headquarters; manufacturing; research/development; administration; service; sales/New York Stock Exchange.

**BRUNSWICK CORPORATION**
One Brunswick Plaza
Skokie IL 60077-1089
708/470-4700
Contact Personnel. One of the nation's leading manufacturers of recreational equipment. Employs 28,400.

**CALSTAR CORPORATION**
1191 South Wheeling Road
Wheeling Il 60090
708/541-9000
Contact Marilyn Alexander, Personnel Manager. Manufactures and sells paint.

**CHICAGO LOCK COMPANY**
4311 West Belmont Avenue
Chicago IL 60641
312/282-7177
Contact Victor Novak, Personnel Director. Manufactures a variety of locks.

**COUNSELOR COMPANY**
2107 Kishwaukee Street
Rockford IL 61101
815/968-9621
Contact Tim Jahnke, Director of Employee Relations. A manufacturer of digital and mechanical bathroom scales.

**CUMMINS ALLISON CORPORATION**
891 Feehanville Drive
Mt. Prospect IL 60056
312/299-9550
Contact J.A. Panarale, Vice President, Employee Relations. Manufacturer of office products, mostly for banking use.

**DESOTO, INC.**
1700 South Mount Prospect Road
Box 5030
Des Plaines IL 60017
708/391-9000
Contact Personnel Representative. A diversified manufacturer of coatings (consumer paints and industrial coatings), and specialty products.

**EMPIRE STOVE COMPANY**
918 Freeburg Avenue
P.O. Box 529
Belleville IL 62222
618/233-7420
Contact Betty Senulis, Personnel Director. Manufacturers of gas heating appliances. Employs over 100.

**EUREKA COMPANY**
1201 E. Bell Street
Bloomington IL 61701
309/823-5285
Contact Martha E. Campbell, Employment Manager. A manufacturer of vacuum cleaners.

**HAEGER POTTERIES**
7 Maiden Lane
Dundee IL 60118
708/426-3441
contact Lorraine Ritt, Personnel Manager. Manufactures ceramic artware and decorations.

**KLEIN TOOLS, INC.**
7200 McCormick Boulevard
Chicago IL 60645
312/588-6821
Contact Tom Dragon, Industrial Relations Manager. A manufacturer of utility tools & protective equipment.

**LAKEWOOD ENGINEERING & MANUFACTURING COMPANY**
520 North Sacramento Boulevard
Chicago IL 60612
312/722-4300
Contact Bob Brueck, Director of Personnel. Manufacturers of ventilating fans, electric heaters, etc.

**LEEWARDS**
1200 St. Charles Street
Elgin IL 60120

Contact Mark Walters, Recruiting Manager. A major manufacturer and retailer of crafts and hobby crafts. Common positions include: Buyer; Computer Programmer; Management Trainee. Company benefits include: medical, dental, and life insurance; tuition assistance; disability coverage; employee discounts. Corporate headquarters location. Operations at this facility include: regional headquarters; divisional headquarters; administration.

**LIGHTOLIER**
1600 Fleetwood Drive
Elgin IL 60123
312/742-2266
Contact David Waltmire, Personnel/Labor Relations. Manufacturer of quality lighting fixtures.

**LOCKE HOME PRODUCTS**
4200 St. Clair Avenue
P.O. Box 1040
East St. Louis IL 62204
618/271-1272
Contact Christine Bearden, Personnel Director. Manufacture heat stoves (wood & gas), and gas fired incinerators.

**MITEK CORPORATION**
One Mitek Plaza
Winslow IL 61089
815/367-3000
Contact Dave Roskam, Director, Human Resources. Engaged in the development, manufacuture, and marketing of automotive, home and professional loudspeakers. Common positions include: Accountant; Blue Collar Worker Supervisor; Buyer; Credit Manager; Customer Service Representative; Draftsperson; Electrical Engineer; Department Manager; General Manager; Operations/Production Manager; Makreting Specialist; Personnel & Labor Relations Specialist; Purchasing Agent; Quality Control Supervisor; Sales Representative; Systems Analyst; Transportation and Traffic Specialist. Principal educational backgrounds sought: Accounting; Art/Design; Business Administration; Communications; Computer Science; Engineering; Finance; Marketing. Company benefits include: medical and life insurance; tuition assistance; disability coverage; profit sharing; employee discounts; savings plan; 401k. Corporate headquarters location. Operations at this facility include: manufacturing; research/development; administration; sales; service.

## MOORE BUSINESS FORMS & SYSTEMS DIVISION
275 North Field Drive
Lake Forest IL 60045
708/615-6000
Contact Cindy Leitza, Manager of Personnel Services. National headquarters and administrative offices for the international manufacturer of business systems, forms, and equipment. Company has branches in 39 countries, and maintains 280 sales offices worldwide.

## NUARC COMPANY INC.
6200 West Howard Street
Niles IL 60648
708/967-4400
Contact Barbara Morgenstern, Personnel Director. Manufacturers of graphic art equipment. Corporate headquarters location.

## NYSTROM COMPANY
## A DIVISION OF HERFF JONES, INC.
3333 North Elston Avenue
Chicago IL 60618
312/463-1144. Contact Human Resources Department. Manufactures and publishes charts, maps, globes and other visual learning systems. Common positions include: Blue-Collar Worker Supervisor; Customer Service Representative; Geographer; Department Manager; Purchasing Agent; Sales Representative. Principal educational backgrounds sought: Business Administration; Geology; Marketing; Teaching. Company benefits include: medical insurance; dental insurance; life insurance; tuition assistance; profit sharing; employee discounts. Operations at this facility include: manufacturing; administration.

## OUTBOARD MARINE CORPORATION
100 Sea-Horse Drive
Waukegan IL 60085
708/689-5289
Contact Wayne Applegate, Personnel Director. Several area locations including: Galesburg. Engaged principally in the manufacture of powered products for leisure-time use. Three industry segments and their principal product names are: marine products, which includes Evinrude outboard motors, Johnson outboard motors, OMC stern drive inboard-outboard engines; power mowers, primarily Lawn-Boy rotary power mowers; and other products, which includes Cushman light industrial vehicles, Ryan turf care equipment, and miscellaneous products. Corporate headquarters location. International. New York Stock Exchange.

## R.S. OWENS AND COMPANY INC.
5535 North Lynch Avenue
Chicago IL 60630
312/282-6000

Contact Personnel Department. Manufactures trophies, plaques and awards. Common positions include: Blue-Collar Worker Supervisor; Credit Manager; Mechanical Engineer; Department Manager; Personnel & Labor Relations Specialist; Purchasing Agent; Quality Control Supervisor; Sales Representative. Principal educational backgrounds sought: Business Administration; Computer Science; Finance; Liberal Arts; Marketing. Company benefits include: medical insurance; life insurance; disability coverage; profit sharing; employee discounts; savings plan. Corporate, regional headquarters location. Operations at this facility include: manufacturing; administration; service; sales.

## PAYMASTER CORPORATION
1811 West Winnemac
Chicago IL 60640
312/878-9200
Contact Larry Hamilton, Personnel Director. Manufactures and sells check-writing machines and check protectors. Corporate headquarters location.

## QUASAR COMPANY
1325 Pratt Boulevard
Elk Grove Village IL 60007
708/228-6366
Contact Bill Schupp, Personnel Manager. Manufacturer of consumer electronic appliances such as televisions, microwave ovens, and video tape machines. A subsidiary of Matsushita Electronics Corporation of America. Corporate headquarters location.

## QUILL CORPORATION
100 South Schelter Road
Lincolnshire IL 60069
708/634-5713
Contact Personnel. Mail order office products distributor.

## RAM GOLF CORPORATION
2020 Indian Boundary Drive
Melrose Park IL 60160
708/681-5800
Contact Vicky Duff, Director of Personnel. Manufacturer of golf clubs, bags, balls, and related accessories. Corporate headquarters location. Common positions include: Accountant; Advertising Worker; Computer Programmer; Credit Manager; Marketing Specialist. Principal educational backgrounds sought: Accounting; Business Administration; Computer Science; Finance; Marketing. Company benefits include: medical and life insurance; pension plan; disability coverage; employee discounts; savings plan. Corporate headquarters location. Operations at this facility include: manufacturing.

## ROADMASTER CORPORATION
P.O. Box 344
Olney IL 62450
618/393-2991
Contact Carol Erwin, Personnel Supervisor. Manufactures bicycles, tricycles, and junior riding products for children; and fitness equipment. Other facility sites in Tyler, Texas and Delavan, Wisconsin. Common positions include: Accountant; Blue-Collar Worker Supervisor; Buyer; Chemist; Computer Programmer; Credit Manager; Customer Service Representative; Draftsperson; Industrial Engineer; Mechanical Engineer; Financial Analyst; Department Manager; Operations/Production Manager; Purchasing Agent; Quality Control Supervisor; Sales Representative; Systems Analyst; Technical Writer/Editor; Transporation & Traffic Specialist; Industrial Designer. Principal educational backgrounds sought: Accounting; Art/Design; Business Administration; Engineering; Finance; Marketing; Industrial Technology. Company benefits include: medical insurance; life insurance; tuition assistance; disability coverage; employee discounts. Corporate headquarters location. Operations at this facility include: manufacturing; quality administration; service; sales; accounting; marketing. NASDAQ.

## ROCK-OLA MANUFACTURING CORPORATION
313 South Rohlwing Road
Addison IL 60101
708/629-9200
Contact Bill Beckert, Director of Human Resources. Manufactures juke boxes and soda machines. Corporate headquarters location.

## SCHWINN BICYCLE COMPANY
217 North Jefferson
Chicago IL 60606
312/454-7400
Contact Brian D. Fiala, Vice President, Human Resources. Manufacturer and distributor of bicycles and exercisers. Common positions include: Accountant; Buyer; Computer Programmer; Credit Manager; Draftsperson; Industrial Engineer; Mechanical Engineer; Financial Analyst; Industrial Manager; Department Manager; Management Trainee; Marketing Specialist; Personnel & Labor Relations Specialist; Purchasing Agent; Systems Analyst. Principal educational backgrounds sought: Accounting; Art/Design; Business Administration; Computer Science; Engineering; Finance; Marketing. Internships offered. Company benefits include: medical insurance; pension plan; life insurance; tuition assistance; disability coverage; profit sharing; employee discounts. Corporate headquarters location. Operations at this facility include: national headquarters; administration.

## SERTA INC.
2800 River Road
Des Plaines IL 60018
312/699-9300

Contact Personnel. Headquarters of the major mattress and box springs manufacturer.

## SKIL CORPORATION
4300 West Peterson Avenue
Chicago IL 60646
312/286-7330
Contact Ellen S. Reese, Employee Relations Manager. Several area locations including: Skokie, and Elk Grove Village. Manufacturers of hand and power tools. A subsidiary of Emerson Electric Company. Corporate headquarters location. International. Common positions include: Accountant; Computer Programmer; Credit Manager; Customer Service Representative; Draftsperson; Electrical Engineer; Industrial Engineer; Mechanical Engineer; Financial Analyst; Marketing Specialist; Personnel & Labor Relations Specialist; Purchasing Agent; Quality Control Supervisor; Systems Analyst. Principal educational backgrounds sought: Accounting; Business Administration; Engineering; Marketing. Training programs offered; Internships offered. Company benefits include: medical, dental, and life insurance; pension plan; tuition assistance; disability coverage; employee discounts; savings plan. Corporate headquarters location. Parent company: Emerson Electric. Operations at this facility include: divisional headquarters; research/development; administration.

## SPACEMASTER
1400 North 25th Avenue
Melrose Park IL 60160
708/345-2500
Contact Linda Lazzaro, Personnel Director. Several area locations. Manufactures store fixtures, office furniture and library equipment. Corporate headquarters location.

## SPIEGEL INC.
1515 West 22nd Street
Oak Brook IL 60522
708/986-8800
Contact F. Malcolm Harris, Human Resources Director. A catalog merchandising company specializing in upscale merchandise for the home, as well as current fashion for women, men and children. Corporate headquarters location. Common positions include: Accountant; Advertising Worker; Architect; Attorney; Buyer; Computer Programmer; Customer Service Representative; Industrial Engineer; Financial Analyst; Manager; Department Manager; Management Trainee; Operations/Production Manager; Marketing Specialist; Quality Control Supervisor; Systems Analyst; Fashion Copywriter; Auditing. Principal educational backgrounds sought: Accounting; Business Administration; Communications; Marketing; Fashion Merchandising. Company benefits include: medical insurance; life insurance; tuition assistance; disability coverage; profit sharing; employee discounts; savings plan; dental insurance. NASDAQ.

**SPRING AIR**
6201 South Harlem
Chicago IL 60188
312/586-3000
Contact Personnel. Corporate headquarters of a major mattress manufacturer.

**ST. CHARLES MANUFACTURING**
1611 East Main Street
St. Charles IL 60174
708/584-3800
Contact Ms. Chris Knox, Employee Relations Manager. The company manufactures cabinetry for residential and institutional use through sheet metal fabrication. Institutional users are laboratories, schools and hospitals. The company also makes grocery store checkout counters and wxhaust hoods for fumes in laboratories. There are other plants in North Carolina and Utah. Corporate headquarters location. International.

**UNITED STATES TOBACCO MANUFACTURING COMPANY**
11601 Copenhagen Court
Franklin Park IL 60131
708/595-8200
Contact Mr. Hammad Askia, Personnel Manager. Several area locations, including: Franklin Park. Manufacturing plant for moist, smokeless tobacco products, and warehouse for distribution of various products. Products include Skoal, Copenhagen and Happy Days smokeless tobaccos. Corporate headquarters location: Greenwich, CT. New York Stock Exchange.

**WEN PRODUCTS, INC.**
5810 Northwest Highway
Chicago IL 60631
312/763-6060
Contact Keith Wright, Vice-President of Operations. Manufactures electronic soldering guns, sanders, electric saws, and a complete line of power tools. Corporate headquarters location.

**WICKS ORGAN COMPANY**
1100 Fifth Street
Highland IL 62249
618/654-2191
Contact Martin Wick, President. A prestigious manufacturer of church pipe organs.

**WILSON SPORTING GOODS CO.**
2233 West Street
River Grove IL 60171
708/456-6100

Contact Mary Lally, Personnel Manager. Manufacturer of sporting goods for golf, tennis, and team sports. Approximately $400 million in sales. Common position include: Accountant; Administrator; Architect; Buyer; Chemist; Commercial Artist; Computer Programmer; Credit Manager; Customer Service Representative; Draftsperson; Aerospace Engineer; Chemical Engineer; Electrical Engineer; Industrial Engineer; Mechanical Engineer; Financial Analyst; Operations/Production Manager; Marketing Specialist; Public Relations Worker; Quality Control Supervisor; Sales Representative; Statistician; Technical Writer/Editor. Principal educational backgrounds sought: Accounting; Art/Design; Business Administration; Chemistry; Communications; Computer Science; Economics; Engineering; Finance; Liberal Arts; Marketing; Mathematics; Physics. Company benefits include: medical, dental, and life insurance; pension plan; tuition assistance; disability coverage; employee discounts; savings plan. Corporate headquarters location. Operations at this facility include: regional headquarters; research/development; administration; service; sales.

**ZENITH ELECTRONICS CORPORATION**
1000 Milwaukee Avenue
Glenview IL 60025
708/391-7000
Contact Personnel. Designs, manufactures and markets consumer electronics products including televisions, video cassette recorders, video cameras, related components and systems, and cable television decoders. Products sold through extensive distributor network, most of which are independently owned. Company maintains facilities throughout the U.S. and in Canada, Mexico, Ireland and Taiwan. Common positions include: Computer Programmer; Electrical Engineer; Financial Analyst. Principal educational backgrounds sought: Computer Science; Engineering; Finance. Internships available. Company benefits include: medical insurance; dental insurance; life insurance; tuition assistance; disability coverage; profit sharing; employee discounts; savings plan. Corporate, headquarters location. Operations include: research/development; administration. International. New York Stock Exchange.

## MANUFACTURING: MISCELLANEOUS INDUSTRIAL

For more information on professional employment opportunities in the manufacturing industries, contact the following professional and trade organizations, as listed beginning on page 315:

NATIONAL ASSOCIATION OF MANUFACTURERS
NATIONAL MACHINE TOOL BUILDERS
NATIONAL SCREW MACHINE PRODUCTS ASSOCIATION
NATIONAL TOOLING AND MACHINING ASSOCIATION
THE TOOLING AND MANUFACTURING ASSOCIATION

**ALLIED PRODUCTS CORPORATION**
10 South Riverside Plaza
Suite 1600
Chicago IL 60606
312/454-1020. Contact Mr. Leo Simmermeyer, Vice President. Agricultural equipment, industrial components.

**AMSTED INDUSTRIES**
205 North Michigan Avenue, 44th Floor
Chicago IL 60601
312/645-1700
Contact Shirley Whitesell, Personnel Manager. Manufactures industrial products through 11 subsidiaries.

**ARMSTRONG-BLUM MANUFACTURING CO.**
1441 Business Center Drive
Mount Prospect IL 60056
708/803-4000
Contact Personnel. Manufactures metal cutting saws.

**ARROW GROUP INDUSTRIES**
1101 North 4th Street
Breese IL 62230
618/526-4546
Contact Patty Sellers, Director, Personnel. Manufacturers of utility storage buildings. Employs over 200.

**BARCO**
**A DIVISION OF MARISON INDUSTRIES**
500 North Hough Street
Barrington IL 60010
Contact K.M. Borre, Human Resources Manager. Manufacturers of flexible piping products used for a variety of piping motion applications. Common positions include: Industrial Engineer; Mechanical Engineer; Product Engineer. Principal educational backgrounds sought: Engineering. Company benefits include: medical insurance; dental insurance; life insurance; tuition assistance; disability coverage; profit sharing; savings plan. Corporate headquarters location. Operations at this facility include: manufacturing; sales.

**BEALL MANUFACTURING DIVISION/**
**VARLEN CORP.**
P.O. Box 70
East Alton IL 62024
618/259-8154

Contact Scott Patsaros, Personnel. Manufacturers of spring lock washers, agriculture implement parts, leaf spring steel items, flat washers. Employs over 100.

**BELDING CORPORATION**
130 West Grand Lake Boulevard
West Chicago IL 60185
708/231-5200
Contact Kathy Suba, Personnel Manager. Moves and installs heavy equipment; millwork, ironworking. Common positions include: Accountant; Administrator; Sales Representative. Principal educational backgrounds sought: Accounting; Marketing. Training programs offered. Company benefits include: medical insurance; life insurance; profit sharing. Corporate headquarters location. Operations at this location include: regional headquarters; administration; service; sales.

**BERKELEY-DAVIS, INC.**
1020 Bahls Street
Danville IL 61832
217/446-9500
Contact Phillip J. Thomas, General Manager. Custom designed resistance and arc welding equipment.

**BINKS MANUFACTURING CO.**
9201 West Belmont Avenue
Franklin Park IL 60131
708/671-3000
Contact Jim Linquist, Personnel Director. Spray finishing and coating application equipment.

**BORG-WARNER CORPORATION**
200 South Michigan Avenue
Chicago IL 60604
312/322-8500
Contact Angela D'Aversa, Director, Human Resources. A diversified manufacturing and services company. Most products are components made for manufacturers serving the transportation industry. The company also has extensive operations that provide protective services for business. Common positions include: Accountant; Attorney; Computer Programmer; Personnel & Labor Relations Specialist; Systems Analyst. Principal educational backgrounds sought: Accounting; Business Administration; Computer Science; Economics; Finance. Company benefits include: medical, dental and life insurance; pension plan; tuition assistance; disability coverage; savings plan. Corporate headquarters location. International. Operations at this facility include: administration.

## CARBIDE INTERNATIONAL
5740 North Tripp Avenue
Chicago IL 60646
312/583-6362
Contact Linda Langiner, Human Resources Assistant. Manufacturer of rotary tools, circuit board drills and fibre glass routers, master carbide drills, special tooling, and regrinding. Operations at this facility include: manufacturing; administration. Common positions include: Accountant; Computer Programmer; Customer Service Representative; Industrial Engineer; Mechanical Engineer; Industrial Manager; Operations/Production Manager; Personnel & Labor Relations Specialist; Purchasing Agent; Quality Control Supervisor; Sales Representative; Computer-Aided Manufacturing Engineer. Principal educational backgrounds sought: Accounting; Business Administration; Computer Science; Engineering; Finance. Company benefits include: medical insurance; dental insurance; pension plan; life insurance; tuition assistance; disability coverage; savings plan; 401K. Parent company: Harbour Group.

## CHICAGO BLOWER CORPORATION
1675 Glen Ellyn Road
Glendale Heights IL 60139
708/858-2600
Contact Kathy Reddington, Personnel Manager. Manufactures industrial fans and blowers.

## CHICAGO EXTRUDED METALS COMPANY
1601 South 54th Avenue
Cicero IL 60650
708/656-7900
Contact Kathy Kull, Human Resource Director. Manufactures screw machine products, brass wire rods, & etc. Common positions include: Mettallurgical Engineer. Company benefits include: medical insurance; pension plan; life insurance; tuition assistance; disability coverage; savings plan. Corporate headquarters location.

## CHICAGO FAUCET COMPANY
2100 South Clearwater Drive
Des Plaines IL 60018
312/694-4400
Contact Brian Downing, Personnel Manager. Manufactures brass plumbing fittings.

## CHICAGO RIVET & MACHINE COMPANY
P.O. Box 3061
Naperville IL 60566-7061
708/357-8500
Contact Mr. Steven Voss, Controller. Operates a fastener and wire producting firm.

## CINCH CONNECTORS
1500 Morse Avenue
Elk Grove Village IL 60007
708/981-6000
Contact Randall Hori, Manager, Human Resources. Produces connectors, interconnection systems, IC sockets, relay sockets, tube sockets, terminal strips, barrier blocks, crimp terminals, communications cross-connect systems, harness assemblies, and adapters. Major markets served: Military/Aerospace; Telecommunications; Computer & Instrumentation; and Automotive. Common positions include: Accountant; Buyer; Chemist; Computer Programmer; Customer Service Representative; Draftsperson; Electrical Engineer; Industrial Engineer; Mechanical Engineer; Metallurgical Engineer; Marketing Specialist; Systems Analyst. Principal educational backgrounds sought: Accounting; Chemistry; Computer Science; Engineering; Marketing. Company benefits include: medical insurance; dental insurance; pension plan; life insurance; tuition assistance; disability coverage; savings plan. Operations at this facility include: divisional headquarters; manufacturing; research/development; administration; service; sales.

## COMMERCIAL STAMPING & FORGING, INC.
5757 West 65th Street
Bedford Park IL 60638
312/767-8500
Contact Frank Kosteki, Industrial Relations. Manufactures fabrications for underground tunnels.

## CULLIGAN INTERNATIONAL
1 Culligan Parkway
Northbrook IL 60062
708/205-5902
Contact Debbie Wheeler, Employment Supervisor. Manufacturer of water equipment and systems, including design, start-up, troubleshooting and R&D. Owned by Rapid American Corporation, a subsidiary of Rilkis Family Corporation.

## DANA CORPORATION/VICTOR PRODUCT DIVISION
5750 West Roosevelt Road
Chicago IL 60650
312/287-6180
Contact Jo Ann Green, Human Resources Coordinator. Several locations. Manufacturers of sealing products; gaskets, rubber seals primarily used on heavy-vehicle trucks and earth-moving equipment. Division of Dana Corporation. International foreign affiliate facilities located in Mexico, South America, India, Japan, Singapore, Taiwan, Thailand, and Korea. Corporate headquarters location: Toledo, OH. Victor Divisional headquarters location: Lisle, IL. International. New York Stock Exchange. Common positions

include: Accountnat; Blue-Collar Worker Supervisor; Buyer; Customer Service Representative; Industrial Engineer; Department Manager; Operations/Production Manager; Personnel and Labor/Relations Specialist; Purchasing Agent; Quality Control Supervisor; Factory Workers. Company benefits include: medical insurance; dental insurance; pension plan; life insurance; tuition assistance; disability coverage; profit sharing; savings plan. Corporate headquarters location: Toledo, OH. Operations at this facility include: manufacturing. New York Stock Exchange.

**DANLY MACHINE DIVISION/
CONNELL LIMITED PARTNERSHIP**
2115 South 54th Avenue
Cicero IL 60650
312/242-1800. Contact Gene Elliot, Director of Employee Relations. A manufacturer of machine tools.

**DEERE & COMPANY**
John Deere Road
Moline IL 61265
309/765-8000
Contact Richard Van Bell, Director of Personnel. Manufactures, distributes and finances the sale of heavy equipment and machinery for use in the agricultural equipment and industrial equipment industries. The agricultural equipment sector manufactures tractors, soil, seeding, and harvesting equipment. The industrial equipment segment manufactures a variety of earth moving equipment, tractors, loaders, and excavators; while the consumer products division manufactures a variety of tractors and products for the homeowner. Financial services, including personal and commercial lines of insurance, retail, and managed health care services are offered. Common positions include: Accountant. Principal educational backgrounds sought include: Accounting. Company benefits include: medical, dental, and life insurance; pension plan; tuition assistance; disability coverage; profit sharing; employee discounts; savings plan. Corporate headquarters location. Operations at this facility include: administration. New York Stock Exchange.

**DEXTER CORPORATION**
1 East Water Street
Waukegan IL 60085
708/623-4200
Contact John Nuebel, Manager/Human Resources. Manufacturer of industrial coatings and finishes. A Fortune 500 company heavily engaged in research and development. New York Stock Exchange. Common positions include: Accountant; Chemist; Computer Programmer; Chemical Engineer; General Manager; Operations/Production Manager; Personnel & Labor Relations Specialist; Purchasing Agent; Quality Control Supervisor; Sales Representative; Systems Analyst; Transportation & Traffic Specialist. Principal educational backgrounds sought: Accounting; Chemistry; Engineering. Company benefits include: medical insurance; dental insurance;

pension plan; life insurance; tuition assistance; disability coverage; profit sharing; savings plan. Operations at this facility include: manufacturing; research/development; administration; sales. Corporate headquarters location: Windsor Locks, CT.

### A.B. DICK COMPANY
5700 West Touhy Avenue
Chicago IL 60648
312/763-1900
Contact Karen Harling, Dir. of Employee & Staffing Relations. A manufacturer of office machines.

### THE DO-ALL COMPANY
254 North Laurel Avenue
Des Plaines IL 60016
708/824-1122
Contact Kevin Hennessy, Personnel Director. Distributor of machine tools and other industrial supplies.

### DUDEK & BOCK SPRING MANUFACTURING
5100 West Roosevelt Road
Chicago IL 60650
312/379-4100
Contact Walter Dudek, President. Manufactures springs, platforms, and wire forms.

### DUO-FAST
3702 North River Road
Franklin Park IL 60131
708/678-0100
Contact Ollie Brewer, Manager of Employee Relations/HR. Manufacturer of industrial staples and nailing tools.

### DURO METAL PRODUCTS COMPANY
2649 North Kildare Avenue
Chicago IL 60639
312/235-5000
Contact Jack Fairbrother, Personnel Manager. Manufacturer of mechanic's hand tools.

### EQUIPTO
225 S. Highland Avenue
Aurora IL 60506
708/859-1000
Contact Bill Corrigan, Personnel Director. Manufactures industrial shelving, work benches, lockers.

### FEDERAL SIGNAL CORPORATION
2645 Federal Signal Drive
Chicago Park IL 60466
708/534-3400
Contact Vice President of Human Resources. A diversified manufacturer of signs, signals, and tools.

### FIATALLIS NORTH AMERICA, INC.
245 East North Avenue
Carol Stream IL 60188
708/260-4000
Contact Rosemarie Herrlin, Personnel Administrator. Distributes moving equipment and components.

### FLUID POWER SYSTEMS
511 Glenn Avenue
Wheeling IL 60090
708/459-2800
Contact Personnel Manager. Several locations. A subsidiary of United Technologies (Hartford, CT), a major diversified industrial firm; this company manufactures hydraulic valves. Common positions include: Accountant; Blue-Collar Worker Supervisor; Buyer; Customer Service Representative; Draftsperson; Industrial Engineer; Mechanical Engineer; Department Manager; Personnel & Labor Relations Specialist; Quality Control Supervisor; Sales Representative. Principal educational backgrounds sought: Engineering. Company benefits include: medical insurance; dental insurance; pension plan; life insurance; tuition assistance; disability coverage; employee discounts; savings plan. Corporate headquarters location: Detroit, MI. Parent company: United Technologies Automotive, Inc. Operations at this facility include: manufacturing, administration, service, sales. New York Stock Exchange.

### FOOTE JONES
2102 N. Natchez
Chicago IL 60635
312/622-8000
Contact Personnel Department. Supplies precision gears and gear boxes.

### GBC
One GBC Plaza
Northbrook IL 60062
708/272-3700, ext.6037
Contact Allison Henley, Human Resources Manager. International manufacturer and distributor of office binding and laminating systems and supplies. Common positions include: Accountant; Administrator; Blue-Collar Worker Supervisor; Buyer; Computer Programmer; Credit Manager; Customer Service Representative; Industrial Engineer; Mechanical Engineer; Financial Analyst; Branch Manager; Operations/Production Manager;

Marketing Specialist; Purchasing Agent; Quality Control Supervisor; Sales Representative; Systems Analyst. Principal educational backgrounds sought: Accounting; Business Administration; Computer Science; Engineering; Finance; Liberal Arts; Marketing. Training programs offered. Company benefits include: medical insurance; dental insurance; pension plan; life insurance; tuition assistance; disability coverage; profit sharing; employee discounts; savings plan. Operations at this facility include: manufacturing; research/development; administration.

## HOLLYMATIC CORPORATION
600 East Plainfield Road
Countryside IL 60525
708/579-3700
Contact Marylyn Krische, Human Resources Manager. Manufactures food processing machines and parts, and paper products. Corporate headquarters location.

## IDEAL ROLLER COMPANY/
## DIVISION OF ROTATION DYNAMICS, INC.
2512 West 24th Street
Chicago IL 60608
312/247-5600
Contact Lillian Hastak, Personnel Director. Manufacturer of mechanical and rubber rollers. Owned by Wheelabrator-Frye. Common positions at this facility include: Accountant; Blue-Collar Worker Supervisor; Chemist; Computer Programmer; Credit Manager; Customer Service Representative; Draftsperson; Industrial Engineer; Branch Manager; Department Manager; Management Trainee; Operations/Production Manager; Marketing Specialist; Purchasing Agent; Quality Control Supervisor; Sales Representative. Principal educational backgrounds sought: Accounting; Business Administration; Computer Science; Engineering; Finance; Marketing. Company benefits include: medical insurance; dental insurance; pension plan; life insurance; tuition assistance; disability coverage; profit sharing; savings plan. Corporate headquarters location: Hinsdale, IL. Operations at this facility include: divisional headquarters; manufacturing; research/development; service.

## ILLINOIS TOOL WORKS
3600 West Lake
Glenview IL 60625
708/724-7500
Contact Personnel Manager. Develops, produces, and markets specially engineered products and systems.

## INTERNATIONAL HOUGH DIVISION/DRESSER INDUSTRIES
East Sunnyside Avenue
Libertyville IL 60048
708/367-2000
Contact Personnel Department. Provides crawler dozers, crawler loaders, wheel loaders and scrapers to a variety of customers.

## ITT/FLUID HANDLING DIVISION
8200 North Austin Avenue
Morton Grove IL 60053
708/966-3700
Contact Don Flowers, Manager of Employee Relations. Producer of heat exchangers, plumbing equipment, & pumps.

## ITT McDONNELL & MILLER
3500 North Spaulding Avenue
Chicago IL 60618
312/267-1600
Contact Al Landini, Personnel Director. Produces water control valves and boiler equipment for heating and air conditioning systems.

## MARSH COMPANY
707 East 'B' Street
Belleville IL 62222
618/234-1122
Contact Fred Drayer, Director, Human Resources. A major company engaged in the manufacture of microprocessor controlled and mechanical marking, coding, and packing equipment for industrial use. Common positions include: Buyer; Chemist; Computer Programmer; Customer Service Representative; Draftsperson; Electrical Engineer; Mechanical Engineer; Sales Representative. Principal educational backgrounds sought: Chemistry; Computer Science; Engineering; Marketing. Training programs offered; Internships offered. Company benefits include: medical insurance; dental insurance; life insurance; tuition assistance; disability coverage; savings plan. Corporate headquarters location. Operations at this facility include: manufacturing; research/development; administration; sales.

## MARTIN INDUSTRIES
4200 St. Clair Avenue,
P.O. Box 1040
Washington Park IL 62204
618/271-1272
Contact Rita Enskat, Personnel Director. Manufacture heat stoves (wood & gas), and gas fired incinerators.

## McMASTER-CARR SUPPLY COMPANY
600 North County Line Road
Elmhurst IL 60126
708/834-9600
Contact Karla Kauffman Keehn, Personnel. A distributor of industrial products and supplies. Primary selling tool is the firm's catalog, which contains descriptions of a variety of products necessary to maintain a manufacturing facility. Corporate headquarters location. Common positions include: Computer Programmer; Customer Service Representative; Management Trainee; Purchasing or Marketing Assistant. Principal educational backgrounds sought: Business Administration; Communications; Computer Science; Economics; Engineering; Finance; Liberal Arts; Marketing. Company benefits include: medical insurance; dental insurance; life insurance; pension plan; tuition assistance; disability coverage; profit sharing; employee discounts.

## MILLER FLUID POWER CORPORATION
800 North York Road
Bensenville IL 60106
708/766-3400
Contact Tom Parker, Human Resources Director. Manufacturer of pneumatic and hydraulic cylinders and components. Corporate headquarters location. Common positions include: Accountant; Buyer; Computer Programmer; Credit Manager; Customer Service Representative; Draftsperson; Engineer; Industrial Engineer; Mechanical Engineer; Industrial Designer; Branch Manager; Department Manager; Operations/Production Manager; Marketing Specialist; Personnel & Labor Relations Specialist; Purchasing Agent; Quality Control Engineer; Sales Representative; Systems Analyst; Manufacturing Engineer. Principal educational backgrounds sought: Accounting; Art/Design; Business Administration; Computer Science; Engineering; Finance; Liberal Arts; Marketing. Company benefits include: medical insurance; pension plan; life insurance; tuition assistance; disability coverage; profit sharing; savings plan. Operations at this facility include: manufacturing; research/development; administration; service; sales.

## NAVISTAR INTERNATIONAL CORPORATION
455 North Cityfront Plaza Drive
Chicago IL 60611
312/836-2000
Contact Jim Gats, Personnel Director. Several area locations including: Hinsdale, Libertyville, Broadview, Schaumburg. A worldwide enterprise having numerous subsidiaries, licensees and joint ventures. Manufactures and markets self-propelled heavy machinery and vehicles for use on and off the highways. Corporate headquarters location. International. New York Stock Exchange.

## OLIN CORPORATION
P.O. Box 2219
Patterson Road
Joliet IL 60434
815/727-4901
Contact Vince Cimino, Personnel Manager. Several area locations including: Oak Brook. Manufacturer of organic and inorganic chemicals, specializing in those used in industry and agriculture. Also manufactures metal and paper products, sports and recreational equipment, and energy systems. Operations at this facility include: manufacturing. Corporate headquarters location: Stamford, CT. New York Stock Exchange. International. Common positions include: Accountant; Chemical Engineer; Industrial Engineer; Mechanical Engineer; Operations/Production Manager; Personnel & Labor Relations Specialist. Principal educational backgrounds sought: Business Administration; Engineering. Company benefits include: medical insurance; dental insurance; pension plan; life insurance; tuition assistance; disability coverage; profit sharing; employee discounts; savings plan.

## OTIS ELEVATOR COMPANY
550 West Jackson Boulevard
Chicago IL 60611-5769
312/454-1323
Contact Diane Kosec, Personnel Representative. One of the world's largest producers of elevators and escalators. The company is primarily engaged in the manufacture, installation, and service of elevators and escalators. Corporate headquarters location: Farmington, CT.

## PARKER-HANNIFIN CORPORATION
500 South Wolf Road
Des Plaines IL 60016
708/298-2400
Contact Lou Ford, Personnel Manager. Several area locations. A fluid power firm making one of the most complete lines of components and replacement parts for hydraulic and pneumatic power systems for the industrial, automotive, aviation, space, and marine industries. Company has also recently entered the biomedical market to research and help produce equipment and products for treatment of chronic illnesses. Employs more than 20,000 people at 131 manufacturing plants, 37 administrative and sales offices, and 63 distribution and service centers. Illinois properties are located in Broadview (refrigeration components headquarters), Des Plaines, and Dixon (3 facilities). Corporate headquarters location: Cleveland, OH. International. New York Stock Exchange.

## PEABODY MYERS CORPORATION
1621 South Illinois
Streator IL 61364
815/672-3171

Contact B. W. Collins, Personnel Director. Manufacturer of truck-mounted vacuum loading and cleaning equipment for cleaning city sewer line systems, industrial vacuum cleaning operations, and municipal street cleaning requirements. Common positions include: Accountant; Computer Programmer; Draftsperson; Engineer; Mechanical Engineer; Operations/ Production Manager; Marketing Specialist; Sales Representative. Principal educational backgrounds sought: Accounting; Business Administration; Engineering; Finance. Company benefits include: medical insurance; pension plan; life insurance; tuition assistance; disability coverage; profit sharing; savings plan. Operations at this facility include: manufacturing; research/ development; administration; sales. Corporate headquarters location: Stamford, CT. New York Stock Exchange.

## PIONEER SCREW & NUT COMPANY
2700 York Road
Elk Grove Village IL 60007
Contact Human Resources Manager. A manufacturer of fasteners and nuts and bolts. Parent company of American Cold Heating Corporation. Common positions include: Customer Service Representative; Metallurgical Engineer; Purchasing Agent; Quality Control Supervisor; Sales Representative. Principal educational backgrounds sought: Business Administration; Engineering; Marketing. Company benefits include: medical, dental, and life insurance; tuition assistance; disability coverage; profit sharing; savings plan. Corporate headquarters location. Operations at this facility include: manufacturing.

## PITTWAY CORPORATION
333 Skokie Boulevard
Northbrook IL 60065
708/498-1260
Contact Peggy Odegaard, Administrative Assistant to President. Several area locations, including: Aurora, Crystal Lake, Niles. A diverse corporation engaged in four industry segments: Burglar and Fire Alarms, produces security systems and fire alarms under brand names First Alert and BRK; Packaging, manufactures aerosol valves, pumps and closures; Publishing, publishes 27 national business and trade magazines; and Real Estate Developing, operates a 950-unit condominium in Florida. Corporate headquarters location. International. American Stock Exchange.

## REVCOR, INC.
251 Edwards Avenue
Carpentersville IL 60110
708/428-4411
Contact Larry Brigman, Personnel Director. Manufactures fans and blowers. Corporate headquarters location.

## RICHARDS-WILCOX
600 South Lake Street
Aurora IL 60506
708/897-6951
Contact Larry French, Manager of Human Resources. Engaged in the manufacture and distribution of material handling equipment and office systems products. Products include: Overhead Chain Conveyors, Horizontal and Vertical Carousels, General Hardware, Aurora Shelving, Timer 2 and Mobile Base. Common positions include: Accountant; Administrator; Blue-Collar Worker Supervisor; Buyer; Computer Programmer; Credit Manager; Customer Service Representative; Draftsperson; Electrical Engineer; Industrial Engineer; Mechanical Engineer; Industrial Manager; Operations/Production Manager; Purchasing Agent; Quality Control Supervisor; Sales Representative; Systems Analyst. Principal educational backgrounds sought: Accounting; Business Administration; Computer Science; Engineering; Finance; Liberal Arts; Marketing. Company benefits include: medical insurance; dental insurance; pension plan; life insurance; tuition assistance; disability coverage; employee discounts; savings plan. Corporate headquarters location: Cleveland, OH. Parent company: White Consolidated Industries. Operations at this facility include: divisional headquarters.

## SCIAKY BROTHERS INC/
## MEMBER COMPANY OF ALLEGHENY INTERNATIONAL
4915 West 67th Street
Chicago IL 60638
708/594-3800
Contact James D. Schmitt, Manager/Employee Relations. A leading manufacturer of automated welding systems, including electron beam, laser, resistance and fusion welding systems. A manufacturer of industrial systems automation. Corporate headquarters location: Pittsburgh, PA. New York Stock Exchange. Common positions include: Accountant; Blue-Collar Worker Supervisor; Buyer; Computer Programmer; Draftsperson (CAD/CAM); Electrical Engineer; Industrial Engineer; Mechanical Engineer; Financial Analyst; Industrial Designer; Operations/Production Manager; Marketing Specialist; Personnel & Labor Relations Specialist; Physicist; Quality Control Supervisor; Sales Representative; Systems Analyst; Technical Writer/Editor; Service Engineer. Principal educational backgrounds sought: Art/Design; Business Administration; Computer Science; Engineering; Finance; Marketing; Physics; Metallurgy; Computer Engineering. Company benefits include: medical insurance; dental insurance; pension plan; life insurance; tuition assistance; disability coverage; profit sharing; employee discounts; savings plan. Divisional headuqarters location. Operations include: manufacturing; research/development; administration; service; sales.

## SCULLY-JONES CORPORATION
1901 South Rockwell
Chicago IL 60608
312/247-5900
Contact Gerald Walton, Personnel Director. An employee-owned manufacturer of precision toolholders for machine tools. Operations include: manufacturing; administration. Corporate headquarters location. Common positions include: Accountant; Customer Service Representative; Industrial Engineer; Mechanical Engineer; Programmer; Purchasing Agent; Quality Control Supervisor; Systems Analyst. Principal educational backgrounds sought: Business Administration; Computer Science; Engineering. Company benefits include: medical insurance; dental insurance; life insurance; tuition assistance; disability coverage; profit sharing; savings plan.

## SLOAN VALVE COMPANY
10500 Seymour
Franklin Park IL 60131
708/671-4300
Contact K. Peter Blut, Employment Manager. Manufacturers of a variety of valves such as Royal Flush valves for toilets, railroad car valves, air brake valves and faucets. A privately-owned company. Corporate headquarters location. International. Common positions include: Accountant; Computer Programmer; Industrial Engineer; Mechnical Engineer; Q.A. Engineer. Principal educational backgrounds sought: Accounting; Business Administration; Computer Science; Engineering. Company benefits include: medical, dental, and life insurance; pension plan; tuition assistance; disability coverage; 401K. Corporate headquarters location. Operations at this facility include: manufacturing; research/development; administration.

## SPOTNAILS INC.
1100 Hicks Road
Rolling Meadows IL 60008
708/259-1620
Contact President. Manufactures pneumatic tools and fasteners. Common positions include: Accountant; Administrator; Blue-Collar Worker Supervisor; Customer Service Representative; Industrial Engineer; Mechanical Engineer. Principal educational backgrounds sought: Accounting; Business Administration; Engineering. Company benefits: medical, dental, and life insurance; pension plan; tuition assistance; disability coverage. Corporate headquarters location. Operations include: regional headquarters; manufacturing; administration; service; sales.

## STEPHENS-ADAMSON, INC.
850 Ridgeway Avenue
Aurora IL 60507
708/892-4311
Contact Personnel. A subsidiary of Allis-Chalmers. Manufacturer of heavy equipment used for handling bulk material. Corporate headquarters location.

**TC INDUSTRIES**
P.O. Box 477
Crystal Lake IL 60014
815/459-2400
Contact John McGrath, Personnel Director. A diversified company with interests in commercial heat treating, heavy equipment, and military components. Corporate headquarters location.

**TEMPLETON, KENLY & CO. INC.**
2525 South Gardner Road
Broadview IL 60153
708/865-1500
Contact Ms. Kathleen Mohr, Manager of Personnel. Manufactures hydraulic and mechanical jacks. Common positions include: Accountant; Computer Programmer; Credit Manager; Customer Service Representative; Draftsperson; Industrial Engineer; Mechanical Engineer; General Manager; Operations/Production Manager; Personnel & Labor Relations Specialist; Purchasing Agent; Quality Control Supervisor; Transportation & Traffic Specialist. Principal educational backgrounds sought: Accounting; Computer Science; Engineering; Marketing. Company benefits include: medical, dental, and life insurance; tuition assistance; disability coverage; profit sharing; savings plan; EAP (Employee Assistance Plan). Operations at this facility include: manufacturing; research/development; administration; service; sales. Corporate headquarters location.

**TUTHILL PUMP DIVISION**
12500 South Pulaski
Chicago IL 60658
708/389-2500
Contact Karen Angelucci, Personnel Director. International distributor and manufacturer of pumps (rotary), positive displacement gear, test plugs, and tube connectors. Corporate headquarters location: Hinsdale, IL. International. Common positions include: Accountant; Blue-Collar Worker Supervisor; Buyer; Computer Programmer; Credit Manager; Customer Service Representative; Draftsperson; Engineer; Electrical Engineer; Mechanical Engineer; Metallurgical Engineer; Purchasing Agent; Quality Control Supervisor; Sales Representative.

**UNION CARBIDE CORPORATION/**
**MIDWEST REGION**
10 South Riverside Plaza
Suite 2200
Chicago IL 60606
312/454-2000
Contact Jim Carey, Employee Relations Manager. Among the nation's 25 largest industrial companies with sales over $9 billion. It is engaged in three major lines of business: chemicals and plastics; gases, metals and carbons.

Union Carbide is primarily a manufacturer of basic products used by the chemicals, plastics, and metal industries. Union Carbide is a major multinational company with about one third of its sales coming from international operations. The company employs 100,000 people, operates about 500 plants, mines and mills in over 30 countries, and has over 170,000 stockholders. Corporate headquarters location: Danbury,CT. International. New York Stock Exchange.

**UNITED AIR CLEANER COMPANY/
A UNIT OF DOLLINGER/A FILTRONA COMPANY**
9705 South Cottage Grove Avenue
Chicago IL 60628
312/734-5000
Contact John J. Dreznes, Vice President - Sales. International distributors and manufacturers of air cleaners, and automotive and tractor engines. Corporate headquarters location: Richmond, VA. Parent company is American Filtrona Corporation.

**UPPCO, INC.**
5610 West Bloomingdale
Chicago IL 60639
312/622-7010
Contact Salvador Isais, Personnel Manager. Designs and manufactures specialized motors. Corporate headquarters location.

**VULCAN MATERIALS COMPANY/
MIDWEST DIVISION**
500 West Plainfield Road
Countryside IL 60525
708/482-7000
Contact J. Wayne Houston, Manager, Admin.& Human Resources. A multi-industry company operating in three businesses: one of the nation's largest producers of construction aggregates; a leading chemicals manufacturer; and a principal producer of secondary aluminum, detinned steel scrap and tin chemicals. Chicago operations produce limestone materials. A Fortune 500 company. Common positions include: Accountant; Buyer; Computer Programmer; Credit Manager; Customer Service Representative; Draftsperson; Industrial Engineer; Mining Engineer; Financial Analyst; Geologist; Operations/Production Manager; Marketing Specialist; Personnel & Labor Relations Specialist; Purchasing Agent; Quality Conrol Supervisor; Sales Representative; Systems Analyst. Principal educational background sought: Accounting; Business Administration; Computer Science; Engineering; Finance; Marketing. Training programs offered. Company benfits include: medical, dental, and life insurance; pension plan; tuition assistance; disability coverage; profit sharing; savings plan. Corporate headquarters location: Birmingham, AL. Operations at this facility include: divisional headquarters; administration; sales. New York Stock Exchange.

### WHITING CORPORATION
15700 Lathrop Avenue
Harvey IL 60426
708/331-4000
Contact Manager of Human Resources. Manufacturer of heavy overhead gantry cranes; metallurgical process equipment; transportation maintenance/repair equipment; and special products. Common positions include: Draftsperson; Electrical Engineer; Industrial Engineer; Mechanical Engineer; Metallurgical Engineer; Department Manager; Sales Representative. Principal educational backgrounds sought: Business Administration; Engineering; Finance; Mathematics. Company benefits include: medical insurance; dental insurance; pension plan; life insurance; tuition assistance; disability coverage; profit sharing. Operations at this facility include: manufacturing; service; sales. Corporate headquarters location.

### YEOMANS CHICAGO
1999 North Ruby Street
Melrose Park IL 60160
708/344-9600
Contact John Lillis, Personnel. Director. Several area locations including: Melrose Park, Westmont, Bensenville, Carol Stream. Manufactures and sells goods and services for conveying, controlling, and treating water and waste water. Principal products include ductile iron pressure pipe and fittings, plastic pipe, waterworks valves, fire hydrants, vitrified clay pipe for sewer lines, waste treatment equipment, and water treatment chemicals. Municipalities, water and sewer line contractors, and piping contractors are the principal customers. Products sold by both company salespersons and distributors. Corporate headquarters location. International.

## MISCELLANEOUS SERVICES

### BURNS INTERNATIONAL SECURITY SERVICES
6323 North Avondale
Chicago Il 60631
312/774-6200
Contact Lester Kerr, Personnel Director. Provides private security guards to a variety of users.

### GREAT LAKES MAINTENENCE & SECURITY CORPORATION
201 North Wells Street
Room 408
Chicago IL 60606
312/332-1638
Contact Barbara Dennis, Personnel Department. Provides maintenence, cleaning and security guard services.

## PINKERTON'S, INC.
9930 Derby Lane, Suite 102
Westchester IL 60154
708/450-2360
Contact Michael Hallei, Personnel Manager. Provides uniformed security officers and investigative services. District headquarters. Corporate headquarters location: New York, NY. New York Stock Exchange. Common positions include: Accountant; Blue-Collar Worker Supervisor; Branch Manager; Department Manager; General Manager; Management Trainee; Personnel & Labor Relations Specialist; Sales Representative. Principal educational backgrounds sought: Accounting; Business Administration; Liberal Arts; Law Enforcement. Company benefits include: medical insurance; life insurance; tuition assistance; profit sharing.

## ROTARY INTERNATIONAL
1560 Sherman Avenue
Evanston IL 60201
708/866-3000
Contact Jacquelyn McGuire, Employment Supervisor. Rotary is an international organization of more than one million service-minded business and professional leaders. The Evanston headquarters is involved in administration and service to the clubs, publicity for the organization and the administration of the humanitarian programs funded by the rotary. Common positions include: Accountant; Commercial Artist; Computer Programmer; Financial Analyst; Department Manager; Personnel & Labor Relations Specialist; Public Relations Worker; Editor/Feature Writer. Principal educational backgrounds sought: Accounting; Business Administration; Communications; Finance; Liberal Arts; International Studies; Foreign Languages; Journalism. Company benefits include: medical insurance, dental, and life insurance; pension plan; tuition assistance; disability coverage. Corporate headquarters location.

## SAFETY-KLEEN
777 Big Timber Road
Elgin IL 60123
708/697-8460
Contact Robert Burian, Vice President of Personnel. A company engaged in the cleaning of industrial machinery and the recycling of industrial cleaning solvents after their use.

## SERVICEMASTER L.P.
1 Service Master Way
Downers Grove IL 60515
708/964-1300
Contact Personnel. Company provides management services for health care, industrial and educational facilities. Employs 14,861.

## NEWSPAPER PUBLISHERS

For more information on professional employment opportunities in the newspaper journalism industry, contact the following professional and trade organizations, as listed beginning on pages 315:

AMERICAN NEWSPAPER PUBLISHERS ASSOCIATION
AMERICAN SOCIETY OF NEWSPAPER EDITORS
THE DOW JONES NEWSPAPER FUND
INTERNATIONAL CIRCULATION MANAGERS ASSOCIATION
NATIONAL NEWSPAPER ASSOCIATION
NATIONAL PRESS CLUB
THE NEWSPAPER GUILD
THE NEWSPAPER GUILD/CHICAGO LOCAL

### ALTON TELEGRAPH PRINTING COMPANY
111 East Broadway
Alton IL 62002
618/463-2500
Contact Personnel Department. A major regional newspaper publisher. Employs over 100.

### CHICAGO TRIBUNE
435 North Michigan
Chicago IL 60611
312/222-4572
Contact Ronald Williams, Empolyment Manager. Publishes one of the nation's largest newspapers.

### THE DAILY HERALD-PADDOCK PUBLICATIONS
P.O. Box 280
Arlington Heights IL 60006
708/870-3722
Contact Sharon Nestmann, Employment Recruiters. Publishes a daily newspaper with circulation of 100,000.

### LERNER NEWSPAPERS, INC.
8135 River Drive
Morton Grove IL 60053
708/966-5555
Contact Personnel Director. Publishes 52 mastheads in the Chicago area.

**THE NEWS-SUN/COPLEY PRESS INC.**
100 West Madison
Waukegan IL 60085
708/336-7000
Contact Personnel Director. Several area locations including: Libertyville. communications firm publishing a daily newspaper, The News-Sun (Waukegan) and a weekly newspaper, The Independent-Register (Libertyville).

**SOUTHTOWN ECONOMIST, INC.**
5959 South Harlem Avenue
Chicago IL 60638
312/586-8800
Contact Sue Buckles, Personnel. Publisher of neighborhood newspapers. Corporate headquarters location.

**THE NEWS DEMOCRAT**
120 South Illinois
P.O. Box 427
Belleville IL 62222
618/234-1000
Contact Personnel Director. A major Southern Illinois newspaper publisher.

## PAPER, PACKAGING & FOREST PRODUCTS/ CONTAINERS & GLASS PRODUCTS

For more information on professional employment opportunities in the paper and packaging industries, contact the following professioanl trade organizations, as listed beginning on page 315:

AMERICAN PAPER INSTITUTE
PAPER INDUSTRY MANAGEMENT ASSOCIATION
TECHNICAL ASSOCIATION OF THE PULP AND PAPER INDUSTRY

**ARVEY CORPORATION**
**A DIVISION OF HAMMERHILL PAPER CO.**
3351 West Addison
Chicago IL 60618
312/463-0030
Contact Dave Gruenewald, Corporate V.P. of Human Resources. A manufacturer and retailer of paper products.

## BAGCRAFT OF AMERICA
3900 West 43rd Street
Chicago IL 60632
312/254-8000
Contact Charles F. Gaul, Industrial Relations Manager. Manager of flexible packaging, laminating materials.

## BENNETT INDUSTRIES
515 North First Street
Peotone IL 60468
708/258-3211
Contact Robert Rundin, Director of Industrial Relations. Manufacturers of plastic and metal shipping containers.

## BRADNOR CENTRAL COMPANY
333 South Desplaines Street
Chicago IL 60661
312/454-1852
Contact Personnel. A distributor of fine paper products.

## CENTRAL CAN COMPANY
3200 South Kilbourn Avenue
Chicago IL 60623
312/254-8700
Contact Raymond Mielkus, Assistant Personnel Manager. Manufactures shipping containers and paint cans.

## JOHN CRANE, INC.
6400 W. Oakton Street
Morton Grove IL 60053
708/967-2460
Contact George Pinder, Senior Human Resources Representative. Manufactures & markets mechanical seals & packaging, and Teflon products. Common positions include: Accountant; Buyer; Computer Programmer; Customer Service Representative; Industrial Engineer; Mechanical Engineer; Financial Analyst; Personnel and Labor Relations Specialist; Purchasing Agent; Sales Representative; Systems Analyst; Technical Writer/Editor. Principal educational backgrounds sought: Business Administration; Computer Science; Computer Science; Engineering; Finance. Internships offered. Company benefits include: medical insurance; pension plan; life insurance; tuition assistance; disability coverage; profit sharing; savings plan; 401K. Corporate headquarters location. Operations at this facility include: manufacturing; research/development; administration; service.

## FIELD CONTAINER CORPORATION
1500 North Nicholas Boulevard
Elk Grove Village IL 60007
312/437-1700
Contact Personnel Department. A major producer of folding boxes, paper, and inks.

## GEE COMPANY
2600 W. 79th Street
Chicago IL 60692
312/476-7400
Contact President. A forest products firm with offices throughout the area.

## GEORGIA PACIFIC
P.O. Box 100
Mt. Olive IL 62069
217/999-2511
Contact Personnel Department. One of several area divisions of the well-known diversified manufacturer of packaging products. Company's principal products are glass containers, although the company also produces and sells containerboard, corrugated containers, printing plates and ink, plywood and demension lumber, blown plastic containers, plastic beverage bottles, plastic drums, metal and plastic closures, tamper-resistant closures, plastic and glass prescription containers, pharmaceutical items, labels, and multipack plastic carriers for containers. Specialized glass products made and sold by the company include Libbey Tumblers, stemware, and decorative glassware, television blubs for picture tubes, and Kimble scientific and laboratory ware. Some overseas affiliates also manufacture flat glass and related products.

## GEORGIA-PACIFIC
## HOPPER PAPER DIVISION
P.O. Box 380
Taylorville IL 62568
217/824-9611
Contact Bob Morrison, Personnel Director. Manufactures printing papers.

## GREIF BROTHERS CORPORATION
615 Northwest Avenue
Northlake IL 60164
708/562-1800
Contact Barbara Bradford, Personnel. Manufactures shipping containers for bulk products.

## HIGHLAND SUPPLY CORPORATION
1111 6th Street
Highland IL 62249
618/654-2161
Contact Donald J. Frolker, Personnel Manager. Manufacture foils, polypropolene film, cellophane and film bags (printed and plain). Common positions include: Accountant; Chemist; Computer Programmer; Mechanical Engineer; General Manager; Operations/Production Manager; Quality Control Supervisor; Sales Representative. Principal educational backgrounds sought: Accounting; Business Administration; Chemistry; Computer Science; Engineering; Marketing. Company benefits include: medical insurance; life insurance; tuition assistance. Corporate headquarters location. Operations at this facility include: manufacturing; administration; sales.

## INLANDER-STEINDLER PAPER COMPANY
2100 Devon Avenue
Elk Grove Village IL 60007
708/952-2000
Contact Sales Manager. A paper distributor with five branches in IL, IN, & WI.

## INTERNATIONAL PAPER COMPANY/NORTHLAKE
635 Northwest Avenue
Northlake IL 60164
708/562-6900 or 562-9300
Contact Phil Kohner, Regional Manager/Employee Relations. One of the largest natural resource management companies. It produces solid wood products, including plywood, lumber, poles, and cabinets and a variety of pulp and paper products, packaging, packaging materials, and packaging systems.

## IVEX CORPORATION
50 South Mannheim Road
Hillside IL 60162
708/547-2400
Contact Personnel Director. Manufactures corrugated packaging.

## JEFFERSON SMURFIT CORPORATION/ ALTON PACKAGING CORPORATION
401 Alton Street
Alton IL 62002
618/463-6000
Contact Mr. Tom Hardy, Personnel Director. Mr. Tom Hardy can be contacted at P.O. Box 66820, St. Louis MO 63166. Manufacture paperboard packaging, boxes, paper cores.

## JEFFERSON-SMURFIT/CONTAINER DIVISION
6th and Zscholkke Sts.
Highland IL 62249
618/654-2141
Contact Don Walker, Personnel Controller. A metropolitan manufacturer of corrugated containers.

## KERR GLASS MANUFACTURING CORPORATION
1500 North Route 59
Plainfield IL 60544
312/242-4592
Contact Barry Healy, Manager, Industrial Relations. Manufactures and sells glass containers.

## MILLS-AMERICAN ENVELOPE
3001 North Rockwell
Chicago IL 60618
312/267-3600
Contact John Arciszewski, Human Resource Manager. An envelope manufacturer. A subsidiary of Stanwood Industries. Corporate headquarters location.

## OWENS-ILLINOIS INC./ MACHINE DIVISION
315 Tolle Lane
Godfrey IL 62035
618/466-8811
Contact Verlene Schwalb, Assistant Industrial Relations Director. One of several area divisions of the well-known diversified manufacturer of packaging products. Company's principal products are glass containers, blown plastic containers, plastic beverage bottles, plastic drums, metal and plastic closures, tamper-resistant closures, plastic and glass presciption containers, pharmaceutical items, labels, and multipack plastic carriers for containers. Specialized glass products made and sold by the company include Libbey Tumblers, stemware, and decorative glassware, television blubs for picture tubes, and Kimble scientific and laboratory ware. Some overseas affiliates also manufacture flat glass and related products. Common positions include: Machinist. Training programs offered. Company benefits include: medical, dental, and life insurance; pension plan; tuition assistance; disability coverage; savings plan. Corporate headquarters location: Toledo, OH. Parent company: Owens-Illinois Inc. Operations at this facility include: manufacturing.

## OWENS-ILLINOIS INC./MOLD SHOP
1625 East Broadway
Alton IL 62002
618/463-3130
Contact David Bailey, Personnel Coordinator. One of several area divisions of the well-known diversified manufacturer of packaging products. Company's principal products are glass containers, although the company also produces and sells blown plastic containers, plastic beverage bottles, plastic drums, metal and plastic closures, tamper-resistant closures, plastic and glass presciption containers, pharmaceutical items, labels, and multipack plastic carriers for containers. Specialized glass products made and sold by the company include Libbey Tumblers, stemware, and decorative glassware, television blubs for picture tubes, and Kimble scientific and laboratory ware. Some overseas affiliates also manufacture flat glass and related products. Common positions include: Moldmaker. Principal educational backgrounds sought: Moldmaker Apprenticeship. Training programs offered. Company benefits include: medical, dental, and life insurance; pension plan; tuition assistance; disability coverage; savings plan. Corporate headquarters location: Toledo, OH. Parent company: manufacturing.

## PACKAGING CORPORATION OF AMERICA
1603 Orrington Avenue
Evanston IL 60204
708/492-4458
Contact Barb White, Administrative Assistant. A worldwide manufacturer of paper, corrugated, paper board, aluminum, and plastics packaging material with 60 plant location and 9,000 employees. Products are used in the packaging of food, paper and paper products, metal products, rubber and plastics, automotive products, and point of purchase displays; packaging soap, detergent, and food products; and residential construction. Operates more than 60 plants throughout the Midwest, South, and East. Common positions include: Accountant; Industrial Engineer; Mechanical Engineer; Operations/Production Manager; Sales Representative. Principal educational backgrounds sought: Accounting; Engineering; Marketing. Training programs offered; Internships offered. Company benefits include: medical, dental, and life insurance; tuition assistance; disability coverage; daycare assistance; profit sharing; employee discounts; savings plan. Corporate headquarters location. Parent company: Tenneco Inc. Operations at this facility include: divisional headquarters; research/development; administration. New York Stock Exchange (Tenneco Inc).

## SCHOLLE CORPORATION
200 West North Avenue
Northlake IL 60164
708/562-7290
Contact Kevin Breese, Director of Corporate Personnel. Manufacturer and distributor of flexible film packaging for the food and beverage industries; specialty chemical solutions for coating and related industries; bulk and

packaged acid; and prefabricated industrial buildings. Also manufactures filling equipment for food and beverage bag-in-box. Operations include: manufacturing; research/development; administration; service; sales. Corporate headquarters location. Common positions include: Accountant; Blue-Collar Worker Supervisor; Buyer; Chemist; Credit Manager; Customer Service Representative; Draftsperson; Chemical Engineer; Industrial Engineer; Mechanical Engineer; Financial Analyst; Department Manager; Management Trainee; Operations/Production Manager; Personnel & Labor Relations Specialist; Purchasing Agent; Quality Control Supervisor; Sales Representative; Transportation & Traffic Specialist. Principal educational backgrounds sought: Accounting; Business Administration; Chemistry; Engineering; Finance; Marketing. Company benefits include: medical insurance; dental insurance; pension plan; life insurance; tuition assistance; disability coverage; employee discounts; 401-k plan.

**SHERWIN-WILLIAMS COMPANY**
11541 South Champlain
Chicago IL 60628
312/821-3011
Contact Mr. Murphy, Personnel Director. Operates nationally in six segments: Retail Stores, Coatings, Chemicals, Packaging Products, Specialty Products, and International. Products include Sherwin-Williams, Dutch Boy, Martin Seymour, Baltimore and Kem paints, as well as such related packaging products as paint cans, sprays and labels. Corporate headquarters location: Cleveland, OH. International. New York Stock Exchange.

**SIGNODE INDUSTRIES INC.**
3650 West Lake
Glenview IL 60025
708/724-6100
Contact Manager of Professional Recruiting. Signode is one of the leading manufacturers and distributors of strapping systems for use in packaging and materials handling by a broad range of industries. Common positions include: Accountant; Computer Programmer; Chemical Engineer; Mechanical Engineer; Financial Analyst; Sales Representative; Systems Analyst. Principal educational backgrounds sought: Business Administration; Computer Science; Engineering. Company benefits include: medical insurance; dental plan; life insurance; tuition assistance; disability coverage; profit sharing; savings plan. Operations at this facility include: manufacturing; research/development; administration; sales. Corporate headquarters location.

**H.P. SMITH COMPANY**
**SPECIALTY COATINGS GROUP, INC.**
5001 West 66th Street
Bedford Park IL 60638
708/458-0777
Contact Robert E. Jones, Human Resources Manager. The company does paper converting for the release paper market. Common positions include: Accountant; Chemist; Customer Service Representative; Process Engineer; Project Engineer; Operations/Production Manager; Marketing Specialist; Sales Representative. Principal educational backgrounds sought: Accounting; Chemistry; Engineering; Marketing. Company benefits include: medical, dental, and life insurance; pension plan; tuition assistance; disability coverage; profit sharing; savings plan. Corporate headquarters location: Richmond, VA. Parent company: Specialty Coatings Group, Inc. Operations at this facility include: divisional headquarters; manufacturing; research/development; administration; service; sales. New York Stock Exchange.

**SOLO CUP COMPANY**
1501 East 96th Street
Chicago IL 60628
312/721-3600
Contact Chuck Keegan, Personnel Office. Manufacturer and distributor of paper cups, plates, etc. Corporate headquarters location: Champaign, IL.

**STONE CONTAINER CORPORATION**
150 North Michigan Avenue
Chicago IL 60601
312/346-6600
Contact Jeanne Seufert, Recruiting Specialist. A major multinational paper company, operating principally in the production and sale of commodity pulp, paper, and packaging products. tems and natural gas. More than 100 locations nationwide. Common positions include: Accountant; Computer Programmer; Credit Manager; Customer Service Representative; Financial Analyst; Systems Analyst; Transportation & Traffic Specialist. Principal educational backgrounds sought: Accounting; Business Administration; Computer Science; Finance. Company benefits include: medical, dental and life insurance; pension plan; tuition assistance; disability coverage; employee discounts; savings plan. Corporate headquarters location. New York Stock Exchange.

**SWEETHEART CUP CORP.**
7575 South Kostner
Chicago IL 60652
312/767-3300
Contact Dorothy Stanis, Employment Manager. Several area locations. Engaged in the manufacture and distribution of a variety of food serviceware including plates, cups, bowls, drinking straws, ice cream cones, as well as containers for use in packaging food and dairy products. Principal

trademarkes include Sweetheart, Guildware, and Eat-it-All. Corporate headquarters location: Green Bay, WI. Parent company: Fort Howard Paper Company. New York Stock Exchange

**WALDORF CORPORATION**
4200 South Pulaski Road
Chicago IL 60632
312/847-2500
Contact Personnel Department. Manufacturer of folding cartons for foods, detergents, personal hygiene products, and soaps. Principal educational background sought: Business Administration. Company benefits include: medical insurance; dental insurance; pension plan; life insurance; disability coverage; profit sharing; savings plan. Operations at this facility include: manufacturing; sales. Corporate headquarters location: St. Paul, MN.

**WESTERN KRAFT PAPER GROUP**
1001 Knell Street
Montgomery IL 60538
708/896-2061
Contact Personnel Department. Manufacturers of corrugated cartons. Common positions include: Customer Service Representative; General Manager; Sales Representative. Principal educational backgrounds sought: Accounting; Marketing. Company benefits include: medical insurance; dental insurance; pension plan; life insurance; tuition assistance; disability coverage; profit sharing; employee discounts; savings plan. Operations at this facility include: manufacturing. Corporate headquarters location: Portland, OR.

**WEYERHAEUSER PAPER COMPANY**
3001 Otto Street
Belleville IL 62223
618/233-5460
Contact Human Resource Manager. Manufacturer of corrugated cardboard shipping containers. Common positions include: Accountant; Customer Service Representative; Electrical Engineer; Industrial Engineer; Mechanical Engineer; Department Manager; Management Trainee; Operations/ Production Manager; Marketing Specialist; Personnel & Labor Relations Specialist; Purchasing Agent; Quality Control Supervisor; Sales Representative. Principal educational backgrounds sought: Accounting; Business Administration; Engineering. Training programs offered; Internships offered. Company benefits include: medical, dental, and life insurance; pension plan; tuition assistance; disability coverage; profit sharing; savings plan. Corporate headquarters location: Tacoma, Washington. Operations at this facility include: manufacturing; administration; service; sales. New York Stock Exchange. American Stock Exchange.

**WEYERHAEUSER PAPER COMPANY**
3001 Otto Street
Belleville IL 62223
618/233-5460
Contact Human Resource Manager. Manufacturer of corrugated cardboard shipping containers. Common positions include: Accountant; Customer Service Representative; Electrical Engineer; Industrial Engineer; Mechanical Engineer; Department Manager; Management Trainee; Operations/Production Manager; Marketing Specialist; Personnel & Labor Relations Specialist; Purchasing Agent; Quality Control Supervisor; Sales Representative. Principal educational backgrounds sought: Accounting; Business Administration; Engineering. Training programs offered; Internships offered. Company benefits include: medical, dental, and life insurance; pension plan; tuition assistance; disability coverage; profit sharing; savings plan. Corporate headquarters location: Tacoma, Washington. Operations at this facility include: manufacturing; administration; service; sales. New York Stock Exchange. American Stock Exchange.

## PETROLEUM & ENERGY RELATED: MINING & DRILLING

For more information on professional employment opportunities in the petroleum, engergy, and mining industries, contact the following profesional and trade organizations, as listed beginning on page 315:

**AMERICAN ASSOCIATION OF PETROLEUM GEOLOGISTS**
**AMERICAN GAS ASSOCIATION**
**AMERICAN GEOLOGICAL INSTITUTE**
**AMERICAN INSTITUTE OF MINING, METALLURGICAL AND PETROLEUM**
**AMERICAN INSTITUTE OF MINING, METALLURGICAL AND PETROLEUM/CHICAGO**
**AMERICAN NUCLEAR SOCIETY**
**AMERICAN PETROLEUM INSTITUTE**
**CLEAN ENERGY RESEARCH INSTITUTE**
**GEOLOGICAL SOCIETY OF AMERICA**
**SOCIETY OF EXPLORATION GEOPHYSICISTS**
**SOCIETY OF TRIBOLOGISTS AND LUBRICATION ENGINEERS**

**AMOCO PETROLEUM ADDITIVES COMPANY**
P.O. Box 182
Wood River IL 62095
618/251-2200
Contact Mr. George A Preston, Manager, Human Resources. Manufacturers of petroleum additives products. Employs over 300.

## AMOCO CORPORATION
200 E. Randolph Drive
Chicago IL 60601
312/856-5551
Contact Human Resources Department. One of the nation's leading energy and petroleum companies.

## BLACKSTONE MANUFACTURING COMPANY
4630 West Harrison Street
Chicago IL 60644
312/378-7800
Contact Juan J. Gomez, Personnel Manager. A manufacturer of fuel pumps. Divisional headquarters.

## CLARK OIL & REFINING
131st and Kedzie Avenue
Blue Island IL 60406
708/385-5000
Contact Tom Fredette, Personnel Director. A refiner and retail marketer of gasoline.

## CLARK OIL AND REFINING CORPORATION
P.O. Box 7
Hartford IL 62048
618/254-7301
Contact Roger Kline, Manager of Industrial Relations. Manufacturers of petroleum products. Employs over 300.

## COLUMBIA QUARRY COMPANY/ PLANTS #9, #3, AND #1
800 Quarry Road
Valmeyer IL 62295
618/935-2201
Contact Kevin Wilder, Superintendant. Manufacturers of calcium carbonate and crushed stone. Employs over 100.

## ELGIN NATIONAL INDUSTRIES
120 South Riverside Plaza
Chicago IL 60606
312/454-1900
Contact Administration. Business company involved in engineering and coal manufacturing.

**GOODMAN EQUIPMENT CORPORATION**
5430 W. 70th Place
Bedford Park IL 60638
708/496-1188
Contact Employee Relations Manager. Manufacturer of underground mining locomotives.

**T.J. GUNDLACH MACHINE COMPANY**
1 Freedom Drive
P.O. Box 385
Belleville IL 62222
618/233-7208
Contact T.E. Dinges, Vice President, Administration. Engaged in the manufacture and sales of mining machinery and equipment.

**LIQUID AIR CORPORATION/
AMERICAN AIR LIQUIDE**
5230 South East Avenue
Countryside IL 60525
708/482-8400
Contact Ronald J. Nowak, Manager of Administration. Engaged in the sale of industrial gases and related.

**LIQUID CARBONIC CORPORATION**
135 Lasalle Street
Chicago IL 60603
312/855-2834
Contact Carol Bosco, Director of Employee Relations. Produces a wide range of gas products.

**MARTIN OIL MARKETING, LTD. AND AFFILIATED COS.**
4501 West 127th Street
Alsip IL 60658
708/358-6500
Contact Personnel. A retailer and wholesale marketer of gasoline and diesel fuels.

**MISSISSIPPI LIME COMPANY**
P.O. Box 2247
Alton IL 62002
618/465-7741
Contact Personnel Department. A leading St. Louis company engaged in the manufacture of limestone, sand and rock.

**TORCO HOLDINGS**
624 South Michigan Avenue
Chicago IL 60605-1975
312/341-1600
Contact Personnel. A holding company whose subsidiaries are engaged in the following businesses: petroleum marketing and transportation; auto leasing.

## PRINTING & GRAPHIC ARTS

For more information on professional employment opportunities in the printing and graphic arts industries, contact the following professional and trade organizations, as listed beginning on page 315:

ASSOCIATION OF GRAPHIC ARTS
BINDING INDUSTRIES OF AMERICA
NATIONAL ASSOCIATION OF PRINTERS AND LITHOGRAPHERS
PRINTING INDUSTRIES OF AMERICA
TECHNICAL ASSOCIATION OF THE GRAPHIC ARTS

**AM INTERNATIONAL**
333 W. Wacker Drive, Suite 900
Chicago IL 60606-1265
312/558-7934
Contact Marianne Gruber, Manager of Personnel. Sells and services design and display products.

**ALDEN PRESS, INC.**
2000 Arthur Avenue
Elk Grove Village IL 60007
708/640-6000
Contact Jim Lillie, Personnel Director. A commercial printing company.

**AMERICAN PRINTERS AND LITHOGRAPHERS**
6701 West Oakton
Chicago IL 60648
312/267-6500
Contact William Wahl, Director of Purchasing. A commercial printer.

**INTERNATIONAL PAPER COMPANY/PEORIA**
8401 North University
Peoria IL 61615
309/692-7221
Contact Charles Harper or Bernice Sommer, Supervisor, Employee Relations. A large printing facility of consumer labels.

## SCHAWK GRAPHICS INC.
1695 River Road
Des Plaines IL 60018
312/694-9080
Contact Bob Drew, Personnel Director. Several area locations. Lithographers with clients in the printing, publishing and advertising industries. Corporate headquarters location: Park Ridge, IL.

## UARCO INC.
700 West Main Street
Barrington IL 60010
708/381-7000
Contact Mr. Fritz Kauffmann, Personnel Manager. Several area locations, including: Chicago and Watseka. Engaged in the design, manufacture and sale of business forms. Forms are used by data processing equipment firms as well as for typical business concerns. Products include such items as sales slips, invoices, purchase orders, and payroll checks. Company has 19 plants and 230 sales offices nationwide. Parent company: Pace Industries, NY. Common job positions include: Accountant; Chemist; Computer Programmer; Credit Manager; Chemical Engineer; Industrial Engineer; Mechanical Engineer; Sales Representative (resumes referred from Barrington to appropriate location near applicant's home). Principal educational backgrounds sought: Accounting; Business Administration; Chemistry; Computer Science; Engineering; Marketing. Company benefits include: medical insurance; dental insurance; pension plan; life insurance; disability coverage. Corporate headquarters location. Operations at this facility include: research/development; administration.

## WILSON JONES COMPANY
3201 Old Glenview Road
Wilmette IL 60091-2942
708/256-8800
Contact Industrial Relations Manager. Manufactures business forms and binders. A subsidiary of American Brands, Inc. (New York, NY). Corporate headquarters location.

---

### REAL ESTATE: SERVICES/MANAGEMENT/DEVELOPMENT
---

For more information on professional employment opportunities in the real state industry, contact the following professioanl and trade organizations, as listed beginning on page 315:

APARTMENT OWNERS AND MANAGERS ASSOCIATION
BUILDING OWNERS AND MANAGERS ASSOCIATION
BUILDING OWNERS AND MANAGERS ASSOCIATION/SUBURBAN
    CHICAGO

INSTITUTE OF REAL ESTATE MANAGEMENT
INTERNATIONAL ASSOCIATION OF CORPORATE REAL ESTATE
 EXECUTIVES/CHICAGO CHAPTER
NATIONAL ASSOCIATION OF REALTORS
INTERNATIONAL ASSOCIATION OF CORPORATE REAL ESTATE
 EXECUTIVES
INTERNATIONAL REAL ESTATE INSTITUTE
NATIONAL ASSOCIATION OF REAL ESTATE INVESTMENT TRUSTS


**BAIRD & WARNER**
200 W. Madison Street
Chicago IL 60606
312/368-5864
Contact Norb Michalak, Vice President of Human Resources. Full service real estate company.

**CHICAGO TITLE & TRUST COMPANY**
30 North LaSalle Street Suite 3700
Chicago IL 60602
312/630-2408
Contact Brenda Barbera, Human Resources Officer. Provides title insurance on real estate property as well as conventional trust services and escrow services. Parent company: Alleghany Corporation. Common positions include: Accountant; Attorney; Computer Programmer; Financial Analyst; Personnel & Labor Relations Specialist; Sales Representative; Systems Analyst; Title Examiner; Escrow Closer. Principal educational backgrounds sought: Accounting; Business Administration; Computer Science; Finance; Law; Title Insurance Related. Company benefits include: medical insurance; dental insurance; pension plan; life insurance; tuition assistance; long term & short term disability coverage; 401K - savings and profit sharing plan. Corporate headquarters location. Parent company: Alleghany Corp. Operations at this facility include: administration; service; sales.

**SHELDON GOOD & CO.**
West Wacker Drive
Suite 450
Chicago IL 60606
312/346-1500
Company is engaged in real estate marketing and auctions.

**INLAND REAL ESTATE AND AFFILIATES**
2901 West Butterfield Road
Oak Brook IL 60521
708/218-8000
Contact Personnel. Company is engaged in a variety of real estate services, including financing, insurance, and brokerage. Employs 1,500.

### JMB REALTY CORPORATION
900 North Michigan Avenue
Chicago IL 60611
312/440-4800
Contact Robyn Ralston, Recruitment Specialist. The nation's leader in real estate investment, management, and development. Common positions include: Accountant; Architect; Management Trainee. Principal educational backgrounds sought: Accounting. Training programs offered; Internships offered. Company benefits include: medical insurance; dental insurance; pension plan; life insurance; tuition assistance; disability coverage; daycare assistance; employee discounts; savings plan. Corporate headquarters location. Operations at this facility include: regional headquarters; administration; service; sales.

### LANE INDUSTRIES
1200 Shermer Road
Northbrook IL 60062
708/498-6789
Contact Personnel. Holding company with diversified interests including ranching, real estate, and banking. Employs over 3,000.

### MERCHANDISE MART PROPERTIES, INC.
470 Mart Plaza
Chicago IL 60654
312/527-7792
Contact Tom Fitzpatrick, Director of Human Resources. Management and leasing agent for the Merchandise Mart Building. Common positions include: Accountant; Advertising Worker; Attorney; Computer Programmer; Credit Manager; Draftsperson; Construction Project Engineer; Mechanical Engineer; Financial Analyst; Department Manager; Marketing Specialist; Personnel & Labor Relations Specialist; Purchasing Agent; Systems Analyst; Sales Representative; Technical Writer/Editor. Principal educational backgrounds sought: Accounting; Communications; Computer Science; Engineering. Company benefits include: medical, dental and life insurance; pension plan; tuition assistance; disability coverage; profit sharing. Corporate headquarters location. Operations at this facility include: administration; service.

## RESEARCH AND DEVELOPMENT

### FERMI NATIONAL ACCELERATOR LABORATORY
P.O. Box 500
Batavia IL 60510
708/840-3324
Contact James L. Thompson, Employment Manager. A federally-funded, not-for-profit organization dedicated to basic research in the field of high

energy physics. Parent company: Universities Research Association. Common positions include: Computer Programmer; Electrical Engineer; Mechanical Engineer. Principal educational backgrounds sought: Computer Science; Engineering; Physics. Internships available. Company benefits include: medical insurance; dental insurance; pension plan; life insurance; tuition assistance; disability coverage; savings plan. Corporate headquarters location: Washington, D.C. Operations at this facility: research/development.

**SARGENT-WELCH SCIENTIFIC COMPANY**
P.O Box 1026
Skokie IL 60076-1026
708/677-0600
Contact Personnel Director. For over 130 years, this company has supplied material for scientific research, education and applied science. Both a distributor and manufacturer of a wide range of analytical instruments, scientific apparatus, lab equipment, supplies, chemicals and specialized furniture. Common positions include: Accountant; Administrator; Advertising Worker; Attorney; Biochemist; Blue-Collar Worker Supervisor; Buyer; Chemist; Computer Programmer; Credit Manager; Customer Service Representative; Draftsperson; Electrical Engineer; Industrial Engineer; Mechanical Engineer; Financial Analyst; Branch Manager; Department Manager; Operations/Production Manager; Marketing Specialist; Personnel & Labor Relations Specialist; Physicist; Purchasing Agent; Quality Control Supervisor; Sales Representative; Systems Analyst; Technical Writer/Editor. Principal educational backgrounds sought: Accounting; Biology; Business Administration; Chemistry; Computer Science; Engineering; Finance; Liberal Arts; Marketing; Physics. Company benefits include: medical insurance; dental insurance; life insurance; tuition assistance; disability coverage; profit sharing; employee discounts; savings plan. Corporate headquarters location. Parent company: Artra Group. Operations at this facility include: manufacturing; research/development; administration; service; sales. International. New York Stock Exchange.

## RUBBER AND PLASTICS

For more information on professional employment opportunities in the rubber and plastics industries, contact the following professional and trade organizations, as listed beginning on page 315:

SOCIETY OF PLASTIC ENGINEERS
SOCIETY OF PLASTICS INDUSTRY
SOCIETY OF PLASTICS INDUSTRY/DES PLAINES

## BP CHEMICAL COMMERICAL COMPOSITES
333 North 6th Street
St. Charles IL 60174
708/584-3130
Contact Ms. Jan Johnson, Assistant Personnel Manager. Manufactures cones and plastic products for stereos.

## FLEX-O-GLASS
4647 West Augusta Boulevard
Chicago IL 60651
312/261-5200
Contact Paul Neville, Personnel Director. A plastics manufacturer.

## GOODYEAR TIRE AND RUBBER COMPANY
1501 Nicholas Boulevard
Elk Grove Village IL 60007
708/640-5000
Contact Personnel Department. One of the largest makers of tire and rubber products.

## HOFFER PLASTICS CORPORATION
500 Collins Street
South Elgin IL 60177
708/741-5740, ext. 275
Contact Personnel Director. A custom injection molder of thermoplastics products.

## INGRID DIVISION OF SEVKO, INC.
1419 Lake Cook Road, Suite 200
Deerfield IL 60015
708/940-8788
Contact Personnel. Manufacturer of plastic housewares and other plastic parts.

## MIDWEST RUBBER RECLAIMING COMPANY
3101 Mississippi Avenue
Box 2349
East St. Louis IL 62202
618/337-6400
Contact Horace Drake, Personnel Director. A leading St. Louis company engaged in the manufacture of reclaimed rubber.

## PANDUIT CORPORATION
17301 South Ridgeland Avenue
Tinley Park IL 60477
312/532-1800, ext. 1246

Contact Employment Department. Several area locations including: Tinley Park, New Lenox, Burr Ridge, Romeoville. Manufactures plastic wiring devices, mass-terminated connectors, terminals, and installation tools associated with these products. Multinational manufacturing facilities with sales and distribution offices in most major world capitals. Operations at this facility include: manufacturing; research/development; administration. Corporate headquarters location. International. Common positions include: Computer Programmer; Draftsperson; Mechanical Engineer; Systems Analyst; Sales Representative. Principal educational backgrounds sought: Business Administration; Computer Science; Engineering; Marketing. Company benefits include: medical insurance; dental insurance; pension plan; life insurance; tuition assistance; disability coverage; profit sharing; employee discounts; savings plan. Operations at this facility include: manufacturing; research/development; administration; service; sales.

**PLASTOFILM INDUSTRIES, INC.**
P.O. Box 531
Wheaton IL 60189
708/668-2838
Contact Sue Finley, Personnel Manager. A manufacturer of plastic packaging for pharmaceuticals, cosmetics, toys and small tools. Corporate headquarters location.

**PREMARK INTERNATIONAL**
1717 Deerfield Road
Deerfield IL 60015
708/405-6000
Contact Pat Lloyd, Human Resources Manager. A holding company with several subsidiaries operating in the area of plastics manufacturing.

**W.H. SALISBURY & COMPANY**
7520 North Long Avenue
Skokie IL 60077
312/679-6700
Contact Vice President. Several area locations. A manufacturer of molded, extruded and cut rubber products such as electrician's gloves.

**SIGNAL PLASTICS**
3445 North Kimball Avenue
Chicago IL 60618
312/267-3100
Contact Human Resources. Molds and manufactures plastic tail lights for cars. A division of T.L. Swint Industries, Inc. Common positions at this facility include: Accountant; Administrator; Blue-Collar Worker Supervisor; Buyer; Customer Service Representative; Draftsperson; Purchasing Agent; Quality Control Supervisor; Sales Representative. Principal educational backgrounds sought: Accounting; Business Administration; Engineering; Marketing. Company benefits include: medical insurance; life insurance;

tuition assistance; disability coverage. Operations at this facility include: manufacturing; research/development; administration.

## TRANSPORTATION/SHIPPING/AUTOMOTIVE

For more information on professional employment opportunities in the transportation/shipping/automotive industries, contact the following professional and trade organizations, as listed beginning on page 315:

AIR LINE EMPLOYEES ASSOCIATION
AIR TRANSPORT ASSOCIATION OF AMERICA
AMERICAN INSTITUTE OF AERONAUTICS AND ASTRONAUTICS
AMERICAN TRUCKING ASSOCIATION
AMERICAN TRUCKING ASSOCIATION/SEATTLE
ASSOCIATION OF AMERICAN RAILROADS
AUTOMOTIVE SERVICE ASSOCIATION
AUTOMOTIVE SERVICE ASSOCIATION/WASHINGTON OFFICE
AUTOMOTIVE SERVICE INDUSTRY ASSOCIATION
AVIATION MAINTENANCE FOUNDATION
INSTITUTE OF TRANSPORTATION ENGINEERS
MARINE TECHNOLOGY SOCIETY
MOTOR VEHICLE MANUFACTURERS ASSOCIATION
NATIONAL AERONAUTIC ASSOCIATION OF USA
NATIONAL AUTOMOTIVE DEALERS ASSOCIATION
NATIONAL INSTITUTE FOR AUTOMOTIVE SERVICE EXCELLENCE
NATIONAL MARINE MANUFACTURERS ASSOCIATION
PROFESSIONAL AVIATION MAINTENANCE ASSOCIATION
SHIPBUILDERS COUNCIL OF AMERICA


**ABF**
2020 Albright Road
Montgomery IL 60538
708/896-4626
Contact Branch Manager. A common carrier trucking firm.

**AIRCRAFT GEAR CORPORATION**
6633 West 65th Street
Chicago IL 60638
708/594-2100 ext. 701
Contact Kenneth Zuncic, Personnel Manager. Manufacturer of aircraft gears, precision parts, rotors and gear boxes. Corporate headquarters location. Common positions include: Industrial Engineer. Principal educational backgrounds sought: Business Administration; Computer Science; Engineering; Finance; Marketing. Company benefits include: medical insurance; dental insurance; pension plan; life insurance; tuition assistance;

disability coverage; profit sharing. Operations at this facility include: manufacturing; administration; sales.

**ALLEN INDUSTRIES**
Route 2
Herrin IL 62948
Contact Industrial Relations Manager. Suppliers of original equipment to the automotive industry.

**ALLIED VAN LINES/
CORPORATE HEADQUARTERS**
300 Park Plaza
Naperville IL 60563
708/717-3150
Contact Human Resource Department. The world's leading mover of families.

**THE ALTON AND SOUTHERN RAILWAY COMPANY**
1000 S. 22nd Street
East St. Louis IL 62207
618/482-3232
Contact F.E. Cooper, Superintendant. A major metropolitan St. Louis-based railroad. Employs over 400.

**AMERICAN WARRANTY CORPORATION**
7373 North Cicero
Lincolnwood IL 60646
708/677-4800
Contact Human Resources Office. Provides services contracts for extended auto repair.

**AMMCO TOOLS INC.**
Wacker Park
North Chicago IL 60064
708/689-1111
Contact John Lauten, Personnel Manager. Manufacturer of automotive tools and equipment for brake service, engine repair and wheel alignment. Corporate headquarters location.

**ANDERSON INDUSTRIES**
803 North Church Street
Rockford, IL 61103
312/987-9070
A diversified manufacturer of automotive, RV, and electrical components.

**BRINK'S, INC.**
234 East 24th Street
Chicago IL 60616
312/567-7100
Contact Personnel Director. Transports money & valuables domestically & internationally.

**BURTON SPRING**
2441 West 48th Street
Chicago IL 60632
312/376-1200
Contact Sandy Thompson, Personnel Manager. A manufacturer of truck and trailer leaf springs.

**CATERPILLAR TRACTOR COMPANY**
P.O. Box 504.
Joliet IL 60434
815/729-6250
Contact Employee Relations Manager. Designs, manufactures, and markets earthmoving equipment.

**CNW/
CHICAGO NORTHWESTERN CORPORATION**
165 North Canal Street
Chicago IL 60606
312/559-7000
Contact Robert F. Ard, Vice President of Personnel. A major railroad company offering freight rail service.

**CONTINENTAL AIR TRANSPORT**
730 West Lake Street
Chicago IL 60661
312/454-7829
Contact Linda Hawkins, Personnel Director. Provides ground transporation for customers around Chicago and O'Hare Airport.

**ECHLIN MANUFACTURING COMPANY**
1600 North Industrial Drive
McHenry IL 60050
815/385-7000
Contact Rick Neblock, Employment Relations Manager. Supplier of aftermarket parts and supplies for motor vehicles.

**ELECTRO-MOTIVE DIVISION/
GENERAL MOTORS**
9301 West 55th Steet
La Grange IL 60525
708/387-6428

Contact Salaried Employment. Manufacturer of diesel electric locomotives for railroads, mobile electric generating plants, and marine engines.

**ELGIN, JOLIET & EASTERN RAILWAY COMPANY**
P.O. Box 880
Joliet IL 60434-0957
815/740-6738
Contact L.M. Frye, Assistant Dir./Personnel Administration. A common carrier freight line operating in IN & IL. Common positions include: Accountant; Computer Programmer; Civil Engineer; Electrical Engineer; Industrial Engineer; Mechanical Engineer; Financial Analyst. Common positions include: Accounting; Engineering; Finance; Marketing. Company benefits include: medical insurance; pension plan; life insurance; tuition assistance; savings plan. Parent company: Transtar (Monroeville, PA). Operations at this facility: service.

**F&B MANUFACTURING CO.**
5480 North Northwest Highway
Chicago IL 60630
312/774-6300
Contact Dan Powell, Personnel Director. Manufactures small auto parts and components.

**FEL-PRO, INC.**
7450 North McCormick Boulevard
Skokie IL 60076
708/674-7700
Contact Personnel. A major manufacturer and marketer of automotive gaskets.

**FRANK CONSOLIDATED ENTERPRISES, INC.**
666 Garland Place
Des Plaines IL 60016
708/699-7000
Contact Personnel. A holding company whose subsidiaries are engaged in engaged in auto and truck sales and leasing, and corporate travel services. Employs 1,472.

**GARRETT GENERAL AVIATION SERVICES DIVISION**
P.O. Box 2177
Springfield IL 62705
217/544-3431
Contact Jay Davis, Manager Human Resources. Provides a comprehensive group of services to the aircraft industry. Parent company, Allied Signal Corporation, serves a broad spectrum of industries through its more than 40 strategic businesses, which are grouped into three sectors: Aerospace; Automotive; and Engineered Materials. Allied Signal is one of the nation's

largest industrial organizations, and has 115,000 employees in over 30 countries. Common positions include: Accountant; Administrator; Customer Service Representative; Operations/Production Manager; Personnel & Labor Relations Specialist; Purchasing Agent; Quality Control Supervisor; Blue-Collar Worker Supervisor; Computer Programmer; Department Manager; A&P Mechanics; Structural Sheet Metal Trim and Upholsters; Cabinet Makers. Principal educational backgrounds sought: Aviation Applied Sciences; Aviation Management; Aviation Maintenance; Accounting; Liberal Arts; Business Administration; Computer Science; Marketing. Company benefits include: medical, dental, and life insurance; pension plan; tuition assistance; disability coverage; profit sharing; savings plan; paid vacation. Corporate headquarters: Morristown, NJ. Parent company: Allied Signal Inc. New York Stock Exchange

**GE RAILCAR SERVICES CORPORATION**
33 West Monroe
Chicago IL 60603
312/853-5000
Contact Julie Dreixler, Manager of Employment/Hourly Relations. Lease and repair of specialized types of railcars.

**GATX CORPORATION**
120 South Riverside Plaza
Chicago IL 60606
312/621-6200
Contact Maureen A. Kelly, Personnel Manager. Holding company engaged in the lease or sale of rail cars.

**HENDRICKSON INTERNATIONAL**
P.O. Box 249
Burr Ridge IL 60521-0249
312/986-2500
Contact Peter Quagliana, Director, Human Resources. A worldwide supplier of quality engineered products to the truck/automotive industry. Company designs, develops, and manufactures suspension systems, leaf springs, and heavy stampings primarily for heavy-duty trucks. Several area locations include: Chicago, Crest Hill, and Burr Ridge. Common positions at this facility include: Buyer; Draftperson; Industrial Engineer; Mechanical Engineer; Sales Representative. Principal educational backgrounds sought: Business Administration; Engineering; Mathematics; Industrial Technology. Internships offered. Company benfits include: medical, dental, and life insurance; pension plan; tuition assistance; disability coverage; savings plan (401K). Corporate headquarters: Itasca, IL. Parent company: Boler Company. Operations at this facility include: research/development; administration.

## ILLINOIS CENTRAL GULF RAILROAD COMPANY
233 North Michigan Avenue
Chicago IL 60601
312/819-7500
Contact Personnel. Corporate offices for a major midwestern railroad.

## ITEL/PULLMAN
200 South Michigan Avenue
Chicago IL 60604
312/322-7070
Contact Diane Kreja, Personnel Manager. Works in railcar leasing, repair, and administration.

## LAWSON PRODUCTS
1666 East Touhy Avenue
Des Plaines IL 60018
708/827-9666
Contact Hank Kvintus, V.P. of Human Resources. Distributors of automotive and industrial parts.

## ROCKWELL GRAPHIC SYSTEMS
700 Oakmont Lane
Westmont IL 60559
708/850-5600
Contact Anson Cranmer, Personnel Director. Operations are conducted in four industry segments: Automotive (develops, manufactures, and markets various components for heavy-duty trucks, special purpose vehicles, light trucks and passenger cars); Aerospace (engaged in the research, development, and manufacture of space systems and rocket engines, military and general aviation aircraft); Electronics (research, development, and manufacture of guidance controls, avionics, telecommunication, and micro-electronics systems and equipment); and General Industries (Energy Graphics, Textile and Power Tools divisions). International operations. Corporate headquarters location: Pittsburgh, PA. New York Stock Exchange.

## SANTA FE SOUTHERN PACIFIC CORPORATION
1700 East Gulf Road
Schaumberg IL 60173
Contact Mr. Robert Edwards, Human Resources Director. Corporate office of the Atchinson, Topeka, and Santa Fe railway. The company is also involved in the exploration, development, production, and marketing of petroleum and natural resources.

**SUN ELECTRIC COMPANY**
One Sun Parkway
Crystal Lake IL 60014
815/459-7700
Contact Betty Zambon, Supervisor, Human Resources. Several area locations including: Chicago. Designs, manufactures, and markets diagnostic test and service equipment for the transportation industry, utilizing microcomputer applications and advanced electronics. Product line includes engine and emission analyzers; wheel service equipment (balancers, aligners, brake service equipment), a line of hand-held engine test equipment, collision repair equipment, and air conditioning and electrical systems testers. Corporate headquarters location. International. New York Stock Exchange.

**SUNSTRAND**
4949 Harrison Avenue
Rockford IL 61125
815/226-6000
Contact Gary Hedges, Corporate V.P. of Personnel & Public Relations. Corporate office of an aeronautics and aviation equipment parts manufacturer. Designs and develops high-technology components for aerospace, aviation, power transmission, and fluid and heat transfer.

**TERMINAL RAILROAD ASSOCIATION/ST. LOUIS**
2016 Madison Avenue
Granite City IL 62040. 314/231-5378
Contact Mr. R.P. Mathewson, Director Labor Relations/Personnel. Railroad terminal and switching operations.

**TORCO HOLDINGS**
624 South Michigan Avenue
Chicago IL 60605-1975
312/341-1600
Contact Personnel. A holding company whose subsidiaries are engaged in the following businesses: petroleum marketing and transportation; auto leasing.

**TRAILER TRAIN**
101 North Wacker Drive
Chicago IL 60606
312/853-3223
Contact Personnel. Company buy and maintains railroad freight car pools. Employs 950.

**UNITED AIRLINES**
P.O. Box 66100
Chicago IL 60666
708/952-4000
Contact Professional Employment. Passenger and cargo air transportation company. Common positions include: Accountant; Attorney; Buyer;

Computer Programmer; Customer Service Representative; Industrial Engineer; Financial Analyst; Marketing Specialist; Personnel & Labor Relations Specialist; Public Relations Worker; Purchasing Agent; Reporter/Editor; Systems Analyst; Technical Writer/Editor; Transportation & Traffic Specialist. Principal educational backgrounds sought: Accounting; Business Administration; Computer Science; Finance; Marketing. Company benefits include: medical, dental, and life insurance; pension plan; disability coverage; employee discounts. Corporate headquarters location. Parent company: UAL, Inc. Operations at this facility include: administration. New York Stock Exchange.

**VAPOR CORPORATION**
6420 West Howard Street
Niles IL 60648
312/631-9200
Contact Sandi Reid, Recruiting Coordinator. Manufacturers of railroad passenger car heating and air conditioning equipment, steam generators, electronic controls for transit rails, and railroad speed indicating/pacesetting controls. Corporate headquarters location.

## UTILITIES

For more information on professional employment opportunities in the utilities industry, contact the following professional organization, as listed beginning on page 315:

**AMERICAN WATER WORKS ASSOCIATION**


**CENTRAL ILLINOIS PUBLIC SERVICE**
607 East Adams Street
Springfield IL 62739
217/523-3600
Contact Richard Grant, Personnel Manager. An electric and gas utility company serving the Central and Southern Illinois area.

**COMMONWEALTH EDISON COMPANY**
P.O. Box 767
Chicago IL 60690-0767
312/294-4489
Contact Mary Kay McMahon, Supervisor of Professional Placement. An investor-owned utility engaged in electricity. Common positions include: Accountant; Chemist; Computer Programmer; Civil Engineer; Electrical Engineer; Industrial Engineer; Mechanical Engineer; Metallurgical Engineer; Personnel and Labor Relations Specialist; Systems Analyst; Chemical Engineer; Nuclear Engineer; Health Physcist. Educational

backgrounds sought include: Chemistry; Computer Science; Engineering. Internships available. Company benefits include: medical insurance; dental insurance; pension plan; life insurance; tuition assistance; disability coverage; savings plan. Operations at this facility include: administration New York Stock Exchange.

### ILLINOIS POWER COMPANY
330 North 29th Street
East St. Louis IL 62205
618/874-1041
Contact Personnel Department. An electric and gas utility serving the East St. Louis region.

### ILLINOIS POWER COMPANY
1050 West Boulevard
Belleville IL 62221
618/234-3400
Contact Personnel Department. An electric and gas utility servinig the Belleville region.

### ILLINOIS POWER
500 South 27th Street
Decatur IL 62525
217/424-6817
Contact Robert Teel, Professional Recruiting Specialist. An electric utilities company servicing approximately 1/4 of the state of Illinois. Common positions include: Accountant; Chemist; Computer Programmer; Customer Service Representantive; Economist; Civil Engineer; Electrical Engineer; Mechanical Engineer; Marketing Specialist; Public Relations Specialist; Statistician. Principal educational backgrounds sought: Accounting; Business Administration; Chemistry; Communications; Computer Science; Economics; Engineering; Finance; Marketing. Company benefits include: medical and life insurance; pension plan; tuition assistance; disability coverage; 401 K. Corporate headquarters location. Operations at this facility include: administration; sales. New York Stock Exchange.

### NICOR
1700 West Ferry Road
Naperville IL 60563
708/305-9500
Contact Becky Bacidore, Senior Personnel Coordinator. A petroleum and natural gas distributor servicing Illinois.

### NORTHERN ILLINOIS GAS COMPANY
P.O. Box 190
Aurora IL 60507-0190
708/983-8888

Contact Steve Webber, Management Recruiting Administrator. Multiple area locations including: Bellwood, Glen Ellyn, Glenwood, Glenview, Crystal Lake, Joliet, and Rockford. A gas supply company serving many communities in Northern Illinois. A subsidiary of NICOR, Inc. Common positions include: Accountant; Computer Programmer; Chemical, Civil, Petroleum, Industrial, and Mechanical Engineers; Sales Representative. Principal educational backgrounds sought: Accounting; Business Administration; Computer Science; Engineering; Marketing. Company benefits include: medical insurance; dental insurance; pension plan; life insurance; tuition assistance; disability coverage; savings plan. Corporate headquarters location: Naperville, FL. New York Stock Exchange.

**PEOPLES GAS COMPANY**
122 South Michigan Avenue
Chicago IL 60603
312/431-4000
Contact Mr. John Harwig, Personnel Director. A gas distributing company servicing the Chicago area.

# Professional Employment Services

# EMPLOYMENT AGENCIES AND TEMPORARY SERVICES OF GREATER CHICAGO

**APT (ABLE'S POOL OF TEMPORARIES)**
180 North Wabash
Suite 802
Chicago IL 60601
312/580-0380
Contact Claire Alshuler, Director. Temporary help service. Appointment requested. Founded 1982. Specializes in placing older workers aged 50 and over. Positions commonly filled include: Bookkeeper; Clerk; Data Entry Clerk; Legal Secretary; Office Worker; Receptionist; Secretary; Stenographer; Typist. Company pays fee.

**ACCORD INC.**
1543 Westchester Boulevard
Westchester IL 60154
708/345-7900
Contact Chester Dombrowski, Mechanical Manager, or John Fawcett, Electronic Manager. Employment agency. Founded 1981. Specializes in the areas of: Computer Hardware and Software; Engineering; Manufacturing; MIS/EDP; Technical and Scientific. Common positions filled include: Computer Programmer; Customer Service Representative; Draftsperson; EDP Specialist; Electrical Engineer; General Manager; Industrial Designer; Industrial Engineer; MIS Specialist; Mechanical Engineer; Quality Control Supervisor; Sales Representative; Software Engineer; Technical Writer/Editor; Technician. Company pays fee. Number of placements per year: 51-100.

**ACCOUNTANTS ON CALL**
3400 Dundee Rd., Ste. 260
Northbrook IL 60062
708/205-0800
FAX: 312/205-1230
Contact Marge Meyer. Specializes in the area of: accounting/finance.

**AGRA PLACEMENTS LTD, ILLINOIS**
1104 Keokuk
Lincoln IL 62656
217/735-4373
FAX: 217/732-2041
Contact Perry Schneider. Specializes in the areas of: agri-business; chemical; horticulture; international/overseas placement.

## AMERICAN ASSOCIATION OF RETIRED PERSONS
## SENIOR COMMUNITY SERVICE EMPLOYMENT PROGRAM
Post Office Box 630
1210 North Main
Edwardsville IL 62025
618/656-5710
Contact June M. Nealy, Project Director. Employment agency; temporary help agency. Appointment recommended. Founded 1974. This is a fee-free employment office sponsored by American Association of Retired Persons to serve persons 55 years of age and older; we offer subsidized employment for eligible persons (under low income) and help in finding permanent employment and vocational counseling to all over 55 years. Nonprofit. Nonspecialized. Positions commonly filled include: Bookkeeper; Clerk; Dietician/Nutritionist; Driver; General Laborer; Receptionist; Secretary; Typist. Placements per year: 51-100.

## E.J. ASHTON & ASSOCIATES, LTD
3125 N. Wilke Road, Suite A
Arlington Heights IL 60008
708/577-7900
Contact Ed Ashton, President. Employment agency. Appointment required. Founded 1979. Recruiting in and for the Insurance and Financial Services industries with emphasis on insurance professionals and Management. Specializes in the areas of: Accounting; Banking and Finance; Health and Medical; Insurance; Real Estate. Positions commonly filled include: Accountant; Actuary; Attorney; Claims Representative; Economist; Financial Analyst; Insurance Agent/Broker; Management Consultant; Marketing Specialist; Sales Representative; Statistician. Company pays fees. Number of placements per year: 51-100.

## AVAILABILITY, INC.
659 A East Broadway
Alton IL 62002
618/462-8831
Contact Lee J. Hamel, Manager. Employment agency; temporary help service. No appointment required. Founded 1964. Specializes in the areas of: Accounting and Finance; Banking; Clerical; Computer Hardware and Software; Engineering; MIS/EDP; Sales and Marketing; Technical and Scientific. Positions commonly filled include: Accountant; Administrative Assistant; Aerospace Engineer; Agricultural Engineer; Bank Officer/Manager; Biomedical Engineer; Bookkeeper; Ceramics Engineer; Chemical Engineer; Civil Engineer; Claim Representative; Clerk; Computer Operator; Computer Programmer; Credit Manager; Customer Service Representative; Data Entry Clerk; EDP Specialist; Electrical Engineer; Financial Analyst; General Manager; Industrial Engineer; Legal Secretary; MIS Specialist; Marketing Specialist; Mechanical Engineer; Medical Secretary; Metallurgical Engineer; Mining Engineer; Office Worker; Personnel and Labor Relations Specialist; Petroleum Engineer; Public

Relations Worker; Purchasing Agent; Receptionist; Sales Representative; Secretary; Statistician; Stenographer; Systems Analyst; Technical Writer/Editor; Typist; Word Processing Specialist. Company pays fee; individual pays fee. Number of placements per year: 101-200.

**B-W AND ASSOC., INC.**
4415 W. Harrison
Hillside IL 60162
708/449-5400
Contact Ms. Pat Edwards, Owner. Employment agency. Appointment required. Founded 1973. Specializes in the areas of: Architecture; Construction; Engineering; Food Industry; Health and Medical; Manufacturing; Real Estate. Positions commonly filled include: Architect; Civil Engineer; Construction Manager; Electrical Engineer; Mechanical Engineer; Petroleum Engineer. Company pays fee. Number of placements per year: 51-100.

**BANNER PERSONNEL SERVICE, INC.**
122 S. Michigan, Avenue
Suite 1510
Chicago IL 60603
312/704-6000
FAX: 312/580-2515
Contact Emel Singer. Specializes in the areas of: audit; bookkeeping; budgeting; consulting; data processing; EDP audit; engineering (aeronautical; chemical; civil; electrical; environmental/hazardous waste; HVAC; industrial; manufacturing; mechanical; nuclear; packaging); entry level (management trainees; support staff); financial analysis; programming; public accounting; sales; software engineering; tax; manufacturing/production (factory automation; plant management; quality control; robotics; safety; supervisory; technicians); office administration (administrators; clerks; management; receptionists; secretaries; word processing); sales (business products; computers; consumer products; industrial products; international; management; media; medical products; services/intangibles; trainees); scientific research & development (product development; research & development; sales; technicians); temporary services (accounting/bookkeeping; professional industrial; sales; secretaries; technical; word processing).

**BANNER PERSONNEL SERVICE, INC.**
1301 W. 22nd St.
#104 Executive Plaza
Oak Brook IL 60521
708/574-9499
FAX: 708/574-2218
Contact Susan Elliot. Specializes in the areas of: audit; bookkeeping; budgeting; consulting; data processing; EDP audit; engineering (aeronautical; chemical; civil; electrical; environmental/hazardous waste; HVAC; industrial;

manufacturing; mechanical; nuclear; packaging); entry level (management trainees; support staff); financial analysis; programming; public accounting; sales; software engineering; tax; manufacturing/production (factory automation; plant management; quality control; robotics; safety; supervisory; technicians); office administration (administrators; clerks; management; receptionists; secretaries; word processing); sales (business products; computers; consumer products; industrial products; management; media; medical products; services/intangibles; trainees); scientific research & development (product development; research & development; sales; technicians); temporary services (accounting/bookkeeping; professional industrial; sales; secretaries; technical; word processing).

**BANNER PERSONNEL SERVICE, INC.**
1701 E. Woodfield Rd., #611
Schaumburg IL 60193
708/706-9180
FAX: 708/706-9187
Contact Kathy A. Jirak, CPC. Specializes in the areas of: audit; bookkeeping; budgeting; clerical; consulting; data processing; EDP audit; engineering (aeronautical; chemical; civil; electrical; environmental/hazardous waste; HVAC; industrial; manufacturing; mechanical; nuclear; packaging); entry level (management trainees; support staff); financial analysis; programming; public accounting; sales; software engineering; tax; manufacturing/production (factory automation; plant management; quality control; robotics; safety; supervisory; technicians); office administration (administrators; clerks; management; receptionists; secretaries; word processing); sales (business products; computers; consumer products; industrial products; management; media; medical products; services/intangibles; trainees); scientific research & development (product development; research & development; sales; technicians); temporary services (accounting/bookkeeping; professional industrial; sales; secretaries; technical; word processing).

**BANNER PERSONNEL SERVICE, INC.**
700 Pearson St.-Des Plaines Mall
Des Plaines IL 60016
708/803-9440
FAX: 708/803-8357
Contact Beverly Zak. Specializes in the areas of: office administration (administrators; clerks; management; receptionists; secretaries; word processing); temporary services (accounting/bookkeeping; professional industrial; sales; secretaries; technical; word processing).

**BANNER PERSONNEL SERVICES, INC.**
800 East Diehl Rd., Ste. 100
Naperville IL 60563
708/505-8881
FAX: 708/505-4566

Contact Julia Mattei. Specializes in the area of: temporary services (accounting/bookkeeping; professional industrial; sales; secretaries; technical; word processing)

**BRITT ASSOCIATES, INC.**
53 West Jackson Boulevard
Chicago IL 60604
312/427-9450
Contact William Lichtenauer, President. Employment agency. Appointment requested. Founded 1971. Member NAPC. Specializes in the areas of: Distribution; Inventory and Production Control; Materials Management; Transportation. Positions commonly filled include: Buyer; Inventory Controller; Production Controller; Purchasing Agent; Traffic Manager; Warehouse Manager. Company pays fee.

**CPU ASSOCIATES**
1717 North Naper Boulevard
Suite 101
Naperville IL 60563
708/505-0082
Contact L.A. Smith, President. Employment agency; temporary help agency. Appointment required. Founded 1982. CPU Assoc. has expanded into DP Temps to service client needs. Specializes in the areas of: Computer Hardware and Software; MIS/EDP. Positions commonly filled include: Computer Programmer; EDP Specialist; Marketing Specialist; Sales Representative; Systems Analyst. Company pays fee. Number of placements per year: 51-100.

**CAREER MANAGEMENT ASSOCIATES**
262 North Phelps
Box 583
Rockford IL 61125
815/229-7815
Contact Brad Marion, Vice President. Employment agency. No appointment required. Founded 1971. Midwest division of national firm specializing in Health Care, Manufacturing and Financial services. Specializes in the areas of: Accounting; Banking and Finance; Computer Hardware and Software; Engineering; Health and Medical; Insurance; Manufacturing; MIS/EDP; Secretarial and Clerical. Positions commonly filled include: Accountant; Actuary; Administrative Assistant; Aerospace Engineer; Bank Officer/Manager; Bookkeeper; Claims Representative; Clerk; Computer Programmer; Credit Manager; Customer Service Representative; Data Entry Clerk; EDP Specialist; Electrical Engineer; Executive Secretary; Financial Analyst; General Manager; Hotel Manager; Industrial Engineer; Legal Secretary; Management Consultant; Marketing Specialist; Mechanical Engineer; Medical Secretary; Metallurgical Engineer; Nurse; Personnel Director; Purchasing Agent; Receptionist; Sales Representative; Secretary; Stenographer; Systems Analyst; Technical Writer/Editor; Typist;

Underwriter; Word Processor. Company pays fee. Number of placements per year: 201-500.

## CARLSON & ASSOCIATES
20 N. Wacker Dr.
Ste. 2243
Chicago IL 60606
312/704-1444
FAX: 312/704-0729
Contact Lawrence R. Carlson. Specializes in the areas of: hospitality/hotel/restaurant (travel).

## CARLSON/BENNETT CORPORATION
11 South Lasalle
Suite 2000
Chicago IL 60603
312/899-0009
Contact Eric Carlson. Specializes in the areas of: entry level (management trainees); sales (business products; computers; consumer products; industrial products; international; management; media; medical products; services/intangibles).

## CASEY FOR ACCOUNTANTS
632 West Algonquin Road, Suite 202
Des Plaines IL 60016
708/981-0200
Employment agency; temporary help agency. Appointment required. Founded 1975. Permanent and temporary Accounting, Finance and DP. Specializes in the areas of: Accounting; Banking and Finance; Computer Hardware and Software; MIS/EDP. Positions commonly filled include: Accountant; Attorney; Bank Officer/Manager; Bookkeeper; Computer Programmer; Credit Manager; Data Entry Clerk; EDP Specialist; Financial Analyst; Personnel Director; Systems Analyst; Word Processor. Company pays fee. Number of placements per year: 201-500.

## CEMCO SYSTEMS
2015 Spring Road, Suite 250
Oak Brook IL 60521
708/573-5050
Contact David R. Gordon, General Manager. Employment agency. Appointment required. Founded 1974. Provides career counseling, resume assistance and "skills vs. salary" evaluation. Accurate representation to both applicant and client. Specializes in the areas of: Computer Hardware and Software; MIS/EDP. Positions commonly filled include: Computer Programmer; EDP Specialist. Company pays fee. Number of placements per year: 101-500.

## COMPUPRO
312 W. Randolph Street
Suite 250
Chicago IL 60606
312/263-5507
FAX: 312/236-7489
Contact Douglas J. Baniqued. Specializes in the areas of: asset; corporate/computer security; consulting; credit; data processing; EDP audit; investment; lending; programming; sales; software engineering; systems; trainees; sales (computers; management); securities/investments (analysts; brokerage; management; operations; risk management); telecommunications (data; satellite; voice).

## DICKEY & ASSOCIATES, INC.
Post Office Box 1598
Rockford IL 61110
815/968-1883
Contact Ned Dickey, President. Employment agency. Founded 1965. Specializes in the areas of: Engineering; Manufacturing; Personnel/I.R. Positions commonly filled include: Accountant; Aerospace Engineer; Agricultural Engineer; Ceramics Engineer; Electrical Engineer; General Manager; Industrial Engineer; Marketing Specialist; Metallurgical Engineer; Personnel Director; Sales Representative; Purchasing Agent. Company pays fee. Number of placements per year: 0-50.

## DUNHILL OF CHICAGO
230 North Michigan Avenue
30th Floor
Chicago IL 60601
312/346-0933
Contact George Baker, Owner. Employment agency. Founded 1967. Specializes in the areas of: Accounting and Finance; Banking; Computer Hardware and Software; Sales and Marketing. Positions commonly filled include: Accountant; Bank Officer/Manager; Computer Operator; Computer Programmer; Sales Representative.

## DYNAMIC SEARCH SYSTEMS, INC.
3800 N. Wilke Road
Suite 485
Arlington Heights IL 60004
708/259-3444
Contact Michael J. Brindise, Principal. Employment agency. Appointment required. Founded 1983. We provide Data Processing personnel to Chicago and suburban employers. Primary focus covers Applications Development, Technical services and Consulting. Positions commonly filled include: Computer Programmer; EDP Specialist; Systems Analyst. Company pays fee. Number of placements per year: 101-500.

**EDP TEMPS AND CONTRACT SERVICES**
2115 Butterfield Road
Oak Brook IL 60521
708/620-7171
Temporary help service. No appointment required. Founded 1976. Branch offices located in: California; Connecticut; Illinois; Maryland; Massachusetts; Michigan; New York; Ohio; Pennsylvania; Virginia. Specializes in the areas of: Accounting and Finance; Banking; Computer Hardware and Software; Engineering; Insurance; Manufacturing; MIS/EDP; Nonprofit; Personnel and Human Resources; Printing and Publishing; Technical and Scientific. Positions commonly filled include: Computer Operator; Computer Programmer; EDP Specialist; MIS Specialist; Systems Analyst; Technical Writer/Editor. Company pays fee. Number of placements per year: 1001+.

**ESQUIRE PERSONNEL SERVICES, INC.**
222 S. Riverside Plaza, Suite 320
Chicago IL 60606
312/715-1111
312/648-4600
Contact Scott F. Fischer, Vice President. Temp services: Employment agency; temporary help agency. Appointment required. Founded 1955. Specializes in the areas of: Accounting; Advertising; Banking and Finance; Health and Medical; Insurance; Legal; Sales and Marketing; Secretarial and Clerical. Positions commonly filled include: Accountant; Actuary; Administrative Assistant; Advertising Executive; Attorney; Bank Officer/Manager; Claims Representative; Clerk; Computer Programmer; Credit Manager; Customer Service Representative; Data Entry Clerk; EDP Specialist; Executive Secretary; Financial Analyst; Insurance Agent/Broker; Legal Secretary; Marketing Specialist; Medical Secretary; Personnel Director; Public Relations Worker; Purchasing Agent; Receptionist; Sales Representative; Secretary; Statistician; Stenographer; Systems Analyst; Technical Writer/Editor; Typist; Underwriter; Word Processor. Company pays fee. Number of placements per year: 201-500.

**FARDIG ASSOCIATES**
176 W. Adams, Suite 1611
Chicago IL 60603
312/332-1480
Contact Maria Ferry, Vice President. Employment agency. Appointment required. Founded 1969. Specializes in the areas of: Accounting; Banking and Finance; Insurance; Legal; Manufacturing; Sales and Marketing; Secretarial and Clerical. Positions commonly filled include: Accountant; Administrative Assistant; Bookkeeper; Clerk; Customer Service Representative; Data Entry Clerk; Executive Secretary; Legal Secretary; Marketing Specialist; Receptionist; Sales Representative; Secretary; Typist; Word Processor. Company pays fee. Number of placements per year: 51-100.

**FIRST SEARCH**
9025 North Kostner
Skokie IL 60076
708/677-0001
FAX: 708/677-0233
Contact Chuck Szajkovics. Specializes in the area of: telecommunications (data; satellite; voice).

**GANS, GANS AND ASSOCIATES**
2930 S. Michigan
Ste. 102
Chicago IL 60616
312/791-9000
Contact Simone Gans. Specializes in the area of: insurance (actuarial; claims; life/health; pension; property/casualty; rating; reinsurance; sales; underwriting); legal (attorneys; legal administrators; legal secretaries; paralegals).

**GODFREY PERSONNEL INC.**
300 W. Adams, Suite 612
Chicago IL 60606
312/236-4455
Contact James Godfrey, President. Employment agency. Appointment required. Founded 1950. One of the leading Chicago area Insurance placement agencies. Positions commonly filled include: Actuary; Claims Representative; General Manager; Insurance Agent/Broker; Secretary; Typist; Underwriter; Word Processor. Company pays fee. Number of placements per year: 201-500.

**GROVE PERSONNEL SERVICES**
1411 Opus Place
Executive Towers West II
Suite 118
Downers Grove IL 60515
708/968-2771
Contact Raejean Fellows C.P.C., President. Employment agency; temporary help agency. Appointment required. Founded 1979. A progressive personnel agency specializing in permanent and temporary placement of office professionals and entry to mid-level management. Specializes in the areas of: Banking and Finance; Insurance; Sales and Marketing; Secretarial and Clerical. Positions commonly filled include: Accountant; Actuary; Administrative Assistant; Bank Officer/Manager; Bookkeeper; Claims Representative; Customer Service Representative; Data Entry Clerk; EDP Specialist; Executive Secretary; Legal Secretary; Marketing Specialist; Medical Secretary; Personnel Director; Receptionist; Sales Representative; Secretary. Company pays fee. Number of placements per year: 201-500.

## HILTON RESEARCH ASSOCIATES-MID WEST
1920 Highland Avenue
Suite 300
Lombard IL 60148
708/916-3124
Employment agency. Appointment requested. Founded 1979. Specializes in the areas of: Health and Medical; MIS/EDP; Sales and Marketing. Positions commonly filled include: Biochemist; Biomedical Engineer; Chemist; Computer Programmer; Customer Service Representative; MIS Specialist; Marketing Specialist; Nurse; Sales Representative. Company pays fee. Number of placements per year: 201-500.

## INFOQUEST
116 W. Eastman, Suite 209
Arlington Heights IL 60004
708/253-9200
Contact Bill Williams. Specializes in the areas of: architectural design; data processing; drafting; engineering (chemical; civil; electrical; environmental/hazardous waste; HVAC; manufacturing; mechanical; packaging); interior design; operations; programming; sales; software engineering; systems; manufacturing/production (factory automation; plant management; quality control; robotics; safety; technicians); temporary services (professional industrial; technical).

## INTERVIEWING CONSULTANTS, INC.
19 S. LaSalle Street
Suite 900
Chicago IL 60603
312/263-1710
Contact Ron Giambarberee, Owner/Manager. Employment agency. Temporary help agency. On and off-premise recruiting. Appointment requested. Founded 1980. A network of personnel consultants. A multiple listing of job orders and candidates. Positions commonly filled include: Accountant; Administrative Assistant; Bookkeeper; Claims Representative; Clerk; Computer Programmer; Credit Manager; Customer Service Representative; Data Entry Clerk; Electrical Engineer; Executive Secretary; Financial Analyst; General Manager; Industrial Engineer; Legal Secretary; Medical Secretary; Office Manager; Personal Director; Purchasing Agent; Receptionist; Sales Representative; Secretary; Stenographer; Systems Analyst; Technician; Typist; Underwriter; Word Processor. Company pays fee. Number of placements per year: 200+.

## KINGSLEY EMPLOYMENT
208 South LaSalle Street
Suite 1877
Chicago IL 60604
312/726-8190

Contact Edward Friedman, Owner. Employment agency. No appointment required. Founded 1968. Specializes in: Advertising; Banking. Positions commonly filled include: Administrative Assistant; Advertising Worker; Financial Analyst; Office Worker; Receptionist; Secretary; Stenographer; Typist; Word Processing Specialist. Company pays fee. Number of placements per year: 51-100.

**MACINTYRE EMPLOYMENT SERVICES, LTD.**
1250 West NW Highway
Room 207
Mt. Prospect IL 60056
708/577-8860
Contact Elizabeth E. MacIntyre, President. Employment agency. No appointment required. Founded 1980. Specializes in the areas of: Accounting; Advertising; Architecture; Computer Hardware and Software; Construction; Engineering; Health and Medical; Manufacturing; MIS/EDP; Printing and Publishing; Sales and Marketing; Secretarial and Clerical; Technical and Scientific; Transportation. Company pays fee.

**MICHAEL DAVID ASSOCIATES, INC.**
133 East Ogden Avenue
Room 202
Hinsdale IL 60521
708/654-4460
Contact Director, Administrative Services. Employment agency. Appointment requested. Founded 1982. Specializes in the areas of: Accounting and Finance; Clerical; Computer Hardware and Software; Engineering; Food Industry; Health and Medical; Insurance; Legal; Manufacturing; Personnel and Human Resources; Sales and Marketing; Technical and Scientific. Company pays fee. Number of placements per year: 201-500.

**MURPHY EMPLOYMENT SERVICE**
133 Vine Street
Park Ridge IL 60068
708/825-2136
Contact Frances Kenney. Specializes in the areas of: audit; bookkeeping; budgeting; clerical; office administration (administrators; clerks; management; receptionists; secretaries; word processing).

**THE MURPHY GROUP**
122B Calender Court Mall
La Grange IL 60525
708/352-8350
Contact Susan M. Oja, Owner/Manager. Employment agency. No appointment required. Founded 1957. Nonspecialized. Positions commonly filled include: Accountant; Actuary; Administrative Assistant; Advertising Worker; Bank Officer/Manager; Bookkeeper; Buyer; Civil Engineer; Claims

Representative; Clerk; Computer Operator; Computer Programmer; Credit Manager; Customer Service Representative; Data Entry Clerk; Demonstrator; Draftsperson; Driver; EDP Specialist; Economist; Electrical Engineer; Financial Analyst; General Manager; Industrial Designer; Industrial Engineer; Insurance Agent/Broker; Legal Secretary; MIS Specialist; Marketing Specialist; Mechanical Engineer; Medical Secretary; Metallurgical Engineer; Office Worker; Operations/Production Specialist; Personnel and Labor Relations Specialist; Public Relations Worker; Purchasing Agent; Quality Control Supervisor; Receptionist; Reporter/Editor; Sales Representative; Secretary; Statistician; Stenographer; Systems Analyst; Technical Writer/Editor; Technician; Typist; Underwriter; Word Processing Specialist. Company pays fee. Number of placements per year: 101-200.

## THE MURPHY GROUP
150 East Cook Avenue
Libertyville IL 60048
708/362-6100
FAX: 708/362-1826
Contact Leah Kayle, CPC. Specializes in the areas of: accounting/finance; hospitality/hotel/restaurant (food service; hotel; institutional; restaurant; travel); office administration.

## THE MURPHY GROUP
6 S. 235 Steeple Run Drive
Naperville IL 60540
708/355-7030
FAX: 708/355-8670
Contact Ethel Berendson, CPC. Specializes in the area of: office administration (administrators; clerks; management; receptionists; secretaries; word processing).

## THE MURPHY GROUP
1211 West 22, Suite 221
Oak Brook IL 60521
708/574-2840
Contact William A. Murphy II, Vice President/General Manager. Employment agency; temporary help agency. Founded 1957. A regional network of personnel consultants, the only one in existence. A multiple listing of job orders and candidates. Specializes in the areas of: Accounting; Advertising; Banking and Finance; Computer Hardware and Software; Engineering; Food Industry; Insurance; Manufacturing; MIS/EDP; Printing and Publishing; Sales and Marketing; Secretarial and Clerical; Technical and Scientific. Positions commonly filled include: Accountant; Administrative Assistant; Advertising Executive; Bookkeeper; Civil Engineer; Claims Representative; Clerk; Computer Programmer; Credit Manager; Customer Service Representative; Data Entry Clerk; Draftsperson; EDP Specialist; Electrical Engineer; Executive Secretary; Financial Analyst; General

Manager; Industrial Engineer; Legal Secretary; Marketing Specialist; Mechanical Engineer; Medical Secretary; Personnel Director; Purchasing Agent; Receptionist; Sales Representative; Secretary; Stenographer; Systems Analyst; Technician; Typist; Underwriter; Word Processor. Company pays fee. Number of placements per year: 1000+

**THE MURPHY GROUP**
205 S. Hale Avenue
Wheaton IL 60187
708/653-3660
Contact William Murphy, II. Specializes in the areas of: asset; credit; credit & collection (commercial; consumer; retail; wholesale); investment; lending; trainees; insurance (claims; life/health; pension; property/casualty; rating; reinsurance; sales; underwriting); manufacturing/production (factory automation; plant management; quality control; robotics; safety; supervisory; technicians); marketing (consumer products; business products/computers; industrial products; market research; medical products; sales promotion).

**THE MURPHY GROUP OF DEERFIELD,**
570 Lake Cook Rd. #414
Deerfield IL 60015
708/945-4950
Contact Sallie Elwell, CPC. Specializes in the areas of: office administration (administrators; clerks; management; receptionists; secretaries; word processing); sales (business products; computers; consumer products; industrial products; management; medical products; services/ intangibles; trainees).

**OMNI ONE**
2200 E. Devon Avenue, Suite 246
Des Plaines IL 60018
708/299-1233
Contact Steve Leibovitz, Agency Manager. Employment agency. No appointment required. Founded 1893. GEE owns and operates 28 branches throughout the U.S. and Canada. "Service Second to None." Specializes in the areas of: Computer Hardware and Software; Engineering; MIS/EDP; Technical and Scientific. Positions commonly filled include: Biomedical Engineer; Computer Programmer; EDP Specialist; Electrical Engineer; Mechanical Engineer; Systems Analyst; Technical Writer/Editor; Technician. Company pays fees. Number of placements per year: 201-500.

## OPERATION ABLE/
## ABLE WORKER INSTITUTE
180 North Wabash
Eighth Floor
Chicago IL 60601
312/580-0390

Individual job search assistance and outplacement counseling. Appointment requested. Founded 1977. Specializes in the areas of: Clerical; Elderly; Minorities; Nonprofit; Sales and Marketing; Technical and Scientific; Women. Positions commonly filled include: Accountant; Administrative Assistant; Advertising Worker; Bookkeeper; Chemical Engineer; Chemist; Claims Representative; Clerk; Computer Programmer; Data Entry Clerk; Demonstrator; Draftsperson; Electrical Engineer; Factory Worker; Financial Analyst; Food Technologist; General Laborer; General Manager; Hotel Manager/Assistant Manager; Industrial Engineer; Insurance Agent/Broker; Light Industrial Worker; Marketing Specialist; Mechanical Engineer; Nurse; Office Worker; Operations and Production Specialist; Purchasing Agent; Quality Control Supervisor; Receptionist; Sales Representative; Secretary; Stenographer; Systems Analyst; Typist. Individual pays fee.

## OPERATION ABLE/
## OAK PARK TOWNSHIP SENIOR EMPLOYMENT CENTER
500 South Maple
Oak Park IL 60304
708/386-6445

Employment agency. Appointment requested. Founded 1980. Specializes in the areas of: Elderly; Nonprofit. Positions commonly filled include: Administrative Assistant; Babysitter; Bookkeeper; Clerk; Companion; Customer Service Representative; Demonstrator; Driver; General Laborer; Handyman; Housekeeper; Janitor/Custodian; Light Industrial Worker; Maintenance Worker; Messenger; Office Worker; Receptionist; Sales Representative; Secretary; Typist. Number of placements per year: 501-1000.

## OPPORTUNITIES UNLIMITED
53 West Jackson, Ste. 1060
Chicago IL 60604
312/922-8898
FAX: 312/347-1206

Contact Roxi Pistilli. Specializes in the areas of: legal (legal administrators; legal secretaries; paralegals); office administration (administrators; clerks; management; receptionists; secretaries; word proccessing).

## OPPORTUNITY PERSONNEL SERVICE
200 West Adams
Suite 1702
Chicago IL 60606
312/704-9898

Contact Gwen Hudson, President; Marian Long, Executive Director; Charlene Langford, Consultant; or John Drykacz, Consultant. Employment agency. Appointment requested. Founded 1955. Specializes in the areas of: Accounting and Finance; Clerical; Computer Hardware and Software; Insurance; Legal; Manufacturing; Personnel and Human Resources; Sales and Marketing. Positions commonly filled include: Accountant; Actuary; Administrative Assistant; Bank Officer/Manager; Bookkeeper; Buyer; Claims Representative; Clerk; Computer Operator; Credit Manager; Customer Service Representative; Data Entry Clerk; Financial Analyst; General Manager; Hotel Manager/Assistant Manager; Legal Secretary; Office Worker; Purchasing Agent; Receptionist; Sales Representative; Secretary; Stenographer; Typist; Underwriter; Word Processing Specialist. Company pays fee; individual pays fee.

**OPPORTUNITY SPECIALISTS, INC.**
709 N. Gilbert
Danville IL 61832
217/446-2940
FAX: 217/446-2991
Contact Sharon L. Ady. Specializes in the area of: temporary services.

**PAIGE PERSONNEL/PAIGE TEMPORARY**
5215 Old Orchard Road, Suite 940
Skokie IL 60077
708/966-0700
Employment agency; temporary help service. No appointment required. Founded 1964. Specializes in the area of: Clerical. Positions commonly filled include: Administrative Assistant; Bookkeeper; Clerk; Computer Operator; Customer Service Representative; Data Entry Clerk; Legal Secretary; Medical Secretary; Office Worker; Personnel and Labor Relations Specialist; Public Relations Worker; Purchasing Agent; Receptionist; Secretary; Stenographer; Typist; Word Processing Specialist. Company pays fee. Number of placements per year: 501-1000.

**PAHLMAN MURPHY AND ATTRIDGE, INC.**
180 North Michigan Avenue
Suite 329
Chicago IL 60601
312/236-9036
Contact Alice Huntsha, President. Clerical and Executive Placement; Resume Service. Specializing in the areas of administration and advertising, communication, and market research.

**PERMANENT PEOPLE, INC.**
1419 Lake Cook Road
Suite 150
Deerfield IL 60015
708/966-1220
Contact Miriam Walchirk, Manager. Employment agency. Appointment required. Specializes in the areas of: Secretarial and Clerical. Positions commonly filled include: Customer Service Representative; Executive Secretary; Legal Secretary; Medical Secretary; Personnel Director; Receptionist; Secretary; Typist; Word Processor. Company pays fee. Number of placements per year: 51-100.

**PERSONNEL POOL**
2680 Bellvedere Road
Waukegan IL 60085
708/336-0164
Temporary help service. Appointment requested. Founded 1954. A member of Victor Temporary Services. Victor Temporary Services has over 100 offices throughout the United States. Nonspecialized. Positions commonly filled include: Bookkeeper; Clerk; Computer Operator; Customer Service Representative; Data Entry Clerk; Demonstrator; Draftsperson; Electronic Assembler; Factory Worker; General Laborer; Legal Secretary; Light Industrial Worker; Medical Secretary; Office Worker; Receptionist; Secretary; Stenographer; Technician; Typist; Word Processing Specialist. Company pays fee. Number of placements per year: 1001+.

**PERSONNEL POOL**
1608 Maple Street
Evanston IL 60201
708/475-2707
Temporary help service. Appointment requested. Founded 1954. Victor Temporary Services has over 100 offices throughout the United States. Nonspecialized. Positions commonly filled include: Bookkeeper; Clerk; Computer Operator; Customer Service Representative; Data Entry Clerk; Demonstrator; Draftsperson; Electronic Assembler; Factory Worker; General Laborer; Legal Secretary; Light Industrial Worker; Medical Secretary; Office Worker; Receptionist; Secretary; Stenographer; Technician; Typist; Word Processing Specialist. Company pays fee. Number of placements per year: 1001+.

**PERSONNEL POOL**
700 North Milwaukee
Suite 102
Vernon Hills IL 60001
708/680-3875
Temporary help service. Appointment requested. Founded 1954. A member of Victor Temporary Services. Victor Temporary Services has over 100 offices throughout the United States. Nonspecialized. Positions commonly

filled include: Bookkeeper; Clerk; Computer Operator; Customer Service Representative; Data Entry Clerk; Demonstrator; Draftsperson; Electronic Assembler; Factory Worker; General Laborer; Legal Secretary; Light Industrial Worker; Medical Secretary; Office Worker; Receptionist; Secretary; Stenographer; Technician; Typist; Word Processing Specialist. Company pays fee. Number of placements per year: 1001+.

**PERSONNEL POOL**
2625 Butterfield Road
Suite 112 South
Oak Brook IL 60521
708/571-8350
Temporary help service. Appointment requested. Founded 1954. Victor Temporary Services has over 100 offices throughout the United States. Nonspecialized. Positions commonly filled include: Bookkeeper; Clerk; Computer Operator; Customer Service Representative; Data Entry Clerk; Demonstrator; Draftsperson; Electronic Assembler; Factory Worker; General Laborer; Legal Secretary; Light Industrial Worker; Medical Secretary; Office Worker; Receptionist; Secretary; Stenographer; Technician; Typist; Word Processing Specialist. Company pays fee. Number of placements per year: 1001+.

**POLLAK AND SKAN, INC.**
120 W. Center Court
Schaumburg IL 60195
708/359-5227
Contact Central Recruiting. Temporary help agency. No appointment required. Founded 1951. Pollak and Skan is a diversified contract technical services company serving a wide range of technologies for over 30 years. The agency is a charter member of the National Technical Services Assoc. and practice its code of ethics. Specializes in the areas of: Computer Hardware and Software; Engineering; Industrial and Interior Design; Manufacturing; MIS/EDP; Technical and Scientific. Positions commonly filled include: Aerospace Engineer; Agricultural Engineer; Biochemist/Chemist; Biomedical Engineer; Ceramics Engineer; Civil Engineer; Computer programmer; Draftsperson; EDP Specialist; Electrical Engineer; Industrial Designer; Industrial Engineer; Mechanical Engineer; Metallurgical Engineer; Mining Engineer; Petroleum Engineer; Systems Analyst; Technical Writer/Editor; Technician.

**PRESTIGE PERSONNEL INC.**
2066 Ridge Road
Homewood IL 60430
708/798-9010
FAX: 708/798-9099
Contact Estelle Harris, CPC. Specializes in the areas of: engineering (civil; electrical; industrial; manufacturing; mechanical); manufacturing/production (factory automation; international; plant management; quality control; safety;

supervisory; technicians); office administration (administrators; clerks; management; receptionists; secretaries; word processing); sales (business products; computers; consumer products; industrial products; international; management; medical products; services/intangibles); temporary services (accounting/bookkeeping; professional industrial; secretaries; technical; word processing).

**PRESTIGE TEMPORARIES-CALUMET DIVISION**
2066 Ridge Road
Homewood IL 60430
219/931-1171
708/798-7666
Contact Estelle Harris, Vice President/Manager. Temporary help agency. Appointment preferred. Founded 1976. Specializes in the areas of: Secretarial and Clerical. Positions commonly filled include: Accountant; Administrative Assistant; Bookkeeper; Clerk; Computer Programmer; Construction Worker; Customer Service Representative; Data Entry Clerk; Executive Secretary; Factory Worker; General Laborer; Legal Secretary; Light Industrial Worker; Marketing Specialist; Medical Secretary; Receptionist; Secretary; Stenographer; Typist; Word Processor. Company pays fee. Number of placements per year: 1000+.

**PRESTIGE TEMPORARIES-HOMEWOOD DIVISION**
2066 Ridge Road
Homewood IL 60430
708/798-4490
Contact Estelle Harris, Vice President/Manager. Temporary help agency. Appointment preferred. Founded 1976. Specializes in the areas of: Accounting; Advertising; Construction; Health and Medical; Legal; Manufacturing; MIS/EDP; Real Estate; Sales and Marketing; Secretarial and Clerical; Transportation. Positions commonly filled include: Administrative Assistant; Bank Officer/Manager; Bookkeeper; Civil Engineer; Claims Representative; Commercial Artist; Computer Programmer; Credit Manager; Customer Service Representative; Data Entry Clerk; Draftsperson; Executive Secretary; Financial Analyst; Industrial Designer; Legal Secretary; Light Industrial Worker; Mechanical Engineer; Medical Secretary; Public Relations Worker; Purchasing Agent; Receptionist; Sales Representative; Secretary; Stenographer; Systems Analyst; Technical Writer/Editor; Technician; Typist; Word Processor. Company pays fee. Number of placements per year: 100+.

**PROFILE PERSONNEL, INC.**
55 West Wacker Drive, Suite 400
Chicago IL 60601
312/641-0540
Contact David Hodge, Operations Manager. Employment agency. Appointment preferred. Founded 1969. Specializes in the areas of: Advertising; Banking; Bilingual; Clerical; Insurance; Legal; Manufacturing;

Personnel and Human Resources; Real Estate; Sales and Marketing; Secretarial. Positions commonly filled include: Actuary; Administrative Assistant; Bank Teller; Bookkeeper; Claims Representative; Clerk; Computer Operator; Customer Service Representative; Data Entry Clerk; Insurance Agent/Broker; Legal Secretary; Medical Secretary; Office Worker; Public Relations Worker; Receptionist; Sales Representative; Secretary; Stenographer; Typist; Underwriter; Word Processing Specialist. Company pays fee. Number of placements per year: 1001+.

**PROFILE TEMPORARY SERVICE, INC.**
55 West Wacker Drive, Suite 400
Chicago IL 60601
312/641-1920
Contact Cheryl L. Davis, C.P.C., Executive Director. Temporary help service. Appointment preferred. Founded 1979. Specializes in the areas of: Accounting and Finance; Advertising; Banking; Clerical; Insurance; Legal; Manufacturing; Real Estate. Positions commonly filled include: Accountant; Administrative Assistant; Advertising Worker; Bookkeeper; Claims Representative; Clerk; Customer Service Representative; Data Entry Clerk; Demonstrator; Legal Secretary; Light Industrial Worker; Model; Office Worker; Receptionist; Secretary; Statistician; Stenographer; Typist; Word Processing Specialist. Company pays fee. Number of placements per year: 1001+.

**RITT - RITT AND ASSOCIATES**
1400 E. Touhy Avenue
Des Plaines IL 60018
708/298-2510
Contact Art Ritt, President. Employment agency. Appointment required. Founded 1976. One of the largest independent executive placement firms in the country specializing in Hospitality. All account executives have previous experience working in the Food and Hospitality industries in top positions. "We speak the language." Highly professional and recognized as one of the best companies to work with. Positions commonly filled include: Accountant; Advertising Executive; Architect; Dietician/Nutritionist; Economist; Food and Hospitality Specialist; General Manager; Hotel Manager; Marketing Specialist; Purchasing Agent. Company pays fee. Number of placements per year: 201-500.

**SALEM TECHNICAL SERVICES OF OAK BROOK**
1333 Butterfield Road
Downers Grove IL 60515
800/323-7200
Contact Mike Hind, Manager. Temporary help service. No appointment required. Founded 1967. Branch offices located in: Atlanta, GA; Austin, TX; Beloit, WI; Bloomington, MN; Burlington, MA; Charlotte, NC; Cincinnati, OH; Cleveland, OH; Dallas, TX; Grand Rapids, MI; McLean, VA; Houston, TX; Milwaukee, WI; Phoenix, AZ; San Jose, CA; Golden, CO; San Jose, CA.

Specializes in the areas of: Architecture; Computer Hardware and Software; Engineering; Manufacturing; MIS/EDP; Personnel and Human Resources; Technical and Scientific. Positions commonly filled include: Aerospace Engineer; Architect; Buyer; Chemical Engineer; Chemist; Civil Engineer; Commercial Artist; Computer Operator; Computer Programmer; Data Entry Clerk; Draftsperson; Driver; EDP Specialist; Electrical Engineer; Industrial Designer; Industrial Engineer; MIS Specialist; Manufacturing Engineer; Mechanical Engineer; Metallurgical Engineer; Operations and Production Specialist; Personnel and Labor Relations Specialist; Purchasing Agent; Quality Control Supervisor; Reporter/Editor; Software Engineer; Systems Analyst; Technical Illustrator; Technical Recruiter; Technical Writer/Editor; Technician; Word Processing Specialist. Number of placements per year: 201-500.

**SEARCH DYNAMICS INC.**
9420 West Foster Avenue
Suite 200
Chicago IL 60656
312/992-3900
Contact George Apostle, President. Employment agency. Appointment requested. Founded 1979. Specializes in the areas of: Computer Hardware and Software; Engineering; Manufacturing; Technical and Scientific. Positions commonly filled include: Aerospace Engineer; Agricultural Engineer; Architect; Biomedical Engineer; Ceramics Engineer; Chemical Engineer; Civil Engineer; Draftsperson; Electrical Engineer; General Manager; Industrial Engineer; Marketing Specialist; Mechanical Engineer; Metallurgical Engineer; Mining Engineer; Petroleum Engineer; Physicist; Quality Control Supervisor. Company pays fee. Number of placements per year: 101-200.

**SELECTABILITY PERSONNEL**
1011 East State Street
Rockford IL 61104
815/964-0078
Temporary help service. Appointment requested. Founded 1954. A member of Victor Temporary Services. Victor Temporary Services has over 100 offices throughout the United States. Nonspecialized. Positions commonly filled include: Bookkeeper; Clerk; Computer Operator; Customer Service Representative; Data Entry Clerk; Demonstrator; Draftsperson; Electronic Assembler; Factory Worker; General Laborer; Legal Secretary; Light Industrial Worker; Medical Secretary; Office Worker; Receptionist; Secretary; Stenographer; Technician; Typist; Word Processing Specialist. Company pays fee. Number of placements per year: 1001+.

**SELLERS & ASSOCIATES**
805 Augusta Ave.
Elgin IL 60120
708/888-1568
FAX: 708/888-0028
Contact Stephen E. Sellers, president. Specializes in the area of: engineering (chemical; electrical; mechanical; packaging; physics).

**SEVILLE TEMPORARY SERVICES**
180 N. Michigan Avenue
Suite 707
Chicago IL 60601
312/368-1144
Contact Matt Bukozy. Temporary help agency. Appointment required. Founded 1979. Specializes in the areas of: Accounting; Clerical; Secretarial. Positions commonly filled include: Accountant; Bookkeeper; Data Entry Clerk; Executive Secretary; Legal Secretary; Medical Secretary; Receptionist; Secretary; Stenographer; Typist; Word Processor. Company pays fee.

**SHEETS EMPLOYMENT SERVICE, INC.**
Four West Miner Street
Arlington Heights IL 60004
708/392-6100
Contact Glenn E. Sheets, President. Employment agency. Appointment required. Specializes in the areas of: Accounting; Manufacturing; Secretarial and Clerical. Positions commonly filled include: Accountant; Administrative Assistant; Bookkeeper; Clerk; Computer Programmer; Credit Manager; Customer Service Representative; Data Entry Clerk; Draftsperson; EDP Specialist; Executive Secretary; Legal Secretary; Personnel Director; Purchasing Agent; Secretary; Stenographer; Typist; Underwriter; Typist; Word Processor. Company pays fee. Number of placements per year: 201-500.

**SNELLING AND SNELLING OF DES PLAINES**
999 East Touhy Avenue
Suite 160
Des Plaines IL 60018
708/296-1026
Contact Tom Malloy, President. Employment agency. Appointment requested. Founded 1974. Specializes in the areas of: Clerical; Food Industry; Sales and Marketing. Positions commonly filled include: Accountant; Clerk; Credit Manager; Customer Service Representative; Data Entry Clerk; General Manager; Office Worker; Receptionist; Sales Representative; Secretary; Stenographer. Company pays fee. Number of placements per year: 101-200.

## SNELLING AND SNELLING OF ROLLING MEADOWS
5105 Tollview Drive, Suite 120
Rolling Meadows IL 60008
708/255-2770
Contact James Salerno, Manager. Employment agency. No appointment required. Founded 1979. Specializes in the areas of: Banking; Clerical; Food Industry; Sales and Marketing. Positions commonly filled include: Accountant; Bookkeeper; Clerk; Legal Secretary; Office Worker; Receptionist; Sales Representative; Secretary; Typist. Company pays fee. Number of placements per year: 51-100.

## STAFF BUILDERS INC. OF ILLINOIS
28 East Jackson
Chicago IL 60604
312/263-0834
Temporary help service. Appointment requested. Founded 1961. Branch offices located in: Arizona; California; Connecticut; District of Columbia; Florida; Georgia; Illinois; Indiana; Kansas; Louisiana; Maryland; Massachusetts; Michigan; Minnesota; Missouri; Nevada; New Jersey; New Mexico; New York; Ohio; Oklahoma; Oregon; Pennsylvania; Rhode Island; Tennessee; Texas; Virginia; Washington. Nonspecialized. Positions commonly filled include: Accountant; Administrative Assistant; Bookkeeper; Clerk; Companion; Computer Operator; Computer Programmer; Customer Service Representative; Data Entry Clerk; Demonstrator; Draftsperson; Driver; EDP Specialist; Factory Worker; General Laborer; Health Aide; Legal Secretary; Light Industrial Worker; Medical Secretary; Nurse; Office Worker; Public Relations Worker; Receptionist; Sales Representative; Secretary; Stenographer; Technician; Typist; Word Processing Specialist. Company pays fee. Number of placements per year: 1001+.

## STIVERS TEMPORARY PERSONNEL, INC.
1225 Corporate Boulevard
Suite 200
Aurora IL 60504
708/851-9330
Temporary help service. Appointment requested. Founded 1945. Specializes in the areas of: Accounting and Finance; Banking; Clerical; Engineering; Health and Medical; Insurance; Legal; Manufacturing; MIS and EDP; Personnel and Human Resources; Real Estate; Transportation. Positions commonly filled include: Administrative Assistant; Bookkeeper; Claims Representative; Clerk; Customer Service Representative; Data Entry Clerk; EDP Specialist; Legal Secretary; Medical Secretary; Office Worker; Receptionist; Secretary; Stenographer; Systems Analyst; Typist; Underwriter; Word Processing Specialist.

**STONE ENTERPRISES, LTD**
405 North Wabash Street
Suite 1702
Chicago IL 60611
312/836-0470
Contact Susan L. Stone, President. Employment agency and executive search firm. Appointment requested. Founded 1980. Specializes in the areas of: Accounting and Finance; Advertising; Banking; Clerical; Legal; Personnel and Human Resources. Positions commonly filled include: Accountant; Actuary; Administrative Assistant; Advertising Worker; Attorney; Bookkeeper; Claims Representative; Clerk; Computer Operator; Computer Programmer; Credit Manager; Customer Service Representative; Financial Analyst; Hotel Manager and Assistant Manager; Insurance Agent and Broker; Legal Secretary; MIS Specialist; Marketing Specialist; Medical Secretary; Office Worker; Purchasing Agent; QC Supervisor; Receptionist; Sales Representative; Secretary; Stenographer; Systems Analyst; Typist; Underwriter; Word Processing Specialist. Company pays fee. Number of placements per year: 201-500.

**SURE HIRE SERVICE, INC.**
140 S. Dearborn
Suite 820
Chicago IL 60603
312/419-0373
FAX: 312/419-8953
Contact Timothy J. Jadwin, CPC. Specializes in the areas of: account management; art; copy; direct marketing; media; production/traffic; research; sales promotion; office administration (administrators; clerks; management; receptionists; secretaries; word processing).

**SYSTEMS RESEARCH INC.**
1051 Perimeter
Schaumburg IL 60173
708/330-1222
Contact Bonnie Albrecht, Administrative Assistant. Employment agency. Appointment requested. Founded 1969. Specializes in the areas of: Engineering; Manufacturing; Technical and Scientific. Positions commonly filled include: Aerospace Engineer; Agricultural Engineer; Biomedical Engineer; Ceramics Engineer; Chemical Engineer; Draftsperson; Electrical Engineer; Industrial Designer; Industrial Engineer; Marketing Specialist; Mechanical Engineer; Metallurgical Engineer; Mining Engineer; Petroleum Engineer; Operations/Production Specialist; Purchasing Agent; Quality Control Supervisor; Systems Analyst; Technical Writer/Editor; Technician. Company pays fee. Number of placements per year: 201-500.

## TALENT TREE OF ILLINOIS
2 North LaSalle
Suite 950
Chicago IL 60602
312/855-1390
Contact Area Manager. Employment agency. No appointment required. Founded 1964. Specializes in the area of: Clerical. Positions commonly filled include: Administrative Assistant; Bookkeeper; Clerk; Customer Service Representative; Data Entry Clerk; Demonstrator; Legal Secretary; Medical Secretary; Office Worker; Personnel and Labor Relations Specialist; Receptionist; Secretary; Stenographer; Typist; Word Processing Specialist. Company pays fee.

## TEMP FORCE OF ILLINOIS
227 South Water Street
Decatur IL 62523
217/429-7147
Contact Dawn McKinney, Manager. Temporary help service. No appointment required. Founded 1965. Branch offices located in: Alabama; Arkansas; California; Colorado; Connecticut; Florida; Illinois; Indiana; Kansas; Maryland; Massachusetts; Michigan; Mississippi; Nevada; New Jersey; New Mexico; New York; Ohio; Oklahoma; Pennsylvania; Tennessee; Utah; Vermont; Virginia. Nonspecialized. Positions commonly filled include: Accountant; Bookkeeper; Clerk; Computer Operator; Computer Programmer; Customer Service Representative; Data Entry Clerk; Demonstrator; Driver; Factory Worker; General Laborer; Legal Secretary; Light Industrial Worker; Medical Secretary; Office Worker; Purchasing Agent; Receptionist; Secretary; Statistician; Stenographer; Typist; Word Processing Specialist.

## TEMP FORCE OF ILLINOIS
2201 5th Avenue
Suite 11
Moline IL 61265
309/797-1108
Contact Juanita Herrell, Manager. Temporary help service. No appointment required. Founded 1965. Branch offices located in: Alabama; Arkansas; California; Colorado; Connecticut; Florida; Illinois; Indiana; Kansas; Maryland; Massachusetts; Michigan; Mississippi; Nevada; New Jersey; New Mexico; New York; Ohio; Oklahoma; Pennsylvania; Tennessee; Utah; Vermont; Virginia. Nonspecialized. Positions commonly filled include: Accountant; Bookkeeper; Clerk; Computer Operator; Computer Programmer; Customer Service Representative; Data Entry Clerk; Demonstrator; Driver; Factory Worker; General Laborer; Legal Secretary; Light Industrial Worker; Medical Secretary; Office Worker; Purchasing Agent; Receptionist; Secretary; Statistician; Stenographer; Typist; Word Processing Specialist.

**TEMPFLEET INC.**
180 North Michigan Avenue
Suite 329
Chicago IL 60601
312/236-0155
Contact Kaye Ruddy, Personnel Interviewer. Specializes in word processing, accounting and secretarial placement with major Chicago employers. Part of a permanent placement agency.

**TEMPORARY OPPORTUNITIES, INC.**
53 W. Jackson
Suite 1035
Chicago IL 60604
312/922-5400
FAX: 312/347-1206
Contact Eileen Griffin. Specializes in the area of: temporary services (secretaries; word processing).

**TEMPSTATT, INC.**
202 Campbell Street
Geneva IL 60134
708/232-1883
Contact Manager. Temporary help agency. Founded 1981. Specializes in the areas of: Computer Hardware and Software; Health and Medical; Legal; Manufacturing. Positions commonly filled include: Administrative Assistant; Customer Service Representative; Executive Secretary; General Laborer; Legal Secretary; Light Industrial Worker; Medical Secretary; Nurse; Secretary; Stenographer; Systems Analyst; Typist; Word Processor.

**THIRTY THREE PERSONNEL CENTER**
33 North Dearborn St.
Ste. 1630
Chicago IL 60602
312/236-2023
Contact Harri Burt, CPC. Specializes in the areas of: entry level (management trainees; support staff); human resources (benefits; compensation; EEO; labor relations; management; personnel/industrial relations; recruiting/staffing; training/development); office administration (administrators; clerks; management; receptionists; secretaries; word processing); temporary services (secretaries; word processing).

**TRI-ASSOCIATES, INC.**
529 South Wabash Street
Suite 200
Chicago IL 60605
312/663-1851
Contact Don McCrimon, Supervisor of Recruitment and Placement. Employment agency; temporary help service. Founded 1976. Nonspecialized.

Positions commonly filled include: Accountant; Administrative Assistant; Bookkeeper; Claims Representative; Clerk; Computer Operator; Computer Programmer; Customer Service Representative; Data Entry Clerk; EDP Specialist; Electrical Engineer; Financial Analyst; Industrial Engineer; Legal Secretary; MIS Specialist; Marketing Specialist; Mechanical Engineer; Medical Secretary; Operations/Production Specialist; Personnel and Labor Relations Specialist; Receptionist; Sales Representative; Secretary; Stenographer; Systems Analyst; Technical Writer/Editor; Technician; Typist; Word Processing Specialist. Company pays fee. Number of placements per year: 101-200.

WILLS & CO., INC.
333 E. Ontario
Suite 2205-7B
Chicago IL 60611
312/236-5356
FAX: 312/236-0468
Contact Donald L. Wills, CPC. Specializes in the areas of: consulting; programming; systems.

RICHARD ALLEN WINTER ASSOC. INC.
2275 Half Day Road
Bannockburn IL 60015
708/948-8222
Recruiting agency. Appointment required. Founded 1961. Nonspecialized. Positions commonly filled include: Accountant; Actuary; Advertising Executive; Aerospace Engineer; Agricultural Engineer; Architect; Attorney; Bank Officer/Manager; Biochemist/Chemist; Biologist; Biomedical Engineer; Bookkeeper; Ceramics Engineer; Civil Engineer; Claims Representative; Commercial Artist; Computer Programmer; Credit Manager; Customer Service Rep; Industrial Designer; Dietician/Nutritionist; EDP Specialist; Economist; Electrical Engineer; Financial Analyst; General Manager; Hotel Manager; Industrial Engineer; Management Consultant; Marketing Specialist; Mechanical Engineer; Metallurgical Engineer; Mining Engineer; Personnel Director; Petroleum Engineer; Phyicist; Public Relations Worker; Purchasing Agent; Reporter/Editor; Sales Representative; Statistician; Systems Analyst; Technical Writer/Editor; Underwriter. Number of placements per year: 51-100.

WORD PROCESSORS PERSONNEL SERVICE
233 N. Michigan, #2229
Chicago IL 60601
312/856-1117
Employment agency; temporary agency. Appointment required. Founded 1978. Corporate office in Palo Alto, CA with 13 branches nationwide. Specializes in Word Processing and PC, Office Administration staffing, temporary and permanent. Positions commonly filled include: Administrative Assistant; Executive Secretary; Legal Secretary; Medical Secretary; PC

Operator; Receptionist; Secretary; Statistician; Typist; Word Processing Supervisor; Word Processor. Company pays fee. Number of placements per year: 0-50(permanent); 501-1000+(temporary).

**WORKING WORLD TEMPORARY PERSONNEL**
Post Office Box 1036
14 North Walkup Street
Crystal Lake IL 60014
815/455-4490

Contact Barbara Kalemba, President. Temporary help agency. Appointment required. Founded 1980. Specializes in the areas of: Manufacturing; Secretarial and Clerical. Positions commonly filled include: Bookkeeper; Clerk; Computer Programmer; Construction Worker; Customer Service Representative; Data Entry Clerk; Draftsperson; Driver; Executive Secretary; Factory Worker; General Laborer; Legal Secretary; Light Industrial Worker; Marketing Specialist; Medical Secretary; Public Relations Worker; Receptionist; Sales Representative; Secretary; Stenographer; Typist; Underwriter; Word Processor. Number of placements per year: 1000+

## EXECUTIVE SEARCH FIRMS OF GREATER CHICAGO

**AP EXECUTIVE SEARCH**
P.O. Box 18118
Chicago IL 60618-0118
312/583-0466

Contact Ahmed Patel, Recruiting Consultant. Executive Search and Recruiting firm.

**ACCORD, INC.**
1543 Westchester Boulevard
Westchester IL 60154
708/345-7900

Contact Chester Dombrowski, Manager (Mechanical) or John Fawcett, Manager (Electronic). Executive search firm. Founded 1981. Specializes in the areas of: Computer Hardware and Software; Engineering; Manufacturing; MIS/EDP; Technical and Scientific. Number of searches conducted per year: 51-100.

## JOHN R. ADY & ASSOCIATES
514 North Neil Street, Suite A
Champaign IL 61820
217/359-8080
FAX: 217/356-8440
Contact John R. Ady, President. Executive, Management and Professional level search firm. Appointment required; no telephone calls; unsolicited resumes accepted. Member Inter-city Personnel Associates, a 240 member nationwide organization of search firms who assist each other with job assignments and candidate placements. Also maintains membership in the National Association of Personnel Consultants and Illinois Association of Personnel consultants. Specializes in positions $25,000-$125,000 per annum within the areas of accounting; administration; MIS/EDP; finance; chemical, electrical, and environmental engineering; computer hardware and software; general management; health and medical; human resources; operations management; sales and marketing. Contingency and retained search.

## E.J. ASHTON & ASSOCIATES, LTD.
3125 North Wilke Road
Suite A
Arlington Heights IL 60008
708/577-7900
Contact Ed Ashton, President. Executive search firm. Appointment requested; unsolicited resumes accepted. Founded 1979. Specializes in the areas of: Accounting; Banking; Insurance. Contingency; noncontingency. Number of searches conducted per year: 26-50.

## CATALYST SEARCH, INC.
900 Jorie Boulevard
Suite 110
Oak Brook IL 60521
708/990-8610
Contact Manager. Executive search firm. Appointment requested. Founded 1977. Member of National Association of Physician Recruiters. Specializes in the areas of: Health and Medical. Number of searches conducted per year: 50.

## CHICAGO FINANCIAL SEARCH
2 North Riverside Plaza
Suite 2400
Chicago IL 60606
312/207-0400
Contact Mike Kelly, Vice President. Executive search firm. Appointment requested; unsolicited resumes accepted. Founded 1983. Specializes in the areas of: Banking; Brokerage; Commodities. Number of searches conducted per year: 101-200.

## CORPORATE ENVIRONMENT, LTD.
Post Office Box 798
Crystal Lake IL 60014
815/455-6070
Contact Thomas P. McDermott, President. Executive search firm. Appointment required; no phone calls; unsolicited resumes accepted. Founded 1979. Key specialists, mid-management and senior level executives in heavy Technical Industries, Environmental, Chemical Process, Equipment/Instruments and other industries requiring a technological background. Functions include Management; Engineering; Manufacturing; and Sales and Marketing. Specializes in the areas of: Chemicals and Pharmaceuticals; Construction; Engineering; Food Industry; General Management; Manufacturing; Operations Management; Sales and Marketing; Technical and Scientific. Noncontingency. Number of searches conducted per year: 0-50.

## CREATIVE STAFFING ENTERPRISES, INC.
164 Division Street
Suite 310
Elgin IL 60120
708/888-4691
Contact Donald Taylor, President. Executive search firm. Appointment requested; unsolicited resumes accepted. Specializes in the areas of: Computer Hardware and Software; Engineering; Technical and Scientific. Number of searches conducted per year: 51-100.

## DUNHILL PERSONNEL SYSTEM OF ILLINOIS
2500 South Highland
Suite 103
Lombard IL 60148
708/916-7300
Contact Tom Barbeau, Owner. Executive search firm. Specializes in the areas of: Sales and Marketing.

## ELSKO EXECUTIVE SEARCH
3601 Algonquin
Suite 130
Rolling Meadows IL 60008
708/394-2400
Executive search firm. Appointment requested; unsolicited resumes accepted. Founded 1976. Specializes in the areas of: Accounting; Finance. Contingency. Number of searches conducted per year: 101-200.

**FIRST SEARCH, INC.**
9025 North Kostner Avenue
Skokie IL 60076
708/677-0001
Contact Michael Zarnek, President. Executive search firm. No appointment required; unsolicited resumes accepted. Founded 1984. Specializes in Telecommunication/Data Comm. industry nationwide, Engineering to Executive levels. Specializes in the areas of: Communications; Engineering; Sales and Marketing; Technical and Scientific; Telecommunications. Contingency. Number of searches conducted per year: 0-50.

**FORESIGHT**
414 Plaza Drive, Suite 306
Westmont IL 60559
708/655-0550
Contact Greg Hufford or Joe Scavuzza, Co-owners. Executive search firm. No appointment required; unsolicited resumes accepted. Founded 1978. Specializes in the areas of: Voice and Data Communications for R&D, Marketing, Technical Marketing, and Sales. Additionally, company specializes in Medical Devices Engineering. 50% Contingency/50% Retained. Number of searches conducted per year: 26-50.

**GEER, GRICE & HOLDENER**
39 South Barrington Road
South Barrington IL 60010
708/382-2950
Contact Michael Geers, Vice President. Executive search firm. Appointment required. Founded 1978. Low-profile; results-oriented. Specializes in the areas of: Computer Hardware and Software; MIS/EDP; Sales and Marketing. Positions commonly filled include: Computer Programmer; EDP Specialist; Management Consultant; Marketing Specialist; Sales Representative; Systems Analyst. Company pays fee. Number of placements per year: 51-100.

**HEALTH STAFFERS**
5636 North Broadway
Chicago IL 60660
312/561-5400
Contact Rose Houston, President. Executive search firm. Appointment requested; unsolicited resumes accepted. Founded 1975. Specializes in the areas of: Health and Medical. Contingency; noncontingency. Number of searches conducted per year: 50.

**J.C.G. LIMITED, INC.**
2300 E. Higgins Road
Elk Grove Village IL 60007
708/439-1400

Contact James Greene, President. Employment agency. Appointment required. Founded 1970. Specializes in the areas of: Engineering; Manufacturing; Transportation. Positions commonly filled include: Accountant; Bank Officer/Manager; Bookkeeper; Civil Engineer; Credit Manager; Draftsperson; Electrical Engineer; Executive Secretary; Insurance Agent/Broker; Marketing Specialist; Mechanical Engineer; Medical Secretary; Physicist; Receptionist; Sales Representative; Secretary; Systems Analyst; Technical Writer/Editor; Underwriter. Company pays fee. Number of placements per year: 51-100.

## JACOBSON ASSOCIATES
150 N. Wacker Drive
Suite 1120
Chicago IL 60606
312/726-1578
Contact David Jacobson, President. Executive search firm. Appointment required. Founded 1971. National executive recruiting firm providing comprehensive professional service to the insurance and related industries. Positions commonly filled include: Actuary; EDP Specialist; Management Consultant. Company pays fee.

## MANAGEMENT RECRUITERS OF ALBION
129 South 4th Street
Albion IL 62806
618/445-2333
FAX: 618/445-4061
Contact Tom Christensen, Manager. Executive search firm. Appointment required; no phone calls; unsolicited resumes accepted. Founded 1965. World's largest contingency search firm. Five hundred offices nationwide, doing business under the names "Management Recruiters", "Sales Consultants", "CompuSearch" and "OfficeMates5". Specializes in mid-management/professional positions, $25,000-75,000 per annum. Specializes in the areas of: Accounting; Administration, MIS/EDP; Advertising; Affirmative Action; Architecture; Banking and Finance; Chemicals and Pharmaceuticals; Communications; Computer Hardware and Software; Construction; Electrical; Engineering; Food Industry; General Management; Health and Medical; Human Resources; Industrial and Interior Design; Insurance; Legal; Manufacturing; Operations Management; Printing and Publishing; Procurement; Real Estate; Retailing; Sales and Marketing; Technical and Scientific; Textiles; Transportation. Contingency.

## MANAGEMENT RECRUITERS OF BANNOCKBURN
2205 Lakeside Drive
Bannockburn IL 60015
708/295-6780
Contact Dennis Gross, Manager. Executive search firm. Appointment required; no phone calls; unsolicited resumes accepted. Founded 1965. World's largest contingency search firm. Five hundred offices nationwide,

doing business under the names "Management Recruiters", "Sales Consultants", "CompuSearch" and "OfficeMates5". Specializes in mid-management/professional positions, $25,000-75,000 per annum. Specializes in the areas of: Accounting; Administration, MIS/EDP; Advertising; Affirmative Action; Architecture; Banking and Finance; Chemicals and Pharmaceuticals; Communications; Computer Hardware and Software; Construction; and Electrical; Engineering; Food Industry; General Management; Health and Medical; Human Resources; Industrial and Interior Design; Insurance; Legal; Manufacturing; Operations Management; Printing and Publishing; Procurement; Real Estate; Retailing; Sales and Marketing; Technical and Scientific; Textiles; Transportation. Contingency.

**MANAGEMENT RECRUITERS OF BARRINGTON HILLS**
P.O. Box 65
960 Route 22
Fox River Grove IL 60021-1954
708/639-1112
Contact Ed Leed, Manager. Executive search firm. Appointment required; no phone calls; unsolicited resumes accepted. Founded 1965. World's largest contingency search firm. Five hundred offices nationwide, doing business under the names "Management Recruiters", "Sales Consultants", "CompuSearch" and "OfficeMates5". Specializes in mid-management/professional positions, $25,000-75,000 per annum. Specializes in the areas of: Accounting; Administration, MIS/EDP; Advertising; Affirmative Action; Architecture; Banking and Finance; Chemicals and Pharmaceuticals; Communications; Computer Hardware and Software; Construction; Electrical; Engineering; Food Industry; General Management; Health and Medical; Human Resources; Industrial and Interior Design; Insurance; Legal; Manufacturing; Operations Management; Printing and Publishing; Procurement; Real Estate; Retailing; Sales and Marketing; Technical and Scientific; Textiles; Transportation. Contingency.

**MANAGEMENT RECRUITERS OF CHAMPAIGN**
2110 North Market Street
Champaign IL 61821
217/398-0050
FAX: 217/398-2043
Contact Ken Williams, Manager. Executive search firm. Appointment required; no phone calls; unsolicited resumes accepted. Founded 1965. World's largest contingency search firm. Five hundred offices nationwide, doing business under the names "Management Recruiters", "Sales Consultants", "CompuSearch" and "OfficeMates5". Specializes in mid-management/professional positions, $25,000-75,000 per annum. Specializes in the areas of: Accounting; Administration, MIS/EDP; Advertising; Affirmative Action; Architecture; Banking and Finance; Chemicals and Pharmaceuticals; Communications; Computer Hardware and Software; Construction; Electrical; Engineering; Food Industry; General Management; Health and Medical; Human Resources; Industrial and Interior Design;

Insurance; Legal; Manufacturing; Operations Management; Printing and Publishing; Procurement; Real Estate; Retailing; Sales and Marketing; Technical and Scientific; Textiles; Transportation. Contingency.

## MANAGEMENT RECRUITERS OF CHERRY VALLEY
Point East
1740 Bell School Road
Cherry Valley IL 61016
815/332-5646
Contact D. Michael Carter, Manager. Executive search firm. Appointment required; no phone calls; unsolicited resumes accepted. Founded 1965. World's largest contingency search firm. Five hundred offices nationwide, doing business under the names "Management Recruiters", "Sales Consultants", "CompuSearch" and "OfficeMates5". Specializes in mid-management/professional positions, $25,000-75,000 per annum. Specializes in the areas of: Accounting; Administration, MIS/EDP; Advertising; Affirmative Action; Architecture; Banking and Finance; Chemicals and Pharmaceuticals; Communications; Computer Hardware and Software; Construction; Electrical; Engineering; Food Industry; General Management; Health and Medical; Human Resources; Industrial and Interior Design; Insurance; Legal; Manufacturing; Operations Management; Printing and Publishing; Procurement; Real Estate; Retailing; Sales and Marketing; Technical and Scientific; Textiles; Transportation. Contingency.

## MANAGEMENT RECRUITERS OF CHICAGO (DOWNTOWN)
Two North Riverside Plaza
Suite 1815
Chicago IL 60606
312/648-1800
Contact Dave Baranski, Manager. Executive search firm. Appointment required; no phone calls; unsolicited resumes accepted. Founded 1965. World's largest contingency search firm. Five hundred offices nationwide, doing business under the names "Management Recruiters", "Sales Consultants", "CompuSearch" and "OfficeMates5". Specializes in mid-management/professional positions, $25,000-75,000 per annum. Specializes in the areas of: Accounting; Administration, MIS/EDP; Advertising; Affirmative Action; Architecture; Banking and Finance; Chemicals and Pharmaceuticals; Communications; Computer Hardware and Software; Construction; Electrical; Engineering; Food Industry; General Management; Health and Medical; Human Resources; Industrial and Interior Design; Insurance; Legal; Manufacturing; Operations Management; Printing and Publishing; Procurement; Real Estate; Retailing; Sales and Marketing; Technical and Scientific; Textiles; Transportation. Contingency.

## MANAGEMENT RECRUITERS OF CHICAGO-SOUTHWEST
College Drive Office Center
7804 West College Drive
Palos Heights IL 60463-1010
708/361-8778
Contact Victor Persico, Manager. Executive search firm. Appointment required; no phone calls; unsolicited resumes accepted. Founded 1965. World's largest contingency search firm. Five hundred offices nationwide, doing business under the names "Management Recruiters", "Sales Consultants", "CompuSearch" and "OfficeMates5". Specializes in mid-management/professional positions, $25,000-75,000 per annum. Specializes in the areas of: Accounting; Administration, MIS/EDP; Advertising; Affirmative Action; Architecture; Banking and Finance; Chemicals and Pharmaceuticals; Communications; Computer Hardware and Software; Construction; Electrical; Engineering; Food Industry; General Management; Health and Medical; Human Resources; Industrial and Interior Design; Insurance; Legal; Manufacturing; Operations Management; Printing and Publishing; Procurement; Real Estate; Retailing; Sales and Marketing; Technical and Scientific; Textiles; Transportation. Contingency.

## MANAGEMENT RECRUITERS OF DES PLAINES
1400 East Touhy Avenue
Suite 220
Des Plaines IL 60018-3374
708/297-7102
FAX 708/297-8477
Contact Richard Kurz, Manager. Executive search firm. Appointment required; no phone calls; unsolicited resumes accepted. Founded 1965. World's largest contingency search firm. Five hundred offices nationwide, doing business under the names "Management Recruiters", "Sales Consultants", "CompuSearch" and "OfficeMates5". Specializes in mid-management/professional positions, $25,000-75,000 per annum. Specializes in the areas of: Accounting; Administration, MIS/EDP; Advertising; Affirmative Action; Architecture; Banking and Finance; Chemicals and Pharmaceuticals; Communications; Computer Hardware and Software; Construction; Electrical; Engineering; Food Industry; General Management; Health and Medical; Human Resources; Industrial and Interior Design; Insurance; Legal; Manufacturing; Operations Management; Printing and Publishing; Procurement; Real Estate; Retailing; Sales and Marketing; Technical and Scientific; Textiles; Transportation. Contingency.

## MANAGEMENT RECRUITERS OF ELGIN
472 North McLean Boulevard
Suite 201
Elgin IL 60123
708/697-2201
Contact Ron Reeves, Manager. Executive search firm. Appointment required; no phone calls; unsolicited resumes accepted. Founded 1965.

World's largest contingency search firm. Five hundred offices nationwide, doing business under the names "Management Recruiters", "Sales Consultants", "CompuSearch" and "OfficeMates5". Specializes in mid-management/professional positions, $25,000-75,000 per annum. Specializes in the areas of: Accounting; Administration, MIS/EDP; Advertising; Affirmative Action; Architecture; Banking and Finance; Chemicals and Pharmaceuticals; Communications; Computer Hardware and Software; Construction; Electrical; Engineering; Food Industry; General Management; Health and Medical; Human Resources; Industrial and Interior Design; Insurance; Legal; Manufacturing; Operations Management; Printing and Publishing; Procurement; Real Estate; Retailing; Sales and Marketing; Technical and Scientific; Textiles; Transportation. Contingency.

**MANAGEMENT RECRUITERS OF ST. CHARLES**
10 East State Avenue
Suite 201
St. Charles IL 60174-1470
708/377-6466
Contact Daniel Lasse, Manager. Executive search firm. Appointment required; no phone calls; unsolicited resumes accepted. Founded 1965. World's largest contingency search firm. Five hundred offices nationwide, doing business under the names "Management Recruiters", "Sales Consultants", "CompuSearch" and "OfficeMates5". Specializes in mid-management/professional positions, $25,000-75,000 per annum. Specializes in the areas of: Accounting; Administration, MIS/EDP; Advertising; Affirmative Action; Architecture; Banking and Finance; Chemicals and Pharmaceuticals; Communications; Computer Hardware and Software; Construction; Electrical; Engineering; Food Industry; General Management; Health and Medical; Human Resources; Industrial and Interior Design; Insurance; Legal; Manufacturing; Operations Management; Printing and Publishing; Procurement; Real Estate; Retailing; Sales and Marketing; Technical and Scientific; Textiles; Transportation. Contingency.

**OFFICEMATES5 OF NORTHFIELD**
181 Waukegan Road, Suite 103
Northfield IL 60093
708/446-7737
FAX: 708/446-0990
Contact Lynne Goldberg, Manager. Executive search firm. Appointment required; no phone calls; unsolicited resumes accepted. Founded 1965. World's largest contingency search firm. Five hundred offices nationwide, doing business under the names "Management Recruiters", "Sales Consultants", "CompuSearch" and "OfficeMates5". Specializes in mid-management/professional positions, $25,000-75,000 per annum. Specializes in the areas of: Accounting; Administration, MIS/EDP; Advertising; Affirmative Action; Architecture; Banking and Finance; Chemicals and Pharmaceuticals; Communications; Computer Hardware and Software; Construction; Electrical; Engineering; Food Industry; General Management;

Health and Medical; Human Resources; Industrial and Interior Design; Insurance; Legal; Manufacturing; Operations Management; Printing and Publishing; Procurement; Real Estate; Retailing; Sales and Marketing; Technical and Scientific; Textiles; Transportation. Contingency.

**OFFICEMATES5 OF WHEELING**
401 South Milwaukee Avenue
Wheeling IL 60090
708/459-6160
Contact Manager. Executive search firm. Appointment required; no phone calls; unsolicited resumes accepted. Founded 1965. World's largest contingency search firm. Five hundred offices nationwide, doing business under the names "Management Recruiters", "Sales Consultants", "CompuSearch" and "OfficeMates5". Specializes in mid-management/professional positions, $25,000-75,000 per annum. Specializes in the areas of: Accounting; Administration, MIS/EDP; Advertising; Affirmative Action; Architecture; Banking and Finance; Chemicals and Pharmaceuticals; Communications; Computer Hardware and Software; Construction; Electrical; Engineering; Food Industry; General Management; Health and Medical; Human Resources; Industrial and Interior Design; Insurance; Legal; Manufacturing; Operations Management; Printing and Publishing; Procurement; Real Estate; Retailing; Sales and Marketing; Technical and Scientific; Textiles; Transportation. Contingency.

**PINKERTON AND ASSOCIATES, INC.**
320 North Michigan Avenue
Suite 2100
Chicago IL 60601
312/266-8669
Contact Tom Pinkerton, President. Executive search firm. Appointment required; unsolicited resumes accepted. Founded 1979. A small firm dedicated to quality search work on retainer assignments only in middle and upper management positions. Specializes in the areas of: Accounting; Administration, MIS/EDP; Advertising; Banking and Finance; Broadcasting; Chemicals and Pharmaceuticals; Communications; Construction; Education; Electrical; Engineering; Food Industry; General Management; Health and Medical; Human Resources; Industrial and Interior Design; Insurance; Legal; Manufacturing; Nonprofit; Operations Management; Printing and Publishing; Procurement; Real Estate; Retailing; Sales and Marketing; Technical and Scientific; Textiles; Transportation; Women. Noncontingency. Number of searches conducted per year: 0-50.

**PROFILE TEMPORARY SERVICE**
55 West Wacker Drive
Suite 400
Chicago IL 60601
312/641-1920

Contact Joseph Lagattuta, Owner/Controller. Executive search firm. Appointment requested. Founded 1977. Specializes in the areas of: Accounting and Finance; Banking; Insurance; Manufacturing. Number of searches conducted per year: 501+.

## RECRUITING RESOURCES GROUP
35 East Wacker Drive
Suite 2700
Chicago IL 60601
312/836-1200
Contact Glenda Peters, Vice President. Executive search firm. Appointment required; unsolicited resumes accepted. Founded 1966. Specializes in the areas of: Accounting; Administration, MIS/EDP; Advertising; Banking and Finance; Chemicals and Pharmaceuticals; Communications; Computer Hardware and Software; Engineering; Food Industry; General Management; Health and Medical; Human Resources; Insurance; Legal; Manufacturing; Nonprofit; Operations Management; Printing and Publishing; Real Estate; Sales and Marketing; Technical and Scientific; Textiles; Transportation; Women. Contingency. Number of searches conducted per year: 501+.

## GRAHAM ROBERTS ASSOCIATES
4300 North Brandywine Drive
Suite 104
Peoria IL 61614
309/685-6225
Contact Robert M. Evans, C.P.C., President. Executive search firm. Appointment requested; unsolicited resumes accepted. Founded 1967. Specializes in the areas of: Accounting; Administration, MIS/EDP; Advertising; Computer Hardware and Software; Engineering; Food Industry; Insurance; Manufacturing; Personnel and Human Resources; Printing and Publishing; Sales and Marketing; Technical and Scientific. Contingency; noncontingency. Number of searches conducted per year: 51-100.

## ROMAC AND ASSOCIATES OF CHICAGO, INC.
20 N. Wacker
Suite 2420
Chicago IL 60606
312/263-0902
Contact Receptionist. Executive search firm. Appointment required. Specializes in the areas of Accounting; Banking and Finance. Positions commonly filled include: Accountant; Bank Officer/Manager; Financial Analyst. Company pays fee.

## SRS DATA SEARCH
6 N. Michigan
Suite 1401
Chicago IL 60602
312/346-6383
Contact William Scothorn, Partner. Executive search firm. Appointment required; unsolicited resumes accepted. Founded 1980. Specializes in the Data Processing field, in the Chicago area; Blue chip client base; employees average 7+ years in business, placing programmers through managers. Specializes in the areas of: Administration, MIS/EDP; Computer Hardware and Software. Contingency. Number of searches conducted per year: 201-500.

## SALES CONSULTANTS OF CHICAGO (DOWNTOWN)
420 North Wabash
Suite 201
Chicago IL 60611
312/836-9100
Contact Bob Bowes, Manager. Executive search firm. Appointment required; no phone calls; unsolicited resumes accepted. Founded 1965. World's largest contingency search firm. Five hundred offices nationwide, doing business under the names "Management Recruiters", "Sales Consultants", "CompuSearch" and "OfficeMates5". Specializes in mid-management/professional positions, $25,000-75,000 per annum. Specializes in the areas of: Accounting; Administration, MIS/EDP; Advertising; Affirmative Action; Architecture; Banking and Finance; Chemicals and Pharmaceuticals; Communications; Computer Hardware and Software; Construction; Electrical; Engineering; Food Industry; General Management; Health and Medical; Human Resources; Industrial and Interior Design; Insurance; Legal; Manufacturing; Operations Management; Printing and Publishing; Procurement; Real Estate; Retailing; Sales and Marketing; Technical and Scientific; Textiles; Transportation. Contingency.

## SALES CONSULTANTS OF CHICAGO (SOUTHWEST)
6420 127th Street
Suite 209
Palos Heights IL 60463-2248
708/371-9677
Contact Carroll White or Jack White, Co-Managers. Executive search firm. Appointment required; no phone calls; unsolicited resumes accepted. Founded 1965. World's largest contingency search firm. Five hundred offices nationwide, doing business under the names "Management Recruiters", "Sales Consultants", "CompuSearch" and "OfficeMates5". Specializes in mid-management/professional positions, $25,000-75,000 per annum. Specializes in the areas of: Accounting; Administration, MIS/EDP; Advertising; Affirmative Action; Architecture; Banking and Finance; Chemicals and Pharmaceuticals; Communications; Computer Hardware and Software; Construction; Electrical; Engineering; Food Industry; General Management; Health and Medical; Human Resources; Industrial and Interior Design;

Insurance; Legal; Manufacturing; Operations Management; Printing and Publishing; Procurement; Real Estate; Retailing; Sales and Marketing; Technical and Scientific; Textiles; Transportation. Contingency.

## SALES CONSULTANTS OF FOX VALLEY
150 Houston Street
Suite 305
Batavia IL 60510
708/879-1890
Contact John Seebert, Manager. Executive search firm. Appointment required; no phone calls; unsolicited resumes accepted. Founded 1965. World's largest contingency search firm. Five hundred offices nationwide, doing business under the names "Management Recruiters", "Sales Consultants", "CompuSearch" and "OfficeMates5". Specializes in mid-management/professional positions, $25,000-75,000 per annum. Specializes in the areas of: Accounting; Administration, MIS/EDP; Advertising; Affirmative Action; Architecture; Banking and Finance; Chemicals and Pharmaceuticals; Communications; Computer Hardware and Software; Construction; Electrical; Engineering; Food Industry; General Management; Health and Medical; Human Resources; Industrial and Interior Design; Insurance; Legal; Manufacturing; Operations Management; Printing and Publishing; Procurement; Real Estate; Retailing; Sales and Marketing; Technical and Scientific; Textiles; Transportation. Contingency.

## SALES CONSULTANTS OF LINCOLNSHIRE
Oak Tree Corners
Suite 6
430 Milwaukee Avenue
Prairie View IL 60069
708/634-0300
Contact Steve Briody, General Manager, or Caroline Wright, Manager. Executive search firm. Appointment required; no phone calls; unsolicited resumes accepted. Founded 1965. World's largest contingency search firm. Five hundred offices nationwide, doing business under the names "Management Recruiters", "Sales Consultants", "CompuSearch" and "OfficeMates5". Specializes in mid-management/professional positions, $25,000-75,000 per annum. Specializes in the areas of: Accounting; Administration, MIS/EDP; Advertising; Affirmative Action; Architecture; Banking and Finance; Chemicals and Pharmaceuticals; Communications; Computer Hardware and Software; Construction; Electrical; Engineering; Food Industry; General Management; Health and Medical; Human Resources; Industrial and Interior Design; Insurance; Legal; Manufacturing; Operations Management; Printing and Publishing; Procurement; Real Estate; Retailing; Sales and Marketing; Technical and Scientific; Textiles; Transportation. Contingency.

## SALES CONSULTANTS OF OAK BROOK
The Corporate Center, Suite 210
1100 Jorie Boulevard
Oak Brook IL 60521-2273
708/990-8233
FAX 708/990-2973
Contact Gary Miller, Manager. Executive search firm. Appointment required; no phone calls; unsolicited resumes accepted. Founded 1965. World's largest contingency search firm. Five hundred offices nationwide, doing business under the names "Management Recruiters", "Sales Consultants", "CompuSearch" and "OfficeMates5". Specializes in mid-management/professional positions, $25,000-75,000 per annum. Specializes in the areas of: Accounting; Administration, MIS/EDP; Advertising; Affirmative Action; Architecture; Banking and Finance; Chemicals and Pharmaceuticals; Communications; Computer Hardware and Software; Construction; Electrical; Engineering; Food Industry; General Management; Health and Medical; Human Resources; Industrial and Interior Design; Insurance; Legal; Manufacturing; Operations Management; Printing and Publishing; Procurement; Real Estate; Retailing; Sales and Marketing; Technical and Scientific; Textiles; Transportation. Contingency.

## SALES CONSULTANTS OF SCHAUMBURG
1701 E. Woodfield Road
Schaumburg IL 60173
708/330-1110
Contact Steve Briody, Manager. Executive search firm. Appointment required; no phone calls; unsolicited resumes accepted. Founded 1965. World's largest contingency search firm. Five hundred offices nationwide, doing business under the names "Management Recruiters", "Sales Consultants", "CompuSearch" and "OfficeMates5". Specializes in mid-management/professional positions, $25,000-75,000 per annum. Specializes in the areas of: Accounting; Administration, MIS/EDP; Advertising; Affirmative Action; Architecture; Banking and Finance; Chemicals and Pharmaceuticals; Communications; Computer Hardware and Software; Construction; Electrical; Engineering; Food Industry; General Management; Health and Medical; Human Resources; Industrial and Interior Design; Insurance; Legal; Manufacturing; Operations Management; Printing and Publishing; Procurement; Real Estate; Retailing; Sales and Marketing; Technical and Scientific; Textiles; Transportation. Contingency.

## SAMUELSON ASSOCIATES
68 East Wacker Place
Suite 800
Chicago IL 60601
312/263-0033
Contact Don S. Samuelson, Owner. Executive search firm. Appointment requested; unsolicited resumes accepted. Founded 1983. Specializes in the

area of: Legal. Contingency; noncontingency. Number of searches conducted per year: 26-50.

**SYNERGISTICS ASSOCIATES**
320 North Michigan Avenue
Suite 1803
Chicago IL 60601
312/346-8782
Contact Al Borenstine, President. Executive search firm. Appointment required. Founded 1971. Specializes in the areas of: Computer Software and Hardware; MIS/EDP. Positions commonly filled include: EDP Executive; EDP Specialist; Management Consultant. Company pays fee. Number of placements per year: 0-50.

**T-A-DAVIS & ASSOCIATES, INC.**
500 Davis Center
Suite 1000
Evanston IL 60201
708/475-8900
Contact Thomas G. Davis, President. Executive search firm. Appointment requested; no phone calls accepted; unsolicited resumes accepted. Founded 1979. Specializes in the area of: Food Industry. Contingency; noncontingency. Number of searches conducted per year: 26-50.

**ROY TALMAN & ASSOCIATES**
203 North Wabash
Suite 1120
Chicago IL 60601
312/630-0130
Contact R. Talman, President. Executive search firm. Appointment requested; unsolicited resumes accepted. Founded 1983. Specializes in the areas of: Computer Hardware and Software; Engineering; Technical and Scientific. Contingency. Number of searches conducted per year: 50-100.

**WESTCOTT ASSOCIATES INC.**
1000 North Lake Shore Plaza
Chicago IL 60611-1335
312/337-3373
Contact Robert F. Westcott, President. Executive search firm. Appointment required; unsolicited resumes accepted. Founded 1966. Independent management consulting firm which concentrates on organization planning, executive search, recruiting and appraisals. Specializes in the areas of: Administration, MIS/EDP; Advertising; Affirmative Action; Architechture; Banking and Finance; Broadcasting; Chemicals and Pharmaceuticals; Communications; Computer Hardware and Software; Construction; Electrical; Engineering; Food Industry; General Management; Health and Medical; Human Resources; Industrial and Interior Design; Insurance; Legal; Manufacturing; Nonprofit; Operations Management; Printing and

Publishing; Procurement; Real Estate; Retailing; Sales and Marketing; Technical and Scientific; Textiles; Transportation; Women. Noncontingency. Number of searches conducted per year: 51-100.

**PHILIP WIELAND & ASSOCIATES**
2525 Greenwood Avenue
Wilmette IL 60091
708/256-8666
Contact Philip J. Wieland, President. Executive search firm. Specializes in the area of: Legal.

## RESUME AND CAREER COUNSELING SERVICES OF GREATER CHICAGO

**PETER K. HUNTER & ASSOCIATES**
180 N. LaSalle
Suite 2405
Chicago IL 60601
312/372-3050
Contact Casey Fredericks, Director of Career Development Services. Complete "Strategic Career Development" Program, including: career assessment and planning; career counseling; motivational training; job retention counseling; career changing & other special workshops; testing services (Myers-Briggs); oral & written communications training & other seminars; career resource library; videotape interview training; lead source development; resume writing & preparation; comprehensive follow-up support services.

**PROFESSIONAL RESUME SERVICE, INC.**
180 N. LaSalle
Suite 2405
Chicago IL 60601
312/368-8888
Contact Peter Komendowski, President. Chicago's largest resume writing servcie. Ten offices in metropolitan Chicago; branch office in Champaign, IL. Comprehensive career development services include: resume preparation; career assessment and planning; cover letters; photocopies; government job application forms; business & professional speechwriting; interview preparation; lifetime update service for clients; serve groups from entry-level to executive.

# Professional and Trade Associations

Anyone who has conducted a job search has heard the dictum, "It's not what you know, it's who you know." While the validity of this comment has just as often been exaggerated, it does contain more than a grain of truth. Connections can never replace good old hard work as the best method of finding employment, but they can't hurt.

If you don't have an uncle in high places who can set up some interviews for you with a few of his friends, don't worry. Most people don't. The important thing to remember is that in most instances, connections do not materialize out of thin air -- they are created. That means that anyone who works at it can make them.

One of the best ways to meet people in your area of interest is through professional trade associations. Trade associations exist so that professionals in an industry can meet, share information about trends in the field, and arrange new business. Many of them regularly publish newsletters and magazines that will help you stay abreast of the current state of your industry. In addition, many associations hold regular meetings, and these meetings may present you the opportunity not only to learn more about the field you hope to enter, but also to establish connections.

With this in mind, we have included this directory of professional associations. Many of the addresses listed are for headquarters offices only. Inquire about local chapters in your area.

## ACCOUNTING

**THE EDP AUDITORS ASSOCIATION**
455 Kehoe Boulevard
Suite 106
Carol Stream IL 60188
708/682-1200

**INDEPENDENT ACCOUNTANTS ASSOCIATION OF ILLINOIS**
Carol Tarantur
1776 Ash Street
Northfield IL 60093
708/441-7800

**INSTITUTE OF INTERNAL AUDITORS/CHICAGO CHAPTER**
P.O. Box 973
Park Ridge IL 60068


For more information, contact:

**AMERICAN INSTITUTE OF
CERTIFIED PUBLIC ACCOUNTANTS**
1211 Avenue of the Americas
New York NY 10036
212/575-6200

**NATIONAL SOCIETY OF PUBLIC ACCOUNTANTS**
1010 North Fairfax Street
Alexandria VA 22314
703/549-6400


## ADVERTISING, MARKETING, PUBLIC RELATIONS

**AMERICAN MARKETING ASSOCIATION**
250 South Wacker Drive
Suite 200
Chicago IL 60606
312/648-0536

**FINANCIAL RELATIONS BOARD INC.**
875 North Michigan Avenue
Suite 2250
Chicago IL 60611

**TELEVISION BUREAU OF ADVERTISING/CHICAGO**
400 North Michigan Avenue
Suite 616
Chicago IL 60611
312/527-3373


For more information, contact:

**AMERICAN ADVERTISING FEDERATION**
1400 K Street NW
Suite 1000
Washington DC 20005

**AMERICAN ASSOCIATION OF ADVERTISING AGENCIES**
666 Third Avenue, 13th Floor
New York NY 10017
212/682-2500

**BUSINESS-PROFESSIONAL ADVERTISING ASSOCIATION**
Metroplex Corporate Center
100 Metroplex Drive
Edison NJ 08817
201/985-4441

**PUBLIC RELATIONS SOCIETY OF AMERICA**
33 Irving Place
New York NY 10003
212/995-2230

**TELEVISION BUREAU OF ADVERTISING**
477 Madison Avenue
New York NY 10022
212/486-1111

## APPAREL AND TEXTILES

**AMERICAN APPAREL MANUFACTURERS ASSOCIATION**
2500 Wilson Boulevard
Suite 301
Arlington VA 22201
703/524-1864

**AMERICAN TEXTILE MANUFACTURERS INSTITUTE**
1801 K Street NW
Suite 900
Washington DC 20006
202/862-0500

**NORTHERN TEXTILE ASSOCIATION**
230 Congress Street
Boston MA 02110
617/542-8220

**TEXTILE RESEARCH INSTITUTE**
Box 625
Princeton NJ 08542
609/924-3150

## ARTS AND ENTERTAINMENT/LEISURE

**AMERICAN FEDERATION OF MUSICIANS/CHICAGO**
Local 10-208
175 West Washington Street
Chicago IL 60602
312/782-0063

**NATIONAL ENDOWMENT FOR THE ARTS/CHICAGO**
Lois Rubin
P.O. Box 597661
Chicago IL 60659-7661
708/965-6670

**NATIONAL RECREATION AND PARKS ASSOCIATION/CHICAGO**
Walter Johnson
c/o Great Lakes Service Center
650 West Higgins Road
Hoffman Estate IL 60195
708/843-7529


For more information, contact:

**AMERICAN ASSOCIATION OF ZOOLOGICAL PARKS & AQUARIUMS**
Oglebay Park
Wheeling WV 26003
304/242-2160

**AMERICAN FEDERATION OF MUSICIANS**
1501 Broadway, Suite 600
New York NY 10036
212/869-1330

**AMERICAN FEDERATION OF TELEVISION AND RADIO ARTISTS**
260 Madison Avenue
New York NY 10016
212/532-0800

**NATIONAL ENDOWMENT FOR THE ARTS**
1100 Pennsylvania Avenue NW
Washington DC 20506
202/682-5400

**THEATRE COMMUNICATIONS GROUP**
355 Lexington Avenue
New York NY 10017
212/697-5230

## BANKING/SAVINGS AND LOAN

**BANK ADMINISTRATION INSTITUTE**
2550 Golf Road
Rolling Meadows IL 60008
800/323-8552

**COMMUNITY BANKERS ASSOCIATION OF ILLINOIS**
Robert J. Wingert, Executive Director
300 West Edwards Street
Suite 200
Springfield IL 62704
217/753-4331

**ILLINOIS BANKERS ASSOCIATION**
Suite 1111
111 North Canal Street
Chicago IL 60606-7204
312/876-9900

**INSTITUTE OF FINANCIAL EDUCATION**
111 East Wacker Drive
24th Floor
Chicago IL 60601
312/644-3100

For more information, contact:

**AMERICAN BANKERS ASSOCIATION**
1120 Connecticut Avenue NW
Washington DC 20036
202/663-5221

**BANK ADMINISTRATION INSTITUTE**
Plaza 1000, Suite 202
Voorhees NJ 08043
609/424-3233

**INDEPENDENT BANKERS ASSOCIATION OF AMERICA**
One Thomas Circle NW
Suite 950
Washington DC 20005
202/659-8111

**NATIONAL COUNCIL OF SAVINGS INSTITUTIONS**
1101 15th Street NW
Suite 400
Washington DC 20005
202/857-3100

## BOOK AND MAGAZINE PUBLISHING

**AMERICAN BOOKSELLERS ASSOCIATION**
137 West 25th Street, 11th Floor
New York NY 10001
212/463-8450

**ASSOCIATION OF AMERICAN PUBLISHERS**
220 East 23rd Street
New York NY 10010
212/689-8920

**MAGAZINE PUBLISHERS ASSOCIATION**
575 Lexington Avenue, Suite 540
New York NY 10022
212/752-0055

**WRITERS GUILD OF AMERICA EAST, INC.**
555 West 57th Street, Suite 1230
New York NY 10019
212/245-6180

**WRITERS GUILD OF AMERICA WEST, INC.**
8955 Beverly Boulevard
Los Angeles CA 90048
213/550-1000

## BROADCASTING

**FEDERAL COMMUNICATIONS COMMISSION**
Park Ridge Office, Room 306
1550 Northwest Highway
Park Ridge IL 60068
312/353-0196

**ILLINOIS CABLE TELEVISION ASSOCIATION**
c/o Richard J. Prendergast
111 West Washington Street
Suite 1100
Chicago IL 60602
312/641-0881

**NATIONAL ASSOCIATION OF BROADCASTERS/ILLINOIS**
2126 MacArthur Boulevard South
Springfield IL 62704
217/753-2636

**TELEVISION BUREAU OF ADVERTISING/CHICAGO**
400 North Michigan Avenue
Suite 616
Chicago IL 60611
312/527-3373


For more information, contact:

**BROADCAST EDUCATION ASSOCIATION**
1771 N Street NW
Washington DC 20036
202/424-5355

**CABLE TELEVISION ASSOCIATION**
1724 Massachusetts Avenue NW
Washington DC 20036
202/775-3550

**INTERNATIONAL RADIO AND TV SOCIETY**
420 Lexington Avenue
Suite 531
New York NY 10170
212/867-6650

**NATIONAL ASSOCIATION OF BROADCASTERS**
1771 N Street NW
Washington DC 20036
202/429-5300

**NATIONAL ASSOCIATION OF BUSINESS
AND EDUCATIONAL RADIO**
1501 Duke Street
Suite 200
Alexandria VA 22314
703/739-0300

**TELEVISION BUREAU OF ADVERTISING**
477 Madison Avenue
New York NY 10022
212/486-1111

**WOMEN IN RADIO AND TV, INC.**
1101 Connecticut Avenue NW
Suite 700
Washington DC 20036
202/429-5102

**CHARITABLE, NON-PROFIT, HUMANITARIAN**

**NATIONAL ORGANIZATION FOR HUMAN
SERVICE EDUCATION**
National College of Education
2840 Sheridan Road
Evanston IL 60201
708/256-5150

For more information, contact:

**NATIONAL ASSOCIATION OF SOCIAL WORKERS**
7981 Eastern Avenue
Silver Spring MD 20910
301/565-0333

## CHEMICALS & RELATED: PROCESSING, PRODUCTION, DISPOSAL

**AMERICAN INSTITUTE OF CHEMICAL ENGINEERING/CHICAGO**
c/o Paul Rom
957 Highland Avenue
Glen Ellen IL 60137
312/693-1030

**AMERICAN INSTITUTE OF CHEMISTS/CHICAGO**
Marcus Bornfleth
1919 Swift Drive
Oak Brook IL 60521


For more information, contact:

**AMERICAN CHEMICAL SOCIETY**
Career Services
1155 16th Street NW
Washington DC 20036
202/872-4600

**AMERICAN INSTITUTE OF CHEMICAL ENGINEERING**
345 East 47th Street
New York NY 10017
212/705-7338

**AMERICAN INSTITUTE OF CHEMISTS**
7315 Wisconsin Avenue, Suite 525 E
Bethesda MD 20814
301/652-2447

**ASSOCIATION OF STATE & INTERSTATE WATER POLLUTION CONTROL ADMINISTRATORS**
444 North Capital Street NW
Suite #330 N
Washington DC 20001
202/624-7782

**WATER POLLUTION CONTROL FEDERATION**
601 Wythe Street Avenue NW
Alexandria VA 22314
703/684-2400

## COLLEGES AND UNIVERSITIES/EDUCATION

**AMERICAN ASSOCIATION OF SCHOOL ADMINISTRATORS**
1801 North Moore Street
Arlington VA 22209
703/528-0700

**ASSOCIATION OF AMERICAN UNIVERSITIES**
One Dupont Circle NW
Suite 730
Washington DC 20036
202/466-5030

## COMMUNICATIONS

**COMMUNICATIONS WORKERS OF AMERICA/CHICAGO**
650 East Devon Avenue
Suite 154
Itasca IL 60143
708/773-4570

For more information, contact:

**COMMUNICATIONS WORKERS OF AMERICA**
1925 K Street NW
Washington DC 20006
202/728-2300

**UNITED STATES TELEPHONE ASSOCIATION**
900 19th Street NW, Suite 800
Washington DC 20006
202/835-3100

## COMPUTERS: HARDWARE, SOFTWARE AND SERVICES

**ADAPSO/THE COMPUTER SOFTWARE AND SERVICES INDUSTRY ASSOCIATION**
1300 North 17th Street, Suite 300
Arlington VA 22209
703/522-5055

**ASSOCIATION FOR COMPUTER SCIENCE**
P.O. Box 19027
Sacramento CA 95819
916/421-9149

**ASSOCIATION FOR COMPUTING MACHINERY**
11 West 42nd Street, 3rd Floor
New York NY 10036
212/869-7440

**IEEE COMPUTER SOCIETY**
1730 Massachusetts Avenue NW
Washington DC 20036-1903

**SEMICONDUCTOR INDUSTRY ASSOCIATION**
4300 Stevens Clark Boulevard, Suite 271
San Jose CA 95129
408/246-2711

## CONSTRUCTION

**BUILDING OFFICIALS AND CODE ADMINISTRATORS INTERNATIONAL, INC**
4051 West Flossmoor Road
Country Club Hills IL 60478
708/799-2300

**HOME BUILDERS ASSOCIATION OF GREATER CHICAGO**
1010 Jorie Boulevard
Oak Brook IL 60521
708/990-7575

For more information, contact:

**CONSTRUCTION INDUSTRY MANUFACTURERS ASSOCIATION**
111 East Wisconsin Avenue, Suite 940
Milwaukee WI 53202
414/272-0943

**INTERNATIONAL CONFERENCE OF BUILDING OFFICIALS**
5360 South Workman Road
Whittier CA 90601
213/699-0541

**NATIONAL ASSOCIATION OF HOME BUILDERS**
15th & M Streets NW
Washington DC 20005
202/822-0200


## ELECTRICAL AND ELECTRONICS

**AMERICAN ELECTROPLATERS AND SURFACE FINISHERS SOCIETY/CHICAGO BRANCH**
Frank Altmayer
c/o Scientific Control Labs
3158 South Kolin Avenue
Chicago IL 60623
312/254-2406

**INSTITUTE OF ELECTRICAL AND ELECTRONICS ENGINEERS/CHICAGO**
Robert Schrage
c/o Commonwealth Edison
P.O. Box 767, Seed 836
Chicago IL 60690
312/649-2800


For more information, contact:

**AMERICAN ELECTROPLATERS AND SURFACE FINISHERS SOCIETY**
12644 Research Parkway
Orlando FL 32826
407/281-6441

**ELECTROCHEMICAL SOCIETY**
10 South Main Street
Pennington NJ 08534-2896
609/737-1902

**ELECTRONIC INDUSTRIES ASSOCIATION**
2001 Pennsylvania Ave NW
Washington DC 20006
202/457-4900

**ELECTRONICS TECHNICIANS ASSOCIATION**
602 N. Jackson Street
Greencastle IN 46135
317/653-8262

**INSTITUTE OF ELECTRICAL AND ELECTRONICS ENGINEERS**
345 East 47th Street
New York NY 10017
212/705-7900

**INTERNATIONAL BROTHERHOOD OF ELECTRICAL WORKERS**
1125 15th Street NW
Washington DC 20005
202/833-7000

**INTERNATIONAL SOCIETY OF CERTIFIED ELECTRONICS TECHNICIANS**
2708 West Berry
Ft. Worth TX 76109
817/921-9101

**NATIONAL ELECTRICAL MANUFACTURERS ASSOCIATION**
2101 L Street NW, Suite 300
Washington DC 20037
202/457-8400

**NATIONAL ELECTRONICS SALES AND SERVICES ASSOCIATION**
2708 West Berry
Ft. Worth TX 76109
817/921-9061

## ENGINEERING AND ARCHITECTURE

**AMERICAN SOCIETY OF HEATING, REFRIGERATING AND AIR CONDITIONING ENGINEERS/CHICAGO**
Paul Schwarz
c/o Henry Valve
3215 North Avenue
Melrose Park IL 60160
708/344-1100

**AMERICAN SOCIETY OF LANDSCAPE ARCHITECTS/CHICAGO**
c/o Theresa Sudges
501 Hill Avenue
Glen Ellen IL 60137
708/858-2462

**AMERICAN SOCIETY OF SAFETY ENGINEERS**
1800 East Oakton Street
Des Plaines IL 60018-2187
708/692-4121

**ILLINOIS SOCIETY OF PROFESSIONAL ENGINEERS**
1304 South Lowell
Springfield IL 62704
217/544-7424

**INSTITUTE OF INDUSTRIAL ENGINEERS/CHICAGO**
c/o Sarosh Khambatta
14200 Yorktown Drive
Orland Park IL 60462-2127
708/534-3400

**SOCIETY OF FIRE PROTECTION ENGINEERS/CHICAGO**
Barbara Filvis
8749 Summerdale
Chicago IL 60656


For more information, contact:

**AMERICAN INSTITUTE OF ARCHITECTS**
1735 New York Ave NW
Washington DC 20006
202/626-7300

**AMERICAN SOCIETY OF CIVIL ENGINEERS**
345 East 47th Street
New York NY 10017
212/705-7496

**AMERICAN SOCIETY FOR ENGINEERING EDUCATION**
11 Dupont Circle NW
Suite 200
Washington DC 20036
202/293-7080

**AMERICAN SOCIETY OF HEATING, REFRIGERATING AND AIR CONDITIONING ENGINEERS**
1791 Tullie Circle NE
Atlanta GA 30329
404/636-8400

**AMERICAN SOCIETY OF NAVAL ENGINEERS**
1452 Duke Street
Alexandria VA 22314
703/836-6727

**AMERICAN SOCIETY OF PLUMBING ENGINEERS**
3617 Thousand Oaks Boulevard
Suite #210
Westlake CA 91362
805/495-7120

**ILLUMINATING ENGINEERING SOCIETY OF NORTH AMERICA**
345 East 47th Street
New York NY 10017
212/705-7926

**INSTITUTE OF INDUSTRIAL ENGINEERS**
25 Technology Park
Norcross GA 30092
404/449-0460

**NATIONAL ACADEMY OF ENGINEERING**
2101 Constitution Avenue NW
Washington DC 20418
202/334-3200

**NATIONAL SOCIETY OF PROFESSIONAL ENGINEERS**
1420 King Street
Alexandria VA 22314
703/684-2800

**SOCIETY OF FIRE PROTECTION ENGINEERS**
60 Batterymarch Street
Boston MA 02110
617/482-0686

**UNITED ENGINEERING TRUSTEES**
345 East 47th Street
New York NY 10017
212/705-7000

## FABRICATED METAL PRODUCTS/PRIMARY METALS

**AMERICAN CASTE METALS ASSOCIATION**
455 State Street
Des Plaines IL 60016
708/299-9156

**NATIONAL ASSOCIATION OF METAL FINISHERS**
111 East Wacker Drive, Suite 600
Chicago IL 60601
312/644-6610

For more information, contact:

**AMERICAN POWDER METALLURGY INSTITUTE**
105 College Road East
Princeton NJ 08540
609/452-7700

**ASSOCIATION OF IRON AND STEEL ENGINEERS**
Three Gateway Center
Suite 2350
Pittsburgh PA 15222
412/281-6323

## FINANCIAL SERVICES/MANAGEMENT CONSULTING

**AMERICAN SOCIETY OF APPRAISERS/CHICAGO**
Charles Oeler
c/o Household International
2700 Sanders Road
Mt. Prospect IL 60070
708/564-6055

**CHICAGO ASSOCIATION OF BUSINESS ECONOMISTS**
John Sylvia
c/o Kemper Financial Services
120 South LaSalle
Chicago IL 60603
312/845-1755

**CHICAGO ASSOCIATION OF CREDIT MANAGEMENT**
315 South Northwest Highway
Park Ridge IL 60068
708/696-3000

**FINANCIAL ANALYSTS FEDERATION/CHICAGO**
600 South Federal Street, Suite 400
Chicago IL 60605
312/922-6222

**FINANCIAL EXECUTIVES INSTITUTE/CHICAGO**
Kent Lampkin
c/o Ameritech
30 South Wacker
Chicago IL 60606
312/750-5168

**INSTITUTE OF FINANCIAL EDUCATION**
111 East Wacker Drive, 24th Floor
Chicago IL 60601
312/644-3100

**INSTITUTE OF MANAGMENT CONSULTANTS/
GREATER CHICAGO CHAPTER**
John Chapin
c/o Coopers & Lybrand
203 North LaSalle Street
Chicago IL 60601
312/701-5500

For more information, contact:

AMERICAN FINANCIAL SERVICES ASSOCIATION
Fourth Floor, 1101 14th Street NW
Washington DC 20005
202/289-0400

AMERICAN SOCIETY OF APPRAISERS
P.O. Box 17265
Washington DC 20041
202/478-2228

ASSOCIATION OF MANAGEMENT CONSULTING FIRMS
230 Park Avenue, Suite 544
New York NY 10169
212/697-9693

COUNCIL OF CONSULTANT ORGANIZATIONS
230 Park Avenue
Suite 544
New York NY 10169
212/697-8262

FEDERATION OF TAX ADMINISTRATORS
444 North Capital Street NW
Washington DC 20001
202/624-5890

FINANCIAL ANALYSTS FEDERATION
1633 Broadway
Room 1602
New York NY 10019
212/957-2860

FINANCIAL EXECUTIVES INSTITUTE
10 Madison Avenue
P.O. Box 1938
Morristown NJ 07962-1938
201/898-4600

NATIONAL ASSOCIATION OF CREDIT MANAGEMENT
8815 Centre Park Drive
Suite 200
Columbia MD 21045-2117
301/740-5560

NATIONAL ASSOCIATION OF REAL ESTATE INVESTMENT TRUSTS
1129 20th Street NW
Suite 705
Washington DC 20036
202/785-8717

NATIONAL CORPORATE CASH
 MANAGEMENT ASSOCIATION
52 Church Hill Road
Newtown CT 06470
203/426-3007

SECURITIES INDUSTRY ASSOCIATION
120 Broadway
New York NY 10271
212/608-1500

## FOOD: PROCESSING, PRODUCTION, AND DISTRIBUTION

ILLINOIS ASSOCIATION OF CEREAL CHEMISTS
Ronald Deis
c/o Nutra Sweet Co.
601 Kensington Road
Mt. Prospect IL 60056
708/506-4239

NATIONAL DAIRY COUNCIL
6300 North River Road
Rosemont IL 60018
708/696-1020

For more information, contact:

AMERICAN ASSOCIATION OF CEREAL CHEMISTS
3340 Pilot Knob Road
St. Paul MN 55121
612/454-7250

AMERICAN SOCIETY OF AGRICULTURAL ENGINEERS
2950 Niles Road
St. Joseph MI 49085
616/429-0300

**AMERICAN SOCIETY OF BREWING CHEMISTS**
3340 Pilot Knob Road
St. Paul MN 55121
612/454-7250

**DAIRY AND FOOD INDUSTRIES SUPPLY ASSOCIATION**
6245 Executive Boulevard
Rockville MD 20852
301/984-1444

**NATIONAL AGRICULTURAL CHEMICALS ASSOCIATION**
1155 15th Street NW
Suite 900
Washington DC 20005
202/296-1585

**UNITED FOOD AND COMMERCIAL WORKERS INTERNATIONAL UNION**
1775 K Street NW
Washington DC 20006
202/223-3111

## GENERAL MERCHANDISE: RETAIL AND WHOLESALE

**NATIONAL RETAIL MERCHANTS ASSOCIATION**
100 West 31st Street
New York NY 10001
212/244-8780

## HEALTH CARE AND PHARMACEUTICALS/HOSPITALS

**AMERICAN COLLEGE OF HEALTHCARE EXECUTIVES**
840 North Lake Shore Drive
Chicago IL 60611
312/943-0544

**AMERICAN DENTAL ASSOCIATION**
211 East Chicago Avenue
Chicago IL 60611
312/440-2500

**AMERICAN MEDICAL ASSOCIATION**
515 North State Street
Chicago IL 60610
312/645-5000

**AMERICAN VETERINARY MEDICAL ASSOCIATION**
930 North Meacham Road
Schaumburg IL 60196
708/605-8070

**CHICAGO PHYSICAL THERAPY ASSOCIATION**
Susan Suria
c/o NTS
3071 South Wolf Road
Westchester IL 60154
312/562-0999

**ILLINOIS ACADEMY OF PHYSICIAN ASSISTANTS**
20 North Michigan Avenue, Suite 700
Chicago IL 60602
312/263-7150

**ILLINOIS SOCIETY OF HOSPITAL PHARMACISTS**
c/o PAS
P.O. Box 6565
Athens GA 30604
404/613-0100

**MEDICAL GROUP MANAGEMENT ASSOCIATION/ SPRINGFIELD BRANCH**
Jan Garmong
c/o Moline Radiology Associates
1505 7th Street
Moline IL 61265-2992
309/762-1072


For more information, contact:

**AMERICAN ACADEMY OF PHYSICIAN ASSISTANTS**
950 North Washington Street
Alexandria VA 22314
703/836-2272

**AMERICAN HEALTH CARE ASSOCIATION**
1201 L Street NW
Washington DC 20005
202/842-4444

**AMERICAN OCCUPATIONAL THERAPY ASSOCIATION**
1383 Piccard Drive
Rockville MD 20850
301/948-9626

**AMERICAN PHARMACEUTICAL ASSOCIATION**
2215 Constitution Avenue NW
Washington DC 20037
202/628-4410

**AMERICAN PHYSICAL THERAPY ASSOCIATION**
1111 North Fairfax Street
Alexandria VA 22314
703/684-2782

**AMERICAN SOCIETY FOR BIOCHEMISTRY
 AND MOLECULAR BIOLOGY**
9650 Rockville Pike
Bethesda MD 20814
301/530-7145

**AMERICAN SOCIETY OF HOSPITAL PHARMACISTS**
4630 Montgomery Avenue
Bethesda MD 20814
301/657-3000

**CARDIOVASCULAR CREDENTIALING INTERNATIONAL**
P.O. Box 611
Dayton OH 45419
513/294-5225

**MEDICAL GROUP MANAGEMENT ASSOCIATION**
1355 South Colorado Boulevard
Suite 900
Denver CO 80222
303/753-1111

**NATIONAL HEALTH COUNCIL**
350 5th Avenue, Suite 1118
New York NY 10018
212/268-8900

**NATIONAL MEDICAL ASSOCIATION**
1012 Tenth Street NW
Washington DC 20001
202/347-1895

## HOTEL AND RESTAURANT RELATED

**THE EDUCATION FOUNDATION OF THE NATIONAL RESTAURANT ASSOCIATION**
250 South Wacker Drive
14th Floor
Chicago IL 60606
312/715-1010

For more information, contact:

**THE AMERICAN HOTEL AND MOTEL ASSOCIATION**
295 Lafayette Street, 7th Floor
New York NY 10012
212/941-5858

**COUNCIL ON HOTEL, RESTAURANT AND INSTITUTIONAL EDUCATION**
1200 17th Street NW
Washington DC 20036
202/331-5990

## INSURANCE

**ALLIANCE OF AMERICAN INSURERS**
1501 Woodfield Road
Suite 400 West
Schaumburg IL 60173-4980
708/330-8500

**INSURANCE INFORMATION INSTITUTE OF CHICAGO**
John Maes
10 South Riverside Plaza, Suite 1620
Chicago IL 60606

**SOCIETY OF ACTUARIES**
475 North Martingale Road
Suite 800
Schaumburg IL 60173-2226
708/706-3500

For more information, contact:

**AMERICAN COUNCIL OF LIFE INSURANCE**
1001 Pennsylvania Avenue NW
Washington DC 20004-2599
202/624-2000

**AMERICAN INSURANCE ASSOCIATION**
1130 Connecticut Avenue NW
Suite 1000
Washington DC 20036
202/828-7100

**INSURANCE INFORMATION INSTITUTE**
110 William Street
New York NY 10038
212/669-9200

**NATIONAL ASSOCIATION OF LIFE UNDERWRITERS**
1922 F Street NW
Washington DC 20006
202/331-6000

## LEGAL SERVICES

**AMERICAN BAR ASSOCIATION**
750 North Lake Shore Drive
Chicago IL 60611
312/988-5000

**FEDERAL BAR ASSOCIATION/CHICAGO CHAPTER**
Lou Hegeman
c/o Gould & Ratner
222 North LaSalle
Chicago IL 60601
312/236-3003

**NATIONAL FEDERATION OF PARALEGAL ASSOCIATIONS**
Suite 201
104 Wilmot Road
Deerfield IL 60015
708/940-8800

For more information, contact:

**FEDERAL BAR ASSOCIATION**
1815 H Street NW, Suite 408
Washington DC 20006
202/638-0252

**NATIONAL ASSOCIATION FOR LAW PLACEMENT**
1666 Connecticut Avenue, Suite 450
Washington DC 20009
202/667-1666

**NATIONAL ASSOCIATION OF LEGAL ASSISTANTS**
1601 South Main Street, Suite 300
Tulsa OK 74119
918/587-6828

**NATIONAL PARALEGAL ASSOCIATION**
P.O. Box 629
Doylestown PA 18901
215/297-8333

## MISCELLANEOUS ASSOCIATIONS

**AMERICAN FEDERATION OF SMALL BUSINESS**
407 South Dearborn Street, Suite 500
Chicago IL 60605
312/427-0206

For more information, contact:

**NATIONAL COOPERATIVE BUSINESS ASSOCIATION**
1401 New York Avenue NW
Suite #1100
Washington DC 20005
202/638-6222

**NATIONAL SMALL BUSINESS UNITED**
1155 15th Street NW
Suite 710
Washington DC 20005
202/293-8830

## MISCELLANEOUS MANUFACTURING

**NATIONAL ASSOCIATION OF MANUFACTURERS/
PARK RIDGE BRANCH**
315 South Northwest Highway
Park Ridge IL 60068
708/698-3838

**NATIONAL TOOLING AND MACHINING ASSOCIATION/
CHICAGO CHAPTER**
Egon Jaeggin
c/o Numerical Precision Inc.
2200 Foster Avenue
Wheeling IL 60090
708/394-3610

**NATIONAL SCREW MACHINE PRODUCTS ASSOCIATION/
NORTHERN ILLINOIS CHAPTER**
Robert Kepler
c/o Commercial Tool Works, Inc.
3738 North River Road
Schiller Park IL 60176
708/678-9000

**For more information, contact:**

**NATIONAL ASSOCIATION OF MANUFACTURERS**
1331 Pennsylvania Avenue, NW
Suite 1500
Washington DC 20004
202/637-3000

**NATIONAL MACHINE TOOL BUILDERS**
7901 Westpark Drive
McLean VA 22102-4269
703/893-2900

NATIONAL SCREW MACHINE PRODUCTS ASSOCIATION
6700 West Snowville Road
Breckville OH 44141
216/526-0300

NATIONAL TOOLING AND MACHINING ASSOCIATION
9300 Livingston Road
Fort Washington MD 20744
301/248-1250

## NEWSPAPER PUBLISHING

THE NEWSPAPER GUILD/CHICAGO LOCAL
230 North Michigan Avenue
Suite 1525
Chicago IL 60601
312/236-4924

For more information, contact:

AMERICAN NEWSPAPER PUBLISHERS ASSOCIATION
Box 17407
Dulles International Airport
Washington DC 20041
703/648-1000

AMERICAN SOCIETY OF NEWSPAPER EDITORS
P.O. Box 17004
Washington DC 20041
202/648-1144

THE DOW JONES NEWSPAPER FUND
P.O. Box 300
Princeton NJ 08543-0300
609/520-4000

INTERNATIONAL CIRCULATION MANAGERS ASSOCIATION
P.O. Box 17420
Washington DC 20041
703/620-9555

**NATIONAL NEWSPAPER ASSOCIATION**
1627 K Street NW
Suite 400
Washington DC 20006
202/466-7200

**NATIONAL PRESS CLUB**
529 14th St. NW
Washington DC 20045
202/662-7500

**THE NEWSPAPER GUILD**
133 West 44th Street
New York NY 10036
212/575-1580

## PAPER PRODUCTS AND PACKAGING/CONTAINERS

**PAPER INDUSTRY MANAGEMENT ASSOCIATION**
2400 East Oakton Street
Arlington Heights IL 60005
708/956-0250

For more information, contact:

**AMERICAN PAPER INSTITUTE**
260 Madison Avenue
New York NY 10016
212/340-0600

**TECHNICAL ASSOCIATION OF THE PULP AND PAPER INDUSTRY**
P.O. Box 105113
Atlanta GA 30348
404/446-1400

## PETROLEUM AND ENERGY RELATED/MINING AND DRILLING

**AMERICAN INSTITUTE OF MINING, METALLURGICAL AND PETROLEUM/CHICAGO**
Douglas Hambley
1051 North Oakley Drive West
Westmont IL 60559
708/972-6478

**AMERICAN NUCLEAR SOCIETY**
555 North Kensington Avenue
La Grange Park IL 60525
708/352-6611

**SOCIETY OF TRIBOLOGISTS AND LUBRICATION ENGINEERS**
838 Busse Highway
Park Ridge IL 60068
708/825-5536

For more information, contact:

**AMERICAN ASSOCIATION OF PETROLEUM GEOLOGISTS**
P.O. Box 979
Tulsa OK 74101
918/584-2555

**AMERICAN GAS ASSOCIATION**
1515 Wilson Boulevard
Arlington VA 22209
703/841-8400

**AMERICAN GEOLOGICAL INSTITUTE**
4220 King Street
Alexandria VA 22302
703/379-2480

**AMERICAN INSTITUTE OF MINING, METALLURGICAL AND PETROLEUM**
345 East 47th Street
New York NY 10017
212/705-7695

**AMERICAN PETROLEUM INSTITUTE**
1220 L Street NW
Washington DC 20005
202/682-8000

**CLEAN ENERGY RESEARCH INSTITUTE**
P.O. Box 248294
Coral Gables FL 33124
305/284-4666

**GEOLOGICAL SOCIETY OF AMERICA**
3300 Penrose Place
P.O. Box 9140
Boulder CO 80301
303/447-2020

**SOCIETY OF EXPLORATION GEOPHYSICISTS**
P.O. Box 702740
Tulsa OK 74170-2740
918/493-3516

## PRINTING

**BINDING INDUSTRIES OF AMERICA**
70 East Lake Street
Chicago IL 60601-5905
312/372-7606

For more information, contact:

**ASSOCIATION OF GRAPHIC ARTS**
5 Penn Plaza
New York NY 10001
212/279-2100

**NATIONAL ASSOCIATION OF PRINTERS AND LITHOGRAPHERS**
780 Pallisade Avenue
Teaneck NJ 07666
201/342-0700

PRINTING INDUSTRIES OF AMERICA
1730 North Lynn Street
Arlington VA 22209
703/841-8100

TECHNICAL ASSOCIATION OF THE GRAPHIC ARTS
Box 9887
Rochester NY 14614
716/272-0557

## REAL ESTATE

BUILDING OWNERS AND MANAGERS ASSOCIATION/
 SUBURBAN CHICAGO
3158 River Road, Suite123
Des Plaines IL 60018
708/635-6709

INSTITUTE OF REAL ESTATE MANAGEMENT
430 North Michigan Avenue
Chicago IL 60611
312/661-1930

INTERNATIONAL ASSOCIATION OF CORPORATE
 REAL ESTATE EXECUTIVES/CHICAGO CHAPTER
Ed O'Donohue
c/o Illinois Bell
225 West Randolph, Room 25A
Chicago IL 60606
312/727-3905

NATIONAL ASSOCIATION OF REALTORS
430 North Michigan Avenue
Chicago IL 60611
312/329-8200


For more information, contact:

APARTMENT OWNERS AND MANAGERS ASSOCIATION
65 Cherry Plaza
Watertown CT 06795
203/274-2589

BUILDING OWNERS AND MANAGERS ASSOCIATION
1521 Ritchie Highway, P.O. Box 9709
Arnold MD 21012
301/261-2882

INTERNATIONAL ASSOCIATION OF CORPORATE
REAL ESTATE EXECUTIVES
440 Columbia Drive, Suite 100
West Palm Beach FL 33409
407/683-8111

INTERNATIONAL REAL ESTATE INSTITUTE
8383 East Evans Road
Scottsdale AZ 85260
602/998-8267

NATIONAL ASSOCIATION OF REAL ESTATE INVESTMENT TRUSTS
1129 20th Street NW
Suite 705
Washington DC 20036
202/785-8717

**RUBBER AND PLASTICS**

SOCIETY OF PLASTICS INDUSTRY/DES PLAINES
2400 East Devon Avenue, Suite 301
Des Plaines IL 60018
708/297-6150

**For more information, contact:**

SOCIETY OF PLASTIC ENGINEERS
14 Fairfield Drive
Brookfield Centre CT 06804
203/775-0471

SOCIETY OF PLASTICS INDUSTRY
355 Lexington Avenue
New York NY 10017
212/370-7340

## TRANSPORTATION/SHIPPING/AUTOMOTIVE

**AIR LINE EMPLOYEES ASSOCIATION**
5600 South Central Avenue
Chicago IL 60638
312/767-3333

**AIR TRANSPORT ASSOCIATION OF CHICAGO**
2128 South Road
Des Plaines IL 60018
708/299-7690

**ASSOCIATION OF AMERICAN RAILROADS/CHICAGO**
3140 South Federal Street
Chicago IL 60616
312/567-3606

**AUTOMOTIVE SERVICE ASSOCIATION/CHICAGO**
Mike Lane
c/o PAMS Inc.
625 South 2nd Street
Springfield IL 62704
217/528-5230

**AUTOMOTIVE SERVICE INDUSTRY ASSOCIATION**
444 North Michigan Avenue
Chicago IL 60611
312/836-1300

**ILLINOIS TRUCKING ASSOCIATION**
2000 5th Avenue
River Grove IL 60171
708/452-3500

**NATIONAL MARINE MANUFACTURERS ASSOCIATION**
401 North Michigan Avenue
Suite 1150
Chicago IL 60611
312/836-4747

**NATIONAL MARINE MANUFACTURERS ASSOCIATION**
401 North Michigan Avenue
Suite 1150
Chicago IL 60611
312/836-4747

**For more information, contact:**

**AIR TRANSPORT ASSOCIATION OF AMERICA**
1709 New York Ave NW
Washington DC 20006
202/626-4000

**AMERICAN INSTITUTE OF AERONAUTICS AND ASTRONAUTICS**
555 West 57th Street
New York NY 10019
212/247-6500

**AMERICAN TRUCKING ASSOCIATION**
2200 Mill Road
Alexandria VA 22314-4677
703/838-1700

**ASSOCIATION OF AMERICAN RAILROADS**
50 F Street NW
Washington DC 20001
202/639-2100

**AUTOMOTIVE SERVICE ASSOCIATION**
1901 Airport Freeway, Suite 100
Bedford TX 76021
817/283-6205

**AVIATION MAINTENANCE FOUNDATION**
P.O. Box 2826
Redmond WA 98073
206/828-3917

**INSTITUTE OF TRANSPORTATION ENGINEERS**
Suite 410
525 School Street SW, Suite 410
Washington DC 20024
202/554-8050

**MARINE TECHNOLOGY SOCIETY**
1825 K Street NW
Suite 218
Washington DC 20006
202/775-5966

**MOTOR VEHICLE MANUFACTURERS ASSOCIATION**
7430 2nd Avenue
Suite 300
Detroit MI 48202
313/872-4311

**NATIONAL AERONAUTIC ASSOCIATION OF USA**
1815 North Fort Meyer Drive
Arlington VA 22209
202/265-8720

**NATIONAL AUTOMOTIVE DEALERS ASSOCIATION**
8400 Westpark Drive
McLean VA 22102
703/821-7000

**NATIONAL INSTITUTE FOR AUTOMOTIVE SERVICE EXCELLENCE**
13505 Dulles Technology Drive
Herndon VA 22071
703/742-3800

**PROFESSIONAL AVIATION MAINTENANCE ASSOCIATION**
500 NW Plaza, Suite 809
St. Ann MO 63074
314/739-2580

**SHIPBUILDERS COUNCIL OF AMERICA**
1110 Vermont Ave. NW, Suite 1250
Washington DC 20005
202/775-9060

## UTILITIES

**AMERICAN WATER WORKS FOUNDATION/CHICAGO**
William Plautz
c/o Consoer, Townsend & Associates
303 East Wacker Drive, Suite 600
Chicago IL 60601
312/938-0300

For more information, contact:

**AMERICAN WATER WORKS ASSOCIATION**
6666 West Quincy Avenue
Denver CO 80235
303/794-7711

# Index

**Alphabetical Index to Greater Chicago Employers**

**A**

ABB RAYMOND COMBUSTION ENGINEERING INC., 163
ABF, 260
AON CORPORATION, 205
ARA SERVICES, 202
ABBOTT LABORATORIES, 194
ACCO INTERNATIONAL, 212
ACE HARDWARE CORP., 212
ADAMS ADVERTISING AGENCY, 112
ADVANCE TRANSFORMER CO., 154
ADVANCED SYSTEM APPLICATIONS, 145
ADVERTISING METAL DISPLAY, 112
AETNA BANK, 120
AIRCRAFT GEAR CORP., 260
ALBANY BANK & TRUST CO., 120
ALBERTO-CULVER CO., 194
ALDEN PRESS, INC., 253
ALLEN INDUSTRIES, 261
ALLIED PRODUCTS CORP., 222
ALLIED VAN LINES, 261
ALLSTATE INSURANCE CO., 206
ALLSTEEL INC., 167
ALLTEL ILLINOIS, INC., 143
ALTON & SOUTHERN RAILWAY, 261
ALTON MEMORIAL HOSPITAL, 194
ALTON MENTAL HEALTH CENTER, 194
ALTON TELEGRAPH PRINTING, 240
AM INTERNATIONAL, 253
AMERICAN BAR ASSN., 210
AMERICAN DENTAL ASSN., 195
AMERICAN HOSPITAL ASSN., 195
AMERICAN LIBRARY ASSN., 126
AMER. NATIONAL BANK & TRUST, 120
AMERICAN PRINTERS AND LITHOGRAPHERS, 253
AMERICAN RED CROSS, 132
AMERICAN SPRING AND WIRE SPECIALTY CO., 167
AMERICAN STEEL FOUNDRIES, 167
AMERICAN WARRANTY CORP., 261
AMERITECH SERVICES, 143
AMMCO TOOLS INC., 261
AMOCO CORP., 251
AMOCO PETROLEUM ADDITIVES, 250
AMSTED INDUSTRIES, 222
ANDERSEN CONSULTING, 175
ANDERSON INDUSTRIES, 261
ANDREW CORP., 143
ANIXTER BROTHERS, INC., 143
ANNING-JOHNSON CO., 149
APPLETON ELECTRIC CO., 149, 154
APPLIED LEARNING INT'L, 145
ARATEX SERVICES, INC., 117
ARCHER DANIEL MIDLAND CO., 180
ARMSTRONG-BLUM MFG. CO., 222
ARNSTEIN AND LEHR, 210
ARROW GROUP INDUSTRIES, 222
ARTEX INT'L INC., 118
ARTRA GROUP, 212
ARVEY CORP., 241
AUSTIN BANK OF CHICAGO, 120
AUSTIN CO., 164
AUTOMATIC DATA PROCESSING, 175
N.W. AYER INC, 112

**B**

B-LINE SYSTEMS INC., 167
BBDO CHICAGO INC., 112
BP CHEMICAL, 258
BAGCRAFT OF AMERICA, 242
BAIRD & WARNER, 255
BAKER & McKENZIE, 211
GEORGE J. BALL, INC., 180
BALLY MFG., 116
BALLY MFG./GAMING DIVISION, 212
BANKERS LIFE AND CASUALTY, 206
BARBER-GREENE CO., 149
BARCO, 222
BARNES & REINECKE, INC., 146
BASLER ELECTRIC CO., 154
BAXTER HEALTHCARE, 195
BEALL MFG. DIVISION, 222
BEATRICE CORP., 180

BELDING CORP., 223
BELL & HOWELL CO., 126
BELLEVILLE AREA COLLEGE, 139
BELLEVILLE SHOE MFG. CO., 118
BENEFIT TRUST LIFE
 INSURANCE, 206
BENNETT INDUSTRIES, 242
BERKELEY-DAVIS, INC., 223
BEVERLY BANK, 120
BEVERLY FARM FOUNDATION, 195
BIG RIVER ZINC CORP., 167
BINKS MFG. CO., 223
BLACKSTONE MFG. CO., 251
BLUE M ELECTRIC CO., 155
BOATMEN'S NAT'L. BANK OF
 BELLEVILLE, 120
BODINE ELECTRIC CO., 155
BOISE CASCADE OFFICE
 PRODUCTS, 180
BORG-WARNER CORP., 223
BOULEVARD BANK NAT'L. ASSN., 121
BOZELL, 113
BRADFORD EXCHANGE, 188
BRADLEY UNIVERSITY, 140
BRADNOR CENTRAL CO., 242
R.A. BRIGGS & CO., 118
BRINK'S, INC., 262
BRUNSWICK CORP., 213
BRUSH FUSES INC., 155
LEO BURNETT CO., 113
BURNS INT'L
 SECURITY SERVICES, 238
BURTON SPRING, 262

C

CBI INDUSTRIES INC., 168
CF INDUSTRIES, 134
CPC INT'L/BEST FOODS, 180
CALSTAR CORP., 213
CARBIDE INT'L, 224
CARSON PIRIE SCOTT, 202
A.M. CASTLE & CO., 168
CATERPILLAR TRACTOR CO., 262
CECO CORP., 149
CENTEL CORP., 143
CENTRAL CAN CO., 242
CENTRAL GROWERS COOP, INC., 181

CENTRAL IL PUBLIC SERVICE, 267
CENTRAL STEEL AND WIRE CO., 168
CENTREVILLE TOWNSHIP
 HOSPITAL, 196
CERTIFIED GROCERS MIDWEST, 181
CHAPMAN AND CUTLER, 211
CHEMICAL WASTE
 MANAGEMENT, 134
THE CHERRY CORP., 155
CHICAGO BLOWER CORP., 224
CHICAGO BOARD OF OPTIONS
 EXCHANGE, 176
THE CHICAGO BOARD OF TRADE, 176
CHICAGO DISPLAY CO., 113
CHICAGO EDUCATIONAL
 TELEVISION ASSN., 131
CHICAGO EXTRUDED METALS, 224
CHICAGO FAUCET CO., 224
CHICAGO LOCK CO., 213
CHICAGO MERCANTILE
 EXCHANGE, 176
CHICAGO METROPOLITAN MUTUAL
 ASSURANCE CO., 176
CHICAGO MILWAUKEE CORP., 176
CHICAGO NAT'L. LEAGUE BALL
 CLUB, INC., 116
CHICAGO NORTHWESTERN, 262
CHICAGO RIVET & MACHINE CO., 224
CHICAGO STADIUM CORP., 116
CHICAGO STATE UNIVERSITY, 140
CHICAGO TITLE & TRUST CO., 255
CHICAGO TRIBUNE, 240
CHILDREN'S PRESS, 126
CHRISTIANITY TODAY, INC., 127
CHURCH'S CHICKEN INC., 202
CINCH CONNECTORS, 225
CITIBANK FSB, 121
CLARK FOODSERVICE, INC., 181
CLARK OIL & REFINING, 251
CLIFTON GUNDERSON & CO., 111
CNA INSURANCE COMPANIES, 206
COLE TAYLOR BANK, 121
COLLINSVILLE HOLIDAY INN, 202
COLLINSVILLE MAC INC., 202
COLUMBIA COLLEGE, 140
COLUMBIA QUARRY CO., 251
COMDISCO, 146
COMMERCE CLEARING HOUSE, 127

COMMERCIAL LIGHT CO., 155
COMMERCIAL STAMPING &
    FORGING, INC., 225
COMMONWEALTH EDISON CO., 267
COMPREHENSIVE BUSINESS
    SERVICES OF CANADA, 111
COMPUTER POWER GROUP, 146
CONSOER, TOWNSEND, & ASSOC., 164
CONTINENTAL AIR TRANSPORT, 262
THE CONTINENTAL CORP., 176
CONTINENTAL GRAIN CO., 181
CONTINENTAL ILLINOIS NAT'L.
    BANK, 121
CONTINENTAL TELEPHONE CO. OF
    ILLINOIS, 144
CONTRACTING & MATERIAL CO., 149
COOK ELECTRIC DIVISION, 144
COOPER POWER SYSTEMS, 156
COTTER CO., 188
COUNSELOR CO., 213
COUNTRY COMPANIES, 206
JOHN CRANE, 242
CULINARY FOODS, INC., 181
CULLIGAN INT'L, 225
CUMMINS ALLISON CORP., 213

## D

DAILY HERALD-PADDOCK
    PUBLICATIONS, 240
DAMON LABS, 196
DANA CORP./
    VICTOR PRODUCT DIV., 225
DANLY MACHINE DIVISION/, 226
DANVILLE METAL STAMPING, 168
DAVID C. COOK PUBLISHING CO., 127
DAVY McKEE CORP., 165
DDB NEEDHAM WORLDWIDE, 113
DEERE & CO., 226
DePAUL UNIVERSITY, 140
DESOTO, INC., 214
DEXTER CORP., 226
A.B. DICK CO., 227
DO-ALL CO., 227
DOMINICK'S FINER FOODS, 181
DON TECH, 127
DRAKE HOTEL, 203
DRESSER INDUSTRIES, 230

DRESSER KOMATSU DIVISION, 177
R. DRON ELECTRICAL CO. INC., 156
DUCHOSSOIS INDUSTRIES, INC., 156
DUDEK & BOCK SPRING MFG., 227
DUO-FAST, 227
DURO METAL PRODUCTS CO., 227
DYNASCAN CORP., 156

## E

EASTERN ILLINOIS UNIVERSITY, 140
EATON CONTROLS DIVISION, 156
ECHLIN MFG. CO., 262
ECONOMY MECHANICAL
    INDUSTRIES, 149
EDWARD DON & CO., 181
EDWARD GRAY CORP., 150
ELECTRO-MOTIVE DIVISION, 262
ELGIN, JOLIET & EASTERN
    RAILWAY, 263
ELGIN NAT'L. INDUSTRIES, 164, 251
EMPIRE STOVE CO., 214
ENCYCLOPAEDIA BRITANNICA, 128
ENVIRODYNE INDUSTRIES, INC., 182
EQUIFAX INC., 177
EQUIPTO, 227
EUREKA CO., 214
EVANS, INC., 189
EXECUTIVE HOUSE HOTEL, 203

## F

F&B MFG. CO., 263
F.E. MORAN, 151
FABER ENTERPRISES, 203
FAIRMONT RACE TRACK, 116
FARLEY INDUSTRIES, 200
FEDERAL KEMPER INSURANCE, 207
FEDERAL RESERVE BANK OF
    CHICAGO, 121
FEDERAL SIGNAL CORP., 228
FEL-PRO, INC., 263
FERALLOY CORP., 168
FERMI NAT'L. ACCELERATOR
    LABORATORY, 256
FIATALLIS NORTH AMERICA, 228
FIELD CONTAINER CORP., 243

FIELD MUSEUM OF NATURAL
    HISTORY, 117
A. FINKL & SONS, 168
FIRESTONE TIRE, 189
FIRST CHICAGO CORP., 121
FIRST FINANCIAL BANK, FSB, 122
FIRST NAT'L. BANK/BELLEVILLE, 122
FISCHER'S RESTAURANT, 203
FLEX-O-GLASS, 258
FLORSHEIM SHOE CO., 118
FLOUR DANIEL, 164
FLOUR MILLS DIVISION, 182
FLUID POWER SYSTEMS, 228
FMC CORP., 135
FOLLETT CORP., 189
FOOTE CONE AND BELDING
    COMMUNICATIONS, 114
FOOTE JONES, 228
FOUR FOUNTAINS
    CONVALESCENT, 196
FOURTH DEARBORN LIFE
    INSURANCE CO., 207
FOXMEYER, 196
FRANCISCAN HERALD PRESS, 128
FRANK CONSOLIDATED
    ENTERPRISES, INC., 263
FURNAS ELECTRIC CO., 156

## G

G&W ELECTRIC CO., 157
GARDNER, CARTON, & DOUGLAS, 211
GARRETT GENERAL AVIATION, 263
GATELY'S PEOPLE STORE, 189
GATX CORP., 264
GBC, 228
GE RAILCAR SERVICES CORP., 264
GEE CO., 243
GENERAL FIRE EXTINGUISHER, 135
GEORGIA PACIFIC, 243
GERMANIA FEDERAL SAVINGS AND
    LOAN ASSN., 122
GLOBE INDUSTRIES, 149
GOLD BOND BUILDING, 150
GOLDEN GRAIN, 182
GONNELLA BAKING CO., 182
GOODMAN EQUIPMENT CORP., 252
GOODYEAR TIRE AND RUBBER, 258

GOVERNORS STATE UNIVERSITY, 140
W.R. GRACE/DEARBORN, 135
GRANITE CITY STEEL DIVISION, 169
GREAT LAKES MAINTENENCE &
    SECURITY CORP., 238
GREELEY AND HANSEN, 165
GREIF BROTHERS CORP., 243
GROEN CO., 182
GUARDIAN ELECTRIC MFG. CO., 157
GUNDLACH MACHINE CO., 252

## H

HADDON ADVERTISING, INC., 114
HAEGER POTTERIES, 214
H.H. HALL CONSTRUCTION CO., 150
HANDY BUTTON MACHINE, 169
HARCROS PIGMENTS INC., 135
HARRIS TRUST & SAVINGS BANK, 123
HARRIS-HUB/DRESHER, 169
HARTMARX CORP., 118
HELENE CURTIS INDUSTRIES, 196
HELLER FINANCIAL, 177
HENDRICKSON INT'L, 264
HIGHLAND SUPPLY CORP., 244
BERNARD HODES ADVERTISING, 114
HOEFFKEN BROS. INC., 150
HOFFER PLASTICS CORP., 258
THE HOFFMAN GROUP, INC., 150
HOLIDAY INNS, INC., 203
HOLLYMATIC CORP., 229
HOME NURSERY GREENHOUSES, 189
HONEYWELL, 146
HOUSEHOLD INT'L, 177
HUMISTON-KEELING, 196
HYATT REGENCY CHICAGO, 203
HYRE ELECTRIC CO., 157
HYSAN CORP., 135

## I

IBM, 147
IDEAL ROLLER CO., 229
ILLINOIS BELL, 144
ILLINOIS CENTRAL GULF
    RAILROAD, 265
ILLINOIS CONSOLIDATED
    TELEPHONE CO., 144

ILLINOIS FARM BUREAU, 182
ILLINOIS FARMERS INSURANCE, 207
ILLINOIS INSTITUTE OF
    TECHNOLOGY, 140
ILLINOIS POWER, 268
ILLINOIS STATE UNIVERSITY, 140
ILLINOIS TOOL WORKS, 229
IMCERA GROUP, 196
INFORMATION RESOURCES, 114
INGRID DIVISION OF SEVKO, 258
INLAND REAL ESTATE
    & AFFILIATES, 255
INLAND STEEL INDUSTRIES, 169
INLANDER-STEINDLER PAPER, 244
INTERMATIC, 157
INT'L ASSN. OF LIONS CLUBS, 132
INT'L MINERALS AND CHEMICAL, 135
INT'L PAPER CO./NORTHLAKE, 244
INT'L PAPER CO./PEORIA, 253
INTERSTATE BRANDS CORP., 183
ITEL, 200
ITEL/PULLMAN, 265
ITT McDONNELL & MILLER, 230
ITT/FLUID HANDLING DIVISION, 230
IVEX CORP., 244

J

JAKEL INCORPORATED, 158
JAY'S FOODS, 183
JEFFERSON SMURFIT CORP., 244
JEFFERSON-SMURFIT/CONTAINER
    DIVISION, 245
JMB REALTY CORP., 256
JOHNSON CONTROLS, 158
JOHNSON PUBLISHING CO., 128
JONES INTERCABLE CO., 131

K

K'S MERCHANDISE, 189
KALMUS & ASSOCIATES, 158
A.T. KEARNEY, 177
KECK, MAHIN, & CATE, 211
KEEBLER CO., 183
KENNY CONSTRUCTION CO., 150
KERR GLASS MFG. CORP., 245
KETCHUM COMMUNICATIONS, 114

KITCHENS OF SARA LEE, 183
KLEIN TOOLS, 214
LESTER B. KNIGHT & ASSOC., 178
KNOWLES ELECTRONICS, 158
KNOX COUNTY COUNCIL/DEVELOP-
    MENTAL DISABILITIES, 133
KPMG/PEAT MARWICK, 111
KRAFT HOLLEB, 184
KRAFT, 184
KROCH'S & BRENTANO'S, 190
KROPP FORGE DIVISION, 169

L

LAKE SHORE NAT'L. BANK, 123
LAKEWOOD ENGINEERING
    & MFG., 214
LANDMARK BANK, 123
LANE BRYANT, 190
LANE INDUSTRIES, 256
LASALLE BANK LAKE VIEW, 123
LASALLE NAT'L., 124
LAWSON PRODUCTS, 265
LEAF, 184
LEEWARDS, 214
LERNER NEWSPAPERS, 240
LERNER STORES CORP., 190
CHARLES LEVY CIRCULATING, 128
THE CHARLES LEVY CO., 147
LEWIS & CLARK COMMUNITY
    COLLEGE, 141
LIBERTY MUTUAL INSURANCE, 207
LIGHTOLIER, 215
LINDBERG CORP., 169
LIQUID AIR CORP., 252
LIQUID CARBONIC CORP., 252
LOCKE HOME PRODUCTS, 215
LORD, BISSELL, & BROOK, 211
LOYOLA UNIVERSITY AND MEDICAL
    CENTER, 141

M

MARSH CO., 230
MARTIN INDUSTRIES, 230
MARTIN OIL MARKETING, LTD. AND
    AFFILIATED COS., 252
MAY & SPEH DATA PROCESSING, 147

McDONALD'S CORP., 203
McDONALD'S RESTAURANT
    OFFICE, 202
McKENDREE COLLEGE, 141
McMASTER-CARR SUPPLY CO., 231
McMILLAN INFORMATION SERVICES
    GROUP, 129
MEDLINE INDUSTRIES, 197
MEMORIAL HOSPITAL, 197
MERCHANDISE MART
    PROPERTIES, 256
MERCHANDISE NAT'L. BANK, 124
MERRILL LYNCH, 178
METHODE ELECTRONICS 159
MICHIGAN AVENUE NAT'L. BANK OF
    CHICAGO, 124
MIDWEST RUBBER RECLAIMING, 258
MIDWEST STOCK EXCHANGE 178
MIDWEST TELEVISION, 131
MILLER FLUID POWER CORP., 231
MILLER-DAVIS CO., 151
MILLS-AMERICAN ENVELOPE, 245
MISSISSIPPI LIME CO., 252
MITEK CORP., 215
MODERN DROP FORGE CO., 169
MOLEX INCORPORATED, 159
MONTGOMERY WARD & CO., 190
MOORE BUSINESS FORMS & SYSTEMS
    DIVISION, 216
MORTON INT'L INC., 136
MORTON THIOKOL, 136
MOTIVATION MEDIA, 117
MOTOROLA 159
MUSEUM OF SCIENCE
    & INDUSTRY, 117

N

NALCO CHEMICAL CO., 136
NAT'L. BAKING CO., 184
NAT'L. BROADCASTING CO., 131
NAT'L. CASTINGS DIVISION, 170
NAT'L. LOUIS UNIVERSITY, 141
NAT'L. METALWARES 170
NAT'L. SAFETY COUNCIL, 133
NAT'L. STEEL CORP., 170
NAVISTAR INT'L CORP., 231
NCR CORP., 147

NESCO STEEL BARREL CO., 170
NESTLE FOODS CORP., 184
NEWARK ELECTRONICS, 160
NEWELL, 200
NEWS DEMOCRAT, 241
NEWS-SUN/COPLEY PRESS 241
NICOR, 268
A.C. NIELSEN, 132
NORTH AMERICAN CO., 208
NORTHEASTERN ILLINOIS U., 141
NORTHERN ILLINOIS GAS CO., 268
THE NORTHERN TRUST CO., 124
NORTHWEST NAT'L. BANK, 124
NORTHWESTERN STEEL & WIRE, 171
NORTHWESTERN UNIVERSITY, 141
NUARC CO. 216
NYSTROM CO., 216

O

O'BRYAN BROTHERS, 118
OAK SWITCH SYSTEMS INC., 160
OLD KENT BANK, 124
OLIN CORP., 136, 137, 232
W.E. O'NEIL CONSTRUCTION, 151
ORVAL KENT FOOD CO., 185
OSCAR MAYER FOODS CORP., 185
OTIS ELEVATOR CO., 232
OUTBOARD MARINE CORP., 216
R.S. OWENS AND CO. 216
OWENS-ILLINOIS INC., 245
OWENS-ILLINOIS/MOLD SHOP, 246
OXFORD CLOTHES, 119
OZITE CORP., 119

P

PACKAGING CORP. OF AMERICA, 246
PACKARD INSTRUMENT CO., 197
PANDUIT CORP., 258
PANSOPHIC SYSTEM, 148
PARKER-HANNIFIN CORP., 232
PARKVIEW METAL PRODUCTS, 171
PASCHEN CONTRACTORS 151
PAYMASTER CORP., 217
PEABODY MYERS CORP., 232
J.C. PENNEY CO. INC., 190
PEOPLES GAS CO., 269

PEPPER COMPANIES, 151
PETERSON, ROSS, SCHLOERB &
    SEIDEL, 211
PHEASANT RUN 204
PHILLIPS, GETSCHOW CO., 152
PINKERTON'S, 239
PIONEER BANK & TRUST CO., 125
PIONEER SCREW & NUT CO., 233
PITMAN-MOORE, 197
PITTWAY CORP., 233
PLASTOFILM INDUSTRIES, 259
PLAYBOY ENTERPRISES, 129
POLK BROTHERS, 191
PRAIRIE FARMS DAIRY 185
PREMARK INT'L, 259
PRICE WATERHOUSE, 111

**Q**

QST INDUSTRIES, 119
QUAKER OATS CO., 186
QUASAR CO., 217
QUILL CORP., 217

**R**

R&D THIEL 152
RAM GOLF CORP., 217
RAMADA HOTEL O'HARE, 204
RAND McNALLY & CO., 129
RAULAND-BORG CORP., 161
RELIABLE ELECTRIC CO., 144
RESPIRATORY CARE INC. (RCI), 198
REVCOR, 233
REYNOLDS METALS CO., 171
RHONE-POULENC BASIC
    CHEMICALS, 137
RICHARDS BRICK CO., 152
RICHARDS-WILCOX, 234
RICHARDSON ELECTRONICS, 161
RITZ CARLTON HOTEL, 204
ROADMASTER CORP., 218
THE ROBERTSON-CECO CORP., 152
ROCK-OLA MFG. CORP., 218
ROCKWELL GRAPHIC SYSTEMS, 265
ROCKWELL INT'L, 144
ROESCH 172
ROOSEVELT UNIVERSITY, 142

ROTARY INT'L, 239
RUDNICK & WOLFE, 212
RUST-OLEUM CORP., 137

**S**

S&C ELECTRIC, 161
SAATCHI SAATCHI DFS, 114
SAFECO INSURANCE COS, 208
SAFETY-KLEEN, 239
ST. ANTHONY'S HOSPITAL, 198
ST. CHARLES MFG., 220
ST. CLEMENT HOSPITAL, 198
ST. ELIZABETH'S HOSPITAL, 198
ST. JOSEPH HOSPITAL, 199
ST. LOUIS NAT'L. STOCK YARDS, 201
ST. PAUL FEDERAL BANK FOR
    SAVINGS, 125
ST. PAUL'S HOMES
    FOR THE AGED, 199
SAKS FIFTH AVENUE, 191
SALEM TECHNICAL SERVICES, 165
W.H. SALISBURY & CO., 259
SALTER BROADCASTING CO., 132
SANTA FE SOUTHERN PACIFIC, 265
SARA LEE, 186
SARGENT & LUNDY, 165
SARGENT-WELCH SCIENTIFIC, 257
SAXON PAINT & HOME CARE
    CENTERS, 191
SCHAWK GRAPHICS 254
SCHMIDT, GARDEN & ERIKSON, 166
SCHOLLE CORP., 246
SCHUMACHER ELECTRIC CORP., 161
SCHWINN BICYCLE CO., 218
SCIAKY BROTHERS INC, 234
SCOTT, FORESMAN AND CO., 129
SCRIPTURE PRESS, 129
SCULLY-JONES CORP., 235
SEARLE & CO., 199
SEARS, ROEBUCK & CO., 191
SENTRY INSURANCE CO., 208
SERTA 218
SERVICEMASTER L.P., 239
SHEFFIELD STEEL CORP., 152
SHELDON GOOD & CO., 255
SHERWIN-WILLIAMS CO., 137, 192, 247
SHURE BROTHERS, 161

SHURFINE-CENTRAL CORP., 186
SIGNAL PLASTICS, 259
SIGNODE INDUSTRIES, 247
SIX FLAGS GREAT AMERICA, 117
SKIL CORP., 219
SLOAN VALVE CO., 235
H.P. SMITH CO., 248
JOHN M. SMYTH'S HOMEMAKERS, 192
SOLA ELECTRIC, 162
GEORGE SOLLITT
    CONSTRUCTION, 152
SOLO CUP CO., 248
SOUTHERN IL U./CARBONDALE, 142
SOUTHERN IL U./
    EDWARDSVILLE, 142
SOUTHTOWN ECONOMIST, 241
SPACEMASTER, 219
SPIEGEL INC., 219
SPOTNAILS INC., 235
SPRING AIR, 220
SQUARE D CO., 162
STANDARD EDUCATIONAL
    CORP., 130
STEIN ROE & FARNHAM, 178
STEPAN CO., 138
STEPHENS-ADAMSON, INC., 235
STONE CONTAINER CORP., 248
SUN CHEMICAL CORP., 138
SUN ELECTRIC CO., 266
SUNSHINE-SALEMO, INC., 186
SUNSTAR FOODS INC., 186
SUNSTRAND, 266
SUPERIOR COFFEE CO., 186
SWEETHEART CUP CORP., 248
SWITCHCRAFT, INC., 162
SYMONS CORP., 153
SYSCO FOOD SERVICES, 187
SYSTEM SOFTWARE ASSOCIATES, 148

**T**

TC INDUSTRIES, 236
TAD TECHNICAL SERVICES, 166
TALMAN HOME FEDERAL S&L, 125
TARACORP INDUSTRIES, 172
TATHAM-LAIRD & KUDNER, 115
TELEPHONE & DATA SYSTEMS, 145
TEMPEL STEEL CO., 172

TEMPLETON, KENLY & CO. INC., 236
TERMINAL RAILROAD ASSN., 266
THOMPSON STEEL CO., 172
J. WALTER THOMPSON USA INC., 115
TICOR TITLE INSURANCE, 209
TOPCO ASSOCIATES, INC., 187
TORCO HOLDINGS, 253, 266
TRAILER TRAIN, 266
TRAVELERS INSURANCE CO., 209
TRI-R VENDING SERVICE, 205
TRIBUNE CO./BROADCASTING
    DIVISION, 132
TUTHILL PUMP DIVISION, 236
TYNDALE HOUSE PUBLISHERS,, 130

**U**

U.S. SAMPLE CO., INC., 130
UARCO INC., 254
UDDEHOLM CORP., 173
UNION CARBIDE CORP., 236
UNITED AIR CLEANER CO., 237
UNITED AIRLINES, 266
UNITED EQUITABLE INSURANCE
    GROUP, 209
UNITED STATES TOBACCO MFG., 220
UNITED STATIONERS SUPPLY, 192
UNIVERSITY OF CHICAGO, 142
UNIVERSITY OF ILLINOIS AT
    CHICAGO, 142
UNIVERSITY OF ILLINOIS AT
    URBANA-CHAMPAIGN, 142
UNR INDUSTRIES, INC., 201
UPPCO, INC., 237
USG CORP., 153
USS/A DIVISION OF USX CORP., 173

**V**

VAPOR CORP., 267
VEDDER, PRICE, KAUFMAN, &
    KAMMHOLZ, 212
VENTURE STORES, 192
VERSON, 173
VIENNA BEEF LTD., 187
VULCAN MATERIALS CO., 237

## W

WALDORF CORP., 249
WALLACE COMPUTER SERVICES, 148
WASHINGTON NAT'L. CORP., 179
WASTE MANAGEMENT INC., 138
WAUSAU INSURANCE COS, 209
WEBER MARKING SYSTEMS, INC., 162
WELDED TUBE CO. OF AMERICA, 174
WELLS MFG. CO., 174
WELLS-GARDNER ELECTRONICS, 163
WEN PRODUCTS, INC., 220
WESLEY-JESSEN CORP., 199
WESTERN ILLINOIS UNIVERSITY, 142
WESTERN KRAFT PAPER GROUP, 249
WESTIN HOTEL, CHICAGO, 204
WEYERHAEUSER PAPER CO., 249, 250
WHITE HEN PANTRY, 187
WHITING CORP., 238
WICKS ORGAN CO., 220
WILSON JONES CO., 254
WILSON SPORTING GOODS CO., 220
WITCO CORP., 139
WOOD RIVER TOWNSHIP HOSPITAL, 200
WOODLAWN ORGANIZATION, 133
WOODWORK CORP. OF AMERICA, 153
WOOLWORTH CO., 193
WORLD'S FINEST CHOCOLATE, 188
WM. WRIGLEY, JR. CO., 188
YEOMANS CHICAGO, 238
YOUNG & RUBICAM/CHICAGO, 115
ZENITH ELECTRONICS CORP., 221
ZURICH-AMERICAN INSURANCE, 210

**Alphabetical Index to Greater Chicago Employment Services**

## A

ACCORD INC., 273, 299
ACCOUNTANTS ON CALL, 273
AGRA PLACEMENTS LTD, IL, 273
AMERICAN ASSN. OF RETIRED PERSONS, 274
APT (ABLE'S POOL OF TEMPORARIES), 273
ASHTON & ASSOCIATES, LTD, 274
AVAILABILITY, INC., 274

## B

B-W AND ASSOC., INC., 275
BANNER PERSONNEL SERVICE, 275, 276
BANNER PERSONNEL SERVICES, 276
BRITT ASSOCIATES, INC., 277

## C

CAREER MANAGEMENT ASSOC., 277
CARLSON & ASSOCIATES, 278
CARLSON/BENNETT CORP., 278
CASEY FOR ACCOUNTANTS, 278
CATALYST SEARCH, INC., 300
CEMCO SYSTEMS, 278
CHICAGO FINANCIAL SEARCH, 300
COMPUPRO, 279
CORPORATE ENVIRONMENT, 301
CPU ASSOCIATES, 277
CREATIVE STAFFING ENTERPRISES, 301
DICKEY & ASSOCIATES, INC., 279
DUNHILL OF CHICAGO, 279
DUNHILL PERSONNEL SYSTEM OF IL, 301
DYNAMIC SEARCH SYSTEMS, INC., 279
E.J. ASHTON & ASSOCIATES, LTD., 300
EDP TEMPS AND CONTRACT SERVICES, 280
ELSKO EXECUTIVE SEARCH, 301
ESQUIRE PERSONNEL SERVICES, 280

## F

FARDIG ASSOCIATES, 280
FIRST SEARCH, 281
FIRST SEARCH, INC., 281, 302
FORESIGHT, 302

**G**

GANS, GANS AND ASSOCIATES, 281
GEER, GRICE & HOLDENER, 302
GODFREY PERSONNEL INC., 281
GRAHAM ROBERTS ASSOCIATES, 309
GROVE PERSONNEL SERVICES, 281

**H**

HEALTH STAFFERS, 302
HILTON RESEARCH ASSOCIATES-MID WEST, 282
HUNTER & ASSOCIATES, 314

**I**

INFOQUEST, 282
INTERVIEWING CONSULTANTS, 282

**J**

J.C.G. LIMITED, INC., 302
JACOBSON ASSOCIATES, 303
JOHN R. ADY & ASSOCIATES, 300

**K**

KINGSLEY EMPLOYMENT, 282

**M**

MACINTYRE EMPLOYMENT SERVICES, LTD., 283
MANAGEMENT RECRUITERS OF ALBION, 303
MANAGEMENT RECRUITERS OF BANNOCKBURN, 303
MANAGEMENT RECRUITERS OF BARRINGTON HILLS, 304
MANAGEMENT RECRUITERS OF CHAMPAIGN, 304
MANAGEMENT RECRUITERS OF CHERRY VALLEY, 305
MANAGEMENT RECRUITERS OF CHICAGO (DOWNTOWN), 305
MANAGEMENT RECRUITERS OF CHICAGO-SOUTHWEST, 306

MANAGEMENT RECRUITERS OF DES PLAINES, 306
MANAGEMENT RECRUITERS OF ELGIN, 306
MANAGEMENT RECRUITERS OF ST. CHARLES, 307
MICHAEL DAVID ASSOCIATES, 283
MURPHY EMPLOYMENT SERVICE, 283
MURPHY GROUP, 283, 284, 285
MURPHY GROUP OF DEERFIELD,, 285

**O**

OFFICEMATES5 OF NORTHFIELD, 307
OFFICEMATES5 OF WHEELING, 308
OMNI ONE, 285
OPERATION ABLE, 286
OPPORTUNITIES UNLIMITED, 286
OPPORTUNITY PERSONNEL SERVICE, 286
OPPORTUNITY SPECIALISTS, INC., 287

**P**

PAHLMAN MURPHY & ATTRIDGE, 287
PAIGE PERSONNEL/ PAIGE TEMPORARY, 287
PERMANENT PEOPLE, INC., 288
PERSONNEL POOL, 288, 289
PHILIP WIELAND & ASSOCIATES, 314
PINKERTON AND ASSOCIATES, 308
POLLAK AND SKAN, INC., 289
PRESTIGE PERSONNEL INC., 289
PRESTIGE TEMPORARIES-CALUMET DIVISION, 290
PRESTIGE TEMPORARIES-HOMEWOOD DIVISION, 290
PROFESSIONAL RESUME SERVICE, 314
PROFILE PERSONNEL, INC., 290
PROFILE TEMPORARY SERVICE, 308
PROFILE TEMPORARY SERVICE, 291

**R**

RECRUITING RESOURCES GROUP, 309
RICHARD ALLEN WINTER, 298

RITT - RITT AND ASSOCIATES, 291
ROMAC AND ASSOCIATES OF
    CHICAGO, INC., 309

**S**

SALEM TECHNICAL SERVICES OF
    OAK BROOK, 291
SALES CONSULTANTS OF CHICAGO
    (DOWNTOWN), 310
SALES CONSULTANTS OF CHICAGO
    (SOUTHWEST), 310
SALES CONSULTANTS OF FOX
    VALLEY, 311
SALES CONSULTANTS OF
    LINCOLNSHIRE, 311
SALES CONSULTANTS OF OAK
    BROOK, 312
SALES CONSULTANTS OF
    SCHAUMBURG, 312
SAMUELSON ASSOCIATES, 312
SEARCH DYNAMICS INC., 292
SELECTABILITY PERSONNEL, 292
SELLERS & ASSOCIATES, 293
SEVILLE TEMPORARY SERVICES, 293
SHEETS EMPLOYMENT SERVICE, 293
SNELLING AND SNELLING OF DES
    PLAINES, 293
SNELLING AND SNELLING OF
    ROLLING MEADOWS, 294
SRS DATA SEARCH, 310
STAFF BUILDERS INC. OF ILLINOIS,
    294
STIVERS TEMPORARY
    PERSONNEL, 294
STONE ENTERPRISES, LTD, 295
SURE HIRE SERVICE, INC., 295
SYNERGISTICS ASSOCIATES, 313
SYSTEMS RESEARCH INC., 295

**T**

T-A-DAVIS & ASSOCIATES, INC., 313
TALENT TREE OF ILLINOIS, 296
TALMAN & ASSOCIATES, 313
TEMP FORCE OF ILLINOIS, 296
TEMPFLEET INC., 297
TEMPORARY OPPORTUNITIES, 297

TEMPSTATT, INC., 297
THIRTY THREE PERSONNEL
    CENTER, 297
TRI-ASSOCIATES, INC., 297

**W**

WESTCOTT ASSOCIATES INC., 313
WILLS & CO., INC., 298
WORD PROCESSORS PERSONNEL
    SERVICE, 298
WORKING WORLD TEMPORARY
    PERSONNEL, 299

## Index of Professional Associations

ADAPSO/THE COMPUTER
    SOFTWARE & SERVICES, 327
AIR LINE EMPLOYEES ASSN., 349
AIR TRANSPORT ASSN.
    OF AMERICA, 350
AIR TRANSPORT ASSN.
    OF CHICAGO, 349
ALLIANCE OF
    AMERICAN INSURERS, 339
AMERICAN ACADEMY OF PHYSICIAN
    ASSISTANTS, 337
AMERICAN ADVERTISING
    FEDERATION, 318
AMERICAN APPAREL MFRS ASSN., 319
AMER. ASSN. OF ADVERTISING
    AGENCIES, 319
AMER. ASSN. OF
    CEREAL CHEMISTS, 335
AMER. ASSN. OF PETROLEUM
    GEOLOGISTS, 345
AMER. ASSN. OF SCHOOL
    ADMINISTRATORS, 326
AMER. ASSN. OF ZOOLOGICAL
    PARKS & AQUARIUMS, 320
AMERICAN BANKERS ASSN., 321
AMERICAN BAR ASSN., 340
AMERICAN BOOKSELLERS ASSN., 322
AMER. CASTE METALS ASSN., 332
AMERICAN CHEMICAL SOCIETY, 325

AMER. COLLEGE OF HEALTHCARE EXECUTIVES, 336
AMERICAN COUNCIL OF LIFE INSURANCE, 340
AMERICAN DENTAL ASSN., 336
AMERICAN ELECTROPLATERS AND SURFACE FINISHERS, 328
AMERICAN FEDERATION OF MUSICIANS, 320
AMERICAN FEDERATION OF MUSICIANS/CHICAGO, 320
AMERICAN FEDERATION OF SMALL BUSINESS, 341
AMERICAN FEDERATION OF TELEVISION AND RADIO ARTISTS, 320
AMER. FINANCIAL SERVICES ASSN., 334
AMERICAN GEOLOGICAL INSTITUTE, 345
AMERICAN HEALTH CARE ASSN., 337
THE AMERICAN HOTEL AND MOTEL ASSN., 339
AMER. INSTITUTE OF AERONAUTICS AND ASTRONAUTICS, 350
AMERICAN INSTITUTE OF ARCHITECTS, 330
AMER. INSTITUTE OF CHEMICAL ENGINEERING, 325
AMERICAN INSTITUTE OF CHEMICAL ENGINEERING/CHICAGO, 325
AMER. INSTITUTE OF CHEMISTS, 325
AMERICAN INSTITUTE OF CHEMISTS/CHICAGO, 325
AMER. INSTITUTE OF MINING,, 345
AMERICAN INSTITUTE OF MINING, METALLURGICAL, 345
AMERICAN INSURANCE ASSN., 340
AMERICAN MARKETING ASSN., 318
AMERICAN MEDICAL ASSN., 337
AMER. NEWSPAPER PUBLISHERS ASSN., 343
AMERICAN NUCLEAR SOCIETY, 345
AMERICAN OCCUPATIONAL THERAPY ASSN., 338
AMERICAN PAPER INSTITUTE, 344
AMERICAN PETROLEUM INSTITUTE, 346

AMERICAN PHARMACEUTICAL ASSN., 338
AMERICAN PHYSICAL THERAPY ASSN., 338
AMERICAN POWDER METALLURGY INSTITUTE, 332
AMER. SOCIETY FOR BIOCHEMISTRY & MOLECULAR BIOLOGY, 338
AMER. SOCIETY FOR ENGINEERING EDUCATION, 331
AMER. SOCIETY OF AGRICULTURAL ENGINEERS, 335
AMER. SOCIETY OF APPRAISERS, 334
AMERICAN SOCIETY OF APPRAISERS/CHICAGO, 333
AMERICAN SOCIETY OF BREWING CHEMISTS, 336
AMERICAN SOCIETY OF CIVIL ENGINEERS, 331
AMERICAN SOCIETY OF HEATING, REFRIGERATING, 331
AMERICAN SOCIETY OF HOSPITAL PHARMACISTS, 338
AMERICAN SOCIETY OF LANDSCAPE ARCHITECTS/CHICAGO, 330
AMERICAN SOCIETY OF NAVAL ENGINEERS, 331
AMERICAN SOCIETY OF NEWSPAPER EDITORS, 343
AMERICAN SOCIETY OF PLUMBING ENGINEERS, 331
AMERICAN SOCIETY OF SAFETY ENGINEERS, 330
AMERICAN TEXTILE MFRS INSTITUTE, 319
AMERICAN TRUCKING ASSN., 350
AMERICAN VETERINARY MEDICAL ASSN., 337
AMERICAN WATER WORKS ASSN., 352
AMERICAN WATER WORKS FOUNDATION/CHICAGO, 351
APARTMENT OWNERS AND MANAGERS ASSN., 347
ASSN. FOR COMPUTER SCIENCE, 327
ASSN. FOR COMPUTING MACHINERY, 327
ASSN. OF AMER. PUBLISHERS, 322
ASSN. OF AMERICAN RAILROADS, 350

ASSN. OF AMERICAN
    RAILROADS/CHICAGO, 349
ASSN. OF AMER. UNIVERSITIES, 326
ASSN. OF GRAPHIC ARTS, 346
ASSN. OF IRON AND STEEL
    ENGINEERS, 332
ASSN. OF MANAGEMENT
    CONSULTING FIRMS, 334
ASSN. OF STATE & INTERSTATE, 325
AUTOMOTIVE SERVICE ASSN., 350
AUTOMOTIVE SERVICE
    ASSN./CHICAGO, 349
AUTOMOTIVE SERVICE INDUSTRY
    ASSN., 349
AVIATION MAINTENANCE
    FOUNDATION, 350

### B

BANK ADMINISTRATION
    INSTITUTE, 321, 322
BINDING INDUSTRIES
    OF AMERICA, 346
BROADCAST EDUCATION ASSN., 323
BUILDING OWNERS AND MANAGERS
    ASSN., 348
BUILDING OWNERS AND MANAGERS
    ASSN., 347
BUSINESS-PROFESSIONAL
    ADVERTISING ASSN., 319

### C

CABLE TELEVISION ASSN., 323
CARDIOVASCULAR CREDENTIALING
    INT'L, 338
CHICAGO ASSN. OF BUSINESS
    ECONOMISTS, 333
CHICAGO ASSN. OF CREDIT
    MANAGEMENT, 333
CHICAGO PHYSICAL
    THERAPY ASSN., 337
CLEAN ENERGY RESEARCH
    INSTITUTE, 346
COMMUNICATIONS WORKERS OF
    AMERICA, 326
COMMUNICATIONS WORKERS OF
    AMERICA/CHICAGO, 326

COMMUNITY BANKERS ASSN. OF
    ILLINOIS, 321
CONSTRUCTION INDUSTRY
    MANUFACTURERS ASSN., 328
COUNCIL OF CONSULTANT
    ORGANIZATIONS, 334
COUNCIL ON HOTEL, RESTAURANT,
    339

### D

DAIRY AND FOOD INDUSTRIES
    SUPPLY ASSN., 336
THE DOW JONES NEWSPAPER FUND,
    343

### E

THE EDP AUDITORS ASSN., 317
ELECTROCHEMICAL SOCIETY, 329
ELECTRONIC INDUSTRIES ASSN., 329
ELECTRONICS TECHNICIANS ASSN.,
    329

### F

FEDERAL BAR ASSN., 341
FEDERAL BAR ASSN./CHICAGO
    CHAPTER, 340
FEDERAL COMMUNICATIONS
    COMMISSION, 323
FEDERATION OF TAX
    ADMINISTRATORS, 334
FINANCIAL ANALYSTS
    FEDERATION, 334
FINANCIAL ANALYSTS
    FEDERATION/CHICAGO, 333
FINANCIAL EXECUTIVES
    INSTITUTE, 334
FINANCIAL EXECUTIVES
    INSTITUTE/CHICAGO, 333
FINANCIAL RELATIONS BOARD, 318

### G

GEOLOGICAL SOCIETY
    OF AMERICA, 346

## H

HOME BUILDERS ASSN.
OF GREATER CHICAGO, 327

## I

IEEE COMPUTER SOCIETY, 327
ILLINOIS ACADEMY OF PHYSICIAN
ASSISTANTS, 337
ILLINOIS ASSN. OF CEREAL
CHEMISTS, 335
ILLINOIS BANKERS ASSN., 321
ILLINOIS CABLE
TELEVISION ASSN., 323
ILLINOIS SOCIETY OF HOSPITAL
PHARMACISTS, 337
ILLINOIS SOCIETY OF PROF-
ESSIONAL ENGINEERS, 330
ILLINOIS TRUCKING ASSN., 349
ILLUMINATING ENGINEERING
SOCIETY OF NORTH
AMERICA, 331
INDEPENDENT ACCOUNTANTS
ASSN. OF ILLINOIS, 317
INDEPENDENT BANKERS ASSN. OF
AMERICA, 322
INSTITUTE OF ELECTRICAL AND
ELECTRONICS, 328
INSTITUTE/ELECTRICAL & ELECT-
RONICS ENGINEERS, 329
INSTITUTE OF FINANCIAL
EDUCATION, 321, 333
INSTITUTE OF INDUSTRIAL
ENGINEERS, 331
INSTITUTE OF INDUSTRIAL
ENGINEERS/CHICAGO, 330
INSTITUTE OF INTERNAL
AUDITORS/CHICAGO, 318
INSTITUTE OF MANAGMENT
CONSULTANTS, 333
INSTITUTE OF REAL ESTATE
MANAGEMENT, 347
INSTITUTE OF TRANSPORTATION
ENGINEERS, 350
INSURANCE INFORMATION
INSTITUTE, 340
INSURANCE INFORMATION
INSTITUTE OF CHICAGO, 339
INT'L ASSN. OF CORPORATE, 347, 348
INT'L BROTHERHOOD OF
ELECTRICAL WORKERS, 329
INT'L CIRCULATION MANAGERS
ASSN., 343
INT'L CONFERENCE OF BUILDING
OFFICIALS, 328
INT'L RADIO AND TV SOCIETY, 323
INT'L REAL ESTATE INSTITUTE, 348
INT'L SOCIETY OF CERTIFIED, 329

## M

MAGAZINE PUBLISHERS ASSN., 322
MARINE TECHNOLOGY SOCIETY, 350
MEDICAL GROUP MANAGEMENT
ASSN., 338
MEDICAL GROUP MANAGEMENT
ASSN., 337
MOTOR VEHICLE MANUFACTURERS
ASSN., 351

## N

NAT'L. ACADEMY
OF ENGINEERING, 331
NAT'L. AERONAUTIC ASSN.
OF USA, 351
NAT'L. AGRICULTURAL CHEMICALS
ASSN., 336
NAT'L. ASSN. FOR
LAW PLACEMENT, 341
NAT'L. ASSN. OF BROADCASTERS, 324
NAT'L. ASSN. OF BROADCASTERS/
ILLINOIS, 323
NAT'L. ASSN. OF BUSINESS, 324
NAT'L. ASSN. OF CREDIT
MANAGEMENT, 334
NAT'L. ASSN./HOME BUILDERS, 328
NAT'L. ASSN./
LEGAL ASSISTANTS, 341
NAT'L. ASSN. OF LIFE
UNDERWRITERS, 340
NAT'L. ASSN./MANUFACTURERS, 342
NAT'L. ASSN./METAL FINISHERS, 332

NAT'L. ASSN. OF PRINTERS AND LITHOGRAPHERS, 346
NAT'L. ASSN. OF REAL ESTATE INVESTMENT TRUSTS, 335, 348
NAT'L. ASSN. OF REALTORS, 347
NAT'L. ASSN./SOCIAL WORKERS, 324
NAT'L. AUTOMOTIVE DEALERS ASSN., 351
NAT'L. COOPERATIVE BUSINESS ASSN., 341
NAT'L. CORPORATE CASH MANAGEMENT ASSN., 335
NAT'L. COUNCIL OF SAVINGS INSTITUTIONS, 322
NAT'L. DAIRY COUNCIL, 335
NAT'L. ELECTRICAL MANUFACTURERS ASSN., 329
NAT'L. ELECTRONICS SALES AND SERVICES ASSN., 329
NAT'L. ENDOWMENT FOR THE ARTS, 321
NAT'L. ENDOWMENT FOR THE ARTS/CHICAGO, 320
NAT'L. FEDERATION OF PARALEGAL ASSN.S, 340
NAT'L. HEALTH COUNCIL, 338
NAT'L. INSTITUTE FOR AUTOMOTIVE SERVICE EXCELLENCE, 351
NAT'L. MACHINE TOOL BUILDERS, 342
NAT'L. MARINE MANUFACTURERS ASSN., 349
NAT'L. MEDICAL ASSN., 338
NAT'L. NEWSPAPER ASSN., 344
NAT'L. ORGANIZATION FOR HUMAN SERVICE, 324
NAT'L. PARALEGAL ASSN., 341
NAT'L. PRESS CLUB, 344
NAT'L. RECREATION AND PARKS ASSN./CHICAGO, 320
NAT'L. RETAIL MERCHANTS ASSN., 336
NAT'L. SCREW MACHINE PRODUCTS ASSN., 343
NAT'L. SCREW MACHINE PRODUCTS ASSN., 342
NAT'L. SMALL BUSINESS UNITED, 342
NAT'L. SOCIETY OF PROFESSIONAL ENGINEERS, 331
NAT'L. SOCIETY OF PUBLIC ACCOUNTANTS, 318
NAT'L. TOOLING AND MACHINING ASSN., 343
NAT'L. TOOLING AND MACHINING ASSN., 342
THE NEWSPAPER GUILD, 344
THE NEWSPAPER GUILD/CHICAGO LOCAL, 343
NORTHERN TEXTILE ASSN., 319

**P**

PAPER INDUSTRY MANAGEMENT ASSN., 344
PETROLEUM AND ENERGY RELATED/MINING AND DRILLING, 345
PRINTING INDUSTRIES OF AMERICA, 347
PROFESSIONAL AVIATION MAINTENANCE ASSN., 351
PUBLIC RELATIONS SOCIETY OF AMERICA, 319

**S**

SECURITIES INDUSTRY ASSN., 335
SEMICONDUCTOR INDUSTRY ASSN., 327
SHIPBUILDERS COUNCIL OF AMERICA, 351
SOCIETY OF ACTUARIES, 339
SOCIETY OF EXPLORATION GEOPHYSICISTS, 346
SOCIETY OF FIRE PROTECTION ENGINEERS, 332
SOCIETY OF FIRE PROTECTION ENGINEERS/CHICAGO, 330
SOCIETY OF PLASTIC ENGINEERS, 348
SOCIETY OF PLASTICS INDUSTRY, 348
SOCIETY OF PLASTICS INDUSTRY/DES PLAINES, 348
SOCIETY OF TRIBOLOGISTS, 345

## T

TECHNICAL ASSN. OF THE GRAPHIC
 ARTS, 347
TECHNICAL ASSN. OF THE PULP
 AND PAPER INDUSTRY, 344
TELEVISION BUREAU OF
 ADVERTISING, 319, 324
TELEVISION BUREAU OF ADVERT-
 ISING/CHICAGO, 318, 323
TEXTILE RESEARCH INSTITUTE, 320
THEATRE COMMUNICATIONS
 GROUP, 321

## U

UNITED ENGINEERING
 TRUSTEES, 332
UNITED FOOD
 AND COMMERCIAL, 336
UNITED STATES
 TELEPHONE ASSN., 326

## W

WATER POLLUTION CONTROL
 FEDERATION, 325
WOMEN IN RADIO AND TV, INC., 324
WRITERS GUILD OF
 AMERICA EAST, 322
WRITERS GUILD OF
 AMERICA WEST, INC., 322

## AVAILABLE AT YOUR LOCAL BOOKSTORE

*Knock 'em Dead With Great Answers to Tough Interview Questions*
Will you have the answers when the recruiter asks: Why do you want to work here? What can you do for us that someone else cannot? How much money do you want? Why do you want to change jobs? In *Knock 'em Dead*, Martin Yate gives you not only the best answers to these and scores of more difficult questions, but also the best way to answer--so that you'll be able to field any tough question, and get the job and salary that you deserve. 6x9 inches, 204 pages, paperback, $7.95.

*Resumes that Knock 'em Dead*
In *Resumes that Knock 'em Dead*, Martin Yate reviews the marks of a great resume: what type of resume is right for each applicant, what always goes in, what always stays out, and why. Every single resume in *Resumes that Knock 'em Dead* was used by a real individual to successfully obtain a job. No other book provides the hard facts for producing an exemplary resume. 8 1/2x11 inches, 216 pages, $7.95.

*Cover Letters that Knock 'em Dead*
*Cover Letters that Knock 'em Dead* shows not just how to write a "correct" cover letter, but how to write a cover letter that offers a powerful competitive advantage in today's tough job market. *Cover Letters that Knock 'em Dead* gives the essential information on composing a cover that wins attention, interest and job offers. 8 1/2x11 inches, 184 pages, $7.95.

## ALSO OF INTEREST...
*The JobBank Series*
There are now 18 *JobBank* books, each providing extensive, up-to-date employment information on hundreds of the largest employers in each job market. Recommended as an excellent place to begin your job search by *The New York Times, The Los Angeles Times, The Boston Globe, The Chicago Tribune*, and many other publications, *JobBank* books have been used by hundreds of thousands of people to find jobs.

Books available: *The Atlanta JobBank--The Boston JobBank--The Chicago JobBank--The Dallas-Ft. Worth JobBank--The Denver JobBank--The Detroit JobBank--The Florida JobBank--The Houston JobBank--The Los Angeles JobBank--The Minneapolis JobBank--The New York JobBank--The Ohio JobBank--The Philadelphia JobBank--The Phoenix JobBank--The St. Louis JobBank--The San Franciso JobBank--The Seattle JobBank--The Washington DC JobBank*. Each book is 6x9 inches, over 250 pages, paperback, $12.95.

If you cannot find a book at your local bookstore, you may order it directly from the publisher. Please send payment including $3.75 for shipping and handling (for the entire order) to : Bob Adams, Inc., 260 Center Street, Holbrook, MA 02343. Credit card holders may call 1-800-USA-JOBS (in Massachusetts, 617-767-8100). Please first check at your local bookstore.